Lord Lytton

Kenelm Chillingly

His Adventures and Opinions

Lord Lytton

Kenelm Chillingly
His Adventures and Opinions

ISBN/EAN: 9783337176556

Printed in Europe, USA, Canada, Australia, Japan

Cover: Foto ©ninafisch / pixelio.de

More available books at **www.hansebooks.com**

FRONTISPIECE.

Kenelm Chillingly

Adventures and Opinions

BY

THE RIGHT HON. LORD LYTTON

LONDON
GEORGE ROUTLEDGE AND SONS
BROADWAY, LUDGATE HILL
GLASGOW AND NEW YORK
—
1888

KENELM CHILLINGLY.

BOOK I.

CHAPTER I.

SIR PETER CHILLINGLY, of Exmundham, Baronet, F.R.S. and F.A.S., was the representative of an ancient family, and a landed proprietor of some importance. He had married young, not from any ardent inclination for the connubial state, but in compliance with the request of his parents. They took the pains to select his bride; and if they might have chosen better they might have chosen worse, which is more than can be said for many men who choose wives for themselves. Miss Caroline Brotherton was in all respects a suitable connection. She had a pretty fortune, which was of much use in buying a couple of farms, long desiderated by the Chillinglys as necessary for the rounding of their property into a ring-fence. She was highly connected, and brought into the county that experience of fashionable life acquired by a young lady who has attended a course of balls for three seasons, and gone out in matrimonial honours, with credit to herself and her chaperon. She was handsome enough to satisfy a husband's pride, but not so handsome as to keep perpetually on the *qui vive* a husband's jealousy. She was considered highly accomplished; that is, she played upon the pianoforte so that any musician would say she "was very well taught;" but no musician would go out of his way to hear her a second time. She painted in water-colours—well enough to amuse herself. She knew French and Italian with an elegance so lady-like, that, without having read more than selected extracts from authors in those languages, she spoke them both with an accent more correct than we have any reason to attribute to Rousseau or Ariosto. What else a young lady may acquire in order to be styled highly accomplished I do not pretend to know, but I am sure that the young lady in question fulfilled that requirement in the opinion of the best masters. It was not only an eligible match for Sir Peter Chillingly,—it was a brilliant match. It was also a very unexceptionable match for Miss Caroline Brotherton. This excellent couple got on together as most excellent couples do. A short time after marriage, Sir Peter, by the death of his parents—who, having married their heir, had nothing left in life worth the trouble of living for—succeeded to the hereditary estates; he lived for nine months of the year at Exmundham, going to town for the other three months. Lady Chillingly and himself were both very glad to go to town, being bored at Exmundham; and very glad to go back to Exmundham, being bored in town. With one exception it was an exceedingly happy marriage, as marriages go. Lady Chillingly had her way in small things; Sir Peter his way in great. Small things happen every day, great things once in three years. Once in three years Lady Chillingly gave way to Sir Peter; households so managed go on regularly. The exception to their connubial happiness was, after all, but of a negative description. Their affection was such that they sighed for a pledge of it; fourteen years had he and Lady Chillingly remained unvisited by the little stranger.

Now, in default of male issue, Sir Peter's estates passed to a distant cousin as heir-at-law; and during the last four years this heir-at-law had evinced his belief that, practically speaking, he was already heir-apparent; and (though Sir Peter was a much younger man than himself, and as healthy as any man well can be) had made his expectations of a speedy succession unpleasantly conspicuous. He had refused his consent to a small exchange of lands with a neighbouring squire, by which Sir Peter would have obtained some good arable land for an outlying unprofitable wood that produced nothing but faggots and rabbits, with the blunt declaration that he, the heir-at-law, was fond of rabbit-shooting, and that the wood would be convenient to him next season if he came into the property by that time, which he very possibly might. He disputed Sir Peter's right to make his customary fall of timber, and had even threatened him with a bill in Chancery on that subject. In short, this heir-at-law was exactly one of those persons to spite whom a landed proprietor would, if single, marry at the age of eighty in the hope of a family.

Nor was it only on account of his very natural wish to frustrate the expectations of this unamiable relation, that Sir Peter Chillingly lamented the absence of the little stranger. Although belonging to that class of country gentlemen to whom certain political reasoners deny the intelligence vouchsafed to other members of the community, Sir Peter was not without a considerable degree of book-learning, and a great taste for speculative philosophy. He sighed for a legitimate inheritor to the stores of his erudition, and, being a very benevolent man, for a more active and useful dispenser of those benefits to the human race which philosophers confer by striking hard against each other; just as, how full soever of sparks a flint may be, they might lurk concealed in the flint till doomsday, if the flint were not hit by the steel. Sir Peter, in short, longed for a son amply endowed with the combative quality, in which he himself was deficient, but which is the first essential to all seekers after renown, and especially to benevolent philosophers.

Under these circumstances one may well conceive the joy that filled the household of Exmundham and extended to all the tenantry on that venerable estate, by whom the present possessor was much beloved, and the prospect of an heir-at-law with a special eye to the preservation of rabbits much detested, when the medical attendant of the Chillinglys declared that 'her ladyship was in an interesting way;' and to what height that joy culminated when, in due course of time, a male baby was safely enthroned in his cradle. To that cradle Sir Peter was summoned. He entered the room with a lively bound and a radiant countenance: he quitted it with a musing step and an overclouded brow.

Yet the baby was no monster. It did not come into the world with two heads, as some babies are said to have done; it was formed as babies are in general—was on the whole a thriving baby, a fine baby. Nevertheless, its aspect awed the father as already it had awed the nurse. The creature looked so unutterably solemn. It fixed its eyes upon Sir Peter with a melancholy reproachful stare; its lips were compressed and drawn downward as if discontentedly meditating its future destinies. The nurse declared in a frightened whisper that it had uttered no cry on facing the light. It had taken possession of its cradle in all the dignity of silent sorrow. A more saddened and a more thoughtful countenance a human being could not exhibit if he were leaving the world instead of entering it.

"Hem!" said Sir Peter to himself on regaining the solitude of his library; "a philosopher who contributes a new inhabitant to this vale of tears takes upon himself very anxious responsibilities——"

At that moment the joy-bells rang out from the neighbouring church-tower, the summer sun shone into the windows, the bees hummed among the flowers on the lawn: Sir Peter roused himself and looked forth—"After all," said he, cheerily, "the vale of tears is not without a smile."

CHAPTER II.

A FAMILY council was held at Exmundham Hall to deliberate on the name by which this remarkable infant should be admitted into the Christian community. The junior branches of that ancient house consisted, first, of the obnoxious heir-at-law — a Scotch branch — named Chillingly Gordon. He was the widowed father of one son, now of the age of three, and happily unconscious of the injury inflicted on his future prospects by the advent of the new-born; which could not be truthfully said of his Caledonian father. Mr. Chillingly Gordon was one of those men who get on in the world without our being able to discover why. His parents died in his infancy, and left him nothing; but the family interest procured him an admission into the Charter House School, at which illustrious academy he obtained no remarkable distinction. Nevertheless, as soon as he left it the State took him under its special care, and appointed him to a clerkship in a public office. From that moment he continued to get on in the world, and was now a commissioner of customs, with a salary of £1500 a-year. As soon as he had been thus enabled to maintain a wife, he selected a wife who assisted to maintain himself. See was an Irish peer's widow, with a jointure of £2000 a-year.

A few months after his marriage, Chillingly Gordon effected insurances on his wife's life, so as to secure himself an annuity of £1000 a-year in case of her decease. As she appeared to be a fine healthy woman, some years younger than her husband, the deduction from his income effected by the annual payments for the insurance seemed an over-sacrifice of present enjoyment to future contingencies. The result bore witness to his reputation for sagacity, as the lady died in the second year of their wedding, a few months after the birth of her only child, and of a heart-disease which had been latent to the doctors, but which, no doubt, Gordon had affectionately discovered before he had insured a life too valuable not to need some compensation for its loss. He was now, then, in the possession of £2500 a-year, and was therefore very well off, in the pecuniary sense of the phrase. He had, moreover, acquired a reputation which gave him a social rank beyond that accorded to him by a discerning State. He was considered a man of solid judgment, and his opinion upon all matters, private and public, carried weight. The opinion itself, critically examined, was not worth much, but the way he announced it was imposing. Mr. Fox said that 'No one ever was so wise as Lord Thurlow looked.' Lord Thurlow could not have looked wiser than Mr. Chillingly Gordon. He had a square jaw and large red bushy eyebrows, which he lowered down with great effect when he delivered judgment. He had another advantage for acquiring grave reputation. He was a very unpleasant man. He could be rude if you contradicted him; and as few persons wish to provoke rudeness, so he was seldom contradicted.

Mr. Chillingly Mivers, another cadet of the house, was also distinguished, but in a different way. He was a bachelor, now about the age of thirty-five. He was eminent for a supreme well-bred contempt for everybody and everything. He was the originator and chief proprietor of a public journal called 'The Londoner,' which had lately been set up on that principle of contempt, and, we need not say, was exceedingly popular with those leading members of the community who admire nobody and believe in nothing. Mr. Chillingly Mivers was regarded by himself and by others as a man who might have achieved the highest success in any branch of literature, if he had deigned to exhibit his talents therein. But he did not so deign, and therefore he had full right to imply that, if he had written an epic, a drama, a novel, a history, a metaphysical treatise, Milton, Shakespeare, Cervantes, Hume, Berkeley, would have been nowhere. He held greatly to the dignity of the anonymous; and even in the journal which he originated, nobody could ever ascertain what he wrote. But, at all events, Mr. Chillingly Mivers was what Mr. Chillingly Gordon was not—viz., a very clever man, and by no means an unpleasant one in general society.

The Rev. John Stalworth Chillingly was a decided adherent to the creed of what is called 'muscular Christianity,' and a very fine specimen of it too. A tall stout man with broad shoulders, and that division of lower limb which intervenes between the knee and the ankle powerfully developed. He would have knocked down a deist as soon as looked at him. It is told by the Sieur de Joinville, in his Memoir of Louis, the sainted king, that an assembly of divines and theologians convened the Jews of an Oriental city for the purpose of arguing with them on the truths of Christianity, and a certain knight, who was at that time crippled, and supporting himself on crutches, asked and obtained permission to be present at the debate. The Jews flocked to the summons, when a prelate, selecting a learned rabbi, mildly put to him the leading question whether he owned the divine conception of our Lord. "Certainly not," replied the rabbi; whereon the pious knight, shocked by such blasphemy, uplifted his crutch and felled the rabbi, and then flung himself among the other misbelievers, whom he soon dispersed in ignominious flight and in a very belaboured condition. The conduct of the knight was reported to the sainted king, with a request that it should be properly reprimanded; but the sainted king delivered himself of this wise judgment:—

"If a pious knight is a very learned clerk, and can meet in fair argument the doctrines of the misbeliever, by all means let him argue fairly; but if a pious knight is not a learned clerk, and the argument goes against him, then let the pious knight cut the discussion short by the edge of his good sword."

The Rev. John Stalworth Chillingly was of the same opinion as St. Louis; otherwise, he was a mild and amiable man. He encouraged cricket and other manly sports among his rural parishioners. He was a skilful and bold rider, but he did not hunt; a convivial man—and took his bottle freely. But his tastes in literature were of a refined and peaceful character, contrasting therein the tendencies one might have expected from his muscular development of Christianity. He was a great reader of poetry, but he disliked Scott and Byron, whom he considered flashy and noisy: he maintained that Pope was only a versifier, and that the greatest poet in the language was Wordsworth; he did not care much for the ancient classics; he refused all merit to the French poets; he knew nothing of the Italian, but he dabbled in German, and was inclined to bore one about the Hermann and Dorothea of Goethe. He was married to a homely little wife, who revered him in silence, and thought there would be no schism in the Church if he were in his right place as Archbishop of Canterbury; in this opinion he entirely agreed with his wife.

Besides these three male specimens of the Chillingly race, the fairer sex was represented, in the absence of her ladyship, who still kept her room, by three female Chillinglys—sisters of Sir Peter—and all three spinsters. Perhaps one reason why they had remained single was, that externally they were so like each other that a suitor must have been puzzled which to choose, and may have been afraid that if he did choose one, he should be caught next day kissing another one in mistake. They were all tall, all thin, with long throats—and beneath the throats a fine development of bone. They had all pale hair, pale eyelids, pale eyes, and pale complexions. They all dressed exactly alike, and their favourite colour was a vivid green: they were so dressed on this occasion.

As there was such similitude in their persons, so, to an ordinary observer, they were exactly the same in character and mind. Very well behaved, with proper notions of female decorum—very distant and reserved in manner to strangers—very affectionate to each other and their relations or favourites—very good to the poor, whom they looked upon as a different order of creation, and treated with that sort of benevolence which humane people bestow upon dumb animals. Their minds had been nourished on the same books— what one read the others had read. The books were mainly divided into two classes—novels, and what they called "good books." They had a habit of taking a specimen of each alternately—one day a novel, then a good book, then a novel again, and so on. Thus if the imagination was overwarmed on Monday, on Tuesday it was cooled down to a proper temperature; and if frost-bitten on Tuesday, it took a tepid bath on Wednesday. The novels they chose were indeed rarely of a nature to raise the intellectual thermometer into blood heat: the heroes and heroines were models of correct conduct. Mr. James's novels were then in vogue, and they united in saying that those "*were* novels a father might allow his daughters to read." But though an ordinary observer might have failed to recognize any distinction between these three ladies, and, finding them habitually dressed in green, would have said they were as much alike as one pea is to another, they had their idiosyncratic differences, when duly examined. Miss Margaret, the eldest, was the commanding one of the three; it was she who regulated their household (they all lived together), kept the joint purse, and decided every doubtful point that arose,—whether they should or should not ask Mrs. So-and-so to tea—whether Mary should or should not be discharged—whether or not they should go to Broadstairs or to Sandgate for the month of October. In fact, Miss Margaret was the WILL of the body corporate.

Miss Sibyl was of milder nature and more melancholy temperament; she had a poetic turn of mind, and occasionally wrote verses. Some of these had been printed on satin paper, and sold for objects of beneficence at charity bazaars. The county newspapers said that the verses "were characterized by all the elegance of a cultured and feminine mind." The other two sisters agreed that Sibyl was the genius of the household, but, like all geniuses, not sufficiently practical for the world. Miss Sarah Chillingly, the youngest of the three, and now just in her forty-fourth year, was looked upon by the others as 'a dear thing, inclined to be naughty, but such a darling that nobody could have the heart to scold her.' Miss Margaret said 'she was a giddy creature.' Miss Sibyl wrote a poem on her, entitled—

"Warning to a young Lady against the Pleasures of the World."

They all called her Sally; the other two sisters had no diminutive synonyms. Sally is a name indicative of fastness. But this Sally would not have been thought fast in another household, and she was now little likely to sally out of the one she belonged to. These sisters, who were all many years older than Sir Peter, lived in a handsome old-fashioned red-brick house, with a large garden at the back, in the principal street of the capital of their native county. They had each £10,000 for portion; and if he could have married all three, the heir-at-law would have married them, and settled the aggregate £30,000 on himself. But we have not yet come to recognize Mormonism as legal, though, if our social progress continues to slide in the same grooves as at present, heaven only knows what triumphs over the prejudices of our ancestors may not be achieved by the wisdom of our descendants!

CHAPTER III.

SIR PETER stood on his hearthstone, surveyed the guests seated in semicircle, and said: "Friends,—in Parliament, before anything affecting the fate of a Bill is discussed, it is, I believe, necessary to introduce the Bill." He paused a moment, rang the bell, and said to the servant who entered, "Tell nurse to bring in the Baby."

MR. GORDON CHILLINGLY.—"I don't see the necessity for that, Sir Peter. We may take the existence of the Baby for granted."

MR. MIVERS.—"It is an advantage to the reputation of Sir Peter's work to preserve the incognito. *Omne ignotum pro magnifico.*"

THE REV. JOHN STALWORTH CHILLINGLY.—"I don't approve the cynical levity of such remarks. Of course we must all be anxious to see, in the earliest stage of being, the future representative of our name and race. Who would not wish to contemplate the source, however small, of the Tigris or the Nile!——"

Miss SALLY (tittering).—"He! he!"

Miss MARGARET.—"For shame, you giddy thing!"

The Baby enters in the nurse's arms. All rise and gather round the Baby, with one exception—Mr. Gordon, who has ceased to be heir-at-law.

The Baby returned the gaze of its relations with the most contemptuous indifference. Miss Sibyl was the first to pronounce an

opinion on the Baby's attributes. Said she, in a solemn whisper—
"What a heavenly mournful expression! it seems so grieved to have left the angels!"

THE REV. JOHN.—"That is prettily said, cousin Sibyl; but the infant must pluck up its courage and fight its way among mortals with a good heart, if it wants to get back to the angels again. And I think it will; a fine child." He took it from the nurse, and moving it deliberately up and down, as if to weigh it, said cheerfully, "Monstrous heavy! by the time it is twenty it will be a match for a prizefighter of fifteen stone!"

Therewith he strode to Gordon, who, as if to show that he now considered himself wholly apart from all interest in the affairs of a family that had so ill-treated him in the birth of that Baby, had taken up the 'Times' newspaper and concealed his countenance beneath the ample sheet. The Parson abruptly snatched away the 'Times' with one hand, and, with the other substituting to the indignant eyes of the *ci-devant* heir-at-law the spectacle of the Baby, said, "Kiss it."

"Kiss it!" echoed Chillingly Gordon, pushing back his chair—"kiss it! pooh, sir, stand off! I never kissed my own baby; I shall not kiss another man's. Take the thing away, sir; it is ugly; it has black eyes."

Sir Peter, who was near-sighted, put on his spectacles and examined the face of the new-born. "True," said he, "it has black eyes—very extraordinary—portentous; the first Chillingly that ever had black eyes."

"Its mamma has black eyes," said Miss Margaret; "it takes after its mamma; it has not the fair beauty of the Chillinglys, but it is not ugly."

"Sweet infant!" sighed Sibyl; "and so good—does not cry."

"It has neither cried nor crowed since it was born," said the nurse; "bless its little heart!"

She took the Baby from the Parson's arms, and smoothed back the frill of its cap, which had got ruffled.

"You may go now, nurse," said Sir Peter.

CHAPTER IV.

"I AGREE with Mr. Shandy," said Sir Peter, resuming his stand on the hearthstone, "that among the responsibilities of a parent, the choice of a name which his child is to bear for life is one of the gravest. And this is especially so with those who belong to the order of baronets. In the case of a peer, his Christian name, fused into his titular designation, disappears. In the case of a Mister, if his baptismal be cacophonous or provocative of ridicule, he need not ostentatiously parade it; he may drop it altogether on his visiting cards, and may be imprinted as Mr. Jones instead of Mr. Ebenezer Jones. In his signature, save where the forms of the law demand Ebenezer in full, he may only use an initial, and be your obedient servant E. Jones, leaving it to be conjectured that E. stands for Edward or Ernest— names inoffensive, and not suggestive of a Dissenting Chapel, like Ebenezer. If a man called Edward or Ernest be detected in some youthful indiscretion, there is no indelible stain on his moral character; but if an Ebenezer be so detected, he is set down as a hypocrite—it produces that shock on the public mind which is felt when a professed saint is proved to be a bit of a sinner. But a baronet never can escape from his baptismal—it cannot lie *perdu*, it cannot shrink into an initial, it stands forth glaringly in the light of day; christen him Ebenezer, and he is Sir Ebenezer in full, with all its perilous consequences if he ever succumb to those temptations to which even baronets are exposed. But, my friends, it is not only the effect that the sound of a name has upon others which is to be thoughtfully considered; the effect that his name produces on the man himself is perhaps still more important. Some names stimulate and encourage the owner, others deject and paralyse him; I am a melancholy instance of that truth. Peter has been for many generations, as you are aware, the baptismal to which the eldest-born of our family has been devoted. On the altar of that name I have been sacrificed. Never has there been a Sir Peter Chillingly who has, in any way, distinguished himself above his fellows. That name has been a dead weight on my intellectual energies. In the catalogue of illustrious Englishmen there is, I think, no immortal Sir Peter, except Sir Peter Teazle, and he only exists on the comic stage."

MISS SIBYL.—"Sir Peter Lely?"

SIR PETER CHILLINGLY.—"That painter was not an Englishman. He was born in Westphalia, famous for hams. I confine my remarks to the children of our native land. I am aware that in foreign countries the name is not an extinguisher to the genius of its owner. But why? In other countries its sound is modified. Pierre Corneille was a great man; but I put it to you whether, had he been an Englishman, he could have been the father of European tragedy as Peter Crow?"

Miss Sibyl.—"Impossible!"

Miss Sally.—"He! he!"

Miss Margaret.—"There is nothing to laugh at, you giddy child!"

Sir Peter.—"My son shall not be petrified into Peter."

Mr. Gordon Chillingly.—"If a man is such a fool—and I don't say your son will not be a fool, cousin Peter—as to be influenced by the sound of his own name, and you want the booby to turn the world topsy-turvy, you had better call him Julius Cæsar, or Hannibal, or Attila, or Charlemagne."

Sir Peter (who excels mankind in imperturbability of temper). —"On the contrary, if you inflict upon a man the burthen of one of those names, the glory of which he cannot reasonably expect to eclipse or even to equal, you crush him beneath the weight. If a poet were called John Milton or William Shakespeare, he could not dare to publish even a sonnet. No; the choice of a name lies between the two extremes of ludicrous insignificance and oppressive renown. For this reason I have ordered the family pedigree to be suspended on yonder wall. Let us examine it with care, and see whether, among the Chillinglys themselves or their alliances, we can discover a name that can be borne with becoming dignity by the destined head of our house—a name neither too light nor too heavy."

Sir Peter here led the way to the family tree—a goodly roll of parchment, with the arms of the family emblazoned at the top. Those arms were simple, as ancient heraldic coats are—three fishes *argent* on a field *azur*; the crest a mermaid's head. All flocked to inspect the pedigree except Mr. Gordon, who resumed the 'Times' newspaper.

"I never could quite make out what kind of fishes these are," said the Rev. John Stalworth. "They are certainly not pike, which formed the emblematic blazon of the Hotofts, and are still grim enough to frighten future Shakespeares, on the scutcheon of the Warwickshire Lucys."

"I believe they are tenches," said Mr. Mivers. "The tench is a fish that knows how to keep itself safe, by a philosophical taste for an obscure existence in deep holes and slush."

SIR PETER.—" No, Mivers; the fishes are dace, a fish that, once introduced into any pond, never can be got out again. You may drag the water—you may let off the water—you may say 'Those dace are extirpated,'—vain thought!—the dace reappear as before; and in this respect the arms are really emblematic of the family. All the disorders and revolutions that have occurred in England since the Heptarchy have left the Chillinglys the same race in the same place. Somehow or other the Norman Conquest did not despoil them; they held fiefs under Eudo Dapifer as peacefully as they had held them under King Harold; they took no part in the Crusades, nor the Wars of the Roses, nor the Civil Wars between Charles the First and the Parliament. As the dace sticks to the water, and the water sticks by the dace, so the Chillinglys stuck to the land and the land stuck by the Chillinglys. Perhaps I am wrong to wish that the new Chillingly may be a little less like a dace."

"Oh!" cried Miss Margaret, who, mounted on a chair, had been inspecting the pedigree through an eye-glass, "I don't see a fine Christian name from the beginning, except Oliver."

SIR PETER.—"That Chillingly was born in Oliver Cromwell's Protectorate, and named Oliver in compliment to him, as his father, born in the reign of James I., was christened James. The three fishes always swam with the stream. Oliver!—Oliver not a bad name, but significant of radical doctrines."

MR. MIVERS.—"I d n't think so. Oliver Cromwell made short work of radicals and their doctrines; but perhaps we can find a name less awful and revolutionary."

"I have it—I have it," cried the Parson. "Here is a descent from Sir Kenelm Digby and Venetia Stanley. Sir Kenelm Digby! No finer specimen of muscular Christianity. He fought as well as he wrote;—eccentric, it is true, but always a gentleman. Call the boy Kenelm!"

"A sweet name," said Miss Sibyl—"it breathes of romance."

"Sir Kenelm Chillingly! It sounds well—imposing!" said Miss Margaret.

"And," remarked Mr. Mivers, "it has this advantage—that while it has sufficient association with honourable distinction to affect the mind of the namesake and rouse his emulation, it is not that of so stupendous a personage as to defy rivalry. Sir Kenelm Digby was certainly an accomplished and gallant gentleman; but what with his silly superstition about sympathetic powders, &c., any man now-a-days might be clever in comparison without being a prodigy. Yes, let us decide on Kenelm."

Sir Peter meditated. "Certainly," said he, after a pause—

"certainly the name of Kenelm carries with it very crotchety associations; and I am afraid that Sir Kenelm Digby did not make a prudent choice in marriage. The fair Venetia was no better than she should be: and I should wish my heir not to be led away by beauty, but wed a woman of respectable character and decorous conduct."

MISS MARGARET.—"A British matron, of course!"

THREE SISTERS (in chorus).—"Of course—of course!"

"But," resumed Sir Peter, "I am crotchety myself, and crotchets are innocent things enough; and as for marriage, the Baby cannot marry to-morrow, so that we have ample time to consider that matter. Kenelm Digby was a man any family might be proud of; and, as you say, sister Margaret, Kenelm Chillingly does not sound amiss—Kenelm Chillingly it shall be!"

The Baby was accordingly christened Kenelm, after which ceremony its face grew longer than before.

CHAPTER V.

BEFORE his relations dispersed, Sir Peter summoned Mr. Gordon into his library.

"Cousin," said he, kindly, "I do not blame you for the want of family affection, or even of humane interest, which you exhibit towards the New-born."

"Blame me, cousin Peter! I should think not. I exhibit as much family affection and humane interest as could be expected from me—circumstances considered."

"I own," said Sir Peter, with all his wonted mildness, "that after remaining childless for fourteen years of wedded life, the advent of this little stranger must have occasioned you a disagreeable surprise. But, after all, as I am many years younger than you, and, in the course of nature, shall outlive you, the loss is less to yourself than to your son, and upon that I wish to say a few words. You know too well the conditions on which I hold my estate not to be aware that I have not legally the power to saddle it with any bequest to your boy. The New-born succeeds to the fee-simple as last in tail. But I intend, from this moment, to lay by something every year for your son out of my income; and, fond as I am of London for a part of the year, I shall now give up my town-house. If I live to the years the Psalmist allots to man, I shall thus accumulate something handsome for your son, which may be taken in the way of compensation."

Mr. Gordon was by no means softened by this generous speech. However, he answered more politely than was his wont, "My son will be very much obliged to you, should he ever need your intended bequest." Pausing a moment, he added, with a cheerful smile, "A large percentage of infants die before attaining the age of twenty-one."

"Nay, but I am told your son is an uncommonly fine healthy child."

"My son, cousin Peter! I was not thinking of my son, but of yours. Yours has a big head. I should not wonder if he had water in it. I don't wish to alarm you, but he may go off any day, and in that case it is not likely that Lady Chillingly will condescend to replace him. So you will excuse me if I still keep a watchful eye on my rights; and however painful to my feelings, I must still dispute your right to cut a stick of the field timber."

"That is nonsense, Gordon. I am tenant for life without impeachment of waste, and can cut down all timber not ornamental."

"I advise you not, cousin Peter. I have told you before that I shall try the question at law, should you provoke it—amicably, of course. Rights are rights; and if I am driven to maintain mine, I trust that you are of a mind too liberal to allow your family affection to me and mine to be influenced by a decree of the Court of Chancery. But my fly is waiting. I must not miss the train."

"Well, good-bye, Gordon. Shake hands."

"Shake hands!—of course—of course. By the bye, as I came through the lodge, it seemed to me sadly out of repair. I believe you are liable for dilapidations. Good-bye."

"The man is a hog in armour," soliloquized Sir Peter, when his cousin was gone; "and if it be hard to drive a common pig in the way he don't choose to go, a hog in armour is indeed undrivable. But his boy ought not to suffer for his father's hoggishness; and I shall begin at once to see what I can lay by for him. After all, it is hard upon Gordon. Poor Gordon!—poor fellow—poor fellow! Still I hope he will not go to law with me. I hate law. And a worm will turn—especially a worm that is put into Chancery."

CHAPTER VI.

DESPITE the sinister semi-predictions of the *ci-devant* heir-at-law, the youthful Chillingly passed with safety, and indeed with dignity through the infant stages of existence.

He took his measles and whooping-cough with philosophical equanimity. He gradually acquired the use of speech, but he did not too lavishly exercise that special attribute of humanity. During the earlier years of childhood he spoke as little as if he had been prematurely trained in the school of Pythagoras. But he evidently spoke the less in order to reflect the more. He observed closely and pondered deeply over what he observed. At the age of eight he began to converse more freely, and it was in that year that he startled his mother with the question—"Mamma, are you not sometimes overpowered by the sense of your own identity?"

Lady Chillingly—I was about to say rushed, but Lady Chillingly never rushed—Lady Chillingly glided less sedately than her wont to Sir Peter, and, repeating her son's question, said, "The boy is growing troublesome, too wise for any woman; he must go to school."

Sir Peter was of the same opinion. But where on earth did the child get hold of so long a word as "identity," and how did so extraordinary and puzzling a metaphysical question come into his head? Sir Peter summoned Kenelm, and ascertained that the boy, having free access to the library, had fastened upon Locke on the Human Understanding, and was prepared to dispute with that philosopher upon the doctrine of innate ideas. Quoth Kenelm, gravely—"A want is an idea; and if, as soon as I was born, I felt the want of food and knew at once where to turn for it, without being taught, surely I came into the world with an 'innate idea.'"

Sir Peter, though he dabbled in metaphysics, was posed, and scratched his head without getting out a proper answer as to the distinction between ideas and instincts. "My child," he said at last, "you don't know what you are talking about; go and take a good gallop on your black pony; and I forbid you to read any books that are not given to you by myself or your mamma. Stick to Puss in Boots."

CHAPTER VII.

SIR PETER ordered his carriage and drove to the house of the stout Parson. That doughty ecclesiastic held a family living a few miles distant from the Hall, and was the only one of the cousins with whom Sir Peter habitually communed on his domestic affairs.

He found the Parson in his study, which exhibited tastes other than clerical. Over the chimney-piece were ranged fencing-foils, boxing-gloves, and staffs for the athletic exercise of single-stick; cricket-bats and fishing-rods filled up the angles. There were sundry prints on the walls: one of Mr. Wordsworth, flanked by two of distinguished race-horses; one of a Leicestershire short-horn, with which the Parson, who farmed his own glebe and bred cattle in its rich pastures, had won a prize at the county show; and on either side of that animal were the portraits of Hooker and Jeremy Taylor. There were dwarf bookcases containing miscellaneous works very handsomely bound. At the open window, a stand of flower-pots, the flowers in full bloom. The Parson's flowers were famous.

The appearance of the whole room was that of a man who is tidy and neat in his habits.

"Cousin," said Sir Peter, "I have come to consult you." And therewith he related the marvellous precocity of Kenelm Chillingly. "You see the name begins to work on him rather too much. He must go to school; and now what school shall it be? Private or public?"

THE REV. JOHN STALWORTH.—"There is a great deal to be said for or against either. At a public school the chances are that Kenelm will no longer be overpowered by a sense of his own identity; he will more probably lose identity altogether. The worst of a public school is that a sort of common character is substituted for individual character. The master, of course, can't attend to the separate development of each boy's idiosyncrasy. All minds are thrown into one great mould, and come out of it more or less in the same form. An Etonian may be clever or stupid, but, as either, he remains emphatically Etonian. A public school ripens talent, but its tendency is to stifle genius. Then, too, a public school for an only son, heir to a good estate, which will be entirely at his own disposal, is apt to encourage reckless and extravagant habits; and your estate requires careful management, and leaves no margin for an heir's notes-of-hand and post-obits. On the whole, I am against a public school for Kenelm."

"Well, then, we will decide on a private one."

"Hold!" said the Parson: "a private school has its drawbacks. You can seldom produce large fishes in small ponds. In private schools the competition is narrowed, the energies stinted. The schoolmaster's wife interferes, and generally coddles the boys. There is not manliness enough in those academies; no fagging, and very little fighting. A clever boy turns out a prig; a boy of feebler intellect turns out a well-behaved young lady in trousers. Nothing muscular in the system. Decidedly the namesake and descendant of Kenelm Digby should not go to a private seminary."

"So far as I gather from your reasoning," said Sir Peter, with characteristic placidity, "Kenelm Chillingly is not to go to school at all."

"It does look like it," said the Parson, candidly; "but, on consideration, there is a medium. There are schools which unite the best qualities of public and private schools, large enough to stimulate and develop energies mental and physical, yet not so framed as to melt all character in one crucible. For instance, there is a school which has at this moment one of the first scholars in Europe for head-master—a school which has turned out some of the most remarkable men of the rising generation. The master sees at a glance if a boy be clever, and takes pains with him accordingly. He is not a mere teacher of hexameters and sapphics. His learning embraces all literature, ancient and modern. He is a good writer and a fine critic—admires Wordsworth. He winks at fighting, his boys know how to use their fists, and they are not in the habit of signing post-obits before they are fifteen. Merton School is the place for Kenelm."

"Thank you," said Sir Peter. "It is a great comfort in life to find somebody who can decide for one. I am an irresolute man myself, and in ordinary matters willingly let Lady Chillingly govern me."

"I should like to see a wife govern *me*," said the stout Parson.

"But you are not married to Lady Chillingly. And now let us go into the garden and look at your dahlias."

CHAPTER VIII.

THE youthful confuter of Locke was despatched to Merton School, and ranked, according to his merits, as lag of the penultimate form. When he came home for the Christmas holidays he was more saturnine than ever—in fact, his countenance bore the impression of some absorbing grief. He said, however, that he liked school very well, and eluded all other questions. But early the next morning he mounted his black pony and rode to the Parson's rectory. The reverend gentleman was in his farm-yard examining his bullocks when Kenelm accosted him thus briefly:—

"Sir, I am disgraced, and I shall die of it if you cannot help to set me right in my own eyes."

"My dear boy, don't talk in that way. Come into my study."

As soon as they entered that room, and the Parson had carefully closed the door, he took the boy's arm, turned him round to the light, and saw at once that there was something very grave on his mind. Chucking him under the chin, the Parson said cheerily, "Hold up your head, Kenelm. I'm sure you have done nothing unworthy of a gentleman."

"I don't know that. I fought a boy very little bigger than myself, and I have been licked. I did not give in, though; but the other boys picked me up, for I could not stand any longer—and the fellow is a great bully—and his name is Butt—and he's the son of a lawyer—and he got my head into chancery—and I have challenged him to fight again next half—and unless you can help me to lick him, I shall never be good for anything in the world—never. It will break my heart."

"I am very glad to hear you have had the pluck to challenge him. Just let me see how you double your fist. Well, that's not amiss. Now, put yourself into a fighting attitude, and hit out at me—hard—harder! Pooh! that will never do. You should make your blows as straight as an arrow. And that's not the way to stand. Stop—so; well on your haunches—weight on the left leg—good! Now, put on these gloves, and I'll give you a lesson in boxing."

Five minutes afterwards Mrs. John Chillingly, entering the room to summon her husband to breakfast, stood astounded to see him with his coat off, and parrying the blows of Kenelm, who flew at him like a young tiger. The good pastor at that moment might certainly have appeared a fine type of muscular Christianity, but not of that kind of Christianity out of which one makes Archbishops of Canterbury.

"Good gracious me!" faltered Mrs. John Chillingly; and then, wife-like, flying to the protection of her husband, she seized Kenelm by the shoulders, and gave him a good shaking. The Parson, who was sadly out of breath, was not displeased at the interruption, but took that opportunity to put on his coat, and said, "We'll begin again to-morrow. Now, come to breakfast." But during breakfast Kenelm's face still betrayed dejection, and he talked little, and ate less.

As soon as the meal was over, he drew the Parson into the garden and said, "I have been thinking, sir, that perhaps it is not fair to Butt, that I should be taking these lessons; and if it is not fair, I'd rather not——"

"Give me your hand, my boy!" cried the Parson, transported. "The name of Kenelm is not thrown away upon you. The natural desire of man in his attribute of fighting animal (an attribute in which, I believe, he excels all other animated beings, except a quail and a gamecock), is to beat his adversary. But the natural desire of that culmination of man which we call gentleman, is to beat his adversary fairly. A gentleman would rather be beaten fairly than beat unfairly. Is not that your thought?"

"Yes," replied Kenelm, firmly; and then, beginning to philosophize, he added,—"And it stands to reason; because if I beat a fellow unfairly, I don't really beat him at all."

"Excellent! But suppose that you and another boy go into examination upon Cæsar's Commentaries or the multiplication table, and the other boy is cleverer than you, but you have taken the trouble to learn the subject and he has not; should you say you beat him unfairly?"

Kenelm meditated a moment, and then said decidedly, "No."

"That which applies to the use of your brains applies equally to the use of your fists. Do you comprehend me?"

"Yes, sir; I do now."

"In the time of your namesake, Sir Kenelm Digby, gentlemen wore swords, and they learned how to use them, because, in case of quarrel, they had to fight with them. Nobody, at least in England, fights with swords now. It is a democratic age, and if you fight at all, you are reduced to fists; and if Kenelm Digby learned to fence, so Kenelm Chillingly must learn to box; and if a gentleman thrashes a drayman twice his size, who has not learned to box, it is not unfair; it is but an exemplification of the truth, that knowledge is power. Come and take another lesson on boxing to-morrow."

Kenelm remounted his pony and returned home. He found his father sauntering in the garden with a book in his hand. "Papa," said Kenelm, "how does one gentleman write to another with whom he has a quarrel, and he don't want to make it up, but he has something to say about the quarrel which it is fair the other gentleman should know?"

"I don't understand what you mean."

"Well, just before I went to school I remember hearing you say that you had a quarrel with Lord Hautfort, and that he was an ass, and you would write and tell him so. When you wrote did you say, 'You are an ass'? Is that the way one gentleman writes to another?"

"Upon my honour, Kenelm, you ask very odd questions. But you cannot learn too early this fact, that irony is to the high-bred what billingsgate is to the vulgar; and when one gentleman thinks another gentleman an ass, he does not say it point-blank—he implies it in the politest terms he can invent. Lord Hautfort denies my right of free warren over a trout-stream that runs through his lands. I don't care a rush about the trout-stream, but there is no doubt of my right to fish in it. He was an ass to raise the question; for, if he had not, I should not have exercised the right. As he did raise the question, I was obliged to catch his trout."

"And you wrote a letter to him?"

"Yes."

"How did you write, papa? What did you say?"

"Something like this. 'Sir Peter Chillingly presents his compliments to Lord Hautfort, and thinks it fair to his lordship to say that he has taken the best legal advice with regard to his rights of free warren, and trusts to be forgiven if he presumes to suggest that Lord Hautfort might do well to consult his own lawyer before he decides on disputing them.'"

"Thank you, papa. I see——"

That evening Kenelm wrote the following letter:—

"Mr. Chillingly presents his compliments to Mr. Butt, and thinks it fair to Mr. Butt to say, that he is taking lessons in boxing, and trusts to be forgiven if he presumes to suggest that Mr. Butt might do well to take lessons himself before fighting with Mr. Chillingly next half."

"Papa," said Kenelm the next morning, "I want to write to a schoolfellow whose name is Butt; he is the son of a lawyer who is called a serjeant. I don't know where to direct to him."

"That is easily ascertained," said Sir Peter. "Serjeant Butt is an eminent man, and his address will be in the Court Guide." The address was found—Bloomsbury Square, and Kenelm directed his letter accordingly. In due course he received this answer:—

"You are an insolent little fool, and I'll thrash you within an inch of your life. ROBERT BUTT."

After the receipt of that polite epistle, Kenelm Chillingly's scruples vanished, and he took daily lessons in muscular Christianity.

Kenelm returned to school with a brow cleared from care, and three days after his return he wrote to the Rev. John:—

"DEAR SIR,—I have licked Butt. Knowledge is power.—Your affectionate KENELM.

"P.S.—Now that I have licked Butt, I have made it up with him."

From that time Kenelm prospered. Eulogistic letters from the illustrious head-master showered in upon Sir Peter. At the age of sixteen Kenelm Chillingly was the head of the school, and quitting it finally, brought home the following letter from his Orbilius to Sir Peter, marked 'confidential:'—

"DEAR SIR PETER CHILLINGLY,—I have never felt more anxious for the future career of any of my pupils than I do for that of your son. He is so clever that, with ease to himself, he may become a great man. He is so peculiar, that it is quite as likely that he may only make himself known to the world as a great oddity. That distinguished teacher, Dr. Arnold, said that the difference between one boy and another was not so much talent as energy. Your son has talent, has energy—yet he wants something for success in life; he wants the faculty of amalgamation. He is of a melancholic and therefore unsocial temperament. He will not act in concert with others. He is lovable enough; the other boys like him, especially the smaller ones, with whom he is a sort of hero; but he has not one intimate friend. So far as school learning is concerned, he might go to college at once, and with the certainty of distinction, provided he chose to exert himself. But if I may venture to offer an advice, I should say employ the next two years in letting him see a little more of real life, and acquire a due sense of its practical objects. Send him to a private tutor who is not a pedant, but a man of letters or a man of the world, and if in the metropolis so much the better. In a word, my young friend is unlike other people; and, with qualities that might do anything in life, I fear, unless you can get him to be like other people, that he will do nothing. Excuse the freedom with which I write, and ascribe it to the singular interest with which your son has inspired me.—I have the honour to be, dear Sir Peter, yours truly,

"WILLIAM HORTON."

Upon the strength of this letter Sir Peter did not indeed summon another family council; for he did not consider that his three maiden sisters could offer any practical advice on the matter. And as to Mr. Gordon, that gentleman having gone to law on the great timber question, and having been signally beaten thereon, had informed Sir Peter that he disowned him as a cousin and despised him as a man—not exactly in those words—more covertly, and therefore more stingingly. But Sir Peter invited Mr. Mivers for a week's shooting, and requested the Rev. John to meet him.

Mr. Mivers arrived. The sixteen years that had elapsed since he was first introduced to the reader, had made no perceptible change in his appearance. It was one of his maxims that in youth a man of the world should appear older than he is; and in middle age, and thence to his dying day, younger. And he announced one secret for attaining that art in these words: "Begin your wig early, thus you never become gray."

Unlike most philosophers, Mivers made his practice conform to his precepts; and while in the prime of youth inaugurated a wig in a fashion that defied the flight of time, not curly and hyacinthine, but straight-haired and unassuming. He looked five-and-thirty from the day he put on that wig at the age of twenty-five. He looked five-and-thirty now at the age of fifty-one.

"I mean," said he, "to remain thirty-five all my life. No better age to stick at. People may choose to say I am more, but I shall not own it. No one is bound to criminate himself."

Mr. Mivers had some other aphorisms on this important subject. One was, "Refuse to be ill. Never tell people you are ill; never own it to yourself. Illness is one of those things which a man should resist on principle at the onset. It should never be allowed to get in the thin end of the wedge. But take care of your constitution, and, having ascertained the best habits for it, keep to them like clock-work." Mr. Mivers would not have missed his constitutional walk in the Park before breakfast, if, by going in a cab to St. Giles's, he could have saved the city of London from conflagration.

Another aphorism of his was, "If you want to keep young, live in a metropolis; never stay above a few weeks at a time in the country. Take two men of similar constitution at the age of twenty-five; let one live in London and enjoy a regular sort of club life; send the other to some rural district, preposterously called 'salubrious.' Look at these men when they have both reached the age of forty-five. The London man has preserved his figure, the rural man has a paunch. The London man has an interesting delicacy of complexion; the face of the rural man is coarse-grained and perhaps jowly."

A third axiom was, "Don't be a family man; nothing ages one like matrimonial felicity and paternal ties. Never multiply cares, and pack up your life in the briefest compass you can. Why add to your carpet-bag of troubles the contents of a lady's imperials and bonnet-boxes, and the travelling *fourgon* required by the nursery. Shun ambition—it is so gouty. It takes a great deal out of a man's life, and gives him nothing worth having till he has ceased to enjoy it."

Another of his aphorisms was this, "A fresh mind keeps the body fresh. Take in the ideas of the day, drain off those of yesterday. As to the morrow, time enough to consider it when it becomes to-day."

Preserving himself by attention to these rules, Mr. Mivers appeared at Exmundham *totus*, *teres*, but not *rotundus*—a man of middle height, slender, upright, with well-cut, small, slight features, thin lips, enclosing an excellent set of teeth, even, white, and not indebted to the dentist. For the sake of those teeth he shunned acid wines, especially hock in all its varieties, culinary sweets, and hot drinks. He drank even his tea cold. "There are," he said, "two things in life that a sage must preserve at every sacrifice, the coats of his stomach and the enamel of his teeth. Some evils admit of consolations: there are no comforters for dyspepsia and toothache." A man of letters, but a man of the world, he had so cultivated his mind as both, that he was feared as the one, and liked as the other. As a man of letters he despised the world; as a man of the world he despised letters. As the representative of both he revered himself.

CHAPTER IX.

ON the evening of the third day from the arrival of Mr. Mivers, he, the Parson, and Sir Peter were seated in the host's parlour, the Parson in an arm-chair by the ingle, smoking a short cutty-pipe; Mivers at length on the couch slowly inhaling the perfumes of one of his own choice *trabucos*. Sir Peter never smoked. There were spirits and hot water and lemons on the table. The Parson was famed for skill in the composition of toddy. From time to time the Parson sipped his glass, and Sir Peter, less frequently, did the same. It is needless to say that Mr. Mivers eschewed toddy: but beside him, on a chair, was a tumbler and large carafe of iced water.

SIR PETER.—"Cousin Mivers, you have now had time to study Kenelm, and to compare his character with that assigned to him in the Doctor's letter."

MIVERS (languidly).—"Ay."

SIR PETER.—"I ask you, as a man of the world, what you think I had best do with the boy. Shall I send him to such a tutor as the Doctor suggests? Cousin John is not of the same mind as the Doctor, and thinks that Kenelm's oddities are fine things in their way, and should not be prematurely ground out of him by contact with worldly tutors and London pavements."

"Ay," repeated Mr. Mivers, more languidly than before. After a pause he added, "Parson John, let us hear you."

The Parson laid aside his cutty-pipe, and emptied his fourth tumbler of toddy, then, throwing back his head in the dreamy fashion of the great Coleridge when he indulged in a monologue, he thus began, speaking somewhat through his nose—

"At the morning of life——"

Here Mivers shrugged his shoulders, turned round on his couch, and closed his eyes with the sigh of a man resigning himself to a homily.

"At the morning of life, when the dews——"

"I knew the dews were coming," said Mivers. "Dry them, if you please; nothing so unwholesome. We anticipate what you mean to say, which is plainly this—When a fellow is sixteen he is very fresh; so he is—pass on—what then?"

"If you mean to interrupt me with your habitual cynicism," said the Parson, "why did you ask to hear me?"

"That was a mistake, I grant; but who on earth could conceive that you were going to commence in that florid style. Morning of life indeed!—bosh!"

"Cousin Mivers," said Sir Peter, "you are not reviewing John's style in 'The Londoner;' and I will beg you to remember that my son's morning of life is a serious thing to his father, and not to be nipped in its bud by a cousin. Proceed, John!"

Quoth the Parson, good-humouredly, "I will adapt my style to the taste of my critic. When a fellow is at the age of sixteen, and very fresh to life, the question is whether he should begin thus prematurely to exchange the ideas that belong to youth for the ideas that properly belong to middle age,—whether he should begin to acquire that knowledge of the world which middle-aged men have acquired and can teach. I think not. I would rather have him yet awhile in the company of the poets—in the indulgence of glorious hopes and beautiful dreams, forming to himself some type of the Heroic, which he will keep before his eyes as a standard when he goes into the world as man. There are two schools of thought for the formation of character—the Real and Ideal. I would form the character in the Ideal school, in order to make it bolder and grander and lovelier when it takes its place in that everyday life which is called the Real. And therefore I am not for placing the descendant of Sir Kenelm Digby, in the interval between school and college, with a man of the world, probably as cynical as cousin Mivers, and living in the stony thoroughfares of London."

MR. MIVERS (rousing himself).—"Before we plunge into that Serbonian bog—the controversy between the Realistic and the Idealistic academicians—I think the first thing to decide is what you want Kenelm to be hereafter. When I order a pair of shoes, I decide beforehand what kind of shoes they are to be—court pumps or strong walking-shoes; and I don't ask the shoemaker to give me a preliminary lecture upon the different purposes of locomotion to which leather can be applied. If, Sir Peter, you want Kenelm to scribble lackadaisical poems, listen to Parson John; if you want to fill his head with pastoral rubbish about innocent love, which may end in marrying the Miller's Daughter, listen to Parson John; if you want him to enter life a soft-headed greenhorn, who will sign any bill carrying 50 per cent. to which a young scamp asks him to be security, listen to Parson John; in fine, if you wish a clever lad to become either a pigeon or a ring-dove, a credulous booby or a sentimental milksop, Parson John is the best adviser you can have."

"But I don't want my son to ripen into either of those imbecile developments of species."

"Then don't listen to Parson John; and there's an end of the discussion."

"No, there is not. I have not heard your advice what to do if John's advice is not to be taken."

Mr. Mivers hesitated. He seemed puzzled.

"The fact is," said the Parson, "that Mivers got up 'The Londoner' upon a principle that regulates his own mind,—find fault with the way everything is done, but never commit yourself by saying how anything can be done better."

"That is true," said Mivers, candidly. "The destructive order of mind is seldom allied to the constructive. I and 'The Londoner' are destructive by nature and by policy. We can reduce a building into rubbish, but we don't profess to turn rubbish into a building. We are critics, and, as you say, not such fools as to commit ourselves to the proposition of amendments that can be criticized by others. Nevertheless, for your sake, cousin Peter, and on the condition that if I give my advice you will never say that I gave it, and if you take it, that you will never reproach me if it turns out, as most advice does, very ill—I will depart from my custom and hazard my opinion."

"I accept the conditions."

"Well, then, with every new generation there springs up a new order of ideas. The earlier the age at which a man seizes the ideas that will influence his own generation, the more he has a start in the race with his contemporaries. If Kenelm comprehends at sixteen those intellectual signs of the time which, when he goes up to college, he will find young men of eighteen or twenty only just prepared to comprehend, he will produce a deep impression of his powers for reasoning, and their adaptation to actual life, which will be of great service to him later. Now the ideas that influence the mass of the rising generation never have their well-head in the generation itself. They have their source in the generation before them, generally in a small minority, neglected or contemned by the great majority which adopt them later. Therefore a lad at the age of sixteen, if he wants to get at such ideas, must come into close contact with some superior mind in which they were conceived twenty or thirty years before. I am consequently for placing Kenelm with a person from whom the new ideas can be learned. I am also for his being placed in the metropolis during the process of this initiation. With such introductions as are at our command, he may come in contact not only with new ideas, but with eminent men in all vocations. It is a great thing to mix betimes with clever people. One picks their brains unconsciously. There is another advantage, and not a small one, in this early entrance into good society. A youth learns manners, self-possession, readiness of resource; and he is much less likely to get into scrapes and contract tastes for low vices and mean dissipation, when he comes into life wholly his own master, after having acquired a predilection for refined companionship, under the guidance of those competent to select it. There, I have talked myself out of breath. And you had better decide at once in favour of my advice; for as I am of a contradictory temperament, myself of to-morrow may probably contradict myself of to-day."

Sir Peter was greatly impressed with his cousin's argumentative eloquence.

The Parson smoked his cutty-pipe in silence until appealed to by Sir Peter, and he then said, "In this programme of education for a Christian gentleman, the part of Christian seems to me left out."

"The tendency of the age," observed Mr. Mivers, calmly, "is towards that omission. Secular education is the necessary reaction from the special theological training which arose in the dislike of one set of Christians to the teaching of another set; and as these antagonists will not agree how religon is to be taught, either there must be no teaching at all, or religion must be eliminated from the tuition."

"That may do very well for some huge system of national education," said Sir Peter, "but it does not apply to Kenelm, as one of a family all of whose members belong to the Established Church. He may be taught the creed of his forefathers without offending a Dissenter."

"Which Established Church is he to belong to?" asked Mr. Mivers—"High Church, Low Church, Broad Church, Puseyite Church, Ritualistic Church, or any other Established Church that may be coming into fashion?"

"Pshaw!" said the Parson. "That sneer is out of place. You know very well that one merit of our Church is the spirit of toleration, which does not magnify every variety of opinion into a heresy or a schism. But if Sir Peter sends his son at the age of sixteen to a tutor who eliminates the religion of Christianity from his teaching, he deserves to be thrashed within an inch of his life; and," continued the Parson, eyeing Sir Peter sternly, and mechanically turning up his cuffs, "I should *like* to thrash him."

"Gently, John," said Sir Peter, recoiling; "gently, my dear kinsman. My heir shall not be educated as a heathen, and Mivers is only bantering us. Come, Mivers, do you happen to know among your London friends some man who, though a scholar and a man of the world, is still a Christian?"

"A Christian as by law established?"

"Well—yes."

"And who will receive Kenelm as a pupil?"

"Of course I am not putting such questions to you out of idle curiosity."

"I know exactly the man. He was originally intended for orders, and is a very learned theologian. He relinquished the thought of the clerical profession on succeeding to a small landed estate by the sudden death of an elder brother. He then came to London and bought experience—that is, he was naturally generous—he became easily taken in—got into difficulties—the estate was transferred to trustees for the benefit of creditors, and on the payment of 400*l.* a-year to himself. By this time he was married and had two children. He found the necessity of employing his pen in order to add to his income, and is one of the ablest contributors to the periodical press. He is an elegant scholar, an effective writer, much courted by public men, a thorough gentleman, has a pleasant house, and receives the best society. Having been once taken in, he defies any one to take him in again. His experience was not bought too dearly. No more acute and accomplished man of the world. The three hundred a-year or so that you would pay for Kenelm would suit him very well. His name is Welby, and he lives in Chester Square."

"No doubt he is a contributor to 'The Londoner,'" said the Parson, sarcastically.

"True. He writes our classical, theological, and metaphysical articles. Suppose I invite him to come here for a day or two, and you can see him and judge for yourself, Sir Peter?"

"Do."

CHAPTER X.

MR. WELBY arrived, and pleased everybody. A man of the happiest manners, easy and courteous. There was no pedantry in him, yet you could soon see that his reading covered an extensive surface, and here and there had dived deeply. He enchanted the Parson by his comments on St. Chrysostom; he dazzled Sir Peter with his lore in the antiquities of ancient Britain; he captivated Kenelm by his readiness to enter into that most disputatious of sciences called metaphysics; while for Lady Chillingly, and the three sisters who were invited to meet him, he was more entertaining, but not less instructive. Equally at home in novels and in good books, he gave to the spinsters a list of innocent works in either; while for Lady Chillingly he sparkled with anecdotes of fashionable life, the newest *bons mots*, the latest scandals. In fact, Mr. Welby was one of those brilliant persons who adorn any society amidst which they are thrown. If at heart he was a disappointed man, the disappointment was concealed by an even serenity of spirits; he had entertained high and justifiable hopes of a brilliant career and a lasting reputation as a theologian and a preacher; the succession to his estate at the age of twenty-three had changed the nature of his ambition. The charm of his manner was such that he sprang at once into the fashion, and became beguiled by his own genial temperament into that lesser but pleasanter kind of ambition which contents itself with social successes, and enjoys the present hour. When his circumstances compelled him to eke out his income by literary profits, he slid into the grooves of periodical composition, and resigned all thoughts of the labour required for any complete work, which might take much time and be attended with scanty profits. He still remained very popular in society, and perhaps his general reputation for ability made him fearful to hazard it by any great undertaking. He was not, like Mivers, a despiser of all men and all things; but he regarded men and things as an indifferent though good-natured spectator regards the thronging streets from a drawing-room window. He could not be called *blasé*, but he was thoroughly *désillusionné*. Once over-romantic, his character now was so entirely imbued with the neutral tints of life that romance offended his taste as an obtrusion of violent colour into a sober woof. He was become a thorough Realist in his code of criticism, and in his worldly mode of action and thought. But Parson John did not perceive this, for Welby listened to that gentleman's eulogies on the Ideal school without troubling himself to contradict them. He had grown too indolent to be combative in conversation, and only as a critic betrayed such pugnacity as remained to him by the polished cruelty of sarcasm.

He came off with flying colours through an examination into his Church orthodoxy instituted by the Parson and Sir Peter. Amid a cloud of ecclesiastical erudition, his own opinions vanished in those of the Fathers. In truth, he was a Realist in religion as in everything else. He regarded Christianity as a type of existent civilization, which ought to be reverenced, as one might recognize the other types of that civilization—such as the liberty of the press, the representative system, white neckcloths and black coats of an evening, &c. He belonged, therefore, to what he himself called the school of Eclectical Christianity, and accommodated the reasonings of Deism to the doctrines of the Church, if not as a creed, at least as an institution. Finally, he united all the Chillingly votes in his favour; and when he departed from the Hall, carried off Kenelm for his initiation into the new ideas that were to govern his generation.

CHAPTER XI.

KENELM remained a year and a half with this distinguished preceptor. During that time he learned much in book-lore; he saw much, too, of the eminent men of the day, in literature, the law, and the senate. He saw, also, a good deal of the fashionable world. Fine ladies, who had been friends of his mother in her youth, took him up, counselled and petted him. One in especial, the Marchioness of Glenalvon, to whom he was endeared by grateful association. For her youngest son had been a fellow-pupil of Kenelm's at Merton School, and Kenelm had saved his life from drowning. The poor boy died of consumption later, and her grief for his loss made her affection for Kenelm yet more tender. Lady Glenalvon was one of the queens of the London world. Though in her fiftieth year, she was still very handsome: she was also very accomplished, very clever, and very kind-hearted, as some of such queens are; just one of those women invaluable in forming the manners and elevating the character of young men destined to make a figure in after-life. But she was very angry with herself in thinking that she failed to arouse any such ambition in the heir of the Chillinglys.

It may here be said that Kenelm was not without great advantages of form and countenance. He was tall, and the youthful grace of his proportions concealed his physical strength, which was extraordinary rather from the iron texture than the bulk of his thews and sinews. His face, though it certainly lacked the roundness of youth, had a grave, sombre, haunting sort of beauty, not artistically regular, but picturesque, peculiar, with large dark expressive eyes, and a certain indescribable combination of sweetness and melancholy in his quiet smile. He never laughed audibly, but he had a quick sense of the comic, and his eye would laugh when his lips were silent. He would say queer, droll, unexpected things, which passed for humour; but, save for that gleam in the eye, he could not have said them with more seeming innocence of intentional joke if he had been a monk of La Trappe looking up from the grave he was digging in order to utter "memento mori."

That face of his was a great 'take in.' Women thought it full of romantic sentiment—the face of one easily moved to love, and whose love would be replete alike with poetry and passion. But he remained as proof as the youthful Hippolytus to all female attraction. He delighted the Parson by keeping up his practice in athletic pursuits, and obtained a reputation at the pugilistic school, which he attended regularly, as the best gentleman boxer about town.

He made many acquaintances, but still formed no friendships. Yet every one who saw him much conceived affection for him. If he did not return that affection, he did not repel it. He was exceedingly gentle in voice and manner, and had all his father's placidity of temper—children and dogs took to him as by instinct.

On leaving Mr. Welby's, Kenelm carried to Cambridge a mind largely stocked with the new ideas that were budding into leaf. He certainly astonished the other freshmen, and occasionally puzzled the mighty Fellows of Trinity and St. John's. But he gradually withdrew himself much from general society. In fact, he was too old in mind for his years; and after having mixed in the choicest circles of a metropolis, college suppers and wine parties had little charm for him. He maintained his pugilistic renown; and on certain occasions, when some delicate undergraduate had been bullied by some gigantic bargeman, his muscular Christianity nobly developed itself. He did not do as much as he might have done in the more intellectual ways of academical distinction. Still, he was always among the first in the college examinations; he won two university prizes, and took a very creditable degree, after which he returned home, more odd, more saturnine—in short, less like other people—than when he had left Merton School. He had woven a solitude round him out of his own heart, and in that solitude he sate still and watchful as a spider sits in his web.

Whether from natural temperament, or from his educational training under such teachers as Mr. Mivers, who carried out the new ideas of reform by revering nothing in the past, and Mr. Welby, who accepted the routine of the present as realistic, and pooh-poohed all visions of the future as idealistic, Kenelm's chief mental characteristic was a kind of tranquil indifferentism. It was difficult to detect in him either of those ordinary incentives to action—vanity or ambition, the yearning for applause or the desire of power. To all female fascinations he had been hitherto star-proof. He had never experienced love, but he had read a good deal about it, and that passion seemed to him an unaccountable aberration of human reason, and an ignominious surrender of the equanimity of thought which it should be the object of masculine natures to maintain undisturbed.

A very eloquent book in praise of celibacy, and entitled 'The Approach to the Angels,' written by that eminent Oxford scholar, Decimus Roach, had produced so remarkable an effect upon his youthful mind, that, had he been a Roman Catholic, he might have become a monk. Where he most evinced ardour, it was a logician's ardour for abstract truth—that is, for what *he* considered truth ; and as what seems truth to one man is sure to seem falsehood to some other man, this predilection of his was not without its inconveniences and dangers, as may probably be seen in the following chapter.

Meanwhile, rightly to appreciate his conduct therein, I entreat thee, O candid Reader (not that any Reader ever is candid), to remember that he is brimful of new ideas, which, met by a deep and hostile undercurrent of old ideas, become more provocatively billowy and surging.

CHAPTER XII.

THERE had been great festivities at Exmundham, in celebration of the honour bestowed upon the world by the fact that Kenelm Chillingly had lived twenty-one years in it.

The young heir had made a speech to the assembled tenants and other admitted revellers, which had by no means added to the exhilaration of the proceedings. He spoke with a fluency and self-possession which were surprising in a youth addressing a multitude for the first time. But his speech was not cheerful.

The principal tenant on the estate, in proposing his health, had naturally referred to the long line of his ancestors. His father's merits as man and landlord had been enthusiastically commemorated, and many happy auguries for his own future career had been drawn, partly from the excellences of his parentage, partly from his own youthful promise in the honours achieved at the university.

Kenelm Chillingly in reply, largely availed himself of those new ideas which were to influence the rising generation, and with which he had been rendered familiar by the journal of Mr. Mivers and the conversation of Mr. Welby.

He briefly disposed of the ancestral part of the question. He observed that it was singular to note how long any given family or dynasty could continue to flourish in any given nook of matter in creation, without any exhibition of intellectual powers beyond those displayed by a succession of vegetable crops. "It is certainly true," he said, "that the Chillinglys have lived in this place from father to son for about a fourth part of the history of the world, since the date which Sir Isaac Newton assigns to the Deluge. But, so far as can be judged by existent records, the world has not been in any way wiser or better for their existence. They were born to eat as long as they could eat, and when they could eat no longer they died. Not that in this respect they were a whit less insignificant than the generality of their fellow-creatures. Most of us now present," continued the youthful orator, "are only born in order to die; and the chief consolation of our wounded pride in admitting this fact, is in the probability that our posterity will not be of more consequence to the scheme of nature than we ourselves are." Passing from that philosophical view of his own ancestors in particular, and of the human race in general, Kenelm Chillingly then touched with serene analysis on the eulogies lavished on his father as man and landlord.

"As man," he said, "my father no doubt deserves all that can be said by man in favour of man. But what, at the best, is man? A crude, struggling, undeveloped embryo, of whom it is the highest attribute that he feels a vague consciousness that he is only an embryo, and cannot complete himself till he ceases to be a man; that is, until he becomes another being in another form of existence. We can praise a dog as a dog, because a dog is a completed *ens*, and not an embryo. But to praise a man as man, forgetting that he is only a germ out of which a form wholly different is ultimately to spring, is equally opposed to Scriptural belief in his present crudity and imperfection, and to psychological or metaphysical examination of a mental construction evidently designed for purposes that he can never fulfil as man. That my father is an embryo not more incomplete than any present, is quite true; but that, you will see on reflection, is saying very little on his behalf. Even in the boasted physical formation of us men, you are aware that the best-shaped amongst us, according to the last scientific discoveries, is only a development of some hideous hairy animal, such as a gorilla; and the ancestral gorilla itself had its own aboriginal forefather in a small marine animal shaped like a two-necked bottle. The probability is that, some day or other, we shall be exterminated by a new development of species.

"As for the merits assigned to my father as landlord, I must respectfully dissent from the panegyrics so rashly bestowed on him. For all sound reasoners must concur in this, that the first duty of an owner of land is not to the occupiers to whom he leases it, but to

C

the nation at large. It is his duty to see that the land yields to the community the utmost it can yield. In order to effect this object, a landlord should put up his farm to competition, exacting the highest rent he can possibly get from responsible competitors. Competitive examination is the enlightened order of the day, even in professions in which the best men would have qualities that defy examination. In agriculture, happily, the principle of competitive examination is not so hostile to the choice of the best men as it must be, for instance, in diplomacy, where a Talleyrand would be excluded for knowing no language but his own; and still more in the army, where promotion would be denied to an officer who, like Marlborough, could not spell. But in agriculture a landlord has only to inquire who can give the highest rent, having the largest capital, subject by the strictest penalties of law to the conditions of a lease dictated by the most scientific agriculturists under penalties fixed by the most cautious conveyancers. By this mode of procedure, recommended by the most liberal economists of our age—barring those still more liberal who deny that property in land is any property at all—by this mode of procedure, I say, a landlord does his duty to his country. He secures tenants who can produce the most to the community by their capital, tested through competitive examination into their bankers' accounts and the security they can give, and through the rigidity of covenants suggested by Liebig and reduced into law by a Chitty. But on my father's land I see a great many tenants with little skill and less capital, ignorant of a Liebig and revolting from a Chitty, and no filial enthusiasm can induce me honestly to say that my father is a good landlord. He has preferred his affection for individuals to his duties to the community. It is not, my friends, a question whether a handful of farmers like yourselves go to the workhouse or not. It is a consumer's question. Do you produce the maximum of corn to the consumer?

"With respect to myself," continued the orator, warming, as the cold he had engendered in his audience became more freezingly felt—"with respect to myself, I do not deny that, owing to the accident of training for a very faulty and contracted course of education, I have obtained what are called 'honours' at the University of Cambridge; but you must not regard that fact as a promise of any worth in my future passage through life. Some of the most useless persons—especially narrow-minded and bigoted— have acquired far higher honours at the university than have fallen to my lot.

"I thank you no less for the civil things you have said of me and of my family; but I shall endeavour to walk to that grave to which we are all bound with a tranquil indifference as to what people may say of me in so short a journey. And the sooner, my friends, we get to our journey's end, the better our chance of escaping a great many pains, troubles, sins, and diseases. So that when I drink to your good healths, you must feel that in reality I wish you an early deliverance from the ills to which flesh is exposed, and which so generally increase with our years, that good health is scarcely compatible with the decaying faculties of old age. Gentlemen, your good healths!"

CHAPTER XIII.

THE morning after these birthday rejoicings, Sir Peter and Lady Chillingly held a long consultation on the peculiarities of their heir, and the best mode of instilling into his mind the expediency either of entertaining more pleasing views, or at least of professing less unpopular sentiments—compatibly of course, though they did not say it, with the new ideas that were to govern his century. Having come to an agreement on this delicate subject, they went forth, arm in arm, in search of their heir. Kenelm seldom met them at breakfast. He was an early riser, and accustomed to solitary rambles before his parents were out of bed.

The worthy pair found Kenelm seated on the banks of a trout-stream that meandered through Chillingly Park, dipping his line into the water, and yawning, with apparent relief in that operation.

"Does fishing amuse you, my boy?" said Sir Peter, heartily.

"Not in the least, sir," answered Kenelm.

"Then why do you do it?" asked Lady Chillingly.

"Because I know nothing else that amuses me more."

"Ah! that is it," said Sir Peter; "the whole secret of Kenelm's oddities is to be found in these words, my dear; he needs amusement. Voltaire says truly, 'amusement is one of the wants of man.' And if Kenelm could be amused like other people, he would be like other people."

"In that case," said Kenelm, gravely, and extracting from the water a small but lively trout, which settled itself in Lady Chillingly's lap—"in that case I would rather not be amused. I have no interest in the absurdities of other people. The instinct of self-preservation compels me to have some interest in my own."

"Kenelm, sir," exclaimed Lady Chillingly, with an animation into which her tranquil ladyship was very rarely betrayed, "take away that horrid damp thing! Put down your rod and attend to what your father says. Your strange conduct gives us cause of serious anxiety."

Kenelm unhooked the trout, deposited the fish in his basket, and raising his large eyes to his father's face, said, "What is there in my conduct that occasions you displeasure?"

"Not displeasure, Kenelm," said Sir Peter, kindly, "but anxiety; your mother has hit upon the right word. You see, my dear son, that it is my wish that you should distinguish yourself in the world. You might represent this county, as your ancestors have done before. I had looked forward to the proceedings of yesterday as an admirable occasion for your introduction to your future constituents. Oratory is the talent most appreciated in a free country, and why should you not be an orator? Demosthenes says that delivery, delivery, delivery, is the art of oratory; and your delivery is excellent, graceful, self-possessed, classical."

"Pardon me, my dear father, Demosthenes does not say delivery, nor action, as the word is commonly rendered; he says, 'acting or stage-play'—$ὑπόκρισις$; the art by which a man delivers a speech in a feigned character—whence we get the word hypocrisy. Hypocrisy, hypocrisy, hypocrisy! is, according to Demosthenes, the triple art of the orator. Do you wish me to become triply a hypocrite?"

"Kenelm, I am ashamed of you. You know as well as I do that it is only by metaphor that you can twist the word ascribed to the great Athenian into the sense of hypocrisy. But assuming it, as you say, to mean not delivery, but acting, I understand why your *début* as an orator was not successful. Your delivery was excellent, your acting defective. An orator should please, conciliate, persuade, prepossess. You did the reverse of all this; and though you produced a great effect, the effect was so decidedly to your disadvantage, that it would have lost you an election on any hustings in England."

"Am I to understand, my dear father," said Kenelm, in the mournful and compassionate tones with which a pious minister of the Church reproves some abandoned and hoary sinner—"am I to understand that you would commend to your son the adoption of deliberate falsehood for the gain of a selfish advantage?"

"Deliberate falsehood! you impertinent puppy!"

"Puppy!" repeated Kenelm, not indignantly but musingly—"puppy!—a well-bred puppy takes after its parents."

Sir Peter burst out laughing.

Lady Chillingly rose with dignity, shook her gown, unfolded her parasol, and stalked away speechless.

"Now, look you, Kenelm," said Sir Peter, as soon as he had

composed himself. "These quips and humours of yours are amusing enough to an eccentric man like myself, but they will not do for the world; and how at your age, and with the rare advantages you have had in an early introduction to the best intellectual society, under the guidance of a tutor acquainted with the new ideas which are to influence the conduct of statesmen, you could have made so silly a speech as you did yesterday, I cannot understand."

"My dear father, allow me to assure you that the ideas I expressed are the new ideas most in vogue—ideas expressed in still plainer, or, if you prefer the epithet, still sillier terms than I employed. You will find them instilled into the public mind by 'The Londoner,' and by most intellectual journals of a liberal character."

"Kenelm, Kenelm, such ideas would turn the world topsy-turvy."

"New ideas always do tend to turn old ideas topsy-turvy. And the world, after all, is only an idea, which is turned topsy-turvy with every successive century."

"You make me sick of the word ideas. Leave off your metaphysics and study real life."

"It is real life which I did study under Mr. Welby. He is the Archimandrite of Realism. It is sham life which you wish me to study. To oblige you I am willing to commence it. I dare say it is very pleasant. Real life is not; on the contrary—dull." And Kenelm yawned again.

"Have you no young friends among your fellow-collegians?"

"Friends! certainly not, sir. But I believe I have some enemies, who answer the same purpose as friends, only they don't hurt one so much."

"Do you mean to say that you lived alone at Cambridge?"

"No, I lived a good deal with Aristophanes, and a little with Conic Sections and Hydrostatics."

"Books. Dry company."

"More innocent, at least, than moist company. Did you ever get drunk, sir?"

"Drunk!"

"I tried to do so once with the young companions whom you would commend to me as friends. I don't think I succeeded, but I woke with a headache. Real life at college abounds with headache."

"Kenelm, my boy, one thing is clear—you must travel."

"As you please, sir. Marcus Antoninus says that it is all one to a stone whether it be thrown upwards or downwards. When shall I start?"

"Very soon. Of course there are preparations to make; you

should have a travelling companion. I don't mean a tutor—you are too clever and too steady to need one—but a pleasant, sensible, well-mannered young person of your own age."

"My own age—male or female?"

Sir Peter tried hard to frown. The utmost he could do was to reply gravely, "FEMALE! If I said you were too steady to need a tutor, it was because you have hitherto seemed little likely to be led out of your way by female allurements. Among your other studies may I inquire if you have included that which no man has ever yet thoroughly mastered—the study of woman?"

"Certainly. Do you object to my catching another trout?"

"Trout be——blest, or the reverse. So you have studied woman. I should never have thought it. Where and when did you commence that department of science?"

"When? ever since I was ten years old. Where? first in your own house, then at college. Hush!—a bite," and another trout left its native element and alighted on Sir Peter's nose, whence it was solemnly transferred to the basket.

"At ten years old, and in my own house. That flaunting hussy Jane, the under-housemaid——"

"Jane! No, sir, Pamela, Miss Byron, Clarissa—females in Richardson, who, according to Dr. Johnson, 'taught the passions to move at the command of virtue.' I trust for your sake that Dr. Johnson did not err in that assertion, for I found all these females at night in your own private apartments."

"Oh!" said Sir Peter, "that's all."

"All I remember at ten years old," replied Kenelm.

"And at Mr. Welby's or at college," proceeded Sir Peter, timorously, "was your acquaintance with females of the same kind?"

Kenelm shook his head. "Much worse; they were very naughty indeed at college."

"I should think so, with such a lot of young fellows running after them."

"Very few fellows run after the females. I mean—rather avoid them."

"So much the better."

"No, my father, so much the worse; without an intimate knowledge of those females there is little use going to college at all."

"Explain yourself."

"Every one who receives a classical education is introduced into their society—Pyrrha and Lydia, Glycera and Corinna, and many more all of the same sort; and then the females in Aristophanes, what do you say to them, sir?"

"Is it only females who lived 2000 or 3000 years ago, or more probably never lived at all, whose intimacy you have cultivated? Have you never admired any real women?"

"Real women! I never met one. Never met a woman who was not a sham, a sham from the moment she is told to be pretty-behaved, conceal her sentiments, and look fibs when she does not speak them. But if I am to learn sham life, I suppose I must put up with sham women."

"Have you been crossed in love that you speak so bitterly of the sex?"

"I don't speak bitterly of the sex. Examine any woman on her oath, and she'll own she is a sham, always has been, and always will be, and is proud of it."

"I am glad your mother is not by to hear you. You will think differently one of these days. Meanwhile, to turn to the other sex, is there no young man of your own rank with whom you would like to travel?"

"Certainly not. I hate quarrelling."

"As you please. But you cannot go quite alone; I will find you a good travelling servant. I must write to town to-day about your preparations, and in another week or so I hope all will be ready. Your allowance will be whatever you like to fix it at; you have never been extravagant, and—boy—I love you. Amuse yourself, enjoy yourself, and come back cured of your oddities, but preserving your honour."

Sir Peter bent down and kissed his son's brow. Kenelm was moved; he rose, put his arm round his father's shoulder, and lovingly said, in an under tone, "If ever I am tempted to do a base thing, may I remember whose son I am—I shall be safe then." He withdrew his arm as he said this, and took his solitary way along the banks of the stream, forgetful of rod and line.

CHAPTER XIV.

THE young man continued to skirt the side of the stream, until he reached the boundary pale of the park. Here, placed on a rough grass mound, some former proprietor, of a social temperament, had built a kind of belvidere, so as to command a cheerful view of the highroad below. Mechanically the heir of the Chillinglys ascended the mound, seated himself within the belvidere, and leant his chin on his hand in a thoughtful attitude. It was rarely that the building was honoured by a human visitor—its habitual occupants were spiders. Of those industrious insects it was a well-populated colony. Their webs, darkened with dust, and ornamented with the wings, and legs, and skeletons of many an unfortunate traveller, clung thick to angle and window-sill, festooned the rickety table on which the young man leant his elbow, and described geometrical circles and rhomboids between the gaping rails that formed the backs of venerable chairs. One large black spider—who was probably the oldest inhabitant, and held possession of the best place by the window, ready to offer perfidious welcome to every winged itinerant who might be tempted to turn aside from the highroad for the sake of a little cool and repose—rushed from its innermost penetralia at the entrance of Kenelm, and remained motionless in the centre of its meshes, staring at him. It did not seem quite sure whether the stranger was too big or not.

"It is a wonderful proof of the wisdom of Providence," said Kenelm, "that whenever any large number of its creatures forms a community or class, a secret element of disunion enters into the hearts of the individuals forming the congregation, and prevents their co-operating heartily and effectually for their common interest. 'The fleas would have dragged me out of bed if they had been unanimous,' said the great Mr. Curran: and there can be no doubt that if all the spiders in this commonwealth would unite to attack me in a body, I should fall a victim to their combined nippers. But spiders, though inhabiting the same region, constituting the same race, animated by the same instincts, do not combine even against a butterfly; each seeks his own special advantage, and not that of the community at large. And how completely the life of each thing resembles a circle in this respect, that it can never touch another circle at more than one point. Nay, I doubt if it quite touches it even there,—there is a space between every atom—self is always selfish; and yet there are eminent masters in the Academe of New Ideas who wish to make us believe that all the working classes of a civilized world could merge every difference of race, creed, intellect, individual propensities and interests, into the construction of a single web, stocked as a larder in common!" Here the soliloquist came to a dead stop, and leaning out of the window, contemplated the highroad. It was a very fine highroad—straight and level, kept in excellent order by turnpikes at every eight miles. A pleasant greensward bordered it on either side, and under the belvidere the benevolence of some mediæval Chillingly had placed a little drinking-fountain for the refreshment of wayfarers. Close to the fountain stood a rude stone bench, overshadowed by a large willow, and commanding from the high table-ground on which it was placed a wide view of corn-fields, meadows, and distant hills, suffused in the mellow light of the summer sun. Along that road there came successively a waggon filled with passengers seated on straw—an old woman, a pretty girl, two children; then a stout farmer going to market in his dog-cart; then three flys carrying fares to the nearest railway station; then a handsome young man on horse-back, a handsome young lady by his side, a groom behind. It was easy to see that the young man and young lady were lovers. See it in his ardent looks and serious lips parted but for whispers only to be heard by her;—see it in her downcast eyes and heightened colour. "'Alas! regardless of their doom,'" muttered Kenelm, "what trouble those 'little victims' are preparing for themselves and their progeny! Would I could lend them Decimus Roach's 'Approach to the Angels'!" The road now for some minutes became solitary and still, when there was heard to the right a sprightly sort of carol, half sung, half recited, in musical voice, with a singularly clear enunciation, so that the words reached Kenelm's ear distinctly. They ran thus:—

> "Black Karl looked forth from his cottage-door,
> He looked on the forest green;
> And down the path, with his dogs before,
> Came the Ritter of Neirestein:
> Singing—singing—lustily singing,
> Down the path, with his dogs before,
> Came the Ritter of Neirestein."

At a voice so English, attuned to a strain so Germanic, Kenelm pricked up attentive ears, and, turning his eye down the road, beheld, emerging from the shade of beeches that overhung the park pales, a figure that did not altogether harmonize with the idea of a Ritter of Neirestein. It was, nevertheless, a picturesque figure enough. The man was attired in a somewhat threadbare suit of Lincoln green, with a high-crowned Tyrolese hat; a knapsack was slung behind his shoulders, and he was attended by a white Pomeranian dog, evidently foot-sore, but doing his best to appear proficient in the chase by limping some yards in advance of his master, and sniffing into the hedges for rats and mice, and such small deer.

By the time the pedestrian had reached to the close of his refrain he had gained the fountain, and greeted it with an exclamation of pleasure. Slipping the knapsack from his shoulder, he filled the iron ladle attached to the basin. He then called to the dog by the name of Max, and held the ladle for him to drink. Not till the animal had satisfied his thirst did the master assuage his own. Then, lifting his hat and bathing his temples and face, the pedestrian seated himself on the bench, and the dog nestled on the turf at his feet. After a little pause the wayfarer began again, though in a lower and slower tone, to chant his refrain, and proceeded, with abrupt snatches, to link the verse on to another stanza. It was evident that he was either endeavouring to remember or to invent, and it seemed rather like the latter and more laborious operation of mind.

"'Why on foot, why on foot, Ritter Karl,' quoth he,
'And not on thy palfrey gray?'

Palfrey gray—hum—gray.

'The run of ill-luck was too strong for me,
And has galloped my steed away.'

That will do—good!"

"Good indeed! He is easily satisfied," muttered Kenelm. "But such pedestrians don't pass the road every day. Let us talk to him." So saying he slipped quietly out of the window, descended the mound, and letting himself into the road by a screened wicket-gate, took his noiseless stand behind the wayfarer and beneath the bowery willow.

The man had now sunk into silence. Perhaps he had tired himself of rhymes; or perhaps the mechanism of verse-making had been replaced by that kind of sentiment, or that kind of reverie, which is common to the temperaments of those who indulge in verse-making. But the loveliness of the scene before him had caught his eye and fixed it into an intent gaze upon wooded landscapes stretching farther and farther to the range of hills on which the heaven seemed to rest.

"I should like to hear the rest of that German ballad," said a voice, abruptly.

The wayfarer started, and turning round, presented to Kenelm's view a countenance in the ripest noon of manhood, with locks and beard of a deep rich auburn, bright blue eyes, and a wonderful nameless charm both of feature and expression, very cheerful, very frank, and not without a certain nobleness of character which seemed to exact respect.

"I beg your pardon for my interruption," said Kenelm, lifting his hat; "but I overheard you reciting; and though I suppose your verses are a translation from the German, I don't remember anything like them in such popular German poets as I happen to have read."

"It is not a translation, sir," replied the itinerant. "I was only trying to string together some ideas that came into my head this fine morning."

"You are a poet, then?" said Kenelm, seating himself on the bench.

"I dare not say poet. I am a verse-maker."

"Sir, I know there is a distinction. Many poets of the present day, considered very good, are uncommonly bad verse-makers. For my part, I could more readily imagine them to be good poets if they did not make verses at all. But can I not hear the rest of the ballad?"

"Alas! the rest of the ballad is not yet made. It is rather a long subject, and my flights are very brief."

"That is much in their favour, and very unlike the poetry in fashion. You do not belong, I think, to this neighbourhood. Are you and your dog travelling far?"

"It is my holiday time, and I ramble on through the summer. I am travelling far, for I travel till September. Life amid summer fields is a very joyous thing."

"Is it indeed?" said Kenelm, with much *naïveté*. "I should have thought that, long before September, you would have got very much bored with the fields and the dog and yourself altogether. But, to be sure, you have the resource of verse-making, and that seems a very pleasant and absorbing occupation to those who practice it—from our old friend Horace, kneading laboured Alcaics into honey in his summer rambles among the watered woodlands of Tibur, to Cardinal Richelieu employing himself on French rhymes in the intervals between chopping off noblemen's heads. It does not seem to signify much whether the verses be good or bad, so far as the pleasure of the verse-maker himself is concerned; for Richelieu was as much charmed with his occupation as Horace was, and his verses were certainly not Horatian."

"Surely at your age, sir, and with your evident education——"

"Say culture; that's the word in fashion nowadays."

"—Well, your evident culture—you must have made verses."

"Latin verses—yes—and occasionally Greek. I was obliged to do so at school. It did not amuse me."

"Try English."

Kenelm shook his head. "Not I. Every cobbler should stick to his last."

"Well, put aside the verse-making: don't you find a sensible enjoyment in those solitary summer walks, when you have Nature all to yourself—enjoyment in marking all the mobile, evanescent changes in her face—her laugh, her smile, her tears, her very frown!"

"Assuming that by Nature you mean a mechanical series of external phenomena, I object to your speaking of a machinery as if it were a person of the feminine gender—*her* laugh, *her* smile, &c. As well talk of the laugh and smile of a steam-engine. But to descend to common-sense. I grant there is some pleasure in solitary rambles in fine weather and amid varying scenery. You say that it is a holiday excursion that you are enjoying: I presume, therefore, that you have some practical occupation which consumes the time that you do not devote to a holiday?"

"Yes; I am not altogether an idler. I work sometimes, though not so hard as I ought. 'Life is earnest,' as the poet says. But I and my dog are rested now, and as I have still a long walk before me, I must wish you good-day."

"I fear," said Kenelm, with a grave and sweet politeness of tone and manner, which he could command at times, and which, in its difference from merely conventional urbanity, was not without fascination—"I fear that I have offended you by a question that must have seemed to you inquisitive—perhaps impertinent; accept my excuse; it is very rarely that I meet any one who interests me; and you do." As he spoke he offered his hand, which the wayfarer shook very cordially.

"I should be a churl indeed if your question could have given me offence. It is rather perhaps I who am guilty of impertinence, if I take advantage of my seniority in years, and tender you a counsel. Do not despise Nature, or regard her as a steam-engine; you will find in her a very agreeable and conversable friend, if you will cultivate her intimacy. And I don't know a better mode of doing so at your age, and with your strong limbs, than putting a knapsack on your shoulders, and turning foot-traveller, like myself."

"Sir, I thank you for your counsel; and I trust we may meet again, and interchange ideas as to the thing you call Nature—a thing which science and art never appear to see with the same eyes. If to an artist Nature has a soul, why, so has a steam-engine. Art gifts with soul all matter that it contemplates; science turns all that is already gifted with soul into matter. Good-day, sir."

Here Kenelm turned back abruptly, and the traveller went his way, silently and thoughtfully.

CHAPTER XV.

KENELM retraced his steps homeward under the shade of his "old hereditary trees." One might have thought his path along the greenswards, and by the side of the babbling rivulet, was pleasanter and more conducive to peaceful thoughts than the broad, dusty thoroughfare along which plodded the wanderer he had quitted. But the man addicted to reverie, forms his own landscapes and colours his own skies.

"It is," soliloquized Kenelm Chillingly, "a strange yearning I have long felt—to get out of myself—to get, as it were, into another man's skin—and have a little variety of thought and emotion. One's self is always the same self; and that is why I yawn so often. But if I can't get into another man's skin, the next best thing is to get as unlike myself as I possibly can do. Let me see what is myself. Myself is Kenelm Chillingly, son and heir to a rich gentleman. But a fellow with a knapsack on his back, sleeping at wayside inns, is not at all like Kenelm Chillingly—especially if he is very short of money, and may come to want a dinner. Perhaps that sort of fellow may take a livelier view of things; he can't take a duller one. Courage, Myself,—you and I can but try."

For the next two days Kenelm was observed to be unusually pleasant. He yawned much less frequently, walked with his father, played piquet with his mother, was more like other people. Sir Peter was charmed; he ascribed this happy change to the preparations he was making for Kenelm's travelling in style. The proud father was in active correspondence with his great London friends, seeking letters of introduction to Kenelm for all the courts of Europe. Portmanteaus, with every modern convenience, were ordered; an experienced courier, who could talk all languages —and cook French dishes if required—was invited to name his terms. In short, every arrangement worthy a young patrician's entrance into the great world was in rapid progress, when suddenly Kenelm Chillingly disappeared, leaving behind him on St. Peter's library table the following letter:—

"MY VERY DEAR FATHER,—Obedient to your desire, I depart in search of real life and real persons, or of the best imitations of them. Forgive me, I beseech you, if I commence that search in my own way. I have seen enough of ladies and gentlemen for the present—they must be all very much alike in every part of the world. You desired me to be amused. I go to try if that be possible. Ladies and gentlemen are not amusing; the more ladylike or gentlemanlike they are, the more insipid I find them. My dear father, I go in quest of adventure like Amadis of Gaul, like Don Quixote, like Gil Blas, like Roderick Random—like, in short, the only people seeking real life—the people who never existed except in books. I go on foot, I go alone. I have provided myself with a larger amount of money than I ought to spend, because every man must buy experience, and the first fees are heavy. In fact, I have put fifty pounds into my pocket-book and into my purse five sovereigns and seventeen shillings. This sum ought to last me a year, but I dare say inexperience will do me out of it in a month, so we will count it as nothing. Since you have asked me to fix my own allowance, I will beg you kindly to commence it this day in advance, by an order to your banker to cash my cheques to the amount of five pounds, and to the same amount monthly—viz., at the rate of sixty pounds a-year. With that sum I can't starve, and if I want more it may be amusing to work for it. Pray don't send after me, or institute inquiries, or disturb the household and set all the neighbourhood talking, by any mention either of my project or of your surprise at it. I will not fail to write to you from time to time.

"You will judge best what to say to my dear mother. If you tell her the truth, which of course I should do did I tell her anything, my request is virtually frustrated, and I shall be the talk of the county. You, I know, don't think telling fibs is immoral, when it happens to be convenient, as it would be in this case.

"I expect to be absent a year or eighteen months; if I prolong my travels it shall be in the way you proposed. I will then take my place in polite society, call upon you to pay all expenses, and fib on my own account to any extent required by that world of fiction which is peopled by illusions and governed by shams.

"Heaven bless you, my dear father, and be quite sure that if I get into any trouble requiring a friend, it is to you I shall turn. As yet I have no other friend on earth, and with prudence and good-luck I may escape the infliction of any other friend.—Yours ever affectionately,

"KENELM.

"*P.S.*—Dear father, I open my letter in your library to say again 'Bless you,' and to tell you how fondly I kissed your old beaver gloves, which I found on the table."

When Sir Peter came to that postscript he took off his spectacles and wiped them—they were very moist.

Then he fell into a profound meditation. Sir Peter was, as I have said, a learned man; he was also in some things a sensible man; and he had a strong sympathy with the humorous side of his son's crotchety character. What was to be said to Lady Chillingly? That matron was quite guiltless of any crime which should deprive her of a husband's confidence in a matter relating to her only son. She was a virtuous matron—morals irreproachable—manners dignified, and *she-baronety*. Any one seeing her for the first time would intuitively say, "Your ladyship." Was this a matron to be suppressed in any well-ordered domestic circle? Sir Peter's conscience loudly answered, "No;" but when, putting conscience into his pocket, he regarded the question at issue as a man of the world, Sir Peter felt that to communicate the contents of his son's letter to Lady Chillingly would be the foolishest thing he could possibly do. Did she know that Kenelm had absconded with the family dignity invested in his very name, no martial authority short of such abuses of power as constitute the offence of cruelty in a wife's action for divorce from social board and nuptial bed, could prevent Lady Chillingly from summoning all the grooms, sending them in all directions, with strict orders to bring back the runaway dead or alive—the walls would be placarded with handbills, "Strayed from his home," &c.,—the police would be telegraphing private instructions from town to town—the scandal would stick to Kenelm Chillingly for life, accompanied with vague hints of criminal propensities and insane hallucinations—he would be ever afterwards pointed out as "THE MAN WHO HAD DISAPPEARED." And to disappear and to turn up again, instead of being murdered, is the most hateful thing a man can do; all the newspapers bark at him, 'Tray, Blanche, Sweetheart, and all;' strict explanations of the unseemly fact of his safe existence are demanded in the name of public decorum, and no explanations are accepted—it is life saved, character lost.

Sir Peter seized his hat and walked forth, not to deliberate whether to fib or not to fib to the wife of his bosom, but to consider what kind of fib would the most quickly sink into the bosom of his wife.

A few turns to and fro on the terrace sufficed for the conception and maturing of the fib selected; a proof that Sir Peter was a practised fibber. He re-entered the house, passed into her ladyship's habitual sitting-room, and said with careless gaiety, "My old friend the Duke of Clareville is just setting off on a tour to

Switzerland with his family. His youngest daughter, Lady Jane, is a pretty girl, and would not be a bad match for Kenelm."

"Lady Jane, the youngest daughter with fair hair, whom I saw last as a very charming child, nursing a lovely doll presented to her by the Empress Eugénie. A good match indeed for Kenelm."

"I am glad you agree with me. Would it not be a favourable step towards that alliance, and an excellent thing for Kenelm generally, if he were to visit the Continent as one of the Duke's travelling party?"

"Of course it would."

"Then you approve what I have done—the Duke starts the day after to-morrow, and I have packed Kenelm off to town, with a letter to my old friend. You will excuse all leave-taking. You know that though the best of sons he is an odd fellow; and seeing that I had talked him into it, I struck while the iron was hot, and sent him off by the express at nine o'clock this morning, for fear that if I allowed any delay he would talk himself out of it."

"Do you mean to say Kenelm is actually gone? Good gracious!"

Sir Peter stole softly from the room, and summoning his valet, said, "I have sent Mr. Chillingly to London. Pack up the clothes he is likely to want, so that he can have them sent at once, whenever he writes for them."

And thus by a judicious violation of truth on the part of his father, that exemplary truth-teller Kenelm Chillingly saved the honour of his house and his own reputation from the breath of scandal and the inquisition of the police. He was not "THE MAN WHO HAD DISAPPEARED."

BOOK II.

CHAPTER I.

KENELM CHILLINGLY had quitted the paternal home at daybreak before any of the household was astir.

"Unquestionably," said he, as he walked along the solitary lanes—"unquestionably I begin the world as poets begin poetry, an imitator and a plagiarist. I am imitating an itinerant verse-maker, as, no doubt, he began by imitating some other maker of verse. But if there be anything in me, it will work itself out in original form. And after all, the verse-maker is not the inventor of ideas. Adventure on foot is a notion that remounts to the age of fable. Hercules, for instance,—that was the way in which he got to heaven, as a foot-traveller. How solitary the world is at this hour! Is it not for that reason that this is of all hours the most beautiful?"

Here he paused, and looked around and above. It was the very height of summer. The sun was just rising over gentle sloping uplands. All the dews on the hedgerows sparkled. There was not a cloud in the heavens. Uprose from the green blades of the corn a solitary skylark. His voice woke up the other birds. A few minutes more, and the joyous concert began. Kenelm reverently doffed his hat and bowed his head in mute homage and thanksgiving.

CHAPTER II.

ABOUT nine o'clock Kenelm entered a town some twelve miles distant from his father's house, and towards which he had designedly made his way, because in that town he was scarcely if at all known by sight, and he might there make the purchases he required without attracting any marked observation. He had selected for his travelling costume a shooting-dress, as the simplest and least likely to belong to his rank as a gentleman. But still in its very cut there was an air of distinction, and every labourer he had met on the way had touched his hat to him. Besides, who wears a shooting-dress in the middle of June, or a shooting-dress at all, unless he be either a game-keeper or a gentleman licensed to shoot?

Kenelm entered a large store-shop for ready-made clothes, and purchased a suit, such as might be worn on Sundays by a small country yeoman or tenant-farmer of a petty holding,—a stout coarse broadcloth upper garment, half coat, half jacket, with waistcoat to match, strong corduroy trousers, a smart Belcher neckcloth, with a small stock of linen and woollen socks in harmony with the other raiment. He bought also a leathern knapsack, just big enough to contain this wardrobe, and a couple of books, which, with his combs and brushes, he had brought away in his pockets. For among all his trunks at home there was no knapsack.

These purchases made and paid for, he passed quickly through the town, and stopped at a humble inn at the outskirts, to which he was attracted by the notice, "Refreshment for man and beast." He entered a little sanded parlour, which at that hour he had all to himself, called for breakfast, and devoured the best part of a fourpenny loaf, with a couple of hard eggs.

Thus recruited, he again sallied forth, and deviating into a thick wood by the roadside, he exchanged the habiliments with which he had left home for those he had purchased, and by the help of one or two big stones sunk the relinquished garments into a small but deep pool which he was lucky enough to find in a bush-grown dell much haunted by snipes in the winter.

"Now," said Kenelm, "I really begin to think I have got out of myself. I am in another man's skin; for what, after all, is a skin but a soul's clothing, and what is clothing but a decenter skin? Of its own natural skin every civilized soul is ashamed. It is the height of impropriety for any one but the lowest kind of savage to show it. If the purest soul now existent upon earth, the Pope of Rome's or the Archbishop of Canterbury's, were to pass down the Strand with the skin which nature gave to it bare to the eye, it would be brought up before a magistrate, prosecuted by the Society for the Suppression of Vice, and committed to jail as a public nuisance.

"Decidedly I am now in another man's skin. Kenelm Chillingly, I no longer
      Remain
       Yours faithfully;
But am,
    With profound consideration,
      Your obedient humble Servant."

With light step and elated crest, the wanderer, thus transformed, sprang from the wood into the dusty thoroughfare.

He had travelled on for about an hour, meeting but few other passengers, when he heard to the right a loud shrill young voice, "Help, help!—I will not go—I tell you, I will not!" Just before him stood, by a high five-barred gate, a pensive gray cob attached to a neat-looking gig. The bridle was loose on the cob's neck, The animal was evidently accustomed to stand quietly when ordered to do so, and glad of the opportunity.

The cries, "Help, help!" were renewed, mingled with louder tones in a rougher voice, tones of wrath and menace. Evidently these sounds did not come from the cob. Kenelm looked over the gate, and saw a few yards distant, in a grass field, a well-dressed boy struggling violently against a stout middle-aged man who was rudely hauling him along by the arm.

The chivalry natural to a namesake of the valiant Sir Kenelm Digby was instantly aroused. He vaulted over the gate, seized the man by the collar, and exclaimed, "For shame! what are you doing to that poor boy!—let him go!"

"Why the devil do you interfere?" cried the stout man—his eyes glaring and his lips foaming with rage. "Ah, are you the villain?—yes, no doubt of it. I'll give it to you, jackanapes," and still grasping the boy with one hand, with the other the stout man darted a blow at Kenelm, from which nothing less than the practised pugilistic skill and natural alertness of the youth thus suddenly assaulted could have saved his eyes and nose. As it was, the stout man had the worst of it; the blow was parried, returned with a dexterous manœuvre of Kenelm's right foot in Cornish fashion, and *procumbit humi bos*—the stout man lay sprawling on his back. The boy, thus released, seized hold of Kenelm by the arm, and hurrying him along up the field, cried, "Come, come before he gets up! save me! save me!" Ere he had recovered his own surprise, the boy had dragged Kenelm to the gate, and jumped into the gig, sobbing forth, "Get in, get in, I can't drive; get in, and drive—you. Quick! quick!"

"But," began Kenelm.

"Get in, or I shall go mad." Kenelm obeyed, the boy gave him the reins, and seizing the whip himself, applied it lustily to the cob. On sprang the cob. "Stop—stop—stop, thief!—villain!—Holloa!—thieves—thieves—thieves!—stop!" cried a voice behind. Kenelm involuntarily turned his head and beheld the stout man perched upon the gate and gesticulating furiously. It was but a glimpse; again the whip was plied, the cob frantically broke into a gallop, the gig jolted and bumped and swerved, and it was not till they had put a good mile between themselves and the stout man that Kenelm succeeded in obtaining possession of the whip, and calming the cob into a rational trot.

"Young gentleman," then said Kenelm, "perhaps you will have the goodness to explain."

"By and by; get on, that's a good fellow; you shall be well paid for it—well and handsomely."

Quoth Kenelm, gravely, "I know that in real life payment and service naturally go together. But we will put aside the payment till you tell me what is to be the service. And first, whither am I to drive you? We are coming to a place where three roads meet; which of the three shall I take?"

"Oh, I don't know; there is a finger-post. I want to get to— but it is a secret; you'll not betray me. Promise—swear."

"I don't swear except when I am in a passion, which, I am sorry to say, is very seldom; and I don't promise till I know what I promise; neither do I go on driving runaway boys in other men's gigs unless I know that I am taking them to a safe place, where their papas and mammas can get at them."

"I have no papa, no mamma," said the boy dolefully, and with quivering lips.

"Poor boy. I suppose that burly brute is your schoolmaster, and you are running away home for fear of a flogging."

The boy burst out laughing; a pretty silvery merry laugh, it thrilled through Kenelm Chillingly. "No, he would not flog me; he is not a schoolmaster; he is worse than that."

"Is it possible? What is he?"

"An uncle."

"Hum! uncles are proverbial for cruelty; were so in the classical days, and Richard III. was the only scholar in his family."

"Eh! classical and Richard III.!" said the boy, startled, and looking attentively at the pensive driver. "Who are you? you talk like a gentleman."

"I beg pardon. I'll not do so again if I can help it. Decidedly," thought Kenelm, "I am beginning to be amused. What a blessing it is to get into another man's skin, and another man's gig too!" Aloud, "Here we are at the finger-post. If you are running away from your uncle, it is time to inform me where you are running to."

Here the boy leaned over the gig and examined the finger-post. Then he clapped his hands joyfully.

"All right! I thought so—'To Tor-Hadham, eighteen miles.' That's the road to Tor-Hadham."

"Do you mean to say I am to drive you all that way—eighteen miles?"

"Yes."

"And to whom are you going?"

"I will tell you by and by. Do go on—do, pray. I can't drive —never drove in my life—or I would not ask you. Pray, pray, don't desert me! If you are a gentleman you will not; and if you are not a gentleman, I have got £10 in my purse, which you shall have when I am safe at Tor-Hadham. Don't hesitate; my whole life is at stake!" And the boy began once more to sob.

Kenelm directed the pony's head towards Tor-Hadham, and the boy ceased to sob.

"You are a good, dear fellow," said the boy, wiping his eyes. "I am afraid I am taking you very much out of your road."

"I have no road in particular, and would as soon go to Tor-Hadham, which I have never seen, as anywhere else. I am but a wanderer on the face of the earth."

"Have you lost your papa and mamma too? Why, you are not much older than I am."

"Little gentleman," said Kenelm, gravely, "I am just of age; and you, I suppose, are about fourteen."

"What fun!" cried the boy, abruptly. "Isn't it fun?"

"It will not be fun if I am sentenced to penal servitude for stealing your uncle's gig, and robbing his little nephew of £10. By the bye, that choleric relation of yours meant to knock down somebody else when he struck at me. He asked, 'Are *you* the villain?' Pray who is the villain? he is evidently in your confidence."

"Villain! he is the most honourable, high-minded—— But no matter now; I'll introduce you to him when we reach Tor-Hadham. Whip that pony; he is crawling."

"It is up-hill; a good man spares his beast."

No art and no eloquence could extort from his young companion any further explanation than Kenelm had yet received; and indeed, as the journey advanced, and they approached their destination, both parties sank into silence. Kenelm was seriously considering that his first day's experience of real life in the skin of another had placed in some peril his own. He had knocked down a man evidently respectable and well to do, had carried off that man's nephew, and made free with that man's goods and chattels—*i.e.*, his gig and horse. All this might be explained satisfactorily to a justice of the peace, but how? By returning to his former skin; by avowing himself to be Kenelm Chillingly, a distinguished university medalist, heir to no ignoble name and some £10,000 a year. But then what a scandal! he who abhorred scandal; in vulgar parlance, what a "row!" he who denied that the very word "row" was sanctioned by any classic authorities in the English language. He would have to explain how he came to be found disguised, carefully disguised, in garments such as no baronet's eldest son—even though that baronet be the least ancestral man of mark whom it suits the convenience of a First Minister to recommend to the Sovereign for exaltation over the rank of Mister—was ever beheld in, unless he had taken flight to the gold-diggings. Was this a position in which the heir of the Chillinglys, a distinguished family, whose coat of arms dated from the earliest authenticated period of English heraldry under Edward III. as Three Fishes *azur*, could be placed without grievous slur on the cold and ancient blood of the Three Fishes.

And then individually to himself, Kenelm, irrespectively of the Three Fishes. What a humiliation! He had put aside his respected father's deliberate preparations for his entrance into real life; he had perversely chosen his own walk on his own responsibility; and here, before half the first day was over, what an infernal scrape he had walked himself into! And what was his excuse? A wretched little boy, sobbing and chuckling by turns, and yet who was clever enough to twist Kenelm Chillingly round his finger; twist *him*—a man who thought himself so much wiser than his parents—a man who had gained honours at the University—a man of the gravest temperament—a man of so nicely a critical turn of mind that there was not a law of art or nature in which he did not detect a flaw,—that he should get himself into this mess was, to say the least of it, an uncomfortable reflection.

The boy himself, as Kenelm glanced at him from time to time, became impish and Will-of-the-Wisp-ish. Sometimes he laughed to himself loudly, sometimes he wept to himself quietly; sometimes, neither laughing nor weeping, he seemed absorbed in reflection. Twice as they came nearer to the town of Tor-Hadham, Kenelm nudged the boy, and said, "My boy, I must talk with you;" and twice the boy, withdrawing his arm from the nudge, had answered dreamily,

"Hush! I am thinking."

And so they entered the town of Tor-Hadham; the cob very much done up.

CHAPTER III.

"NOW, young sir," said Kenelm, in a tone calm, but peremptory—"now we are in the town, where am I to take you? and wherever it be, there to say good-bye."

"No, not good-bye. Stay with me a little bit. I begin to feel frightened, and I am so friendless;" and the boy, who had before resented the slightest nudge on the part of Kenelm, now wound his arm into Kenelm's, and clung to him caressingly.

I don't know what my readers have hitherto thought of Kenelm Chillingly, but amid all the curves and windings of his whimsical humour, there was one way that went straight to his heart—you had only to be weaker than himself, and ask his protection.

He turned round abruptly; he forgot all the strangeness of his position, and replied: "Little brute that you are, I'll be shot if I forsake you if in trouble. But some compassion is also due to the cob—for his sake say where we are to stop."

"I am sure I can't say; I never was here before. Let us go to a nice quiet inn. Drive slowly—we'll look out for one."

Tor-Hadham was a large town, not nominally the capital of the county, but in point of trade, and bustle, and life, virtually the capital. The straight street, through which the cob went as slowly as if he had been drawing a Triumphal Car up the Sacred Hill, presented an animated appearance. The shops had handsome façades and plate-glass windows; the pavements exhibited a lively concourse, evidently not merely of business, but of pleasure, for a large proportion of the passers-by was composed of the fair sex, smartly dressed, many of them young, and some pretty. In fact a regiment of Her Majesty's —th Hussars had been sent into the town two days before, and between the officers of that fortunate regiment, and the fair sex in that hospitable town, there was a natural emulation which should make the greater number of slain and wounded. The advent of these heroes, professional subtracters from hostile, and multipliers of friendly, populations, gave a stimulus to the caterers for those amusements which bring young folks together—archery-meetings, rifle shootings, concerts, balls, announced in bills attached to boards and walls, and exposed at shop-windows.

The boy looked eagerly forth from the gig, scanning especially these advertisements, till at length he uttered an excited exclamation, "Ah, I was right—there it is!"

"There what is?" asked Kenelm. "The Inn?" His companion did not answer, but Kenelm following the boy's eyes perceived an immense hand-bill.

"TO-MORROW NIGHT THEATRE OPENS.
RICHARD III. MR. COMPTON."

"Do just ask where the theatre is," said the boy, in a whisper, turning away his head.

Kenelm stopped the cob, made the inquiry, and was directed to take the next turning to the right. In a few minutes the compo portico of an ugly dilapidated building, dedicated to the Dramatic Muses, presented itself at the angle of a dreary deserted lane. The walls were placarded with play-bills, in which the name of Compton stood forth as gigantic as capitals could make it. The boy drew a sigh. "Now," said he, "let us look out for an inn near here—the nearest."

No inn, however, beyond the rank of a small and questionable-looking public-house, was apparent, until at a distance somewhat remote from the theatre, and in a quaint, old-fashioned, deserted square, a neat newly-whitewashed house displayed upon its frontispiece, in large black letters of funereal aspect, "Temperance Hotel."

"Stop," said the boy; "don't you think that would suit us? it looks quiet."

"Could not look more quiet if it were a tombstone," replied Kenelm.

The boy put his hand upon the reins and stopped the cob. The cob was in that condition that the slightest touch sufficed to stop him, though he turned his head somewhat ruefully, as if in doubt whether hay and corn would be within the regulations of a Temperance Hotel. Kenelm descended and entered the house. A tidy woman emerged from a sort of glass cupboard which constituted the bar, minus the comforting drinks associated with the *beau idéal* of a bar, but which displayed instead two large decanters of cold water with tumblers *à discretion*, and sundry plates of thin buscuits and sponge-cakes. This tidy woman politely inquired what was his "pleasure."

"Pleasure," answered Kenelm, with his usual gravity, "is not the word I should myself have chosen. But could you oblige my horse—I mean *that* horse—with a stall and a feed of oats; and that young gentleman and myself with a private room and a dinner?"

"Dinner!" echoed the hostess—"dinner!"

"A thousand pardons, ma'am. But if the word 'dinner' shock you, I retract it, and would say instead, 'something to eat and drink.'"

"Drink! This is strictly a Temperance Hotel, sir."

"Oh, if you don't eat and drink here," exclaimed Kenelm, fiercely, for he was famished, "I wish you good morning."

"Stay a bit, sir. We do eat and drink here. But we are very simple folks. We allow no fermented liquors."

"Not even a glass of beer?"

"Only ginger-beer. Alcohols are strictly forbidden. We have tea, and coffee, and milk. But most of our customers prefer the pure liquid. As for eating, sir—anything you order, in reason."

Kenelm shook his head and was retreating, when the boy, who had sprung from the gig and overheard the conversation, cried, petulantly, "What does it signify? Who wants fermented liquors? Water will do very well. And as for dinner,—anything convenient. Please, ma'am, show us into a private room; I am so tired." The last words were said in a caressing manner, and so prettily, that the hostess at once changed her tone, and muttering, "poor boy!" and, in a still more subdued mutter, "what a pretty face he has!" nodded, and led the way up a very clean old-fashioned staircase.

"But the horse and gig—where are they to go?" said Kenelm, with a pang of conscience on reflecting how ill-treated hitherto had been both horse and owner.

"Oh, as for the horse and gig, sir, you will find Jukes's livery-stables a few yards farther down. We don't take in horses ourselves —our customers seldom keep them; but you will find the best of accommodation at Jukes's."

Kenelm conducted the cob to the livery-stables thus indicated, and waited to see him walked about to cool, well rubbed down, and made comfortable over half a peck of oats—for Kenelm Chillingly was a humane man to the brute creation—and then, in a state of ravenous appetite, returned to the Temperance Hotel, and was ushered into a small drawing-room, with a small bit of carpet in the centre, six small chairs with cane seats, prints on the walls descriptive of the various effects of intoxicating liquors upon sundry specimens of mankind—some resembling ghosts, others fiends, and all with a general aspect of beggary and perdition, contrasted by Happy-Family pictures—smiling wives, portly husbands, rosy infants, emblematic of the beatified condition of members of the Temperance Society.

A table with a spotless cloth, and knives and forks for two, chiefly, however, attracted Kenelm's attention.

The boy was standing by the window, seemingly gazing on a small aquarium which was there placed, and contained the usual variety of small fishes, reptiles and insects, enjoying the pleasures of Temperance in its native element, including, of course, an occasional meal upon each other.

"What are they going to give us to eat?" inquired Kenelm. "It must be ready by this time I should think."

Here he gave a brisk tug at the bell-pull. The boy advanced from the window, and as he did so Kenelm was struck with the grace of his bearing and the improvement in his looks, now that he was without his hat, and rest and ablution had refreshed from heat and dust the delicate bloom of his complexion. There was no doubt about it that he was an exceedingly pretty boy, and if he lived to be a man would make many a lady's heart ache. It was with a certain air of gracious superiority such as is seldom warranted by superior rank if it be less than royal, and chiefly becomes a marked seniority in years, that this young gentleman, approaching the solemn heir of the Chillinglys, held out his hand and said—

"Sir, you have behaved extremely well, and I thank you very much."

"Your Royal Highness is condescending to say so," replied Kenelm Chillingly, bowing low; "but have you ordered dinner? and what are they going to give us? No one seems to answer the bell here. As it is a Temperance Hotel, probably all the servants are drunk."

"Why should they be drunk at a Temperance Hotel?"

"Why! because, as a general rule, people who flagrantly pretend to anything, are the reverse of that which they pretend to. A man who sets up for a saint is sure to be a sinner, and a man who boasts that he is a sinner, is sure to have some feeble, maudlin, snivelling bit of saintship about him which is enough to make him a humbug. Masculine honesty, whether it be saint-like or sinner-like, does not label itself either saint or sinner. Fancy St. Augustin labelling himself saint, or Robert Burns sinner; and therefore, though, little boy, you have probably not read the Poems of Robert Burns, and have certainly not read the Confessions of St. Augustin, take my word for it, that both those personages were very good fellows; and with a little difference of training and experience, Burns might have written the Confessions, and Augustin the poems. Powers above! I am starving. What did you order for dinner, and when is it to appear?"

The boy, who had opened to an enormous width a naturally large pair of hazel eyes, while his tall companion in fustian trousers and Belcher neckcloth spoke thus patronizingly of Robert Burns and St. Augustin, now replied with rather a deprecatory and shamefaced aspect, "I am sorry I was not thinking of dinner. I was not so mindful of you as I ought to have been. The landlady asked me what we would have. I said, 'What you like;' and the landlady muttered something about——" (here the boy hesitated.)

"Yes. About what? Mutton-chops?"

"No. Cauliflowers and rice-pudding."

Kenelm Chillingly never swore, never raged. Where ruder beings of human mould swore or raged, he vented displeasure in an expression of countenance so pathetically melancholy and lugubrious that it would have melted the heart of an Hyrcanian tiger. He turned his countenance now on the boy, and murmuring "Cauliflower!—Starvation!" sank into one of the cane-bottomed chairs, and added quietly, "so much for human gratitude!"

The boy was evidently smitten to the heart by the bitter sweetness of this reproach. There were almost tears in his voice, as he said falteringly, "Pray forgive me, I *was* ungrateful. I'll run down and see what there is;" and suiting the action to the word, he disappeared.

Kenelm remained motionless; in fact he was plunged into one of those reveries, or rather absorptions of inward and spiritual being, into which it is said that the consciousness of the Indian Dervish can be, by prolonged fasting, preternaturally resolved. The appetite of all men of powerful muscular development is of a nature far exceeding the properties of any reasonable number of cauliflowers and rice-puddings to satisfy. Witness Hercules himself, whose cravings for substantial nourishment were the standing joke of the classic poets. I don't know that Kenelm Chillingly would have beaten the Theban Hercules either in fighting or in eating; but when he wanted to fight or when he wanted to eat, Hercules would have had to put forth all his strength not to be beaten.

After ten minutes' absence, the boy came back radiant. He tapped Kenelm on the shoulder, and said playfully, "I made them cut a whole loin into chops, besides the cauliflower, and such a big rice-pudding, and eggs and bacon too. Cheer up! it will be served in a minute."

"A—h!" said Kenelm.

"They are good people; they did not mean to stint you; but most of their customers, it seems, live upon vegetables and farinaceous food. There is a society here formed upon that principle; the landlady says they are philosophers!"

At the word "philosophers" Kenelm's crest rose as that of a practised hunter at the cry of 'Yoiks! Tally-ho!' "Philosophers!" said he—"philosophers indeed! O ignoramuses, who do not even know the structure of the human tooth! Look you, little boy, if nothing were left on this earth of the present race of man, as we are assured upon great authority will be the case one of these days—and a mighty good riddance it will be—if nothing, I say, of man were left except fossils of his teeth and his thumbs, a philosopher of that superior race which will succeed to man would at once see in those relics all his characteristics and all his history; would say, comparing his thumb with the talons of an eagle, the claws of a tiger, the hoof of a horse, the owner of that thumb must have been lord over creatures with talons and claws and hoofs. You may say the monkey tribe has thumbs. True; but compare an ape's thumb with a man's—could the biggest ape's thumb have built Westminster Abbey? But even thumbs are trivial evidence of man as compared with his teeth. Look at his teeth!"—here Kenelm expanded his jaws from ear to ear and displayed semicircles of ivory, so perfect for the purposes of mastication that the most artistic dentist might have despaired of his power to imitate them—"look, I say, at his teeth!" The boy involuntarily recoiled. "Are the teeth those of a miserable cauliflower-eater? or is it purely by farinaceous food that the proprietor of teeth like man's obtains the rank of the sovereign destroyer of creation? No, little boy, no," continued Kenelm, closing his jaws, but advancing upon the infant, who at each stride receded towards the aquarium—"no; man is the master of the world, because of all created beings he devours the greatest variety and the greatest number of created things. His teeth evince that man can live upon every soil from the torrid to the frozen zone, because man can eat everything that other creatures cannot eat. And the formation of his teeth proves it. A tiger can eat a deer—so can man; but a tiger can't eat an eel—man can. An elephant can eat cauliflowers and rice-pudding—so can man! but an elephant can't eat a beefsteak—man can. In sum, man can live everywhere, because he can eat anything, thanks to his dental formation!" concluded Kenelm, making a prodigious stride towards the boy. "Man, when everything else fails him, eats his own species."

"Don't; you frighten me," said the boy. "Aha!" clapping his hands with a sensation of gleeful relief, "here come the mutton-chops!"

A wonderfully clean, well-washed, indeed well-washed-out, middle-aged parlour-maid now appeared, dish in hand. Putting the dish on the table and taking off the cover, the hand-maiden said civilly, though frigidly, like one who lived upon salad and cold water, "Mistress is sorry to have kept you waiting, but she thought you were Vegetarians."

After helping his young friend to a mutton-chop, Kenelm helped himself, and replied, gravely, "Tell your mistress that if she had only given us vegetables, I should have eaten you. Tell her that though man is partially graminivorous, he is principally carnivorous. Tell her that though a swine eats cabbages and suchlike, yet where a swine can get a baby, it eats the baby. Tell her," continued Kenelm (now at his third chop), "that there is no animal that in digestive organs more resembles man than a swine. Ask her if there is any baby in the house; if so, it would be safe for the baby to send up some more chops."

As the acutest observer could rarely be quite sure when Kenelm Chillingly was in jest or in earnest, the parlour-maid paused a moment and attempted a pale smile. Kenelm lifted his dark eyes, unspeakably sad and profound, and said, mournfully, "I should be so sorry for the baby. Bring the chops!" The parlour-maid vanished. The boy laid down his knife and fork, and looked fixedly and inquisitively on Kenelm. Kenelm, unheeding the look, placed the last chop on the boy's plate.

"No more," cried the boy, impulsively, and returned the chop to the dish. "I have dined—I have had enough."

"Little boy, you lie," said Kenelm; "you have not had enough to keep body and soul together. Eat that chop or I shall thrash you; whatever I say, I do."

Somehow or other the boy felt quelled; he ate the chop in silence, again looked at Kenelm's face, and said to himself, "I am afraid."

The parlour-maid here entered with a fresh supply of chops and a dish of bacon and eggs, soon followed by a rice-pudding baked in a tin dish, and of size sufficient to have nourished a charity school. When the repast was finished, Kenelm seemed to forget the dangerous properties of the carnivorous animal; and stretching himself indolently out, appeared to be as innocently ruminative as the most domestic of animals graminivorous.

Then said the boy, rather timidly, "May I ask you another favour?"

"Is it to knock down another uncle, or to steal another gig and cob?"

"No, it is very simple: it is merely to find out the address of a friend here; and when found to give him a note from me."

"Does the commission press? 'After dinner, rest a while,' saith the proverb; and proverbs are so wise that no one can guess the author of them. They are supposed to be fragments of the philosophy of the antediluvians—came to us packed up in the ark."

"Really, indeed," said the boy, seriously. "How interesting! No, my commission does not press for an hour or so. Do you think, sir, they had any drama before the Deluge?"

"Drama! not a doubt of it. Men who lived one or two thousand years had time to invent and improve everything; and a play could have had its natural length then. It would not have been necessary to crowd the whole history of Macbeth, from his youth to his old age, into an absurd epitome of three hours. One cannot trace a touch of real human nature in any actor's delineation of that very interesting Scotchman, because the actor always comes on the stage as if he were the same age when he murdered Duncan, and when, in his sear and yellow leaf, he was lopped off by Macduff."

"Do you think Macbeth was young when he murdered Duncan?"

"Certainly. No man ever commits a first crime of violent nature, such as murder, after thirty; if he begins before, he may go on up to any age. But youth is the season for commencing those wrong calculations which belong to irrational hope and the sense of physical power. You thus read in the newspapers that the persons who murder their sweethearts are generally from two to six and twenty; and persons who murder from other motives than love—that is, from revenge, avarice, or ambition—are generally about twenty-eight—Iago's age. Twenty-eight is the usual close of the active season for getting rid of one's fellow-creatures—a prize-fighter falls off after that age. I take it that Macbeth was about twenty-eight when he murdered Duncan, and from about fifty-four to sixty when he began to whine about missing the comforts of old age. But can any audience understand that difference of years in seeing a three-hours' play; or does any actor ever pretend to impress it on the audience, and appear as twenty-eight in the first act and a sexagenarian in the fifth?"

"I never thought of that," said the boy, evidently interested. "But I never saw Macbeth. I have seen Richard III.—is not that nice? Don't you dote on the Play? I do. What a glorious life an actor's must be!"

Kenelm, who had been hitherto rather talking to himself than to his youthful companion, here roused his attention, looked on the boy intently, and said—

"I see you are stage-stricken. You have run away from home in order to turn player, and I should not wonder if this note you want me to give is for the manager of the theatre or one of his company."

The young face that encountered Kenelm's dark eye became very flushed, but set and *défiant* in its expression.

"And what if it were—would not you give it?"

"What! help a child of your age, run away from his home, to go upon the stage against the consent of his relations—certainly not."

"I am not a child; but that has nothing to do with it. I don't want to go on the stage, at all events without the consent of the person who has a right to dictate my actions. My note is not to the manager of the theatre, nor to one of his company, but it is to a gentleman who condescends to act here for a few nights—a thorough gentleman—a great actor—my friend, the only friend I have in the world. I say frankly I have run away from home so that he may have that note, and if you will not give it some one else will!"

The boy had risen while he spoke, and he stood erect beside the recumbent Kenelm, his lips quivering, his eyes suffused with suppressed tears, but his whole aspect resolute and determined. Evidently, if he did not get his own way in this world, it would not be for want of will.

"I will take your note," said Kenelm.

"There it is; give it into the hands of the person it is addressed to—Mr. Herbert Compton."

CHAPTER IV.

ENELM took his way to the theatre, and inquired of the doorkeeper for Mr. Herbert Compton. That functionary replied, "Mr. Compton does not act to-night, and is not in the house."

"Where does he lodge?"

The doorkeeper pointed to a grocer's shop on the other side of the way, and said, tersely, "There, private door—knock and ring."

Kenelm did as he was directed. A slatternly maid-servant opened the door, and, in answer to his interrogatory, said that Mr. Compton was at home, but at supper.

"I am sorry to disturb him," said Kenelm, raising his voice, for he heard a clatter of knives and plates within a room hard by at his left, "but my business requires to see him forthwith;" and pushing the maid aside, he entered at once the adjoining banquet-hall.

Before a savoury stew smelling strongly of onions sate a man very much at his ease, without coat or neckcloth, a decidedly handsome man—his hair cut short and his face closely shaven, as befits an actor who has wigs and beards of all hues and forms at his command. The man was not alone; opposite to him sate a lady, who might be a few years younger, of a somewhat faded complexion, but still pretty, with good stage features and a profusion of blond ringlets.

"Mr. Compton, I presume," said Kenelm, with a solemn bow.

"My name is Compton: any message from the theatre? or what do you want with me?"

"I—nothing!" replied Kenelm; and then deepening his naturally mournful voice into tones ominous and tragic, continued—"By whom you are wanted let this explain;" therewith he placed in Mr. Compton's hand the letter with which he was charged, and stretching his arms and interlacing his fingers in the *pose* of Talma as Julius Cæsar, added, "'*Qu'en dis tu, Brute?*'"

Whether it was from the sombre aspect and awe-inspiring delivery, or ὑπόκρισις, of the messenger, or the sight of the handwriting on the address of the missive, Mr. Compton's countenance suddenly fell, and his hand rested irresolute, as if not daring to open the letter.

"Never mind me, dear," said the lady with blond ringlets, in a tone of stinging affability; "read your *billet-doux;* don't keep the young man waiting, love!"

"Nonsense, Matilda, nonsense! *billet-doux* indeed! more likely a bill from Duke the tailor. Excuse me for a moment, my dear. Follow me, sir," and rising, still with shirt-sleeves uncovered, he quitted the room, closing the door after him, motioned Kenelm into a small parlour on the opposite side of the passage, and by the light of a suspended gas-lamp ran his eye hastily over the letter, which, though it seemed very short, drew from him sundry exclamations. "Good heavens! how very absurd! what's to be done?" Then, thrusting the letter into his trousers-pocket, he fixed upon Kenelm a very brilliant pair of dark eyes, which soon dropped before the steadfast look of that saturnine adventurer.

"Are you in the confidence of the writer of this letter?" asked Mr. Compton, rather confusedly.

"I am not the confidant of the writer," answered Kenelm, "but for the time being I am the protector!"

"Protector!"

"Protector."

Mr. Compton again eyed the messenger, and this time fully realizing the gladiatorial development of that dark stranger's physical form, he grew many shades paler, and involuntarily retreated towards the bell-pull.

After a short pause, he said, "I am requested to call on the writer. If I do so, may I understand that the interview will be strictly private?"

"So far as I am concerned, yes—on the condition that no attempt be made to withdraw the writer from the house."

"Certainly not—certainly not; quite the contrary," exclaimed Mr. Compton, with genuine animation. "Say I will call in half an hour."

"I will give your message," said Kenelm, with a polite inclination of his head; "and pray pardon me if I remind you that I styled myself the protector of your correspondent, and if the slightest advantage be taken of that correspondent's youth and inexperience, or the smallest encouragement be given to plans of abduction from home and friends, the stage will lose an ornament, and Herbert Compton vanish from the scene." With those words Kenelm left the player standing aghast. Gaining the street-door, a lad with a bandbox ran against him and was nearly upset.

"Stupid," cried the lad, "can't you see where you are going? Give this to Mrs. Compton."

"I should deserve the title you give if I did for nothing the business for which you are paid," replied Kenelm, sententiously, and striding on.

CHAPTER V.

"HAVE fulfilled my mission," said Kenelm, on rejoining his travelling companion. "Mr. Compton said he would be here in half an hour."

"You saw him?"

"Of course; I promised to give your letter into his own hands."

"Was he alone?"

"No; at supper with his wife."

"His wife? what do you mean, sir?—wife! he has no wife."

"Appearances are deceitful. At least he was with a lady who called him 'dear' and 'love' in as spiteful a tone of voice as if she had been his wife; and as I was coming out of his street-door a lad who ran against me asked me to give a bandbox to Mrs. Compton."

The boy turned as white as death, staggered back a few steps, and dropped into a chair.

A suspicion which, during his absence, had suggested itself to Kenelm's inquiring mind, now took strong confirmation. He approached softly, drew a chair close to the companion whom fate had forced upon him, and said in a gentle whisper—

"This is no boy's agitation. If you have been deceived or misled, and I can in any way advise or aid you, count on me as women under the circumstances count on men and gentlemen."

The boy started to his feet, and paced the room with disordered steps, and a countenance working with passions which he attempted vainly to suppress. Suddenly arresting his steps, he seized Kenelm's hand, pressed it convulsively, and said, in a voice struggling against a sob—

"I thank you—I bless you. Leave me now—I would be alone. Alone, too, I must face this man. There may be some mistake yet; go."

"You will promise not to leave the house till I return?"

"Yes, I promise that."

"And if it be as I fear, you will then let me counsel with and advise you?"

"Heaven help me, if so! Whom else should I trust to? Go—go!"

Kenelm once more found himself in the streets, beneath the mingled light of gas-lamps and the midsummer moon. He walked on mechanically till he reached the extremity of the town. There he halted, and seating himself on a milestone, indulged in these meditations:—

"Kenelm, my friend, you are in a still worse scrape than I thought you were an hour ago. You have evidently now got a woman on your hands. What on earth are you to do with her? A runaway woman, who, meaning to run off with somebody else— such are the crosses and contradictions in human destiny—has run off with you instead. What mortal can hope to be safe? The last thing I thought could befall me when I got up this morning was that I should have any trouble about the other sex before the day was over. If I were of an amatory temperament, the Fates might have some justification for leading me into this snare, but, as it is, those meddling old maids have none. Kenelm, my friend, do you think you ever can be in love? and, if you were in love, do you think you could be a greater fool than you are now?"

Kenelm had not decided this knotty question in the conference held with himself, when a light and soft strain of music came upon his ear. It was but from a stringed instrument and might have sounded thin and tinkling, but for the stillness of the night, and that peculiar addition of fulness which music acquires when it is borne along a tranquil air. Presently a voice in song was heard from the distance accompanying the instrument. It was a man's voice, a mellow and a rich voice, but Kenelm's ear could not catch the words. Mechanically he moved on towards the quarter from which the sounds came, for Kenelm Chillingly had music in his soul, though he was not quite aware of it himself. He saw before him a patch of greensward, on which grew a solitary elm with a seat for wayfarers beneath it. From this sward the ground receded in a wide semicircle bordered partly by shops, partly by the tea-gardens of a pretty cottage-like tavern. Round the tables scattered throughout the gardens were grouped quiet customers, evidently belonging to the class of small tradespeople or superior artisans. They had an appearance of decorous respectability, and were listening intently to the music. So were many persons at the shopdoors, and at the windows of upper rooms. On the sward, a little in advance of the tree, but beneath its shadow, stood the musician, and in that musician Kenelm recognized the wanderer from whose talk he had conceived the idea of the pedestrian excursion which had already brought him into a very awkward position. The instrument on which the singer accompanied himself was a guitar, and his song was evidently a love-song, though, as it was now drawing near to its close, Kenelm could but imperfectly guess at its general meaning. He heard enough to perceive that its words were at least free from the vulgarity which generally characterizes street ballads, and were yet simple enough to please a very homely audience.

When the singer ended there was no applause; but there was evident sensation among the audience—a feeling as if something that had given a common enjoyment had ceased. Presently the white Pomeranian dog, who had hitherto kept himself out of sight under the seat of the elm-tree, advanced, with a small metal tray between his teeth, and, after looking round him deliberately as if to select whom of the audience should be honoured with the commencement of a general subscription, gravely approached Kenelm, stood on his hind-legs, stared at him, and presented the tray.

Kenelm dropped a shilling into that depository, and the dog, looking gratified, took his way towards the tea-gardens.

Lifting his hat, for he was, in his way, a very polite man, Kenelm approached the singer, and, trusting to the alteration in his dress for not being recognized by a stranger who had only once before encountered him, he said—

"Judging by the little I heard, you sing very well, sir. May I ask who composed the words?"

"They are mine," replied the singer.

"And the air?"

"Mine too."

"Accept my compliments. I hope you find these manifestations of genius lucrative?"

The singer, who had not hitherto vouchsafed more than a careless glance at the rustic garb of the questioner, now fixed his eyes full upon Kenelm, and said, with a smile, "Your voice betrays you, sir. We have met before."

"True; but I did not then notice your guitar, nor, though acquainted with your poetical gifts, suppose that you select this primitive method of making them publicly known."

"Nor did I anticipate the pleasure of meeting you again in the character of Hobnail. Hist! let us keep each other's secret. I am known hereabouts by no other designation than that of the 'Wandering Minstrel.'"

"It is in the capacity of minstrel that I address you. If it be not an impertinent question, do you know any songs which take the other side of the case?"

"What case? I don't understand you, sir."

"The song I heard seemed in praise of that sham called love. Don't you think you could say something more new and more true, treating that aberration from reason with the contempt it deserves?"

"Not if I am to get my travelling expenses paid."

"What! the folly is so popular?"

"Does not your own heart tell you so?"

"Not a bit of it—rather the contrary. Your audience at present seem folks who live by work, and can have little time for such idle phantasies—for, as it is well observed by Ovid, a poet who wrote much on that subject, and professed the most intimate acquaintance with it, 'Idleness is the parent of love.' Can't you sing something in praise of a good dinner? Everybody who works hard has an appetite for food."

The singer again fixed on Kenelm his inquiring eye, but not detecting a vestige of humour in the grave face he contemplated, was rather puzzled how to reply, and therefore remained silent.

"I perceive," resumed Kenelm, "that my observations surprise you: the surprise will vanish on reflection. It has been said by another poet, more reflective than Ovid, 'that the world is governed by love and hunger.' But hunger certainly has the lion's share of the government; and if a poet is really to do what he pretends to do—viz., represent nature—the greater part of his lays should be addressed to the stomach." Here, warming with his subject, Kenelm familiarly laid his hand on the musician's shoulder, and his voice took a tone bordering on enthusiasm. "You will allow that a man in the normal condition of health, does not fall in love every day. But in the normal condition of health he is hungry every day. Nay, in those early years when you poets say he is most prone to love, he is so especially disposed to hunger that less than three meals a-day can scarcely satisfy his appetite. You may imprison a man for months, for years, nay, for his whole life—from infancy to any age which Sir Cornewall Lewis may allow him to attain—without letting him be in love at all. But if you shut him up for a week without putting something into his stomach, you will find him at the end of it as dead as a door-nail."

Here the singer, who had gradually retreated before the energetic advance of the orator, sank into the seat by the elm-tree, and said, pathetically, "Sir, you have fairly argued me down. Will you please to come to the conclusion which you deduce from your premises?"

"Simply this, that where you find one human being who cares about love, you will find a thousand susceptible to the charms of a dinner; and if you wish to be the popular minnesinger or troubadour of the age, appeal to nature, sir—appeal to nature; drop all hackneyed rhapsodies about a rosy cheek, and strike your lyre to the theme of a beef-steak."

The dog had for some minutes regained his master's side, standing on his hind-legs, with the tray, tolerably well filled with copper coins, between his teeth; and now, justly aggrieved by the inattention which detained him in that artificial attitude, dropped the tray and growled at Kenelm.

At the same time there came an impatient sound from the audience in the tea-garden. They wanted another song for their money.

The singer rose, obedient to the summons. "Excuse me, sir; but I am called upon to——"

"To sing again?"

"Yes."

"And on the subject I suggest?"

"No, indeed."

"What! love, again?"

"I am afraid so."

"I wish you good evening, then. You seem a well-educated man—more shame to you. Perhaps we may meet once more in our rambles, when the question can be properly argued out."

Kenelm lifted his hat, and turned on his heel. Before he reached the street, the sweet voice of the singer again smote his ears; but the only word distinguishable in the distance, ringing out at the close of the refrain, was "love."

"Fiddle-de-dee," said Kenelm.

CHAPTER VI.

AS Kenelm regained the street dignified by the edifice of the Temperance Hotel, a figure, dressed picturesquely in a Spanish cloak, brushed hurriedly by him, but not so fast as to be unrecognized as the tragedian. "Hem!" muttered Kenelm—"I don't think there is much triumph in that face. I suspect he has been scolded."

The boy—if Kenelm's travelling companion is still to be so designated—was leaning against the mantelpiece as Kenelm re-entered the dining-room. There was an air of profound dejection about the boy's listless attitude and in the drooping tearless eyes.

"My dear child," said Kenelm, in the softest tones of his plaintive voice, "do not honour me with any confidence that may be painful. But let me hope that you have dismissed for ever all thoughts of going on the stage."

"Yes," was the scarce audible answer.

"And now only remains the question, 'What is to be done?'"

"I am sure I don't know, and I don't care."

"Then you leave it to me to know and to care, and assuming for the moment as a fact, that which is one of the greatest lies in this mendacious world—namely, that all men are brothers, you will consider me as an elder brother, who will counsel and control you as he would—an imprudent young——sister. I see very well how it is. Somehow or other you, having first admired Mr. Compton as Romeo or Richard III., made his acquaintance as Mr. Compton. He allowed you to believe him a single man. In a romantic moment you escaped from your home, with the design of adopting the profession of the stage, and of becoming Mrs. Compton."

"Oh," broke out the girl, since her sex must now be declared—"oh," she exclaimed, with a passionate sob, "what a fool I have been! Only do not think worse of me than I deserve. The man did deceive me; he did not think I should take him at his word, and follow him here, or his wife would not have appeared. I should not have known he had one and—and——" here her voice was choked under her passion.

"But now you have discovered the truth, let us thank heaven that you are saved from shame and misery. I must despatch a telegram to your uncle—give me his address."

"No, no."

"There is not a 'No' possible in this case, my child. Your

reputation and your future must be saved. Leave me to explain all to your uncle. He is your guardian. I must send for him; nay, nay, there is no option. Hate me now for enforcing your will, you will thank me hereafter. And listen, young lady; if it does pain you to see your uncle, and encounter his reproaches, every fault must undergo its punishment. A brave nature undergoes it cheerfully, as a part of atonement. You are brave. Submit, and in submitting rejoice!"

There was something in Kenelm's voice and manner at once so kindly and so commanding, that the wayward nature he addressed fairly succumbed. She gave him her uncle's address, "John Bovill, Esq., Oakdale, near Westmere." And after giving it, fixed her eyes mournfully upon her young adviser, and said with a simple, dreary pathos, "Now, will you esteem me more, or rather despise me less?"

She looked so young, nay, so childlike, as she thus spoke, that Kenelm felt a parental inclination to draw her on his lap and kiss away her tears. But he prudently conquered that impulse, and said, with a melancholy half-smile—

"If human beings despise each other for being young and foolish, the sooner we are exterminated by that superior race which is to succeed us on earth the better it will be. Adieu till your uncle comes."

"What! you leave me here—alone?"

"Nay, if your uncle found me under the same roof, now that I know you are his niece, don't you think he would have a right to throw me out of the window? Allow me to practise for myself the prudence I preach to you. Send for the landlady to show you your room, shut yourself in there, go to bed, and don't cry more than you can help."

Kenelm shouldered the knapsack he had deposited in a corner of the room, inquired for the telegraph-office, despatched a telegram to Mr. Bovill, obtained a bedroom at the Commercial Hotel, and fell asleep muttering these sensible words—

"Rochefoucauld was perfectly right when he said, 'Very few people would fall in love if they had not heard it so much talked about.'"

CHAPTER VII.

KENELM CHILLINGLY rose with the sun, according to his usual custom, and took his way to the Temperance Hotel. All in that sober building seemed still in the arms of Morpheus. He turned towards the stables in which he had left the gray cob, and had the pleasure to see that ill-used animal in the healthful process of rubbing down.

"That's right," said he to the ostler. "I am glad to see you are so early a riser."

"Why," quoth the ostler, "the gentleman as owns the pony knocked me up at two o'clock in the morning, and pleased enough he was to see the creature again lying down in the clean straw."

"Oh, he has arrived at the hotel, I presume?—a stout gentleman?"

"Yes, stout enough; and a passionate gentleman too. Came in a yellow and two posters, knocked up the Temperance, and then knocked up me to see for the pony, and was much put out as he could not get any grog at the Temperance."

"I dare say he was. I wish he had got his grog; it might have put him in better humour. Poor little thing!" muttered Kenelm, turning away; "I am afraid she is in for a regular vituperation. My turn next, I suppose. But he must be a good fellow to have come at once for his niece in the dead of the night."

About nine o'clock Kenelm presented himself again at the Temperance Hotel, inquired for Mr. Bovill, and was shown by the prim maid-servant into the drawing-room, where he found Mr. Bovill seated amicably at breakfast with his niece, who, of course, was still in boy's clothing, having no other costume at hand. To Kenelm's great relief, Mr. Bovill rose from the table with a beaming countenance, and, extending his hand to Kenelm, said—

"Sir, you are a gentleman; sit down, sit down, and take breakfast."

Then, as soon as the maid was out of the room, the uncle continued—

"I have heard all your good conduct from this young simpleton. Things might have been worse, sir."

Kenelm bowed his head, and drew the loaf towards him in silence. Then, considering that some apology was due to his entertainer, he said—

"I hope you forgive me for that unfortunate mistake, wher——"

"You knocked me down, or rather tripped me up. All right now. Elsie, give the gentleman a cup of tea. Pretty little rogue, is not she? and a good girl, in spite of her nonsense. It was all my fault letting her go to the play and be intimate with Miss Lockit, a stage-stricken, foolish old maid, who ought to have known better than lead her into all this trouble."

"No, uncle," cried the girl, resolutely; "don't blame her, nor any one but me."

Kenelm turned his dark eyes approvingly towards the girl, and saw that her lips were firmly set; there was an expression, not of grief nor shame, but compressed resolution in her countenance. But when her eyes met his they fell softly, and a blush mantled over her cheeks up to her very forehead.

"Ah!" said the uncle, "just like you, Elsie; always ready to take everybody's fault on your own shoulders. Well, well, say no more about that.—Now, my young friend, what brings you across the country tramping it on foot, eh? a young man's whim?" As he spoke, he eyed Kenelm very closely, and his look was that of an intelligent man not unaccustomed to observe the faces of those he conversed with. In fact a more shrewd man of business than Mr. Bovill is seldom met with on 'Change or in market.

"I travel on foot to please myself, sir," answered Kenelm, curtly, and unconsciously set on his guard.

"Of course you do," cried Mr. Bovill, with a jovial laugh. "But it seems you don't object to a chaise and pony whenever you can get them for nothing—ha, ha!—excuse me—a joke."

Herewith Mr. Bovill, still in excellent good-humour, abruptly changed the conversation to general matters—agricultural prospects—chance of a good harvest—corn trade—money market in general—politics—state of the nation. Kenelm felt there was an attempt to draw him out, to sound, to pump him, and replied only by monosyllables, generally significant of ignorance on the questions broached; and at the close, if the philosophical heir of the Chillinglys was in the habit of allowing himself to be surprised he would certainly have been startled when Mr. Bovill rose, slapped him on the shoulder, and said in a tone of great satisfaction, "Just as I thought, sir; you know nothing of these matters—you are a gentleman born and bred—your clothes can't disguise you, sir. Elsie was right. My dear, just leave us for a few minutes; I have something to say to our young friend. You can get ready meanwhile to go with me."

Elsie left the table and walked obediently towards the doorway. There she halted a moment, turned round, and looked timidly towards Kenelm. He had naturally risen from his seat as she rose, and advanced some paces as if to open the door for her. Thus their looks encountered. He could not interpret that shy gaze of hers; it was tender, it was deprecating, it was humble, it was pleading; a man accustomed to female conquests might have thought it was something more, something in which was the key to all. But that something more was an unknown tongue to Kenelm Chillingly.

When the two men were alone, Mr. Bovill reseated himself and motioned to Kenelm to do the same. "Now, young sir," said the former, "you and I can talk at our ease. That adventure of yours yesterday may be the luckiest thing that could happen to you."

"It is sufficiently lucky if I have been of any service to your niece. But her own good sense would have been her safeguard if she had been alone, and discovered, as she would have done, that Mr. Compton had, knowingly or not, misled her to believe that he was a single man."

"Hang Mr. Compton! we have done with him. I am a plain man, and I come to the point. It is you who have carried off my niece; it is with you that she came to this hotel. Now when Elsie told me how well you had behaved, and that your language and manners were those of a real gentleman, my mind was made up. I guess pretty well what you are; you are a gentleman's son—probably a college youth—not overburthened with cash—had a quarrel with your governor, and he keeps you short. Don't interrupt me. Well, Elsie is a good girl and a pretty girl, and will make a good wife, as wives go; and, hark ye, she has £20,000. So just confide in me—and if you don't like your parents to know about it till the thing's done, and they be only got to forgive and bless you, why, you shall marry Elsie before you can say Jack Robinson."

For the first time in his life Kenelm Chillingly was seized with terror—terror and consternation.—His jaw dropped—his tongue was palsied. If hair ever stands on end, his hair did. At last, with superhuman effort, he gasped out the word, "Marry!"

"Yes—marry. If you are a gentleman you are bound to it. You have compromised my niece—a respectable, virtuous girl, sir —an orphan, but not unprotected. I repeat, it is you who have plucked her from my very arms, and with violence and assault; eloped with her; and what would the world say if it knew? Would it believe in your prudent conduct?—conduct only to be explained by the respect you felt due to your future wife. And where will you find a better? Where will you find an uncle who will part with his ward and £20,000 without asking if you have a sixpence?

and the girl has taken a fancy to you—I see it; would she have given up that player so easily if you had not stolen her heart? Would you break that heart? No, young man—you are not a villain. Shake hands on it!"

"Mr. Bovill," said Kenelm, recovering his wonted equanimity, "I am inexpressibly flattered by the honour you propose to me, and I do not deny that Miss Elsie is worthy of a much better man than myself. But I have inconceivable prejudices against the connubial state. If it be permitted to a member of the Established Church to cavil at any sentence written by St. Paul—and I think that liberty may be permitted to a simple layman, since eminent members of the clergy criticize the whole Bible as freely as if it were the history of Queen Elizabeth by Mr. Froude—I should demur at the doctrine that it is better to marry than to burn; I myself should prefer burning. With these sentiments it would ill become any one entitled to that distinction of 'gentleman' which you confer on me to lead a fellow-victim to the sacrificial altar. As for any reproach attached to Miss Elsie, since in my telegram I directed you to ask for a young gentleman at this hotel, her very sex is not known in this place unless you divulge it. And——"

Here Kenelm was interrupted by a violent explosion of rage from the uncle. He stamped his feet; he almost foamed at the mouth; he doubled his fist, and shook it in Kenelm's face.

"Sir, you are mocking me: John Bovill is not a man to be jeered in this way. You *shall* marry the girl. I'll not have her thrust back upon me to be the plague of my life with her whims and tantrums. You have taken her, and you shall keep her, or I'll break every bone in your skin."

"Break them," said Kenelm, resignedly, but at the same time falling back into a formidable attitude of defence, which cooled the pugnacity of his accuser. Mr. Bovill sank into his chair, and wiped his forehead. Kenelm craftily pursued the advantage he had gained, and in mild accents proceeded to reason—

"When you recover your habitual serenity of humour, Mr. Bovill, you will see how much your very excusable desire to secure your niece's happiness, and, I may add, to reward what you allow to have been forbearing and well-bred conduct on my part, has hurried you into an error of judgment. You know nothing of me. I may be, for what you know, an impostor or swindler; I may have every bad quality, and yet you are to be contented with my assurance, or rather your own assumption, that I am born a gentleman in order to give me your niece and her £20,000. This is temporary insanity on your part. Allow me to leave you to recover from your excitement."

"Stop, sir," said Mr. Bovill, in a changed and sullen tone; "I am not quite the madman you think me. But I dare say I have been too hasty and too rough. Nevertheless the facts are as I have stated them, and I do not see how, as a man of honour, you can get off marrying my niece. The mistake you made in running away with her was, no doubt, innocent on your part; but still there it is; and supposing the case came before a jury, it would be an ugly one for you and your family. Marriage alone could mend it. Come, come, I own I was too business-like in rushing to the point at once, and I no longer say, 'Marry my niece off-hand.' You have only seen her disguised and in a false position. Pay me a visit at Oakdale—stay with me a month—and if, at the end of that time, you do not like her well enough to propose, I'll let you off and say no more about it."

While Mr. Bovill thus spoke, and Kenelm listened, neither saw that the door had been noiselessly opened, and that Elsie stood at the threshold. Now, before Kenelm could reply, she advanced into the middle of the room, and, her small figure drawn up to its fullest height, her cheeks glowing, her lips quivering, exclaimed—

"Uncle, for shame!" Then, addressing Kenelm in a sharp tone of anguish, "Oh, do not believe I knew anything of this!" she covered her face with both hands, and stood mute.

All of chivalry that Kenelm had received with his baptismal appellation was aroused. He sprang up, and, bending his knee as he drew one of her hands into his own, he said—

"I am as convinced that your uncle's words are abhorrent to you as I am that you are a pure-hearted and high-spirited woman, of whose friendship I shall be proud. We meet again." Then releasing her hand, he addressed Mr. Bovill: "Sir, you are unworthy the charge of your niece. Had you not been so, she would have committed no imprudence. If she have any female relation, to that relation transfer your charge."

"I have! I have!" cried Elsie; "my lost mother's sister—let me go to her."

"The woman who keeps a school!" said Mr. Bovill, sneeringly.

"Why not?" asked Kenelm.

"She never would go there. I proposed it to her a year ago. The minx would not go into a school."

"I will now, uncle."

"Well, then, you shall at once; and I hope you'll be put on bread and water. Fool! fool! you have spoilt your own game. Mr. Chillingly, now that Miss Elsie has turned her back on herself, I can convince you that I am not the madman you thought me.

I was at the festive meeting held when you came of age—my brother is one of your father's tenants. I did not recognize your face immediately in the excitement of our encounter and in your change of dress; but in walking home it struck me that I had seen it before, and I knew it at once when you entered the room to-day. It has been a tussle between us which should beat the other. You have beat me; and thanks to that idiot! If she had not put her spoke into my wheel, she would have lived to be 'my lady.' Now goodday, sir."

"Mr. Bovill, you offered to shake hands: shake hands now, and promise me, with the good faith of one honourable combatant to another, that Miss Elsie shall go to her aunt the schoolmistress at once if she wishes it. Hark ye, my friend" (this in Mr. Bovill's ear): "A man can never manage a woman. Till a woman marries, a prudent man leaves her to women; when she does marry, she manages her husband, and there's an end of it."

Kenelm was gone.

"Oh, wise young man!" murmured the uncle. "Elsie, dear, how can we go to your aunt's while you are in that dress?"

Elsie started as from a trance, her eyes directed towards the doorway through which Kenelm had vanished. "This dress," she said, contemptuously—"this dress—is not that easily altered with shops in the town?"

"Gad!" muttered Mr. Bovill, "that youngster is a second Solomon; and if I can't manage Elsie, she'll manage a husband—whenever she gets one."

CHAPTER VIII.

"BY the powers that guard innocence and celibacy," soliloquized Kenelm Chillingly, "but I have had a narrow escape! and had that amphibious creature been in girl's clothes instead of boy's, when she intervened like the deity of the ancient drama, I might have plunged my armorial Fishes into hot water. Though, indeed, it is hard to suppose that a young lady head-over-ears in love with Mr. Compton yesterday could have consigned her affections to me to-day. Still she looked as if she could, which proves either that one is never to trust a woman's heart, or never to trust a woman's looks. Decimus Roach is right. Man must never relax his flight from the women, if he strives to achieve an 'Approach to the Angels.'"

These reflections were made by Kenelm Chillingly as, having turned his back upon the town in which such temptations and trials had befallen him, he took his solitary way along a footpath that wound through meads and corn-fields, and shortened by three miles the distance to a cathedral town at which he proposed to rest for the night.

He had travelled for some hours, and the sun was beginning to slope towards a range of blue hills in the west, when he came to the margin of a fresh rivulet, overshadowed by feathery willows, and the quivering leaves of silvery Italian poplars. Tempted by the quiet and cool of this pleasant spot, he flung himself down on the banks, drew from his knapsack some crusts of bread with which he had wisely provided himself, and, dipping them into the pure lymph as it rippled over its pebbly bed, enjoyed one of those luxurious repasts for which epicures would exchange their banquets in return for the appetite of youth. Then, reclined along the bank, and crushing the wild thyme which grows best and sweetest in wooded coverts, provided they be neighboured by water, no matter whether in pool or rill, he resigned himself to that intermediate state between thought and dream-land which we call 'reverie.' At a little distance he heard the low still sound of the mower's scythe, and the air came to his brow sweet with the fragrance of new-mown hay.

He was roused by a gentle tap on the shoulder, and turning lazily round, saw a good-humoured jovial face upon a pair of massive shoulders, and heard a hearty and winning voice say—

"Young man, if you are not too tired, will you lend a hand to get in my hay? We are very short of hands, and I am afraid we shall have rain pretty soon."

Kenelm rose and shook himself, gravely contemplated the stranger, and replied in his customary sententious fashion, "Man is born to help his fellow-man—especially to get in hay while the sun shines. I am at your service."

"That's a good fellow, and I'm greatly obliged to you. You see I had counted on a gang of roving haymakers, but they were bought up by another farmer. This way,"—and leading on through a gap in the brushwood, he emerged, followed by Kenelm, into a large meadow, one-third of which was still under the scythe, the rest being occupied with persons of both sexes, tossing and spreading the cut grass. Among the latter, Kenelm, stripped to his shirt-sleeves, soon found himself tossing and spreading like the rest, with his usual melancholy resignation of mien and aspect. Though a little awkward at first in the use of his unfamiliar implements, his practice in all athletic accomplishments bestowed on him that invaluable quality which is termed 'handiness,' and he soon distinguished himself by the superior activity and neatness with which he performed his work. Something—it might be in his countenance or in the charm of his being a stranger—attracted the attention of the feminine section of haymakers, and one very pretty girl, who was nearer to him than the rest, attempted to commence conversation.

"This is new to you," she said, smiling.

"Nothing is new to me," answered Kenelm, mournfully. "But allow me to observe, that to do things well you should only do one thing at a time. I am here to make hay, and not conversation."

"My!" said the girl, in amazed ejaculation, and turned off with a toss of her pretty head.

"I wonder if that jade has got an uncle," thought Kenelm.

The farmer, who took his share of work with the men, halting now and then to look round, noticed Kenelm's vigorous application with much approval, and at the close of the day's work shook him heartily by the hand, leaving a two-shilling piece in his palm. The heir of the Chillinglys gazed on that honorarium, and turned it over with the finger and thumb of the left hand.

"Ben't it eno'?" said the farmer, nettled.

"Pardon me," answered Kenelm. "But, to tell you the truth, it is the first money I ever earned by my own bodily labour; and I regard it with equal curiosity and respect. But, if it would not offend you, I would rather that, instead of the money, you had offered me some supper; for I have tasted nothing but bread and water since the morning."

"You shall have the money and supper both, my lad," said the farmer, cheerily. "And if you will stay and help till I have got in the hay, I dare say my good woman can find you a better bed than you'll get at the village inn—if, indeed, you can get one there at all."

"You are very kind. But before I accept your hospitality excuse one question—have you any nieces about you?"

"Nieces!" echoed the farmer, mechanically thrusting his hands into his breeches-pockets, as if in search of something there—"nieces about me! what do you mean? Be that a newfangled word for coppers?"

"Not for coppers, though perhaps for brass. But I spoke without metaphor. I object to nieces upon abstract principle, confirmed by the test of experience."

The farmer stared, and thought his new friend not quite so sound in his mental as he evidently was in his physical conformation, but replied, with a laugh, "Make yourself easy, then. I have only one niece, and she is married to an ironmonger and lives in Exeter."

On entering the farmhouse, Kenelm's host conducted him straight into the kitchen, and cried out, in a hearty voice, to a comely middle-aged dame, who, with a stout girl, was intent on culinary operations, "Hulloa! old woman, I have brought you a guest who has well earned his supper, for he has done the work of two, and I have promised him a bed."

The farmer's wife turned sharply round. "He is heartily welcome to supper. As to a bed," she said, doubtfully, "I don't know." But here her eyes settled on Kenelm; and there was something in his aspect so unlike what she expected to see in an itinerant haymaker, that she involuntarily dropped a curtsy, and resumed, with a change of tone, "The gentleman shall have the guest-room; but it will take a little time to get ready—you know, John, all the furniture is covered up."

"Well, wife, there will be leisure eno' for that. He don't want to go to roost till he has supped."

"Certainly not," said Kenelm, sniffing a very agreeable odour.

"Where are the girls?" asked the farmer.

"They have been in these five minutes, and gone up-stairs to tidy themselves."

"What girls?" faltered Kenelm, retreating towards the door. "I thought you said you had no nieces."

"But I did not say I had no daughters. Why, you are not afraid of them, are you?"

"Sir," replied Kenelm, with a polite and politic evasion of that question, "if your daughters are like their mother, you can't say that they are not dangerous."

"Come," cried the farmer, looking very much pleased, while his dame smiled and blushed—"come, that's as nicely said as if you were canvassing the county. 'Tis not among haymakers that you learned manners, I guess; and perhaps I have been making too free with my betters."

"What!" quoth the courteous Kenelm, "do you mean to imply that you were too free with your shillings? Apologize for that, if you like, but I don't think you'll get back the shillings. I have not seen so much of this life as you have, but, according to my experience, when a man once parts with his money, whether to his betters or his worsers, the chances are that he'll never see it again."

At this aphorism the farmer laughed ready to kill himself, his wife chuckled, and even the maid-of-all-work grinned. Kenelm, preserving his unalterable gravity, said to himself—

"Wit consists in the epigrammatic expression of a commonplace truth, and the dullest remark on the worth of money is almost as sure of successful appreciation as the dullest remark on the worthlessness of women. Certainly I am a wit without knowing it."

Here the farmer touched him on the shoulder—touched it, did not slap it, as he would have done ten minutes before—and said—

"We must not disturb the Missis or we shall get no supper. I'll just go and give a look into the cow-sheds. Do you know much about cows?"

"Yes, cows produce cream and butter. The best cows are those which produce at the least cost the best cream and butter. But how the best cream and butter can be produced at a price which will place them free of expense on a poor man's breakfast-table, is a question to be settled by a Reformed Parliament and a Liberal Administration. In the mean while let us not delay the supper."

The farmer and his guest quitted the kitchen and entered the farmyard.

"You are quite a stranger in these parts?"

"Quite."

"You don't even know my name?"

"No, except that I heard your wife call you John."

"My name is John Saunderson."

"Ah! you come from the north, then? That's why you are so sensible and shrewd. Names that end in 'son' are chiefly borne by the descendants of the Danes, to whom King Alfred, heaven bless him, peacefully assigned no less than sixteen English counties. And when a Dane was called somebody's son, it is a sign that he was the son of a somebody."

"By gosh! I never heard that before."

"If I thought you had I should not have said it."

"Now I have told you my name, what is yours?"

"A wise man asks questions and a fool answers them. Suppose for a moment that I am not a fool."

Farmer Saunderson scratched his head, and looked more puzzled than became the descendant of a Dane settled by King Alfred in the north of England.

"Dash it," said he, at last, "but I think you are Yorkshire too."

"Man, who is the most conceited of all animals, says that he alone has the prerogative of thought, and condemns the other animals to the meaner mechanical operation which he calls instinct. But as instincts are unerring and thoughts generally go wrong, man has not much to boast of according to his own definition. When you say you think, and take it for granted, that I am Yorkshire, you err. I am not Yorkshire. Confining yourself to instinct, can you divine when we shall sup? The cows you are about to visit divine to a moment when they shall be fed."

Said the farmer, recovering his sense of superiority to the guest whom he obliged with a supper, "In ten minutes." Then, after a pause, and in a tone of depreciation, as if he feared he might be thought fine, he continued—"We don't sup in the kitchen. My father did, and so did I till I married; but my Bess, though she's as good a farmer's wife as ever wore shoe-leather, was a tradesman's daughter, and had been brought up different. You see she was not without a good bit of money; but even if she had been, I should not have liked her folks to say I had lowered her—so we sup in the parlour."

Quoth Kenelm, "The first consideration is to sup at all. Supper conceded, every man is more likely to get on in life who would rather sup in his parlour than his kitchen. Meanwhile, I see a pump; while you go to the cows I will stay here and wash my hands of them."

"Hold; you seem a sharp fellow and certainly no fool. I have a son, a good smart chap, but stuck up; crows it over us all; thinks no small beer of himself. You'd do me a service, and him too, if you'd let him down a peg or two."

Kenelm, who was now hard at work at the pump-handle, only replied by a gracious nod. But as he seldom lost an opportunity for reflection, he said to himself, while he laved his face in the stream from the spout, "One can't wonder why every small man thinks it so pleasant to let down a big one, when a father asks a stranger to let down his own son for even fancying that he is not small beer. It is upon that principle in human nature that criticism wisely relinquishes its pretensions as an analytical science, and becomes a lucrative profession. It relies on the pleasure its readers find in letting a man down."

CHAPTER IX.

IT was a pretty, quaint farmhouse, such as might go well with two or three hundred acres of tolerably good land, tolerably well farmed by an active old-fashioned tenant, who, though he did not use mowing-machines, nor steam-ploughs, nor dabble in chemical experiments, still brought an adequate capital to his land, and made the capital yield a very fair return of interest. The supper was laid out in a good-sized though low-pitched parlour with a glazed door, now wide open, as were all the latticed windows, looking into a small garden, rich in those straggling old English flowers which are now-a-days banished from gardens more pretentious and infinitely less fragrant. At one corner was an arbour covered with honeysuckle, and, opposite to it, a row of beehives. The room itself had an air of comfort, and that sort of elegance which indicates the presiding genius of feminine taste. There were shelves suspended to the wall by blue ribbons, and filled with small books neatly bound; there were flower-pots in all the window-sills; there was a small cottage piano; the walls were graced partly with engraved portraits of county magnates and prize oxen; partly with samplers in worsted work, comprising verses of moral character and the names and birthdays of the farmer's grandmother, mother, wife, and daughters. Over the chimney-piece was a small mirror, and above that the trophy of a fox's brush; while niched into an angle in the room was a glazed cupboard, rich with specimens of old china, Indian and English.

The party consisted of the farmer, his wife, three buxom daughters, and a pale-faced, slender lad of about twenty, the only son, who did not take willingly to farming: he had been educated at a superior grammar school, and had high notions about the March of Intellect and the Progress of the Age.

Kenelm, though among the gravest of mortals, was one of the least shy. In fact shyness is the usual symptom of a keen *amour propre;* and of that quality the youthful Chillingly scarcely possessed more than did the three Fishes of his hereditary scutcheon. He felt himself perfectly at home with his entertainers; taking care, however, that his atttentions were so equally divided between the three daughters as to prevent all suspicion of a particular preference. "There is safety in numbers," thought he, "especially in odd numbers. The three Graces never married, neither did the nine Muses."

"I presume, young ladies, that you are fond of music," said Kenelm, glancing at the piano.

"Yes, I love it dearly," said the eldest girl, speaking for the others.

Quoth the farmer, as he heaped the stranger's plate with boiled beef and carrots, "Things are not what they were when I was a boy; then it was only great tenant-farmers who had their girls taught the piano, and sent their boys to a good school. Now we small folks are for helping our children a step or two higher than our own place on the ladder."

"The schoolmaster is abroad," said the son, with the emphasis of a sage adding an original aphorism to the stores of philosophy.

"There is, no doubt, a greater equality of culture than there was in the last generation," said Kenelm. "People of all ranks utter the same commonplace ideas in very much the same arrangements of syntax. And in proportion as the democracy of intelligence extends—a friend of mine, who is a doctor, tells me that complaints formerly reserved to what is called aristocracy (though what that word means in plain English I don't know) are equally shared by the commonalty—*tic-douloureux* and other neuralgic maladies abound. And the human race, in England at least, is becoming more slight and delicate. There is a fable of a man who, when he became exceedingly old, was turned into a grasshopper. England is very old, and is evidently approaching the grasshopper state of development. Perhaps we don't eat as much beef as our forefathers did. May I ask you for another slice?"

Kenelm's remarks were somewhat over the heads of his audience. But the son, taking them as a slur upon the enlightened spirit of the age, coloured up and said, with a knitted brow, "I hope, sir, that you are not an enemy to progress."

"That depends: for instance, I prefer staying here, where I am well off, to going farther and faring worse."

"Well said!" cried the farmer.

Not deigning to notice that interruption, the son took up Kenelm's reply with a sneer, "I suppose you mean that it is to fare worse, if you march with the time."

"I am afraid we have no option but to march with the time; but when we reach that stage when to march any farther is to march into old age, we should not be sorry if time would be kind enough to stand still; and all good doctors concur in advising us to do nothing to hurry him."

"There is no sign of old age in this country, sir; and thank heaven we are not standing still!"

"Grasshoppers never do; they are always hopping and jumping, and making what they think 'progress,' till (unless they hop into the water and are swallowed up prematurely by a carp or a frog) they die of the exhaustion which hops and jumps unremitting naturally produce. May I ask you, Mrs. Saunderson, for some of that rice-pudding?"

The farmer, who, though he did not quite comprehend Kenelm's metaphorical mode of arguing, saw delightedly that his wise son looked more posed than himself, cried with great glee, "Bob, my boy,—Bob! our visitor is a little too much for you!"

"Oh no," said Kenelm modestly. "But I honestly think Mr. Bob would be a wiser man, and a weightier man, and more removed from the grasshopper state, if he would think less and eat more pudding."

When the supper was over the farmer offered Kenelm a clay pipe filled with shag, which that adventurer accepted with his habitual resignation to the ills of life; and the whole party, excepting Mrs. Saunderson, strolled into the garden. Kenelm and Mr. Saunderson seated themselves in the honeysuckle arbour: the girls and the advocate of progress stood without among the garden flowers. It was a still and lovely night, the moon at her full. The farmer, seated facing his hay-fields, smoked on placidly. Kenelm, at the third whiff, laid aside his pipe, and glanced furtively at the three Graces. They formed a pretty group, all clustered together near the silenced beehives, the two younger seated on the grass strip that bordered the flower-beds, their arms over each other's shoulders, the elder one standing behind them, with the moonlight shining soft on her auburn hair.

Young Saunderson walked restlessly by himself to and fro the path of gravel.

"It is a strange thing," ruminated Kenelm, "that girls are not unpleasant to look at if you take them collectively—two or three bound up together; but if you detach any one of them from the bunch, the odds are that she is as plain as a pike-staff. I wonder whether that bucolical grasshopper, who is so enamoured of the hop and jump that he calls 'progress,' classes the society of Mormons among the evidences of civilized advancement. There is a good deal to be said in favour of taking a whole lot of wives as one may buy a whole lot of cheap razors. For it is not impossible that out of a dozen a good one may be found. And then, too, a whole nosegay of variegated blooms, with a faded leaf here and there, must be more agreeable to the eye than the same monotonous solitary lady's smock. But I fear these reflections are naughty; let us change them. Farmer," he said aloud, "I suppose your handsome daughters are too fine to assist you much. I did not see them among the haymakers."

"Oh, they were there, but by themselves, in the back part of the field. I did not want them to mix with all the girls, many of whom are strangers from other places. I don't know anything against them; but as I don't know anything for them, I thought it as well to keep my lasses apart."

"But I should have supposed it wiser to keep your son apart from them. I saw him in the thick of those nymphs."

"Well," said the farmer, musingly, and withdrawing his pipe from his lips, "I don't think lasses not quite well brought up, poor things! do as much harm to the lads as they can do to proper-behaved lasses—leastways my wife does not think so. 'Keep good girls from bad girls,' says she, 'and good girls will never go wrong.' And you will find there is something in that when you have girls of your own to take care of."

"Without waiting for that time—which I trust may never occur—I can recognize the wisdom of your excellent wife's observation. My own opinion is, that a woman can more easily do mischief to her own sex than to ours,—since, of course, she cannot exist without doing mischief to somebody or other."

"And good, to," said the jovial farmer, thumping his fist on the table. "What should we be without the women?"

"Very much better, I take it, sir. Adam was as good as gold, and never had a qualm of conscience or stomach till Eve seduced him into eating raw apples."

"Young man, thou'st been crossed in love. I see it now. That's why thou look'st so sorrowful."

"Sorrowful! Did you ever know a man crossed in love who looked less sorrowful when he came across a pudding?"

"Hey! but thou canst ply a good knife and fork—that I will say for thee." Here the farmer turned round, and gazed on Kenelm with deliberate scrutiny. That scrutiny accomplished, his voice took a somewhat more respectful tone, as he resumed, "Do you know that you puzzle me somewhat?"

"Very likely. I am sure that I puzzle myself. Say on."

"Looking at your dress and—and——"

"The two shillings you gave me? Yes——"

"I took you for the son of some small farmer like myself. But now I judge from your talk that you are a college chap—anyhow, a gentleman. Ben't it so?"

"My dear Mr. Saunderson, I set out on my travels, which is not long ago, with a strong dislike to telling lies. But I doubt if a man can get long through this world without finding that the faculty of lying was bestowed on him by nature as a necessary means of self-preservation. If you are going to ask me any questions about myself, I am sure that I shall tell you lies. Perhaps, therefore, it may be best for both if I decline the bed you proffered me, and take my night's rest under a hedge."

"Pooh! I don't want to know more of a man's affairs than he thinks fit to tell me. Stay and finish the haymaking. And I say, lad, I'm glad you don't seem to care for the girls; for I saw a very pretty one trying to flirt with you—and if you don't mind she'll bring you into trouble."

"How? Does she want to run away from her uncle?"

"Uncle! Bless you, she don't live with him! She lives with her father; and I never knew that she wants to run away. In fact, Jessie Wiles—that's her name—is, I believe, a very good girl, and everybody likes her—perhaps a little too much; but then she knows she's a beauty, and does not object to admiration."

"No woman ever does, whether she's a beauty or not. But I don't yet understand why Jessie Wiles should bring me into trouble."

"Because there is a big hulking fellow who has gone half out of his wits for her; and when he fancies he sees any other chap too sweet on her he thrashes him into a jelly. So, youngster, you just keep your skin out of that trap."

"Hem! And what does the girl say to those proofs of affection? Does she like the man the better for thrashing other admirers into jelly?"

"Poor child! No; she hates the very sight of him. But he swears she shall marry nobody else, if he hangs for it. And to tell you the truth, I suspect that if Jessie does seem to trifle with others a little too lightly, it is to draw away this bully's suspicion from the only man I think she does care for—a poor sickly young fellow who was crippled by an accident, and whom Tom Bowles could brain with his little finger."

"This is really interesting," cried Kenelm, showing something like excitement. "I should like to know this terrible suitor."

"That's easy eno'," said the farmer, dryly. "You have only to take a stroll with Jessie Wiles after sunset, and you'll know more of Tom Bowles than you are likely to forget in a month."

"Thank you very much for your information," said Kenelm, in a soft tone, grateful but pensive. "I hope to profit by it."

"Do. I should be sorry if any harm came to thee; and Tom Bowles in one of his furies is as bad to cross as a mad bull. So now, as we must be up early, I'll just take a look round the stables, and then off to bed; and I advise you to do the same."

"Thank you for the hint. I see the young ladies have already gone in. Good night."

Passing through the garden, Kenelm encountered the junior Saunderson.

"I fear," said the Votary of Progress, "that you have found the governor awful slow. What have you been talking about?"

"Girls," said Kenelm, "a subject always awful, but not necessarily slow."

"Girls—the governor been talking about girls! You joke."

"I wish I did joke, but that is a thing I could never do since I came upon earth. Even in the cradle, I felt that life was a very serious matter, and did not allow of jokes. I remember too well my first dose of castor-oil. You too, Mr. Bob, have doubtless imbibed that initiatory preparation to the sweets of existence. The corners of your mouth have not recovered from the downward curves into which it so rigidly dragged them. Like myself, you are of grave temperament, and not easily moved to jocularity—nay, an enthusiast for Progress is of necessity a man eminently dissatisfied with the present state of affairs. And chronic dissatisfaction resents the momentary relief of a joke."

"Give off chaffing, if you please," said Bob, lowering the didascular intonations of his voice, "and just tell me plainly, did not my father say anything particular about me?"

"Not a word—the only person of the male sex of whom he said anything particular was Tom Bowles."

"What, fighting Tom! the terror of the whole neighbourhood! Ah, I guess the old gentleman is afraid lest Tom may fall foul upon me. But Jessie Wiles is not worth a quarrel with that brute. It is a crying shame in the Government——"

"What! has the Government failed to appreciate the heroism of Tom Bowles, or rather to restrain the excesses of its ardour?"

"Stuff! it is a shame in the Government not to have compelled his father to put him to school. If education were universal——"

"You think there would be no brutes in particular. It may be so, but education is universal in China. And so is the bastinado. I thought, however, that you said the schoolmaster was abroad, and that the age of enlightenment was in full progress."

"Yes, in the towns, but not in these obsolete rural districts; and that brings me to the point. I feel lost—thrown away here. I have something in me, sir, and it can only come out by collision with equal minds. So do me a favour, will you?"

"With the greatest pleasure."

"Give the governor a hint that he can't expect me, after the education I have had, to follow the plough and fatten pigs; and that Manchester is the place for ME."

"Why Manchester?"

"Because I have a relation in business there who will give me a clerkship if the governor will consent. And Manchester rules England."

"Mr. Bob Saunderson, I will do my best to promote your wishes. This is a land of liberty, and every man should choose his own walk in it, so that, at the last, if he goes to the dogs, he goes to them without that disturbance of temper which is naturally occasioned by the sense of being driven to their jaws by another man against his own will. He has then no one to blame but himself. And that, Mr. Bob, is a great comfort. When, having got into a scrape, we blame others, we unconsciously become unjust, spiteful, uncharitable, malignant, perhaps revengeful. We indulge in feelings which tend to demoralize the whole character. But when we only blame ourselves, we become modest and penitent. We make allowances for others. And, indeed, self-blame is a salutary exercise of conscience, which a really good man performs every day of his life. And now, will you show me the room in which I am to sleep, and forget for a few hours that I am alive at all—the best thing that can happen to us in this world, my dear Mr. Bob! There's never much amiss with our days, so long as we can forget all about them the moment we lay our heads on the pillow."

The two young men entered the house amicably, arm in arm. The girls had already retired, but Mrs. Saunderson was still up to conduct her visitor to the guest's chamber—a pretty room which had been furnished twenty-two years ago, on the occasion of the farmer's marriage, at the expense of Mrs. Saunderson's mother, for her own occupation whenever she paid them a visit. And with its dimity curtains and trellised paper it still looked as fresh and new as if decorated and furnished yesterday.

Left alone, Kenelm undressed, and before he got into bed, bared his right arm, and doubling it, gravely contemplated its muscular development, passing his left hand over that prominence in the upper part which is vulgarly called the ball. Satisfied apparently with the size and the firmness of that pugilistic protuberance, he gently sighed forth, "I fear I shall have to lick Thomas Bowles." In five minutes more he was asleep.

CHAPTER X.

THE next day the hay-mowing was completed, and a large portion of the hay already made carted away to be stacked. Kenelm acquitted himself with a credit not less praiseworthy than had previously won Mr. Saunderson's approbation. But instead of rejecting as before the acquaintance of Miss Jessie Wiles, he contrived towards noon to place himself near to that dangerous beauty, and commenced conversation. "I am afraid I was rather rude to you yesterday, and I want to beg pardon."

"Oh," answered the girl, in that simple intelligible English which is more frequent among our village folks nowadays than many popular novelists would lead us into supposing—"oh, I ought to ask pardon for taking a liberty in speaking to you. But I thought you'd feel strange, and I intended it kindly."

"I'm sure you did," returned Kenelm, chivalrously raking her portion of hay as well as his own, while he spoke. "And I want to be good friends with you. It is very near the time when we shall leave off for dinner, and Mrs. Saunderson has filled my pockets with some excellent beef-sandwiches, which I shall be happy to share with you, if you do not object to dine with me here, instead of going home for your dinner."

The girl hesitated, and then shook her head in dissent from the proposition.

"Are you afraid that your neighbours will think it wrong?"

Jessie curled up her lip with a pretty scorn, and said, "I don't much care what other folks say, but isn't it wrong?"

"Not in the least. Let me make your mind easy. I am here but for a day or two; we are not likely ever to meet again; but, before I go, I should be glad if I could do you some little service." As he spoke he had paused from his work, and, leaning on his rake, fixed his eyes, for the first time attentively, on the fair haymaker.

Yes, she was decidedly pretty—pretty to a rare degree—luxuriant brown hair neatly tied up, under a straw hat doubtless of her own plaiting; for, as a general rule, nothing more educates the village maid for the destinies of flirt, than the accomplishment of straw-plaiting. She had large, soft blue eyes, delicate small features, and a complexion more clear in its healthful bloom than rural beauties generally retain against the influences of wind and sun. She smiled and slightly coloured as he gazed on her, and, lifting her eyes, gave him one gentle, trustful glance, which might have bewitched a philosopher and deceived a *roué*. And yet Kenelm, by that intuitive knowledge of character which is often truthfulest where it is least disturbed by the doubts and cavils of acquired knowledge, felt at once that in that girl's mind coquetry, perhaps unconscious, was conjoined with an innocence of anything worse than coquetry as complete as a child's. He bowed his head, in withdrawing his gaze, and took her into his heart as tenderly as if she had been a child appealing to it for protection.

"Certainly," he said inly—"certainly I must lick Tom Bowles; yet stay, perhaps after all she likes him."

"But," he continued aloud, "you do not see how I can be of any service to you. Before I explain, let me ask which of the men in the field is Tom Bowles?"

"Tom Bowles!" exclaimed Jessie, in a tone of surprise and alarm, and turning pale as she looked hastily round; "you frightened me, sir, but he is not here; he does not work in the fields. But how came you to hear of Tom Bowles?"

"Dine with me and I'll tell you. Look, there is a quiet place in yon corner under the thorn-trees by that piece of water. See, they are leaving off work: I will go for a can of beer, and then, pray, let me join you there."

Jessie paused for a moment as if doubtful still; then again glancing at Kenelm, and assured by the grave kindness of his countenance, uttered a scarce audible assent, and moved away towards the thorn-trees.

As the sun now stood perpendicularly over their heads, and the hand of the clock in the village church tower, soaring over the hedgerows, reached the first hour after noon, all work ceased in a sudden silence; some of the girls went back to their homes; those who stayed grouped together, apart from the men, who took their way to the shadows of a large oak-tree in the hedgerow, where beer kegs and cans awaited them.

CHAPTER XI.

"AND now," said Kenelm, as the two young persons, having finished their simple repast, sat under the thorn-trees and by the side of the water, fringed at that part with tall reeds through which the light summer breeze stirred with a pleasant murmur,—"now I will talk to you about Tom Bowles. Is it true that you don't like that brave young fellow?—I say young, as I take his youth for granted."

"Like him! I hate the sight of him."

"Did you always hate the sight of him? You must surely at one time have allowed him to think that you did not?"

The girl winced, and made no answer, but plucked a daffodil from the soil, and tore it ruthlessly to pieces.

"I am afraid you like to serve your admirers as you do that ill-fated flower," said Kenelm, with some severity of tone. "But concealed in the flower you may sometimes find the sting of a bee. I see by your countenance that you did not tell Tom Bowles that you hated him till it was too late to prevent his losing his wits for you."

"No; I wasn't so bad as that," said Jessie, looking, nevertheless, rather ashamed of herself; "but I was silly and giddy-like, I own; and, when he first took notice of me, I was pleased, without thinking much of it, because, you see, Mr. Bowles (emphasis on *Mr.*) is higher up than a poor girl like me. He is a tradesman, and I am only a shepherd's daughter—though, indeed, father is more like Mr. Saunderson's foreman than a mere shepherd. But I never thought anything serious of it, and did not suppose he did—that is, at first."

"So Tom Bowles is a tradesman. What trade?"

"A farrier, sir."

"And, I am told, a very fine young man."

"I don't know as to that: he is very big."

"And what made you hate him?"

"The first thing that made me hate him was, that he insulted father, who is a very quiet, timid man, and threatened, I don't know what, if father did not make me keep company with him. Make me indeed! But Mr. Bowles is a dangerous, bad-hearted, violent man; and—don't laugh at me, sir—but I dreamed one night he was murdering me. And I think he will too, if he stays here; and so does his poor mother, who is a very nice woman, and wants him to go away; but he'll not."

"Jessie," said Kenelm, softly, "I said I wanted to make friends with you. Do you think you can make a friend of me? I can never be more than friend. But I should like to be that. Can you trust me as one?"

"Yes," answered the girl firmly, and, as she lifted her eyes to him, their look was pure from all vestige of coquetry—guileless, frank, grateful.

"Is there not another young man who courts you more civilly than Tom Bowles does, and whom you really could find it in your heart to like?"

Jessie looked round for another daffodil, and not finding one, contented herself with a blue-bell, which she did not tear to pieces but caressed with a tender hand. Kenelm bent his eyes down on her charming face with something in their gaze rarely seen there— something of that unreasoning, inexpressible human fondness, for which philosophers of his school have no excuse. Had ordinary mortals, like you or myself, for instance, peered through the leaves of the thorn-trees, we should have sighed or frowned, according to our several temperaments; but we should all have said, whether spitefully or envyingly, "Happy young lovers!" and should all have blundered lamentably in so saying.

Still, there is no denying the fact that a pretty face has a very unfair advantage over a plain one. And, much to the discredit of Kenelm's philanthropy, it may be reasonably doubted whether, had Jessie Wiles been endowed by nature with a snub nose and a squint, Kenelm would have volunteered his friendly services, or meditated battle with Tom Bowles on her behalf.

But there was no touch of envy or jealousy in the tone with which he said—

"I see there is some one you would like well enough to marry, and that you make a great difference in the way you treat a daffodil and a blue-bell. Who and what is the young man whom the blue-bell represents? Come, confide."

"We were much brought up together," said Jessie, still looking down, and still smoothing the leaves of the blue-bell. "His mother lived in the next cottage; and my mother was very fond of him, and so was father too; and, before I was ten years old, they used to laugh when poor Will called me his little wife." Here the tears which had started to Jessie's eyes began to fall over the flower. "But now father would not hear of it; and it can't be. And I've tried to care for some one else, and I can't, and that's the truth."

"But why? Has he turned out ill?—taken to poaching or drink?"

"No—no—no,—he's as steady and good a lad as ever lived. But—but——"

"Yes; but——"

"He is a cripple now—and I love him all the better for it." Here Jessie fairly sobbed.

Kenelm was greatly moved, and prudently held his peace till she had a little recovered herself; then, in answer to his gentle questionings, he learned that Will Somers—till then a healthy and strong lad—had fallen from the height of a scaffolding, at the age of sixteen, and been so seriously injured that he was moved at once to the hospital. When he came out of it—what with the fall, and what with the long illness which had followed the effects of the accident —he was not only crippled for life, but of health so delicate and weakly that he was no longer fit for outdoor labour and the hard life of a peasant. He was the only son of a widowed mother, and his sole mode of assisting her was a very precarious one. He had taught himself basket-making; and though, Jessie said, his work was very ingenious and clever, still there were but few customers for it in that neighbourhood. And, alas! even if Jessie's father would consent to give his daughter to the poor cripple, how could the poor cripple earn enough to maintain a wife?

"And," said Jessie, "still I was happy, walking out with him on Sunday evenings, or going to sit with him and his mother—for we are both young and can wait. But I daren't do it any more now—for Tom Bowles has sworn that if I do he will beat him before my eyes; and Will has a high spirit, and I should break my heart if any harm happened to him on my account."

"As for Mr. Bowles, we'll not think of him at present. But if Will could maintain himself and you, your father would not object, nor you either, to a marriage with the poor cripple?"

"Father would not; and as for me, if it weren't for disobeying father, I'd marry him to-morrow. *I* can work."

"They are going back to the hay now; but after that task is over, let me walk home with you, and show me Will's cottage and Mr. Bowles's shop or forge."

"But you'll not say anything to Mr. Bowles. He wouldn't mind your being a gentleman, as I now see you are, sir; and he's dangerous—oh, so dangerous!—and so strong."

"Never fear," answered Kenelm, with the nearest approach to a laugh he had ever made since childhood; "but when we are relieved, wait for me a few minutes at yon gate."

CHAPTER XII.

KENELM spoke no more to his new friend in the hayfields; but when the day's work was over he looked round for the farmer to make an excuse for not immediately joining the family supper. However, he did not see either Mr. Saunderson or his son. Both were busied in the stackyard. Well pleased to escape excuse and the questions it might provoke, Kenelm therefore put on the coat he had laid aside and joined Jessie, who had waited for him at the gate. They entered the lane side by side, following the stream of villagers who were slowly wending their homeward way. It was a primitive English village, not adorned on the one hand with fancy or model cottages, nor on the other hand indicating penury and squalor. The church rose before them gray and Gothic, backed by the red clouds in which the sun had set, and bordered by the glebe-land of the half-seen parsonage. Then came the village green, with a pretty schoolhouse; and to this succeeded a long street of scattered white-washed cottages, in the midst of their own little gardens.

As they walked, the moon rose in full splendour, silvering the road before them.

"Who is the squire here?" asked Kenelm. "I should guess him to be a good sort of man and well off."

"Yes, Squire Travers; he is a great gentleman, and they say very rich. But his place is a good way from this village. You can see it if you stay, for he gives a harvest-home supper on Saturday, and Mr. Saunderson and all his tenants are going. It is a beautiful park, and Miss Travers is a sight to look at. Oh, she is lovely!" continued Jessie, with an unaffected burst of admiration; for women are more sensible of the charm of each other's beauty than men give them credit for.

"As pretty as yourself?"

"Oh, pretty is not the word. She is a thousand times handsomer!"

"Humph!" said Kenelm, incredulously.

There was a pause, broken by a quick sigh from Jessie.

"What are you sighing for?—tell me."

"I was thinking that a very little can make folks happy, but that somehow or other that very little is as hard to get as if one set one's heart on a great deal."

"That's very wisely said. Everybody covets a little something for which, perhaps, nobody else would give a straw. But what's the very little thing for which you are sighing?"

"Mrs. Bawtrey wants to sell that shop of hers. She is getting old, and has had fits; and she can get nobody to buy; and if Will had that shop and I could keep it—but 'tis no use thinking of that."

"What shop do you mean?"

"There!"

"Where? I see no shop."

"But it is *the* shop of the village—the only one, where the post-office is."

"Ah! I see something at the windows like a red cloak. What do they sell?"

"Everything—tea and sugar, and candles, and shawls, and gowns, and cloaks, and mouse-traps, and letter-paper; and Mrs. Bawtrey buys poor Will's baskets, and sells them for a good deal more than she pays."

"It seems a nice cottage, with a field and orchard at the back."

"Yes. Mrs. Bawtrey pays £8 a-year for it; but the shop can well afford it."

Kenelm made no reply. They both walked on in silence, and had now reached the centre of the village street when Jessie, looking up, uttered an abrupt exclamation, gave an affrighted start, and then came to a dead stop.

Kenelm's eye followed the direction of hers, and saw, a few yards distant, at the other side of the way, a small red brick house, with thatched sheds adjoining it, the whole standing in a wide yard, over the gate of which leaned a man smoking a small cutty-pipe. "It is Tom Bowles," whispered Jessie, and instinctively she twined her arm into Kenelm's—then, as if on second thoughts, withdrew it, and said, still in a whisper, "Go back now, sir—do."

"Not I. It is Tom Bowles whom I want to know. Hush!"

For here Tom Bowles had thrown down his pipe and was coming slowly across the road towards them.

Kenelm eyed him with attention. A singularly powerful man, not so tall as Kenelm by some inches, but still above the middle height, herculean shoulders and chest, the lower limbs not in equal proportion—a sort of slouching, shambling gait. As he advanced the moonlight fell on his face,—it was a handsome one. He wore no hat, and his hair, of a light brown, curled close. His face was fresh-coloured, with aquiline features; his age apparently about six or seven-and-twenty. Coming nearer and nearer, whatever favourable impression the first glance at his physiognomy might have made on Kenelm was dispelled, for the expression of his face changed and became fierce and lowering.

Kenelm was still walking on, Jessie by his side, when Bowles rudely thrust himself between them, and seizing the girl's arm with one hand, he turned his face full on Kenelm, with a menacing wave of the other hand, and said in a deep burly voice—

"Who be you?"

"Let go that young woman before I tell you."

"If you weren't a stranger," answered Bowles, seeming as if he tried to suppress a rising fit of wrath, "you'd be in the kennel for those words. But I s'pose you don't know that I'm Tom Bowles, and I don't choose the girl as I'm after to keep company with any other man. So you be off."

"And I don't choose any other man to lay violent hands on any girl walking by my side without telling him that he's a brute; and that I only wait till he has both his hands at liberty to let him know that he has not a poor cripple to deal with."

Tom Bowles could scarcely believe his ears. Amaze swallowed up for the moment every other sentiment. Mechanically he loosened his hold of Jessie, who fled off like a bird released. But evidently she thought of her new friend's danger more than her own escape; for instead of sheltering herself in her father's cottage, she ran towards a group of labourers, who, near at hand, had stopped loitering before the public-house, and returned with those allies towards the spot in which she had left the two men. She was very popular with the villagers, who, strong in the sense of numbers, overcame their awe of Tom Bowles, and arrived at the place half running, half striding, in time, they hoped, to interpose between his terrible arm and the bones of the unoffending stranger.

Meanwhile Bowles, having recovered his first astonishment, and scarcely noticing Jessie's escape, still left his right arm extended towards the place she had vacated, and with a quick back-stroke of the left levelled at Kenelm's face, growled contemptuously, "Thou'lt find one hand enough for thee."

But quick as was his aim, Kenelm caught the lifted arm just above the elbow, causing the blow to waste itself on air, and with a simultaneous advance of his right knee and foot, dexterously tripped up his bulky antagonist, and laid him sprawling on his back. The movement was so sudden, and the stun it occasioned so utter, morally as well as physically, that a minute or more elapsed before Tom Bowles picked himself up. And he then stood another minute glowering at his antagonist, with a vague sentiment of awe almost like a superstitious panic. For it is noticeable that, however fierce and fearless a man or even a wild beast may be, yet if either has hitherto been only familiar with victory and triumph, never yet having met with a foe that could cope with its force, the first effect of a defeat, especially from a despised adversary, unhinges and half paralyzes the whole nervous system. But as fighting Tom gradually recovered to the consciousness of his own strength, and the recollection that it had been only foiled by the skilful trick of a wrestler, not the hand-to-hand might of a pugilist, the panic vanished, and Tom Bowles was himself again. "Oh, that's your sort, is it? We don't fight with our heels hereabouts, like Cornishers and donkeys; we fight with our fists, youngster; and since you *will* have a bout at that, why you must."

"Providence," answered Kenelm, solemnly, "sent me to this village for the express purpose of licking Tom Bowles. It is a signal mercy vouchsafed to yourself, as you will one day acknowledge."

Again a thrill of awe, something like that which the demagogue in Aristophanes might have felt when braved by the sausage-maker, shot through the valiant heart of Tom Bowles. He did not like those ominous words, and still less the lugubrious tone of voice in which they were uttered. But resolved, at least, to proceed to battle with more preparation than he had at first designed, he now deliberately disencumbered himself of his heavy fustian jacket and vest, rolled up his shirt-sleeves, and then slowly advanced towards the foe.

E

Kenelm had also, with still greater deliberation, taken off his coat—which he folded up with care, as being both a new and an only one, and deposited by the hedge-side—and bared arms, lean indeed, and almost slight, as compared with the vast muscle of his adversary, but firm in sinew as the hindleg of a stag.

By this time the labourers, led by Jessie, had arrived at the spot, and were about to crowd in between the combatants, when Kenelm waved them back, and said in a calm and impressive voice—

"Stand round, my good friends, make a ring, and see that it is fair play on my side. I am sure it will be fair on Mr. Bowles's. He's big enough to scorn what is little. And now, Mr. Bowles, just a word with you in the presence of your neighbours. I am not going to say anything uncivil. If you are rather rough and hasty, a man is not always master of himself—at least so I am told—when he thinks more than he ought to do about a pretty girl. But I can't look at your face even by this moonlight, and though its expression at this moment is rather cross, without being sure that you are a fine fellow at bottom. And that if you give a promise as man to man you will keep it. Is that so?"

One or two of the bystanders murmured assent; the others pressed round in silent wonder.

"What's all that soft sawder about?" said Tom Bowles, somewhat falteringly.

"Simply this: if in the fight between us I beat you, I ask you to promise before your neighbours that you will not by word or deed molest or interfere again with Miss Jessie Wiles."

"Eh!" roared Tom. "Is it that *you* are after her?"

"Suppose I am, if that pleases you; and, on my side, I promise that, if you beat me, I quit this place as soon as you leave me well enough to do so, and will never visit it again. What! do you hesitate to promise? Are you really afraid I shall lick you?"

"You! I'd smash a dozen of you to powder."

"In that case, you are safe to promise. Come, 'tis a fair bargain. Isn't it, neighbours?"

Won over by Kenelm's easy show of good temper, and by the sense of justice, the bystanders joined in a common exclamation of assent.

"Come, Tom," said an old fellow, "the gentleman can't speak fairer; and we shall all think you be afeard if you hold back."

Tom's face worked; but at last he growled, "Well, I promise—that is, if he beats me."

"All right," said Kenelm. "You hear, neighbours; and Tom Bowles could not show that handsome face of his among you if he broke his word. Shake hands on it."

Fighting Tom sulkily shook hands.

"Well, now, that's what I call English," said Kenelm,—"all pluck and no malice. Fall back, friends, and leave a clear space for us."

The men all receded; and as Kenelm took his ground, there was a supple ease in his posture which at once brought out into clearer evidence the nervous strength of his build, and, contrasted with Tom's bulk of chest, made the latter look clumsy and top-heavy.

The two men faced each other a minute, the eyes of both vigilant and steadfast. Tom's blood began to fire up as he gazed—nor, with all his outward calm, was Kenelm insensible of that proud beat of the heart which is aroused by the fierce joy of combat. Tom struck out first, and a blow was parried, but not returned; another and another blow—still parried—still unreturned. Kenelm, acting evidently on the defensive, took all the advantages for that strategy which he derived from superior length of arm and lighter agility of frame. Perhaps he wished to ascertain the extent of his adversary's skill, or to try the endurance of his wind, before he ventured on the hazards of attack. Tom, galled to the quick that blows which might have felled an ox were thus warded off from their mark, and dimly aware that he was encountering some mysterious skill which turned his brute strength into waste force, and might overmaster him in the long-run, came to a rapid conclusion that the sooner he brought that brute strength to bear, the better it would be for him. Accordingly, after three rounds, in which, without once breaking the guard of his antagonist, he had received a few playful taps on the nose and mouth, he drew back, and made a bull-like rush at his foe—bull-like, for it butted full at him with the powerful down-bent head, and the two fists doing duty as horns. The rush spent, he found himself in the position of a man *milled*. I take it for granted that every Englishman who can call himself a man—that is, every man who has been an English boy, and, as such, been compelled to the use of his fists—knows what a 'mill' is. But I sing not only "pueris," but "virginibus." Ladies,—'a mill'—using, with reluctance and contempt for myself, that slang in which lady-writers indulge, and Girls of the Period know much better than they do their Murray—'a mill'—speaking not to lady-writers, not to Girls of the Period, but to innocent damsels, and in explanation to those foreigners who only understand the English language as taught by Addison and Macaulay—a 'mill,' periphrastically, means this: your adversary, in the noble encounter between fist and fist, has so plunged his head that it gets caught, as in a vice, between the side and doubled left arm of the adversary, exposing that head, unprotected and helpless, to be pounded out of recognizable shape by the right fist of the opponent. It is a situation in which raw superiority of force sometimes finds itself, and is seldom spared by disciplined superiority of skill. Kenelm, his right fist raised, paused for a moment, then, loosening the left arm, releasing the prisoner, and giving him a friendly slap on the shoulder, he turned round to the spectators, and said apologetically,—"he has a handsome face—it would be a shame to spoil it."

Tom's position of peril was so obvious to all, and that good-humoured abnegation of the advantage which the position gave to the adversary seemed so generous, that the labourers actually hurrahed. Tom himself felt as if treated like a child; and alas, and alas for him! in wheeling round, and regathering himself up, his eye rested on Jessie's face. Her lips were apart with breathless terror; he fancied they were apart with a smile of contempt. And now he became formidable. He fought as fights the bull in presence of the heifer, who, as he knows too well, will go with the conqueror.

If Tom had never yet fought with a man taught by a prize-fighter, so never yet had Kenelm encountered a strength which, but for the lack of that teaching, would have conquered his own. He could act no longer on the defensive; he could no longer play, like a dexterous fencer, with the sledge-hammers of those mighty arms. They broke through his guard—they sounded on his chest as on an anvil. He felt that did they alight on his head he was a lost man. He felt also that the blows spent on the chest of his adversary were idle as the stroke of a cane on the hide of a rhinoceros. But now his nostrils dilated, his eyes flashed fire—Kenelm Chillingly had ceased to be a philosopher. Crash came his blow—how unlike the swinging round-about hits of Tom Bowles!—straight to its aim as the rifle-ball of a Tyrolese, or a British marksman at Aldershot—all the strength of nerve, sinew, purpose, and mind concentred in its vigour,—crash just at that part of the front where the eyes meet, and followed up with the rapidity of lightning, flash upon flash, by a more restrained but more disabling blow with the left hand just where the left ear meets throat and jaw-bone.

At the first blow Tom Bowles had reeled and staggered, at the second he threw up his hands, made a jump in the air as if shot through the heart, and then heavily fell forwards, an inert mass.

The spectators pressed round him in terror. They thought he was dead. Kenelm knelt, passed quickly his hand over Tom's lips, pulse, and heart, and then rising, said, humbly and with an air of apology—

"If he had been a less magnificent creature, I assure you on my honour that I should never have ventured that second blow. The first would have done for any man less splendidly endowed by nature. Lift him gently; take him home. Tell his mother, with my kind regards, that I'll call and see her and him to-morrow. And, stop, does he ever drink too much beer?"

"Well," said one of the villagers, "Tom *can* drink."

"I thought so. Too much flesh for that muscle. Go for the nearest doctor. You, my lad?—good—off with you—quick! No danger, but perhaps it may be a case for the lancet."

Tom Bowles was lifted tenderly by four of the stoutest men present and borne into his home, evincing no sign of consciousness; but his face, where not clouted with blood, very pale, very calm, with a slight froth at the lips.

Kenelm pulled down his shirt-sleeves, put on his coat, and turned to Jessie—

"Now, my young friend, show me Will's cottage."

The girl came to him white and trembling. She did not dare to speak. The stranger had become a new man in her eyes. Perhaps he frightened her as much as Tom Bowles had done. But she quickened her pace, leaving the public-house behind, till she came to the further end of the village. Kenelm walked beside her, muttering to himself; and though Jessie caught his words, happily she did not understand, for they repeated one of those bitter reproaches on her sex as the main cause of all strife, bloodshed, and mischief in general, with which the classic authors abound. His spleen soothed by that recourse to the lessons of the ancients, Kenelm turned at last to his silent companion, and said, kindly but gravely—

"Mr. Bowles has given me his promise, and it is fair that I should now ask a promise from you. It is this—just consider how easily a girl so pretty as you can be the cause of a man's death. Had Bowles struck me where I struck him, I should have been past the help of a surgeon."

"Oh!" groaned Jessie, shuddering, and covering her face with both hands.

"And, putting aside that danger, consider that a man may be hit mortally on the heart as well as on the head, and that a woman has much to answer for who, no matter what her excuse, forgets what misery and what guilt can be inflicted by a word from her lip and a glance from her eye. Consider this, and promise that, whether you marry Will Somers or not, you will never again give a man fair cause to think you can like him unless your own heart tells you that you can. Will you promise that?"

"I will, indeed—indeed." Poor Jessie's voice died in sobs.

"There, my child, I don't ask you not to cry, because I know how much women like crying, and in this instance it does you a great deal of good. But we are just at the end of the village; which is Will's cottage?"

Jessie lifted her head, and pointed to a solitary, small thatched cottage.

"I would ask you to come in and introduce me; but that might look too much like crowing over poor Tom Bowles. So good-night to you, Jessie, and forgive me for preaching."

CHAPTER XIII.

KENELM knocked at the cottage door; a voice said faintly, "Come in."

He stooped his head, and stepped over the threshold.

Since his encounter with Tom Bowles his sympathies had gone with that unfortunate lover—it is natural to like a man after you have beaten him; and he was by no means predisposed to favour Jessie's preference for a sickly cripple.

Yet, when two bright, soft, dark eyes, and a pale intellectual countenance, with that nameless aspect of refinement which delicate health so often gives, especially to the young, greeted his quiet gaze, his heart was at once won over to the side of the rival. Will Somers was seated by the hearth, on which a few live embers, despite the warmth of the summer evening, still burned; a rude little table was by his side, on which were laid osier twigs and white peeled chips, together with an open book. His hands, pale and slender, were at work on a small basket half finished. His mother was just clearing away the tea-things from another table that stood by the window. Will rose, with the good breeding that belongs to the rural peasant, as the stranger entered; the widow looked round with surprise, and dropped her simple courtesy—a little thin woman, with a mild patient face.

The cottage was very tidily kept, as it is in most village homes where the woman has it her own way. The deal dresser opposite the door had its display of humble crockery. The whitewashed walls were relieved with coloured prints, chiefly Scriptural subjects from the New Testament, such as the Return of the Prodigal Son, in a blue coat and yellow inexpressibles, with his stockings about his heels.

At one corner there were piled up baskets of various sizes, and at another corner was an open cupboard containing books—an article of decorative furniture found in cottages much more rarely than coloured prints and gleaming crockery.

All this, of course, Kenelm could not at a glance comprehend in detail. But as the mind of a man accustomed to generalization is marvellously quick in forming a sound judgment, whereas a mind accustomed to dwell only on detail is wonderfully slow at arriving at any judgment at all, and when it does, the probability is that it will arrive at a wrong one, Kenelm judged correctly when he came to this conclusion: "I am among simple English peasants; but, for some reason or other, not to be explained by the relative amount of wages, it is a favourable specimen of that class."

"I beg your pardon for intruding at this hour, Mrs. Somers," said Kenelm, who had been too familiar with peasants from his earliest childhood not to know how quickly, when in the presence of their household gods, they appreciate respect, and how acutely they feel the want of it. "But my stay in the village is very short, and I should not like to leave without seeing your son's basket-work, of which I have heard much."

"You are very good, sir," said Will, with a pleased smile that wonderfully brightened up his face. "It is only just a few common things that I keep by me. Any finer sort of work I mostly do by order."

"You see, sir," said Mrs. Somers, "it takes so much more time for pretty work-baskets, and suchlike; and unless done to order, it might be a chance if he could get it sold. But pray be seated, sir," and Mrs. Somers placed a chair for her visitor, "while I just run up-stairs for the work-basket which my son has made for Miss Travers. It is to go home to-morrow, and I put it away for fear of accidents."

Kenelm seated himself, and, drawing his chair near to Will's, took up the half-finished basket which the young man had laid down on the table.

"This seems to me very nice and delicate workmanship," said Kenelm; "and the shape, when you have finished it, will be elegant enough to please the taste of a lady."

"It is for Mrs. Lethbridge," said Will; "she wanted something to hold cards and letters; and I took the shape from a book of drawings which Mr. Lethbridge kindly lent me. You know Mr. Lethbridge, sir? He is a very good gentleman."

"No, I don't know him. Who is he?"

"Our clergyman, sir. This is the book."

To Kenelm's surprise, it was a work on Pompeii, and contained woodcuts of the implements and ornaments, mosaics and frescoes, found in that memorable little city.

"I see this is your model," said Kenelm; "what they call a *patera*, and rather a famous one. You are copying it much more truthfully than I should have supposed it possible to do in substituting basket-work for bronze. But you observe that much of the beauty of this shallow bowl depends on the two doves perched on the brim. You can't manage that ornamental addition."

"Mrs. Lethbridge thought of putting there two little stuffed canary-birds."

"Did she? Good heavens!" exclaimed Kenelm.

"But somehow," continued Will, "I did not like that, and I made bold to say so."

"Why did not you like it?"

"Well, I don't know; but I did not think it would be the right thing."

"It would have been very bad taste, and spoilt the effect of your basket-work; and I'll endeavour to explain why. You see here, in the next page, a drawing of a very beautiful statue. Of course this statue is intended to be a representation of nature—but nature idealized. You don't know the meaning of that hard word, idealized, and very few people do. But it means the performance of a something in art according to the idea which a man's mind forms to itself out of a something in nature. That something in nature must, of course, have been carefully studied before the man can work out anything in art by which it is faithfully represented. The artist, for instance, who made that statue, must have known the proportions of the human frame. He must have made studies of various parts of it—heads and hands, and arms and legs, and so forth—and having done so, he then puts together all his various studies of details, so as to form a new whole, which is intended to personate an idea formed in his own mind. Do you go with me?"

"Partly, sir; but I am puzzled a little still."

"Of course you are; but you'll puzzle yourself right if you think over what I say. Now if, in order to make this statue, which is composed of metal or stone, more natural, I stuck on it a wig of real hair, would not you feel at once that I had spoilt the work—that, as you clearly express it, 'it would not be the right thing?'—and, instead of making the work of art more natural, I should have made it laughably unnatural, by forcing insensibly upon the mind of him who looked at it the contrast between the real life, represented by a wig of actual hair, and the artistic life, represented by an idea embodied in stone or metal. The higher the work of art (that is, the higher the idea it represents as a new combination of details taken from nature), the more it is degraded or spoilt by an attempt to give it a kind of reality which is out of keeping with the materials employed. But the same rule applies to everything in art, however humble. And a couple of stuffed canary-birds at the brim of a basket-work imitation of a Greek drinking-cup, would be as bad taste as a wig from the barber's on the head of a marble statue of Apollo."

"I see," said Will, his head downcast, like a man pondering—"at least I think I see; and I'm very much obliged to you, sir."

Mrs. Somers had long since returned with the work-basket, but stood with it in her hands, not daring to interrupt the gentleman, and listening to his discourse with as much patience and as little comprehension as if it had been one of the controversial sermons upon Ritualism with which on great occasions Mr. Lethbridge favoured his congregation.

Kenelm having now exhausted his critical lecture—from which certain poets and novelists, who contrive to caricature the ideal by their attempt to put wigs of real hair upon the heads of stone statues, might borrow a useful hint or two if they would condescend to do so, which is not likely—perceived Mrs. Somers standing by him, took from her the basket, which was really very pretty and elegant, subdivided into various compartments for the implements in use among ladies, and bestowed on it well-merited eulogium.

"The young lady means to finish it herself with ribbons, and line it with satin," said Mrs. Somers proudly.

"The ribbons will not be amiss, sir?" said Will, interrogatively.

"Not at all. Your natural sense of the fitness of things tells you that ribbons go well with straw and light straw-like work such as this; though you would not put ribbons on those rude hampers and game-baskets in the corner. Like to like; a stout cord goes suitably with them; just as a poet who understands his art employs pretty expressions for poems intended to be pretty and suit a fashionable drawing-room, and carefully shuns them to substitute a simple cord for poems intended to be strong and travel far, despite of rough usage by the way. But you really ought to make much more money by this fancy-work than you could as a day-labourer."

Will sighed. "Not in this neighbourhood, sir, I might in a town."

"Why not move to a town, then?"

The young man coloured, and shook his head.

Kenelm turned appealingly to Mrs. Somers. "I'll be willing

to go wherever it would be best for my boy, sir. But——" and here she checked herself, and a tear trickled silently down her cheeks.

Will resumed, in a more cheerful tone, "I am getting a little known now, and work will come if one waits for it."

Kenelm did not deem it courteous or discreet to intrude further on Will's confidence in the first interview; and he began to feel, more than he had done at first, not only the dull pain of the bruises he had received in the recent combat, but also somewhat more than the weariness which follows a long summer-day's work in the open air. He therefore, rather abruptly, now took his leave, saying that he should be very glad of a few specimens of Will's ingenuity and skill, and would call or write to give directions about them.

Just as he came in sight of Tom Bowles's house on his way back to Mr. Saunderson's, Kenelm saw a man mounting a pony that stood tied up at the gate, and exchanging a few words with a respectable-looking woman before he rode on. He was passing by Kenelm without notice, when that philosophical vagrant stopped him, saying, "If I am not mistaken, sir, you are the doctor. There is not much the matter with Mr. Bowles?"

The doctor shook his head. "I can't say yet. He has had a very ugly blow somewhere."

"It was just under the left ear. I did not aim at that exact spot; but Bowles unluckily swerved a little aside at the moment, perhaps in surprise at a tap between his eyes immediately preceding it: and so, as you say, it was an ugly blow that he received. But if it cures him of the habit of giving ugly blows to other people who can bear them less safely, perhaps it may be all for his good, as, no doubt, sir, your schoolmaster said when he flogged you."

"Bless my soul! are you the man who fought with him—you? I can't believe it."

"Why not?"

"Why not! So far as I can judge by this light, though you are a tall fellow, Tom Bowles must be a much heavier weight than you are."

"Tom Spring was the champion of England; and according to the records of his weight, which history has preserved in her archives, Tom Spring was a lighter weight than I am."

"But are you a prize-fighter?"

"I am as much that as I am anything else. But to return to Mr. Bowles, was it necessary to bleed him?"

"Yes; he was unconscious, or nearly so, when I came. I took away a few ounces, and I am happy to say he is now sensible, but must be kept very quiet."

"No doubt; but I hope he will be well enough to see me to-morrow."

"I hope so too; but I can't say yet. Quarrel about a girl—eh?"

"It was not about money. And I suppose if there were no money and no women in the world, there would be no quarrels, and very few doctors. Good-night, sir."

"It is a strange thing to me," said Kenelm, as he now opened the garden-gate of Mr. Saunderson's homestead, "that though I've had nothing to eat all day, except a few pitiful sandwiches, I don't feel the least hungry. Such arrest of the lawful duties of the digestive organs never happened to me before. There must be something weird and ominous in it."

On entering the parlour, the family party, though they had long since finished supper, were still seated round the table. They all rose at sight of Kenelm. The fame of his achievements had preceded him. He checked the congratulations, the compliments, and the questions which the hearty farmer rapidly heaped upon him, with a melancholic exclamation, "But I have lost my appetite! No honours can compensate for that. Let me go to bed peaceably, and perhaps in the magic land of sleep Nature may restore me by a dream of supper."

CHAPTER XIV.

KENELM rose betimes the next morning somewhat stiff and uneasy, but sufficiently recovered to feel ravenous. Fortunately one of the young ladies who attended specially to the dairy was already up, and supplied the starving hero with a vast bowl of bread and milk. He then strolled into the hayfield, in which there was now very little left to do, and but few hands besides his own were employed. Jessie was not there. Kenelm was glad of that. By nine o'clock his work was over, and the farmer and his men were in the yard completing the ricks. Kenelm stole away unobserved, bent on a round of visits. He called first at the village shop kept by Mrs. Bawtrey, which Jessie had pointed out to him, on pretence of buying a gaudy neckerchief; and soon, thanks to his habitual civility, made familiar acquaintance with the shop-woman. She was a little sickly old lady, her head shaking, as with palsy, somewhat deaf, but still shrewd and sharp, rendered mechanically so by long habits of shrewdness and sharpness. She became very communicative, spoke freely of her desire to give up the shop, and pass the rest of her days with a sister, widowed like herself, in a neighbouring town. Since she had lost her husband, the field and orchard attached to the shop had ceased to be profitable, and become a great care and trouble; and the attention the shop required was wearisome. But she had twelve years unexpired of the lease granted for twenty-one years to her husband on low terms, and she wanted a premium for its transfer, and a purchaser for the stock of the shop. Kenelm soon drew from her the amount of the sum she required for all—£45.

"You ben't thinking of it for yourself?" she asked, putting on her spectacles, and examining him with care.

"Perhaps so, if one could get a decent living out of it. Do you keep a book of your losses and gains?"

"In course, sir," she said, proudly. "I kept the books in my goodman's time, and he was one who could find out if there was a farthing wrong, for he had been in a lawyer's office when a lad."

"Why did he leave a lawyer's office to keep a little shop?"

"Well, he was born a farmer's son in this neighbourhood, and he always had a hankering after the country, and—and besides that——"

"Yes."

"I'll tell you the truth; he had got into a way of drinking speerrits, and he was a good young man, and wanted to break himself of it, and he took the temperance oath; but it was too hard on him, for he could not break himself of the company that led him into liquor. And so, one time when he came into the neighbourhood to see his parents for the Christmas holiday, he took a bit of liking to me; and my father, who was Squire Travers's bailiff, had just died, and left me a little money. And so, somehow or other, we came together, and got this house and the land from the Squire on lease very reasonable; and my goodman being well eddycated, and much thought of, and never being tempted to drink, now that he had a missis to keep him in order, had a many little things put into his way. He could help to measure timber, and knew about draining, and he got some book-keeping from the farmers about; and we kept cows and pigs and poultry, and so we did very well, specially as the Lord was merciful and sent us no children."

"And what does the shop bring in a-year since your husband died?"

"You had best judge for yourself. Will you look at the book, and take a peep at the land and apple-trees? But they's been neglected since my goodman died."

In another minute the heir of the Chillinglys was seated in a neat little back parlour, with a pretty, though confined, view of the orchard and grass slope behind it, and bending over Mrs. Bawtrey's ledger.

Some customers for cheese and bacon coming now into the shop, the old woman left him to his studies. Though they were not of a nature familiar to him, he brought to them, at least, that general clearness of head and quick seizure of important points which are common to most men who have gone through some disciplined training of intellect, and been accustomed to extract the pith and marrow out of many books on many subjects. The result of his examination was satisfactory; there appeared to him a clear balance of gain from the shop alone of somewhat over 40*l.* a-year, taking the average of the last three years. Closing the book, he then let himself out of the window into the orchard, and thence into the neighbouring grass field. Both were, indeed, much neglected; the trees wanted pruning, the field manure. But the soil was evidently of rich loam, and the fruit-trees were abundant and of ripe age, generally looking healthy in spite of neglect. With the quick intuition of a man born and bred in the country, and picking up scraps of rural knowledge unconsciously, Kenelm convinced himself that the land, properly managed, would far more than cover the rent, rates, tithes, and all incidental outgoings, leaving the profits of the shop as the clear income of the occupiers. And no doubt with clever young people to manage the shop, its profits might be increased.

Not thinking it necessary to return at present to Mrs. Bawtrey's, Kenelm now bent his way to Tom Bowles's.

The house-door was closed. At the summons of his knock it was quickly opened by a tall, stout, remarkably fine-looking woman, who might have told fifty years, and carried them off lightly on her ample shoulders. She was dressed very respectably in black, her brown hair braided simply under a neat tight-fitting cap. Her features were aquiline and very regular—altogether there was something about her majestic and Cornelia-like. She might have sat for the model of that Roman matron, except for the fairness of her Anglo-Saxon complexion.

"What's your pleasure?" she asked, in a cold and somewhat stern voice.

"Ma'am," answered Kenelm, uncovering, "I have called to see Mr. Bowles, and I sincerely hope he is well enough to let me do so."

"No, sir, he is not well enough for that; he is lying down in his own room, and must be kept quiet."

"May I then ask you the favour to let me in? I would say a few words to you who are his mother, if I mistake not."

Mrs. Bowles paused a moment as if in doubt; but she was at no loss to detect in Kenelm's manner something superior to the fashion of his dress, and supposing the visit might refer to her son's professional business, she opened the door wider, drew aside to let him pass first, and when he stood midway in the parlour, requested him to take a seat, and to set him the example, seated herself.

"Ma'am," said Kenelm, "do not regret to have admitted me, and do not think hardly of me when I inform you that I am the unfortunate cause of your son's accident."

Mrs. Bowles rose with a start.

"You're the man who beat my boy?"

"No, ma'am, do not say I beat him. He is not beaten. He is so brave and so strong that he would easily have beaten me if I had not, by good luck, knocked him down before he had time to do so. Pray, ma'am, retain your seat and listen to me patiently for a few moments."

Mrs. Bowles, with an indignant heave of her Juno-like bosom, and with a superbly haughty expression of countenance, which suited well with its aquiline formation, tacitly obeyed.

"You will allow, ma'am," recommenced Kenelm, "that this is not the first time by many that Mr. Bowles has come to blows with another man. Am I not right in that assumption?"

"My son is of a hasty temper," replied Mrs. Bowles, reluctantly, "and people should not aggravate him."

"You grant the fact, then?" said Kenelm, imperturbably, but with a polite inclination of head. "Mr. Bowles has often been engaged in these encounters, and in all of them it is quite clear that he provoked the battle; for you must be aware that he is not the sort of man to whom any other would be disposed to give the first blow. Yet, after these little incidents had occurred, and Mr. Bowles had, say, half killed the person who aggravated him, you did not feel any resentment against that person, did you? Nay, if he had wanted nursing, you would have gone and nursed him."

"I don't know as to nursing," said Mrs. Bowles, beginning to lose her dignity of mien; "but certainly I should have been very sorry for him. And as for Tom—though I say it who should not say—he has no more malice than a baby—he'd go and make it up with any man, however badly he had beaten him."

"Just as I supposed; and if the man had sulked and would not make it up, Tom would have called him a bad fellow, and felt inclined to beat him again."

Mrs. Bowles's face relaxed into a stately smile.

"Well, then," pursued Kenelm, "I do but humbly imitate

Mr. Bowles, and I come to make it up and shake hands with him."

"No, sir—no," exclaimed Mrs. Bowles, though in a low voice, and turning pale. "Don't think of it. 'Tis not the blows—he'll get over those fast enough; 'tis his pride that's hurt; and if he saw you there might be mischief. But you're a stranger, and going away;—do go soon—do keep out of his way—do!" And the mother clasped her hands.

"Mrs. Bowles," said Kenelm, with a change of voice and aspect—a voice and aspect so earnest and impressive that they stilled and awed her—"will you not help me to save your son from the dangers into which that hasty temper and that mischievous pride may at any moment hurry him. Does it never occur to you that these are the causes of terrible crime, bringing terrible punishment; and that against brute force, impelled by savage passions, society protects itself by the hulks and the gallows?"

"Sir, how dare you——"

"Hush! If one man kill another in a moment of ungovernable wrath, that is a crime which, though heavily punished by the conscience, is gently dealt with by the law, which calls it only manslaughter; but if a motive to the violence—such as jealousy or revenge—can be assigned, and there should be no witness by to prove that the violence was not premeditated, then the law does not call it manslaughter, but murder. Was it not that thought which made you so imploringly exclaim, 'Go soon; keep out of his way?!'"

The woman made no answer, but sinking back in her chair, gasped for breath.

"Nay, madam," resumed Kenelm, mildly; "banish your fears. If you will help me I feel sure that I can save your son from such perils, and I only ask you to let me save him. I am convinced that he has a good and a noble nature, and he is worth saving." As he thus said he took her hand. She resigned it to him and returned the pressure, all her pride softening as she began to weep.

At length, when she recovered voice, she said—

"It is all along of that girl. He was not so till she crossed him, and made him half mad. He is not the same man since then—my poor Tom!"

"Do you know that he has given me his word, and before his fellow-villagers, that if he had the worst of the fight he would never molest Jessie Wiles again?"

"Yes, he told me so himself; and it is that which weighs on him now. He broods, and broods, and mutters, and will not be comforted; and—and I do fear that he means revenge. And again, I implore you keep out of his way."

"It is not revenge on me that he thinks of. Suppose I go and am seen no more, do you think in your own heart that that girl's life is safe?"

"What! My Tom kill a woman!"

"Do you never read in your newspaper of a man who kills his sweetheart, or the girl who refuses to be his sweetheart? At all events, you yourself do not approve this frantic suit of his. If I have heard rightly, you have wished to get Tom out of the village for some time, till Jessie Wiles is—we'll say, married, or gone elsewhere for good."

"Yes, indeed, I have wished and prayed for it many's the time, both for her sake and for his. And I am sure I don't know what we shall do if he stays, for he has been losing custom fast. The Squire has taken away his, and so have many of the farmers; and such a trade as it was in his good father's time! And if he would go, his uncle, the Veterinary at Luscombe, would take him into partnership; for he has no son of his own, and he knows how clever Tom is;—there ben't a man who knows more about horses; and cows, too, for the matter of that."

"And if Luscombe is a large place, the business there must be more profitable than it can be here, even if Tom got back his custom?"

"Oh yes! five times as good—if he would but go; but he'll not hear of it."

"Mrs. Bowles, I am very much obliged to you for your confidence, and I feel sure that all will end happily, now we have had this talk. I'll not press farther on you at present. Tom will not stir out, I suppose, till the evening."

"Ah, sir, he seems as if he had no heart to stir out again, unless for something dreadful."

"Courage! I will call again in the evening, and then you just take me up to Tom's room, and leave me there to make friends with him, as I have with you. Don't say a word about me in the meanwhile."

"But——"

"'But,' Mrs. Bowles, is a word that cools many a warm impulse, stifles many a kindly thought, puts a dead stop to many a brotherly deed. Nobody would ever love his neighbour as himself if he listened to all the Buts that could be said on the other side of the question."

CHAPTER XV.

ENELM now bent his way towards the parsonage, but just as he neared its glebe-lands he met a gentleman whose dress was so evidently clerical that he stopped and said—
"Have I the honour to address Mr. Lethbridge?"

"That is my name," said the clergyman, smiling pleasantly. "Anything I can do for you?"

"Yes, a great deal, if you will let me talk to you about a few of your parishioners."

"My parishioners! I beg your pardon, but you are quite a stranger to me, and, I should think, to the parish."

"To the parish—no, I am quite at home in it; and I honestly believe that it has never known a more officious busybody thrusting himself into its most private affairs."

Mr. Lethbridge stared, and, after a short pause, said—"I have heard of a young man who has been staying at Mr. Saunderson's, and is indeed at this moment the talk of the village. You are——"

"That young man. Alas! yes."

"Nay," said Mr. Lethbridge, kindly, "I cannot myself, as a minister of the Gospel, approve of your profession, and, if I might take the liberty, I would try and dissuade you from it; but still, as for the one act of freeing a poor girl from the most scandalous persecution, and administering, though in a rough way, a lesson to a savage brute who has long been the disgrace and terror of the neighbourhood, I cannot honestly say that it has my condemnation. The moral sense of a community is generally a right one—you have won the praise of the village. Under all the circumstances, I do not withhold mine. You woke this morning and found yourself famous. Do not sigh 'Alas.'"

"Lord Byron woke one morning and found himself famous, and the result was that he sighed 'Alas' for the rest of his life. If there be two things which a wise man should avoid, they are fame and love. Heaven defend me from both!"

Again the parson stared; but being of compassionate nature, and inclined to take mild views of everything that belongs to humanity, he said, with a slight inclination of his head—

"I have always heard that the Americans in general enjoy the advantage of a better education than we do in England, and their reading public is infinitely larger than ours; still, when I hear one of a calling not highly considered in this country for intellectual cultivation or ethical philosophy cite Lord Byron, and utter a sentiment at variance with the impetuosity of inexperienced youth, but which has much to commend it in the eyes of a reflective Christian impressed with the nothingness of the objects mostly coveted by the human heart, I am surprised, and—Oh, my dear young friend, surely your education might fit you for something better!"

It was among the maxims of Kenelm Chillingly's creed that a sensible man should never allow himself to be surprised; but here he was, to use a popular idiom, 'taken aback,' and lowered himself to the rank of ordinary minds by saying simply, "I don't understand."

"I see," resumed the clergyman, shaking his head gently, "as I always suspected, that in the vaunted education bestowed on Americans, the elementary principles of Christian right and wrong are more neglected than they are among our own humble classes. Yes, my young friend, you may quote poets, you may startle me by remarks on the nothingness of human fame and human love, derived from the precepts of heathen poets, and yet not understand with what compassion, and, in the judgment of most sober-minded persons, with what contempt, a human being who practises your vocation is regarded."

"Have I vocation?" said Kenelm. "I am very glad to hear it. What is my vocation? and why must I be an American?"

"Why—surely I am not misinformed. You are the American—I forget his name—who has come over to contest the belt of prize-fighting with the champion of England. You are silent; you hang your head. By your appearance, your length of limb, your gravity of countenance, your evident education, you confirm the impression of your birth. Your prowess has proved your profession."

"Reverend sir," said Kenelm, with his unutterable seriousness of aspect, "I am on my travels in search of truth, and in flight from shams, but so great a take-in as myself I have not yet encountered. Remember me in your prayers. I am not an American; I am not a prize-fighter. I honour the first as the citizen of a grand republic trying his best to accomplish an experiment in government in which he will find the very prosperity he tends to create will sooner or later destroy his experiment. I honour the last because strength, courage, and sobriety are essential to the prize-fighter, and are among the chiefest ornaments of kings and heroes. But I am neither one nor the other. And all I can say for myself is, that I belong to that very vague class commonly called English gentlemen, and that, by birth and education, I have a right to ask you to shake hands with me as such."

Mr. Lethbridge stared again, raised his hat, bowed, and shook hands.

"You will allow me now to speak to you about your parishioners. You take an interest in Will Somers—so do I. He is clever and ingenious. But it seems there is not sufficient demand here for his baskets, and he would, no doubt, do better in some neighbouring town. Why does he object to move?"

"I fear that poor Will would pine away to death if he lost sight of that pretty girl for whom you did such chivalrous battle with Tom Bowles."

"The unhappy man, then, is really in love with Jessie Wiles? And do you think she no less really cares for him?"

"I am sure of it."

"And would make him a good wife—that is, as wives go?"

"A good daughter generally makes a good wife. And there is not a father in the place who has a better child than Jessie is to hers. She really is a girl of a superior nature. She was the cleverest pupil at our school, and my wife is much attached to her. But she has something better than mere cleverness; she has an excellent heart."

"What you say confirms my own impressions. And the girl's father has no other objection to Will Somers than his fear that Will could not support a wife and family comfortably."

"He can have no other objection save that which would apply equally to all suitors. I mean his fear lest Tom Bowles might do her some mischief, if he knew she was about to marry any one else."

"You think, then, that Mr. Bowles is a thoroughly bad and dangerous person?"

"Thoroughly bad and dangerous, and worse since he has taken to drinking."

"I suppose he did not take to drinking till he lost his wits for Jessie Wiles?"

"No, I don't think he did."

"But, Mr. Lethbridge, have you never used your influence over this dangerous man?"

"Of course, I did try, but I only got insulted. He is a godless animal, and has not been inside a church for years. He seems to have got a smattering of such vile learning as may be found in infidel publications, and I doubt if he has any religion at all."

"Poor Polyphemus! no wonder his Galatea shuns him."

"Old Wiles is terribly frightened, and asked my wife to find Jessie a place as servant at a distance. But Jessie can't bear the thoughts of leaving."

"For the same reason which attaches Will Somers to the native soil?"

"My wife thinks so."

"Do you believe that if Tom Bowles were out of the way, and Jessie and Will were man and wife, they could earn a sufficient livelihood as successors to Mrs. Bawtrey; Will adding the profits of his basket-work to those of the shop and land?"

"A sufficient livelihood! of course. They would be quite rich. I know the shop used to turn a great deal of money. The old woman, to be sure, is no longer up to business, but still she retains a good custom."

"Will Somers seems in delicate health. Perhaps if he had less weary struggle for a livelihood, and no fear of losing Jessie, his health would improve."

"His life would be saved, sir."

"Then," said Kenelm, with a heavy sigh and a face as long as an undertaker's, "though I myself entertain a profound compassion for that disturbance to our mental equilibrium which goes by the name of 'love,' and I am the last person who ought to add to the cares and sorrows which marriage entails upon its victims—I say nothing of the woes destined to those whom marriage usually adds to a population already overcrowded—I fear that I must be the means of bringing these two love-birds into the same cage. I am ready to purchase the shop and its appurtenances on their behalf, on the condition that you will kindly obtain the consent of Jessie's father to their union. As for my brave friend Tom Bowles, I undertake to deliver them and the village from that exuberant nature, which requires a larger field for its energies. Pardon me for not letting you interrupt me. I have not yet finished what I have to say. Allow me to ask if Mrs. Grundy resides in this village."

"Mrs. Grundy! Oh, I understand. Of course; wherever a woman has a tongue, there Mrs. Grundy has a home."

"And seeing that Jessie is very pretty, and that in walking with her I encountered Mr. Bowles, might not Mrs. Grundy say, with a toss of her head—'that it was not out of pure charity that the stranger had been so liberal to Jessie Wiles.' But if the money for the shop be paid through you to Mrs. Bawtrey, and you kindly undertake all the contingent arrangements, Mrs. Grundy will have nothing to say against any one."

Mr. Lethbridge gazed with amaze at the solemn countenance before him.

"Sir," he said, after a long pause, "I scarcely know how to express my admiration of a generosity so noble, so thoughtful, and accompanied with a delicacy, and, indeed, with a wisdom, which—which——"

"Pray, my dear sir, do not make me still more ashamed of myself than I am at present, for an interference in love matters quite alien to my own convictions as to the best mode of making an 'Approach to the Angels.' To conclude this business, I think it better to deposit in your hands the sum of £45, for which Mrs. Bawtrey has agreed to sell the remainder of her lease and stock-in-hand; but, of course, you will not make anything public till I am gone, and Tom Bowles too. I hope I may get him away to-morrow; but I shall know to-night when I can depend on his departure—and till he goes I must stay."

As he spoke, Kenelm transferred from his pocket-book to Mr. Lethbridge's hand bank-notes to the amount specified.

"May I at least ask the name of the gentleman who honours me with his confidence, and has bestowed so much happiness on members of my flock?"

"There is no great reason why I should not tell you my name, but I see no reason why I should. You remember Talleyrand's advice—'If you are in doubt whether to write a letter or not—don't.' The advice applies to many doubts in life besides that of letter-writing. Farewell, sir!"

"A most extraordinary young man," muttered the parson, gazing at the receding form of the tall stranger; then gently shaking his head, he added, "Quite an original." He was contented with that solution of the difficulties which had puzzled him. May the reader be the same.

CHAPTER XVI.

AFTER the family dinner, at which the farmer's guest displayed more than his usual powers of appetite, Kenelm followed his host towards the stackyard, and said—

"My dear Mr. Saunderson, though you have no longer any work for me to do, and I ought not to trespass farther on your hospitality; yet if I might stay with you another day or so, I should be very grateful."

"My dear lad," cried the farmer, in whose estimation Kenelm had risen prodigiously since the victory over Tom Bowles, "you are welcome to stay as long as you like, and we shall be all sorry when you go. Indeed, at all events, you must stay over Saturday, for you shall go with us to the Squire's harvest-supper. It will be a pretty sight, and my girls are already counting on you for a dance."

"Saturday—the day after to-morrow. You are very kind; but merry-makings are not much in my way, and I think I shall be on my road before you set off to the Squire's supper."

"Pooh! you shall stay; and, I say, young un, if you want more to do, I have a job for you quite in your line."

"What is it?"

"Thrash my ploughman. He has been insolent this morning, and he is the biggest fellow in the county, next to Tom Bowles."

Here the farmer laughed heartily, enjoying his own joke.

"Thank you for nothing," said Kenelm, rubbing his bruises. "A burnt child dreads the fire."

The young man wandered alone into the fields. The day was becoming overcast, and the clouds threatened rain. The air was exceedingly still; the landscape, missing the sunshine, wore an aspect of gloomy solitude. Kenelm came to the banks of the rivulet not far from the spot on which the farmer had first found him. There he sate down, and leant his cheek on his hand, with eyes fixed on the still and darkened stream lapsing mournfully away: sorrow entered into his heart and tinged its musings.

"Is it then true," said he, soliloquizing, "that I am born to pass through life utterly alone; asking, indeed, for no sister-half of myself, disbelieving its possibility, shrinking from the thought of it—half scorning, half pitying those who sigh for it?—thing unattainable—better sigh for the moon!

"Yet if other men sigh for it, why do I stand apart from them? If the world be a stage, and all the men and women in it merely players, am I to be the solitary spectator, with no part in the drama, and no interest in the vicissitudes of its plot? Many there are, no doubt, who covet as little as I do the part of 'Lover,' 'with a woeful ballad, made to his mistress' eyebrow;' but then they covet some other part in the drama, such as that of Soldier 'bearded as a pard,' or that of Justice 'in fair round belly with fat capon lined.' But me no ambition fires—I have no longing either to rise or to shine. I don't desire to be a colonel, nor an admiral, nor a member of Parliament, nor an alderman; I do not yearn for the fame of a wit, or a poet, or a philosopher, or a diner-out, or a crack shot at a rifle-match or a *battue*. Decidedly, I am the one looker-on, the one bystander, and have no more concern with the active world than a stone has. It is a horrible phantasmal crotchet of Goethe's, that originally we were all monads, little segregated atoms adrift in the atmosphere, and carried hither and thither by forces over which we had no control, especially by the attraction of other monads, so that one monad, compelled by porcine monads, crystallizes into a pig; another, hurried along by heroic monads, becomes a lion or an Alexander. Now it is quite clear," continued Kenelm, shifting his position and crossing the right leg over the left, "that a monad intended or fitted for some other planet may, on its way to that destination, be encountered by a current of other monads blowing earthward, and be caught up in the stream and whirled on, till, to the marring of its whole proper purpose and scene of action, it settles here—conglomerated into a baby. Probably that lot has befallen me: my monad, meant for another region in space, has been dropped into this, where it can never be at home, never amalgamate with other monads, nor comprehend why they are in such a perpetual fidget. I declare I know no more why the minds of human beings should be so restlessly agitated about things which, as most of them own, give more pain than pleasure, than I understand why that swarm of gnats, which has such a very short time to live, does not give itself a moment's repose, but goes up and down, rising and falling as if it were on a seesaw, and making as much noise about its insignificant alternations of ascent and descent, as if it were the hum of men. And yet, perhaps, in another planet my monad would have frisked, and jumped, and danced, and seesawed with congenial monads, as contentedly and as sillily as do the monads of men and gnats in this alien Vale of Tears."

Kenelm had just arrived at that conjectural solution of his perplexities when a voice was heard singing, or rather modulated to that kind of chant between recitative and song, which is so pleasingly effective where the intonations are pure and musical. They were so in this instance, and Kenelm's ear caught every word in the following song:—

CONTENT.

There are times when the troubles of life are still;
   The bees wandered lost in the depths of June,
And I paused where the chime of a silver rill
   Sang the linnet and lark to their rest at noon.

Said my soul—"See how calmly the wavelets glide,
   Though so narrow their way to their ocean-vent:
And the world that I traverse is wide, is wide,
   And yet is too narrow to hold content."

"O my soul, never say that the world is wide—
   The rill in its banks is less closely pent;
It is thou who art shoreless on every side,
   And thy width will not let thee enclose content."

As the verse ceased Kenelm lifted his head. But the banks of the brook were so curving and so clothed with brushwood, that for some minutes the singer was invisible. At last the boughs before him were put aside, and within a few paces of himself paused the man to whom he had commended the praises of a beefsteak, instead of those which minstrelsy, in its immemorial error, dedicates to love.

"Sir," said Kenelm, half rising, "well met once more. Have you ever listened to the cuckoo?"

"Sir," answered the minstrel, "have you ever felt the presence of the summer?"

"Permit me to shake hands with you. I admire the question by which you have countermet and rebuked my own. If you are not in a hurry, will you sit down and let us talk?"

The minstrel inclined his head and seated himself. His dog—now emerged from the brushwood—gravely approached Kenelm, who with greater gravity regarded him; then, wagging his tail, reposed on his haunches, intent with ear erect on a stir in the neighbouring reeds, evidently considering whether it was caused by a fish or a water-rat.

"I asked you, sir, if you had ever listened to the cuckoo—from no irrelevant curiosity;—for often on summer days, when one is talking with one's self—and, of course, puzzling one's self—a voice breaks out, as it were from the heart of Nature, so far is it and yet so near; and it says something very quieting, very musical, so that one is tempted inconsiderately and foolishly to exclaim, 'Nature replies to me.' The cuckoo has served me that trick pretty often. Your song is a better answer to a man's self-questionings than he can ever get from a cuckoo."

"I doubt that," said the minstrel. "Song, at the best, is but the echo of some voice from the heart of Nature. And if the cuckoo's note seemed to you such a voice, it was an answer to your questionings perhaps more simply truthful than man can utter, if you had rightly construed the language."

"My good friend," answered Kenelm, "what you say sounds very prettily; and it contains a sentiment which has been amplified by certain critics into that measureless domain of dunderheads which is vulgarly called Bosh. But though Nature is never silent, though she abuses the privilege of her age in being tediously gossiping and garrulous—Nature never replies to our questions—she can't understand an argument—she has never read Mr. Mill's work on Logic. In fact, as it is truly said by a great philosopher, 'Nature has no mind.' Every man who addresses her is compelled to force upon her for a moment the loan of his own mind. And if she answers a question which his own mind puts to her, it is only by such a reply as his own mind teaches to her parrot-like lips. And as every man has a different mind, so every man gets a different answer. Nature is a lying old humbug."

The minstrel laughed merrily; and his laugh was as sweet as his chant.

"Poets would have a great deal to unlearn if they are to look upon Nature in that light."

"Bad poets would, and so much the better for them and their readers."

"Are not good poets students of Nature?"

"Students of Nature, certainly—as surgeons study anatomy by dissecting a dead body. But the good poet, like the good surgeon, is the man who considers that study merely as the necessary A B C and not as the all-in-all essential to skill in his practice. I do not give the fame of a good surgeon to a man who fills a book with details, more or less accurate, of fibres, and nerves, and muscles; and I don't give the fame of a good poet to a man who makes an inventory of the Rhine or the Vale of Gloucester. The good surgeon and the good poet are they who understand the living man. What is that poetry of drama which Aristotle justly ranks as the highest? Is it not a poetry in which description of inanimate Nature must of necessity be very brief and general; in which even the external form of man is so indifferent a consideration that it will vary with each actor who performs the part? A Hamlet may be fair or dark. A Macbeth may be short or tall. The merit of dramatic poetry consists in the substituting for what is commonly called Nature (viz., external and material Nature), creatures intellectual, emotional, but so purely immaterial that they may be said to be all mind and soul, accepting the temporary loans of any such bodies at hand as actors may offer, in order to be made palpable and visible to the audience, but needing no such bodies to be palpable and visible to readers. The highest kind of poetry is therefore that which has least to do with external Nature. But every grade has its merit more or less genuinely great, according as it instils into Nature that which is not there—the reason and the soul of man."

"I am not much disposed," said the minstrel, "to acknowledge any one form of poetry to be practically higher than another—that is, so far as to elevate the poet who cultivates what you call the highest with some success, above the rank of the poet who cultivates what you call a very inferior school with a success much more triumphant. In theory, dramatic poetry may be higher than lyric, and 'Venice Preserved' is a very successful drama; but I think Burns a greater poet than Otway."

"Possibly he may be; but I know of no lyrical poet, at least among the moderns, who treats less of Nature as the mere outward form of things, or more passionately animates her framework with his own human heart, than does Robert Burns. Do you suppose when a Greek, in some perplexity of reason or conscience, addressed a question to the oracular oak-leaves of Dodona, that the oak-leaves answered him? Don't you rather believe that the question suggested by his mind was answered by the mind of his fellow-man, the priest, who made the oak-leaves the mere vehicle of communication, as you and I might make such vehicle in a sheet of writing-paper? Is not the history of superstition a chronicle of the follies of man in attempting to get answers from external Nature?"

"But," said the minstrel, "have I not somewhere heard or read that the experiments of Science are the answers made by Nature to the questions put to her by man?"

"They are the answers which his own mind suggests to her, nothing more. His mind studies the laws of matter, and in that study makes experiments on matter; out of those experiments his mind, according to its previous knowledge or natural acuteness, arrives at its own deductions, and hence arise the sciences of mechanics and chemistry, &c. But the matter itself gives no answer; the answer varies according to the mind that puts the question, and the progress of science consists in the perpetual correction of the errors and falsehoods which preceding minds conceived to be the correct answers they received from Nature. It is the supernatural within us—viz., Mind—which can alone guess at the mechanism of the natural—viz., Matter. A stone cannot question a stone."

The minstrel made no reply. And there was a long silence, broken but by the hum of the insects, the ripple of onward waves, and the sigh of the wind through reeds.

CHAPTER XVII.

SAID Kenelm, at last breaking silence—
"Rapiamus, amici,
Occasionem de die, dumque virent genua,
Et decet, obducta solvatur fronte senectus!"

"Is not that quotation from Horace?" asked the minstrel.

"Yes; and I made it insidiously, in order to see if you had not acquired what is called a classical education."

"I might have received such education, if my tastes and my destinies had not withdrawn me in boyhood from studies of which I did not then comprehend the full value. But I did pick up a smattering of Latin at school; and from time to time since I left school, I have endeavoured to gain some little knowledge of the most popular Latin poets—chiefly, I own to my shame, by the help of literal English translations."

"As a poet yourself, I am not sure that it would be an advantage to know a dead language so well that its forms and modes of thought ran, though perhaps unconsciously, into those of the living one in which you compose. Horace might have been a still better poet if he had not known Greek better than you know Latin."

"It is at least courteous in you to say so," answered the singer, with a pleased smile.

"You would be still more courteous," said Kenelm, "if you would pardon an impertinent question, and tell me whether it is for a wager that you wander through the land, Homer-like, as a wandering minstrel, and allow that intelligent quadruped, your companion, to carry a tray in his mouth for the reception of pennies?"

"No, it is not for a wager; it is a whim of mine, which I fancy, from the tone of your conversation, you could understand, being, apparently, somewhat whimsical yourself."

"So far as whim goes, be assured of my sympathy."

"Well, then, though I follow a calling by the exercise of which I secure a modest income—my passion is verse. If the seasons were always summer, and life were always youth, I should like to pass through the world singing. But I have never ventured to publish any verses of mine. If they fell still-born it would give me more pain than such wounds to vanity ought to give to a bearded man; and if they were assailed or ridiculed, it might seriously injure me in my practical vocation. That last consideration, were I quite alone in the world, might not much weigh on me; but there are others for whose sake I should like to make fortune and preserve station. Many years ago—it was in Germany—I fell in with a German student who was very poor, and who did make money by wandering about the country with lute and song. He has since become a poet of no mean popularity, and he has told me that he is sure he found the secret of that popularity in habitually consulting popular tastes during his roving apprenticeship to song. His example strongly impressed me. So I began this experiment; and for several years my summers have been all partly spent in this way. I am only known, as I think I told you before, in the rounds I take as 'The Wandering Minstrel.'. I receive the trifling moneys that are bestowed on me as proofs of a certain merit. I should not be paid by poor people if I did not please; and the songs which please them best are generally those I love best myself. For the rest, my time is not thrown away—not only as regards bodily health, but healthfulness of mind—all the current of one's ideas becomes so freshened by months of playful exercise and varied adventure."

"Yes, the adventure is varied enough," said Kenelm, somewhat ruefully; for he felt, in shifting his posture, a sharp twinge of his bruised muscles. "But don't you find those mischief-makers, the women, always mix themselves up with adventure?"

"Bless them! of course," said the minstrel, with a ringing laugh. "In life, as on the stage, the petticoat interest is always the strongest."

"I don't agree with you there," said Kenelm, dryly. "And you seem to me to utter a claptrap beneath the rank of your understanding. However, this warm weather indisposes one to disputation; and I own that a petticoat, provided it be red, is not without the interest of colour in a picture."

"Well, young gentleman," said the minstrel, rising, "the day is wearing on, and I must wish you good-bye; probably, if you were to ramble about the country as I do, you would see too many pretty girls not to teach you the strength of petticoat interest—not in pictures alone; and should I meet you again, I may find you writing love-verses yourself."

"After a conjecture so unwarrantable, I part company with you less reluctantly than I otherwise might do. But I hope we shall meet again."

"Your wish flatters me much, but, if we do, pray respect the confidence I have placed in you, and regard my wandering minstrelsy and my dog's tray as sacred secrets. Should we not so meet, it is but a prudent reserve on my part if I do not give you my right name and address."

"There you show the cautious common-sense which belongs rarely to lovers of verse and petticoat interest. What have you done with your guitar?"

"I do not pace the roads with that instrument: it is forwarded to me from town to town under a borrowed name, together with other raiment than this, should I have cause to drop my character of wandering minstrel."

The two men here exchanged a cordial shake of the hand. And as the minstrel went his way along the river-side, his voice in chanting seemed to lend to the wavelets a livelier murmur, to the reeds a less plaintive sigh.

CHAPTER XVIII.

IN his room, solitary and brooding, sate the defeated hero of a hundred fights. It was now twilight; but the shutters had been partially closed all day, in order to exclude the sun, which had never before been unwelcome to Tom Bowles, and they still remained so, making the twilight doubly twilight, till the harvest moon, rising early, shot its ray through the crevice, and forced a silvery track amid the shadows of the floor.

The man's head drooped on his breast, his strong hands rested listlessly on his knees; his attitude was that of utter despondency and prostration. But in the expression of his face there were the signs of some dangerous and restless thought which belied, not the gloom but, the stillness of the posture. His brow, which was habitually open and frank, in its defying aggressive boldness, was now contracted into deep furrows, and lowered darkly over his downcast, half-closed eyes. His lips were so tightly compressed that the face lost its roundness, and the massive bone of the jaw stood out hard and salient. Now and then, indeed, the lips opened, giving vent to a deep, impatient sigh, but they reclosed as quickly as they had parted. It was one of those crises in life which find all the elements that make up a man's former self in lawless anarchy; in which the Evil One seems to enter and direct the storm; in which a rude untutored mind, never before harbouring a thought of crime, sees the crime start up from an abyss, feels it to be an enemy, yet yields to it as a fate. So that when, at the last, some wretch, sentenced to the gibbet, shudderingly looks back to the moment 'that trembled between two worlds'—the world of the man guiltless, the world of the man guilty—he says to the holy, highly educated, rational, passionless priest who confesses him and calls him 'brother,' "The devil put it into my head."

At that moment the door opened; at its threshold there stood the man's mother—whom he had never allowed to influence his conduct, though he loved her well in his rough way—and the hated fellow-man whom he longed to see dead at his feet. The door reclosed, the mother was gone, without a word, for her tears choked her; the fellow-man was alone with him. Tom Bowles looked up, recognized his visitor, cleared his brow, and rubbed his mighty hands.

CHAPTER XIX.

KENELM CHILLINGLY drew a chair close to his antagonist's, and silently laid a hand on his.

Tom Bowles took up the hand in both his own, turned it curiously towards the moonlight, gazed at it, poised it, then with a sound between groan and laugh tossed it away as a thing hostile but trivial, rose and locked the door, came back to his seat and said bluffly—

"What do you want with me now?"

"I want to ask you a favour."

"Favour?"

"The greatest which man can ask from man—friendship. You see, my dear Tom," continued Kenelm, making himself quite at home —throwing his arm over the back of Tom's chair, and stretching his legs comfortably as one does by one's own fireside; "you see, my dear Tom, that men like us—young, single, not on the whole bad-looking as men go—can find sweethearts in plenty. If one does not like us, another will; sweethearts are sown everywhere like nettles and thistles. But the rarest thing in life is a friend. Now, tell me frankly, in the course of your wanderings did you ever come into a village where you could not have got a sweetheart if you had asked for one; and if, having got a sweetheart, you had lost her, do you think you would have had any difficulty in finding another? But have you such a thing in the world, beyond the pale of your own family, as a true friend—a man friend; and supposing that you had such a friend—a friend who would stand by you through thick and thin—who would tell you your faults to your face, and praise you for your good qualities behind your back—who would do all he could to save you from a danger, and all he could to get you out of one,—supposing you had such a friend, and lost him, do you believe that if you lived to the age of Methuselah you could find another? You don't answer me; you are silent. Well, Tom, I ask you to be such a friend to me, and I will be such a friend to you."

Tom was so thoroughly 'taken aback' by this address that he remained dumbfounded. But he felt as if the clouds in his soul were breaking, and a ray of sunlight were forcing its way through the sullen darkness. At length, however, the receding rage within him returned, though with vacillating step, and he growled between his teeth—

"A pretty friend indeed! robbing me of my girl! Go along with you!"

"She was not your girl any more than she was or ever can be mine."

"What, you ben't after her?"

"Certainly not; I am going to Luscombe, and I ask you to come with me. Do you think I am going to leave you here?"

"What is it to you?"

"Everything. Providence has permitted me to save you from the most lifelong of all sorrows. For—think! Can any sorrow be more lasting than had been yours if you had attained your wish; if you had forced or frightened a woman to be your partner till death do part—you loving her, she loathing you; you conscious, night and day, that your very love had insured her misery, and that misery haunting you like a ghost!—from that sorrow I have saved you. May Providence permit me to complete my work, and save you also from the most irredeemable of all crimes! Look into your soul, then recall the thoughts which all day long, and not least at the moment I crossed this threshold, were rising up, making reason dumb and conscience blind, and then lay your hand on your heart and say—'I am guiltless of a dream of murder.'"

The wretched man sprang up erect, menacing, and, meeting Kenelm's calm, steadfast, pitying gaze, dropped no less suddenly —dropped on the floor, covered his face with his hands, and a great cry came forth between sob and howl.

"Brother," said Kenelm, kneeling beside him, and twining his arm round the man's heaving breast, "it is over now; with that cry the demon that maddened you has fled for ever."

CHAPTER XX.

WHEN, some time after, Kenelm quitted the room and joined Mrs. Bowles below, he said cheerily, "All right; Tom and I are sworn friends. We are going together to Luscombe the day after to-morrow—Sunday; just write a line to his uncle to prepare him for Tom's visit, and send thither his clothes, as we shall walk, and steal forth unobserved betimes in the morning. Now go up and talk to him; he wants a mother's soothing and petting. He is a noble fellow at heart, and we shall be all proud of him some day or other."

As he walked back towards the farmhouse, Kenelm encountered

Mr. Lethbridge, who said—" I have come from Mr. Saunderson's, where I went in search of you. There is an unexpected hitch in the negotiation for Mrs. Bawtrey's shop. After seeing you this morning I fell in with Mr. Travers's bailiff, and he tells me that her lease does not give her the power to sublet without the Squire's consent; and that as the premises were originally let on very low terms to a favoured and responsible tenant, Mr. Travers cannot be expected to sanction the transfer of the lease to a poor basket-maker —in fact, though he will accept Mrs. Bawtrey's resignation, it must be in favour of an applicant whom he desires to oblige. On hearing this, I rode over to the Park and saw Mr. Travers himself. But he was obdurate to my pleadings. All I could get him to say was— 'Let the stranger who interests himself in the matter come and talk to me. I should like to see the man who thrashed that brute Tom Bowles; if he got the better of him perhaps he may get the better of me. Bring him with you to my harvest-supper to-morrow evening.' Now, will you come?"

"Nay," said Kenelm, reluctantly; "but if he only asks me in order to gratify a very vulgar curiosity, I don't think I have much chance of serving Will Somers. What do you say?"

"The Squire is a good man of business, and though no one can call him unjust or grasping, still he is very little touched by sentiment; and we must own that a sickly cripple like poor Will is not a very eligible tenant. If, therefore, it depended only on your chance with the Squire, I should not be very sanguine. But we have an ally in his daughter. She is very fond of Jessie Wiles, and she has shown great kindness to Will. In fact, a sweeter, more benevolent, sympathizing nature than that of Cecilia Travers does not exist. She has great influence with her father, and through her you may win him."

"I particularly dislike having anything to do with women," said Kenelm churlishly. "Parsons are accustomed to get round them. Surely, my dear sir, you are more fit for that work than I am."

"Permit me humbly to doubt that proposition; one don't get very quickly round the women when one carries the weight of years on one's back. But whenever you want the aid of a parson to bring your own wooing to a happy conclusion, I shall be happy, in my special capacity of parson, to perform the ceremony required."

"*Dii meliora!*" said Kenelm, gravely. "Some ills are too serious to be approached even in joke. As for Miss Travers, the moment you call her benevolent you inspire me with horror. I know too well what a benevolent girl is—officious, restless, fidgety, with a snub-nose, and her pocket full of tracts. I will not go to the harvest-supper."

"Hist!" said the parson, softly. They were now passing the cottage of Mrs. Somers; and while Kenelm was haranguing against benevolent girls, Mr. Lethbridge had paused before it, and was furtively looking in at the window. "Hist! and come here,—gently."

Kenelm obeyed, and looked in through the window. Will was seated—Jessie Wiles had nestled herself at his feet, and was holding his hand in both hers, looking up into his face. Her profile alone was seen, but its expression was unutterably soft and tender. His face, bent downwards towards her, wore a mournful expression; nay—the tears were rolling silently down his cheeks. Kenelm listened, and heard her say, "Don't talk so, Will, you break my heart; it is I who am not worthy of you."

"Parson," said Kenelm, as they walked on, "I must go to that confounded harvest-supper. I begin to think there is something true in the venerable platitude about love in a cottage. And Will Somers must be married in haste, in order to repent at leisure."

"I don't see why a man should repent having married a good girl whom he loves."

"You don't? Answer me candidly. Did you never meet a man who repented having married?"

"Of course I have; very often."

"Well, think again, and answer as candidly. Did you ever meet a man who repented not having married?"

The parson mused, and was silent.

"Sir," said Kenelm, "your reticence proves your honesty, and I respect it." So saying, he bounded off, and left the parson crying out wildly, "But—but——"

CHAPTER XXI.

MR. SAUNDERSON and Kenelm sate in the arbour; the former sipping his grog and smoking his pipe—the latter looking forth into the summer night skies with an earnest yet abstracted gaze, as if he were trying to count the stars in the Milky Way.

"Ha!" said Mr. Saunderson, who was concluding an argument; "you see it now, don't you?"

"I—not a bit of it. You tell me that your grandfather was a

farmer, and your father was a farmer, and that you have been a farmer for thirty years; and from these premises you deduce the illogical and irrational conclusion that therefore your son must be a farmer."

"Young man, you may think yourself very knowing 'cause you have been at the 'Varsity, and swept away a headful of book-learning."

"Stop," quoth Kenelm. "You grant that a university is learned."

"Well, I suppose so."

"But how could it be learned if those who quitted it brought the learning away? We leave it all behind us in the care of the tutors. But I know what you were going to say—that it is not because I had read more books than you have that I was to give myself airs and pretend to have more knowledge of life than a man of your years and experience. Agreed, as a general rule. But does not every doctor, however wise and skilful, prefer taking another doctor's opinion about himself, even though that other doctor has just started in practice? And, seeing that doctors, taking them as a body, are monstrous clever fellows, is not the example they set us worth following? Does it not prove that no man, however wise, is a good judge of his own case? Now, your son's case is really your case—you see it through the medium of your likings and dislikings—and insist upon forcing a square peg into a round hole, because in a round hole you, being a round peg, feel tight and comfortable. Now I call that irrational."

"I don't see why my son has any right to fancy himself a square peg," said the farmer, doggedly, "when his father, and his grandfather, and his great-grandfather, have been round pegs; and it is agin' nature for any creature not to take after its own kind. A dog is a pointer or a sheep-dog according as its forebears were pointers or sheep-dogs. There," cried the farmer, triumphantly, shaking the ashes out of his pipe, "I think I have posed you, young master!"

"No; for you have taken it for granted that the breeds have not been crossed. But suppose that a sheep-dog has married a pointer, are you sure that his son will not be more of a pointer than a sheep-dog?"

Mr. Saunderson arrested himself in the task of refilling his pipe, and scratched his head.

"You see," continued Kenelm, "that you have crossed the breed. You married a tradesman's daughter, and I dare say her grandfather and great-grandfather were tradesmen too. Now, most sons take after their mothers, and therefore Mr. Saunderson, junior, takes after his kind on the distaff side, and comes into the world a square peg, which can only be tight and comfortable in a square hole. It is no use arguing, farmer: your boy must go to his uncle; and there's an end of the matter."

"By goles!" said the farmer, "you seem to think you can talk me out of my senses."

"No; but I think if you had your own way you would talk your son into the workhouse."

"What! by sticking to the land like his father before him? Let a man stick by the land, and the land will stick by him."

"Let a man stick in the mud, and the mud will stick to him. You put your heart in your farm, and your son would only put his foot into it. Courage! Don't you see that Time is a whirligig, and all things come round? Every day somebody leaves the land and goes off into trade. By and by he grows rich, and then his great desire is to get back to the land again. He left it the son of a farmer: he returns to it as a squire. Your son, when he gets to be fifty, will invest his savings in acres, and have tenants of his own: Lord, how he will lay down the law to them! I would not advise you to take a farm under him."

"Catch me at it!" said the farmer. "He would turn all the contents of the 'pothecary's shop into my fallows, and call it 'progress.'"

"Let him physic the fallows when he has farms of his own: keep yours out of his chemical clutches. Come, I shall tell him to pack up and be off to his uncle's next week."

"Well, well," said the farmer, in a resigned tone,—"a wilful man must e'en have his way."

"And the best thing a sensible man can do is not to cross it. Mr. Saunderson, give me your honest hand. You are one of those men who put the sons of good fathers in mind of their own; and I think of mine when I say, 'God bless you!'"

Quitting the farmer, Kenelm re-entered the house, and sought Mr. Saunderson, junior, in his own room. He found that young gentleman still up, and reading an eloquent tract on the Emancipation of the Human Race from all Tyrannical Control—Political, Social, Ecclesiastical, and Domestic.

The lad looked up sulkily and said, on encountering Kenelm's melancholic visage, "Ah! I see you have talked with the old governor, and he'll not hear of it."

"In the first place," answered Kenelm, "since you value yourself on a superior education, allow me to advise you to study the English language, as the forms of it are maintained by the elder authors— whom, in spite of an Age of Progress, men of superior education esteem. No one who has gone through that study—no one, indeed, who has studied the Ten Commandments in the vernacular, commits the mistake of supposing that 'the old governor' is a synonymous expression for 'Father.' In the second place, since you pretend to the superior enlightenment which results from a superior education, learn to know better your own self before you set up as a teacher of mankind. Excuse the liberty I take, as your sincere well-wisher, when I tell you that you are at present a conceited fool—in short, that which makes one boy call another 'an ass.' But when one has a poor head he may redeem the average balance of humanity by increasing the wealth of the heart. Try and increase yours. Your father consents to your choice of your lot at the sacrifice of all his own inclinations. This is a sore trial to a father's pride, a father's affection; and few fathers make such sacrifices with a good grace. I have thus kept my promise to you, and enforced your wishes on Mr. Saunderson's judgment, because I am sure you would have been a very bad farmer. It now remains for you to show that you can be a very good tradesman. You are bound in honour to me and to your father to try your best to be so; and meanwhile leave the task of upsetting the world to those who have no shop in it, which would go crash in the general tumble. And so good-night to you."

To these admonitory words, *sacro digna silentio*, Saunderson junior listened with a dropping jaw and fascinated staring eyes. He felt like an infant to whom the nurse has given a hasty shake, and who is too stupefied by that operation to know whether he is hurt or not.

A minute after Kenelm had quitted the room he re-appeared at the door, and said in a conciliatory whisper, "Don't take it to heart that I called you a conceited fool and an ass. These terms are no doubt just as applicable to myself. But there is a more conceited fool and a greater ass than either of us, and that is, the Age in which we have the misfortune to be born—an Age of Progress, Mr. Saunderson, junior—an Age of Prigs!"

BOOK III.

CHAPTER I.

IF there were a woman in the world who might be formed and fitted to reconcile Kenelm Chillingly to the sweet troubles of love and the pleasant bickerings of wedded life, one might reasonably suppose that that woman could be found in Cecilia Travers. An only daughter, and losing her mother in childhood, she had been raised to the mistress-ship of a household at an age in which most girls are still putting their dolls to bed; and thus had early acquired that sense of responsibility, accompanied with the habits of self-reliance, which seldom fails to give a certain nobility to character; though almost as often, in the case of women, it steals away the tender gentleness which constitutes the charm of their sex.

It had not done so in the instance of Cecilia Travers, because she was so woman-like that even the exercise of power could not make her man-like. There was in the depth of her nature such an instinct of sweetness, that wherever her mind toiled and wandered it gathered and hoarded honey.

She had one advantage over most girls in the same rank of life—she had not been taught to fritter away such capacities for culture as Providence gave her in the sterile nothingnesses which are called feminine accomplishments. She did not paint figures out of drawing in meagre water colours; she had not devoted years of her life to the inflicting on polite audiences the boredom of Italian bravuras, which they could hear better sung by a third-rate professional singer in a metropolitan music-hall. I am afraid she had no other female accomplishments than those by which the sempstress or embroideress earns her daily bread. That sort of work she loved, and she did it deftly.

But if she had not been profitlessly plagued by masters, Cecilia Travers had been singularly favoured by her father's choice of a teacher,—no great merit in him either. He had a prejudice against professional governesses, and it chanced that among his own family connections was a certain Mrs. Campion, a lady of some literary distinction, whose husband had held a high situation in one of our public offices, and living, much to his satisfaction, up to a very handsome income, had died, much to the astonishment of others, without leaving a farthing behind him.

Fortunately, there were no children to provide for. A small government pension was allotted to the widow; and as her husband's house had been made by her one of the pleasantest in London, she was popular enough to be invited by numerous friends to their country seats—among others, by Mr. Travers. She came intending to stay a fortnight. At the end of that time she had grown so attached to Cecilia, and Cecilia to her, and her presence had become so pleasant and so useful to her host, that the Squire entreated her to stay and undertake the education of his daughter. Mrs. Campion, after some hesitation, gratefully consented; and thus Cecilia, from the age of eight to her present age of nineteen, had the inestimable advantage of living in constant companionship with a woman of richly-cultivated mind, accustomed to hear the best criticisms on the best books, and adding to no small accomplishment in literature the refinement of manners and that sort of prudent judgment which result from habitual intercourse with an intellectual and gracefully world-wise circle of society; so that Cecilia herself, without being at all blue or pedantic, became one of those rare young women with whom a well-educated man can converse on equal terms—from whom he gains as much as he can impart to her; while a man who, not caring much about books, is still gentleman enough to value good breeding, felt a relief in exchanging the forms of his native language without the shock of hearing that a bishop was "a swell," or a croquet-party "awfully jolly."

In a word, Cecilia was one of those women whom heaven forms for man's helpmate—who, if he were born to rank and wealth, would, as his partner, reflect on them a new dignity, and add to their enjoyment by bringing forth their duties—who, not less if the husband she chose were poor and struggling, would encourage, sustain, and soothe him, take her own share of his burdens, and temper the bitterness of life with the all-recompensing sweetness of her smile.

Little, indeed, as yet had she ever thought of love or of lovers. She had not even formed to herself any of those ideals which float before the eyes of most girls when they enter their teens. But of two things she felt inly convinced—first, that she could never wed where she did not love; and secondly, that where she did love it would be for life.

And now I close this sketch with a picture of the girl herself. She has just come into her room from inspecting the preparations for the evening entertainment which her father is to give to his tenants and rural neighbours.

She has thrown aside her straw-hat, and put down the large basket which she has emptied of flowers. She pauses before the glass, smoothing back the ruffled bands of her hair—hair of a dark, soft chestnut, silky and luxuriant—never polluted, and never, so long as she lives, to be polluted by auricomous cosmetics :—far from that delicate darkness, every tint of the colours traditionally dedicated to the locks of Judas.

Her complexion, usually of that soft bloom which inclines to paleness, is now heightened into glow by exercise and sunlight. The features are small and feminine, the eyes dark with long lashes, the mouth singularly beautiful, with a dimple on either side, and parted now in a half-smile at some pleasant recollection, giving a glimpse of small teeth glistening as pearls. But the peculiar charm of her face is in an expression of serene happiness, that sort of happiness which seems as if it had never been interrupted by a sorrow, had never been troubled by a sin—that holy kind of happiness which belongs to innocence, the light reflected from a heart and conscience alike at peace.

CHAPTER II.

IT was a lovely summer evening for the Squire's rural entertainment. Mr. Travers had some guests staying with him : they had dined early for the occasion, and were now grouped with their host, a little before six o'clock, on the lawn. The house was of irregular architecture, altered or added to at various periods from the reign of Elizabeth to that of Victoria : at one end, the oldest part, a gable with mullion windows ; at the other, the newest part, a flat-roofed wing, with modern sashes opening to the ground, the intermediate part much hidden by a verandah covered with creepers in full bloom. The lawn was a spacious table-land facing the west, and backed by a green and gentle hill, crowned with the ruins of an ancient priory. On one side of the lawn stretched a flower-garden and pleasure-ground, originally planned by Repton ; on the opposite angles of the sward were placed two large marquees—one for dancing, the other for supper. Towards the south the view was left open, and commanded the prospect of an old English park, not of the stateliest character,— not intersected with ancient avenues, nor clothed with profitless fern as lairs for deer—but the park of a careful agriculturist, uniting profit with show, the sward duly drained and nourished, fit to fatten bullocks in an incredibly short time, and somewhat spoilt to the eye by sub-divisions of wire-fence. Mr. Travers was renowned for skilful husbandry, and the general management of land to the best advantage. He had come into the estate while still in childhood, and thus enjoyed the accumulations of a long minority. He had entered the Guards at the age of eighteen, and having more command of money than most of his contemporaries, though they might be of higher rank and the sons of richer men, he had been much courted and much plundered. At the age of twenty-five he found himself one of the leaders of fashion, renowned chiefly for reckless daring wherever honour could be plucked out of the nettle danger; a steeplechaser, whose exploits made a quiet man's hair stand on end ; a rider across country, taking leaps which a more cautious huntsman carefully avoided. Known at Paris as well as in London, he had been admired by ladies whose smiles had cost him duels, the marks of which still remained in glorious scars on his person. No man ever seemed more likely to come to direst grief before attaining the age of thirty, for at twenty-seven all the accumulations of his minority were gone ; and his estate, which, when he came of age, was scarcely three thousand a-year, but entirely at his own disposal, was mortgaged up to its eyes.

His friends began to shake their heads and call him "poor fellow ;" but with all his wild faults, Leopold Travers had been wholly pure from the two vices out of which a man does not often redeem himself. He had never drunk, and he had never gambled. His nerves were not broken, his brain was not besotted. There was plenty of health in him yet, mind and body. At the critical period of his life he married for love, and his choice was a most felicitous one. The lady had no fortune ; but, though handsome and high-born, she had no taste for extravagance, and no desire for other society than that of the man she loved. So when he said, "Let us settle in the country and try our best to live on a few hundreds, lay by, and keep the old place out of the market," she consented with a joyful heart : and marvel it was to all how this wild Leopold Travers did settle down ; did take to cultivating his home farm with his men from sunrise to sunset, like a common tenant-farmer ; did contrive to pay the interest on the mortgages, and keep his head above water. After some years of pupilage in this school of thrift, during which his habits became formed, and his whole character braced, Leopold Travers suddenly found himself again rich, through the wife whom he had so prudently married without other dower than her love and her virtues. Her only brother, Lord Eagleton, a Scotch peer, had been engaged in marriage to a young lady, considered to be a rare prize in the lottery of wedlock. The marriage was broken off under very disastrous circumstances; but the young Lord, good-looking and agreeable, was naturally expected to seek speedy consolation in some other alliance. Nevertheless he did not do so;—he became a confirmed invalid, and died single, leaving to his sister all in his power to save from the distant kinsman who succeeded to his lands and title,—a goodly sum, which not only sufficed to pay off the mortgages on Neesdale Park, but bestowed on its owner a surplus which the practical knowledge of country life that he had acquired enabled him to devote with extraordinary profit to the general improvement of his estate. He replaced tumble-down old farm buildings with new constructions on the most approved principles; bought or pensioned off certain slovenly incompetent tenants; threw sundry petty holdings into large farms suited to the buildings he constructed; purchased here and there small bits of land, commodious to the farms they adjoined, and completing the integrity of his ring-fence; stubbed up profitless woods which diminished the value of neighbouring arables, by obstructing sun and air, and harbouring legions of rabbits; and then seeking tenants of enterprise and capital, more than doubled his original yearly rental, and perhaps more than tripled the market value of his property. Simultaneously with this acquisition of fortune, he emerged from the inhospitable and unsocial obscurity which his previous poverty had compelled, took an active part in county business, proved himself an excellent speaker at public meetings, subscribed liberally to the Hunt, and occasionally joined in it—a less bold but a wiser rider than of yore. In short, as Themistocles boasted that he could make a small state great, so Leopold Travers might boast with equal truth that, by his energies, his judgment, and the weight of his personal character, he had made the owner of a property which had been at his succession to it of third-rate rank in the county, a personage so considerable that no knight of the shire against whom he declared could have been elected, and if he had determined to stand himself he would have been chosen free of expense.

But he said, on being solicited to become a candidate, "When a man once gives himself up to the care and improvement of a landed estate, he has no time and no heart for anything else. An estate is an income or a kingdom, according as the owner chooses to take it. I take it as a kingdom, and I cannot be *roi fainéant*, with a steward for *maire du palais*. A king does not go into the House of Commons."

Three years after this rise in the social ladder, Mrs. Travers was seized with congestion of the lungs, followed by pleurisy, and died after less than a week's illness. Leopold never wholly recovered her loss. Though still young, and always handsome, the idea of another wife, the love of another woman, were notions which he dismissed from his mind with a quiet scorn. He was too masculine a creature to parade grief. For some weeks, indeed, he shut himself up in his own room, so rigidly secluded that he would not see even his daughter. But one morning he appeared in his fields as usual, and from that day resumed his old habits, and gradually renewed that cordial interchange of hospitalities which had popularly distinguished him since his accession to wealth. Still people felt that the man was changed; he was more taciturn, more grave: if always just in his dealings, he took the harder side of justice, where in his wife's time he had taken the gentler. Perhaps, to a man of strong will, the habitual intercourse with an amiable woman is essential for those occasions in which Will best proves the fineness of its temper by the facility with which it can be bent.

It may be said that Leopold Travers might have found such intercourse in the intimate companionship of his own daughter. But she was a mere child when his wife died, and she grew up to womanhood too insensibly for him to note the change. Besides, where a man has found a wife, his all-in-all, a daughter can never supply her place. The very reverence due to children precludes unrestrained confidence; and there is not that sense of permanent fellowship in a daughter which a man has in a wife,—any day a stranger may appear and carry her off from him. At all events Leopold did not own in Cecilia the softening influence to which he had yielded in her mother. He was fond of her, proud of her, indulgent to her; but the indulgence had its set limits. Whatever she asked solely for herself he granted; whatever she wished for matters under feminine control—the domestic household, the parish school, the alms-receiving poor—obtained his gentlest consideration. But when she had been solicited by some offending out-of-door dependant, or some petty defaulting tenant to use her good offices in favour of the culprit, Mr. Travers checked her interference by a firm 'No,' though uttered in a mild accent; and accompanied with a masculine aphorism to the effect "that there would be no such things as strict justice and disciplined order in the world if a man yielded to a woman's pleadings in any matter of business between man and man." From this it will be seen that Mr. Lethbridge had overrated the value of Cecilia's alliance in the negotiation respecting Mrs. Bawtrey's premium and shop.

CHAPTER III.

IF, having just perused what has thus been written on the biographical antecedents and mental characteristics of Leopold Travers, you, my dear reader, were to be personally presented to that gentleman as he now stands, the central figure of the group gathered round him, on his terrace, you would probably be surprised,—nay, I have no doubt you would say to yourself, "Not at all the sort of man I expected." In that slender form, somewhat below the middle height; in that fair countenance which still, at the age of forty-eight, retains a delicacy of feature and of colouring which is of almost woman-like beauty, and, from the quiet placidity of its expression, conveys at first glance the notion of almost woman-like mildness,—it would be difficult to recognize a man who in youth had been renowned for reckless daring, in maturer years more honourably distinguished for steadfast prudence and determined purpose, and who, alike in faults or in merits, was as emphatically masculine as a biped in trousers can possibly be.

Mr. Travers is listening to a young man of about two-and-twenty, the eldest son of the richest nobleman of the county, and who intends to start for the representation of the shire at the next general election, which is close at hand. The Hon. George Belvoir is tall, inclined to be stout, and will look well on the hustings. He has had those pains taken with his education which an English peer generally does take with the son intended to succeed to the representation of an honourable name and the responsibilities of high station. If eldest sons do not often make as great a figure in the world as their younger brothers, it is not because their minds are less cultivated, but because they have less motive power for action. George Belvoir was well read, especially in that sort of reading which befits a future senator—history, statistics, political economy, so far as that dismal science is compatible with the agricultural interest. He was also well-principled, had a strong sense of discipline and duty, was prepared in politics firmly to uphold as right whatever was proposed by his own party, and to reject as wrong whatever was proposed by the other. At present he was rather loud and noisy in the assertion of his opinions,—young men fresh from the university generally are. It was the secret wish of Mr. Travers that George Belvoir should become his son-in-law—less because of his rank and wealth (though such advantages were not of a nature to be despised by a practical man like Leopold Travers), than on account of those qualities in his personal character which were likely to render him an excellent husband.

Seated on wire benches, just without the verandah, but shaded by its fragrant festoons, were Mrs. Campion and three ladies, the wives of neighbouring squires. Cecilia stood a little apart from them, bending over a long-backed Skye terrier, whom she was teaching to stand on his hind-legs.

But see, the company are arriving! How suddenly that green space, ten minutes ago so solitary, has become animated and populous!

Indeed the Park now presented a very lively appearance: vans, carts, and farmers' chaises were seen in crowded procession along the winding road; foot-passengers were swarming towards the house in all directions. The herds and flocks in the various enclosures stopped grazing to stare at the unwonted invaders of their pasture; yet the orderly nature of the host imparted a respect for order to his ruder visitors; not even a turbulent boy attempted to scale the fences, or creep through their wires; all threaded the narrow turnstiles which gave egress from one subdivision of the sward to another.

Mr. Travers turned to George Belvoir—"I see old farmer Steen's yellow gig. Mind how you talk to him, George. He is full of whims and crotchets, and if you once brush his feathers the wrong way he will be as vindictive as a parrot. But he is the man who must second you at the nomination. No other tenant-farmer carries the same weight with his class."

"I suppose," said George, "that if Mr. Steen is the best man to second me at the hustings, he is a good speaker?"

"A good speaker?—in one sense he is. He never says a word too much. The last time he seconded the nomination of the man you are to succeed, this was his speech: 'Brother Electors, for twenty years I have been one of the judges at our county cattle-show. I know one animal from another. Looking at the specimens before us to-day, none of them are as good of their kind as I've seen elsewhere. But if you choose Sir John Hogg, you'll not get the wrong sow by the ear!'"

"At least," said George, after a laugh at this sample of eloquence unadorned, "Mr. Steen does not err on the side of flattery in his commendations of a candidate. But what makes him such an authority with the farmers? Is he a first-rate agriculturist?"

"In thrift, yes!—in spirit, no! He says that all expensive experiments should be left to gentlemen farmers. He is an authority with other tenants—1stly, Because he is a very keen censor of their landlords; 2n.lly, Because he holds himself thoroughly independent of his own; 3rdly, Because he is supposed to have studied the political bearings of questions that affect the landed interest, and has more than once been summoned to give his opinion on such subjects to Committees of both Houses of Parliament. Here he comes. Observe, when I leave you to talk to him, 1stly, that you confess utter ignorance of practical farming. Nothing enrages him like the presumption of a gentleman farmer like myself; 2ndly, that you ask his opinion on the publication of Agricultural Statistics, just modestly intimating that you, as at present advised, think that inquisitorial researches into a man's business involve principles opposed to the British Constitution. And on all that he may say as to the shortcomings of landlords in general, and of your father in particular, make no reply, but listen with an air of melancholy conviction. How do you do, Mr. Steen, and how's the Mistress? Why have you not brought her with you?"

"My good woman is in the straw again, Squire. Who is that youngster?"

"Hist! let me introduce Mr. Belvoir."

Mr. Belvoir offers his hand.

"No, sir!" vociferates Steen, putting both his own hands behind him. "No offence, young gentleman. But I don't give my hand at first sight to a man who wants to shake a vote out of it. Not that I know anything against you. But, if you be a farmer's friend, rabbits are not, and my Lord your father is a great one for rabbits."

"Indeed you are mistaken there!" cries George, with vehement earnestness. Mr. Travers gave him a nudge, as much as to say, "Hold your tongue." George understood the hint, and is carried off meekly by Mr. Steen down the solitude of the plantations.

The guests now arrived fast and thick. They consisted chiefly not only of Mr. Travers's tenants, but of farmers and their families within the range of eight or ten miles from the Park, with a few of the neighbouring gentry and clergy.

It was not a supper intended to include the labouring class. For Mr. Travers had an especial dislike to the custom of exhibiting peasants at feeding-time, as if they were so many tamed animals of an inferior species. When he entertained work-people, he made them comfortable in their own way; and peasants feel more comfortable when not invited to be stared out of countenance.

"Well, Lethbridge," said Mr. Travers, "where is the young gladiator you promised to bring?"

"I did bring him, and he was by my side not a minute ago.

He has suddenly given me the slip—*abiit, evasit, erupit.* I was looking round for him in vain when you accosted me."

"I hope he has not seen some guest of mine whom he wants to fight."

"I hope not," answered the Parson, doubtfully. "He's a strange fellow. But I think you will be pleased with him—that is, if he can be found. Oh, Mr. Saunderson, how do you do? Have you seen your visitor?"

"No, sir, I have just come. My Mistress, Squire, and my three girls;—and this is my son."

"A hearty welcome to all," said the graceful Squire; (turning to Saunderson junior) "I suppose you are fond of dancing. Get yourself a partner. We may as well open the ball."

"Thank you, sir, but I never dance," said Saunderson junior, with an air of austere superiority to an amusement which the March of Intellect had left behind.

"Then you'll have less to regret when you are grown old. But the band is striking up; we must adjourn to the marquee. George" (Mr. Belvoir, escaped from Mr. Steen, had just made his appearance), "will you give your arm to Cecilia, to whom I think you are engaged for the first quadrille?"

"I hope," said George to Cecilia, as they walked towards the marquee, "that Mr. Steen is not an average specimen of the electors I shall have to canvass. Whether he has been brought up to honour his own father and mother I can't pretend to say, but he seems bent upon teaching me not to honour mine. Having taken away my father's moral character upon the unfounded allegation that he loved rabbits better than mankind, he then assailed my innocent mother on the score of religion, and inquired when she was going over to the Church of Rome—basing that inquiry on the assertion that she had taken away her custom from a Protestant grocer and conferred it on a Papist."

"Those are favourable signs, Mr. Belvoir. Mr. Steen always prefaces a kindness by a great deal of incivility. I asked him once to lend me a pony, my own being suddenly taken lame, and he seized that opportunity to tell me that my father was an impostor in pretending to be a judge of cattle; that he was a tyrant, screwing his tenants in order to indulge extravagant habits of hospitality; and implied that it would be a great mercy if we did not live to apply to him, not for a pony, but for parochial relief. I went away indignant. But he sent me the pony. I am sure he will give you his vote."

"Meanwhile," said George, with a timid attempt at gallantry, as they now commenced the quadrille, "I take encouragement from the belief that I have the good wishes of Miss Travers. If ladies had votes, as Mr. Mill recommends, why, then——"

"Why, then, I should vote as papa does," said Miss Travers, simply. "And if women had votes, I suspect there would be very little peace in any household where they did not vote as the man at the head of it wished them."

"But I believe, after all," said the aspirant to Parliament, seriously, "that the advocates for female suffrage would limit it to women independent of masculine control—widows and spinsters voting in right of their own independent tenements."

"In that case," said Cecilia, "I suppose they would still generally go by the opinion of some man they relied on, or make a very silly choice if they did not."

"You underrate the good sense of your sex."

"I hope not. Do you underrate the good sense of yours, if, in far more than half the things appertaining to daily life, the wisest men say, 'better leave *them* to *the women*'? But you're forgetting the figure—*cavalier seul*."

"By the way," said George, in another interval of the dance, "do you know a Mr. Chillingly, the son of Sir Peter, of Exmundham, in Westshire?"

"No; why do you ask?"

"Because I thought I caught a glimpse of his face: it was just as Mr. Steen was bearing me away down the plantation. From what you say, I must suppose I was mistaken."

"Chillingly! But surely some persons were talking yesterday at dinner about a young gentleman of that name as being likely to stand for Westshire at the next election, but who had made a very unpopular and eccentric speech on the occasion of his coming of age."

"The same man—I was at college with him—a very singular character. He was thought clever—won a prize or two—took a good degree, but it was generally said that he would have deserved a much higher one if some of his papers had not contained covert jests either on the subject or the examiners. It is a dangerous thing to set up as a humourist in practical life—especially public life. They say Mr. Pitt had naturally a great deal of wit and humour, but he wisely suppressed any evidence of those qualities in his Parliamentary speeches. Just like Chillingly, to turn into ridicule the important event of festivities in honour of his coming of age—an occasion that can never occur again in the whole course of his life."

"It was bad taste," said Cecilia, "if intentional. But perhaps he was misunderstood, or taken by surprise."

"Misunderstood—possibly; but taken by surprise—no. The coolest fellow I ever met. Not that I have met him very often. Latterly, indeed, at Cambridge he lived much alone. It was said that he read hard. I doubt that, for my rooms were just over his, and I know that he was much more frequently out of doors than in. He rambled a good deal about the country on foot. I have seen him in by-lanes a dozen miles distant from the town when I have been riding back from the Hunt. He was fond of the water, and pulled a mighty strong oar, but declined to belong to our University crew; yet if ever there was a fight between undergraduates and bargemen, he was sure to be in the midst of it. Yes, a very great oddity indeed, full of contradictions, for a milder, quieter fellow in general intercourse you could not see; and as for the jests of which he was accused in his Examination Papers, his very face should have acquitted him of the charge before any impartial jury of his countrymen."

"You sketch quite an interesting picture of him," said Cecilia. "I wish we did know him; he would be worth seeing."

"And, once seen, you would not easily forget him—a dark, handsome face, with large melancholy eyes, and with one of those spare, slender figures which enable a man to disguise his strength, as a fraudulent billiard-player disguises his play."

The dance had ceased during this conversation, and the speakers were now walking slowly to and fro the lawn amid the general crowd.

"How well your father plays the part of host to these rural folks!" said George, with a secret envy. "Do observe how quietly he puts that shy young farmer at his ease, and now how kindly he deposits that lame old lady on the bench, and places the stool under her feet. What a canvasser he would be; and how young he still looks, and how monstrous handsome!"

This last compliment was uttered as Travers, having made the old lady comfortable, had joined the three Miss Saundersons, dividing his pleasant smile equally between them, and seemingly unconscious of the admiring glances which many another rural beauty directed towards him as he passed along. About the man there was a certain indescribable elegance, a natural suavity free from all that affectation, whether of forced heartiness or condescending civility, which too often characterizes the well-meant efforts of provincial magnates to accommodate themselves to persons of inferior station and breeding. It is a great advantage to a man to have passed his early youth in that most equal and most polished of all democracies—the best society of large capitals. And to such acquired advantage Leopold Travers added the inborn qualities that please.

Later in the evening Travers, again accosting Mr. Lethbridge, said, "I have been talking much to the Saundersons about that young man who did us the inestimable service of punishing your ferocious parishioner, Tom Bowles; and all I hear so confirms the interest your own account inspired me with, that I should really like much to make his acquaintance. Has not he turned up yet?"

"No; I fear he must have gone. But in that case I hope you will take his generous desire to serve my poor basket-maker into benevolent consideration."

"Do not press me; I feel so reluctant to refuse any request of yours. But I have my own theory as to the management of an estate, and my system does not allow of favour. I should wish to explain that to the young stranger himself. For I hold courage in such honour that I do not like a brave man to leave these parts with an impression that Leopold Travers is an ungracious churl. However, he may not have gone. I will go and look for him myself. Just tell Cecilia that she has danced enough with the gentry, and that I have told farmer Turby's son, a fine young fellow, and a capital rider across country, that I expect him to show my daughter that he can dance as well as he rides."

CHAPTER IV.

QUITTING Mr. Lethbridge, Travers turned with quick step towards the more solitary part of the grounds. He did not find the object of his search in the walks of the plantation; and, on taking the circuit of his demesne, wound his way back towards the lawn through a sequestered rocky hollow in the rear of the marquee, which had been devoted to a fernery. Here he came to a sudden pause; for, seated a few yards before him on a gray crag, and the moonlight full on his face, he saw a solitary man, looking upwards with a still and mournful gaze, evidently absorbed in abstract contemplation.

Recalling the description of the stranger which he had heard from Mr. Lethbridge and the Saundersons, Mr. Travers felt sure that he had come on him at last. He approached gently; and, being much concealed by the tall ferns, Kenelm (for that itinerant it was) did not see him advance, until he felt a hand on his shoulder, and, turning round, beheld a winning smile and heard a pleasant voice.

"I think I am not mistaken," said Leopold Travers, "in assuming you to be the gentleman whom Mr. Lethbridge promised to introduce to me, and who is staying with my tenant, Mr. Saunderson?"

Kenelm rose and bowed. Travers saw at once that it was the bow of a man of his own world, and not in keeping with the Sunday costume of a petty farmer. "Nay," said he, "let us talk seated;" and, placing himself on the crag, he made room for Kenelm beside him.

"In the first place," resumed Travers, "I must thank you for having done a public service in putting down the brute force which has long tyrannized over the neighbourhood. Often in my young days I have felt the disadvantage of height and sinews, whenever it would have been a great convenience to terminate dispute or chastise insolence by a resort to man's primitive weapons; but I never more lamented my physical inferiority than on certain occasions when I would have given my ears to be able to thrash Tom Bowles myself. It has been as great a disgrace to my estate that that bully should so long have infested it, as it is to the King of Italy not to be able with all his armies to put down a brigand in Calabria."

"Pardon me, Mr. Travers, but I am one of those rare persons who do not like to hear ill of their friends. Mr. Thomas Bowles is a particular friend of mine."

"Eh!" cried Travers, aghast. "'Friend!' you are joking."

"You would not accuse me of joking if you knew me better. But surely you have felt that there are few friends one likes more cordially, and ought to respect more heedfully, than the enemy with whom one has just made it up."

"You say well, and I accept the rebuke," said Travers, more and more surprised. "And I certainly have less right to abuse Mr. Bowles than you have, since I had not the courage to fight him. To turn to another subject less provocative. Mr. Lethbridge has told me of your amiable desire to serve two of his young parishioners—Will Somers and Jessie Wiles—and of your generous offer to pay the money Mrs. Bawtrey demands for the transfer of her lease. To that negotiation my consent is necessary, and that consent I cannot give. Shall I tell you why?"

"Pray do. Your reasons may admit of argument."

"Every reason admits of argument," said Mr. Travers, amused at the calm assurance of a youthful stranger in anticipating argument with a skilful proprietor on the management of his own property.

"I do not, however, tell you my reasons for the sake of argument, but in vindication of my seeming want of courtesy towards yourself. I have had a very hard and a very difficult task to perform in bringing the rental of my estate up to its proper value. In doing so, I have been compelled to adopt one uniform system, equally applied to my largest and my pettiest holdings. That system consists in securing the best and safest tenants I can, at the rents computed by a valuer in whom I have confidence. To this system, universally adopted on my estate, though it incurred much unpopularity at first, I have at length succeeded in reconciling the public opinion of my neighbourhood. People began by saying I was hard; they now acknowledge I am just. If I once give way to favour or sentiment, I unhinge my whole system. Every day I am subjected to moving solicitations. Lord Twostars—a keen politician—begs me to give a vacant farm to a tenant because he is an excellent canvasser, and has always voted straight with the Party. Mrs. Fourstars, a most benevolent woman, entreats me not to dismiss another tenant, because he is in distressed circumstances, and has a large family—very good reasons perhaps for my excusing him an arrear, or allowing him a retiring pension, but the worst reason in the world for letting him continue to ruin himself and my land. Now, Mrs. Bawtrey has a small holding on lease at the inadequate rent of £8 a-year. She asks £45 for its transfer, but she can't transfer the lease without my consent; and I can get £12 a-year as a moderate rental from a large choice of competent tenants. It will better answer me to pay her the £45 myself, which I have no doubt the incoming tenant would pay me back, at least in part; and if he did not, the additional rent would be good interest for my expenditure. Now, you happen to take a sentimental interest, as you pass through the village, in the loves of a needy cripple, whose utmost industry has but served to save himself from parish relief, and a giddy girl without a sixpence, and you ask me to accept these very equivocal tenants instead of substantial ones, and at a rent one-third less than the market value. Suppose that I yielded to your request, what becomes of my reputation for practical, business-like justice? I shall have made an inroad into the system by which my whole estate is managed, and have invited all manner of solicitations on the part of friends and neighbours, which I could no longer consistently refuse, having shown how easily I can be persuaded into compliance by a stranger whom I may never see again. And are you sure, after all, that, if you did prevail on me, you would do the individual good you aim at? It is, no doubt, very pleasant to think one has made a young couple happy. But if that young couple fail in keeping the little shop to which you would transplant them (and nothing more likely—peasants seldom become good shopkeepers), and find themselves, with a family of children, dependent solely, not on the arm of a strong labourer, but the ten fingers of a sickly cripple, who makes clever baskets, for which there is but slight and precarious demand in the neighbourhood, may you not have insured the misery of the couple you wished to render happy?"

"I withdraw all argument," said Kenelm, with an aspect so humiliated and dejected, that it would have softened a Greenland bear, or a Counsel for the Prosecution. "I am more and more convinced that of all the shams in the world, that of benevolence is the greatest. It seems so easy to do good, and it is so difficult to do it. Everywhere, in this hateful civilized life, one runs one's head against a system. A system, Mr. Travers, is man's servile imitation of the blind tyranny of what in our ignorance we call 'Natural Laws,' a mechanical something through which the world is ruled by the cruelty of General Principles, to the utter disregard of individual welfare. By Natural Laws creatures prey on each other, and big fishes eat little ones upon system. It is, nevertheless, a hard thing for the little fish. Every nation, every town, every hamlet, every occupation, has a system, by which, somehow or other, the pond swarms with fishes, of which a great many inferiors contribute to increase the size of a superior. It is an idle benevolence to keep one solitary gudgeon out of the jaws of a pike. Here am I doing what I thought the simplest thing in the world, asking a gentleman, evidently as good-natured as myself, to allow an old woman to let her premises to a deserving young couple, and paying what she asks for it out of my own money. And I find that I am running against a system, and invading all the laws by which a rental is increased and an estate improved. Mr. Travers, you have no cause for regret in not having beaten Tom Bowles. You have beaten his victor, and I now give up all dream of further interference with the Natural Laws that govern the village which I have visited in vain. I had meant to remove Tom Bowles from that quiet community. I shall now leave him to return to his former habits—to marry Jessie Wiles—which he certainly will do, and——"

"Hold!" cried Mr. Travers. "Do you mean to say that you can induce Tom Bowles to leave the village?"

"I *had* induced him to do it, provided Jessie Wiles married the basket-maker; but as that is out of the question, I am bound to tell him so, and he will stay."

"But if he left, what would become of his business? His mother could not keep it on; his little place is a freehold; the only house in the village that does not belong to me, or I should have ejected him long ago. Would he sell the premises to me?"

"Not if he stays and marries Jessie Wiles. But if he goes with me to Luscombe and settles in that town as a partner to his uncle, I suppose he would be too glad to sell a house of which he can have no pleasant recollections. But what then? You cannot violate your system for the sake of a miserable forge."

"It would not violate my system if, instead of yielding to a sentiment, I gained an advantage; and, to say truth, I should be very glad to buy that forge and the fields that go with it."

"'Tis your affair now, not mine, Mr. Travers. I no longer presume to interfere. I leave the neighbourhood to-morrow: see if *you* can negotiate with Mr. Bowles. I have the honour to wish you a good evening."

"Nay, young gentleman, I cannot allow you to quit me thus. You have declined apparently to join the dancers, but you will at least join the supper. Come!"

"Thank you sincerely, no. I came here merely on the business which your system has settled."

"But I am not sure that it is settled." Here Mr. Travers wound his arm within Kenelm's, and looking him full in the face, said, "I know that I am speaking to a gentleman at least equal in rank to myself, but as I enjoy the melancholy privilege of being the older man, do not think I take an unwarrantable liberty in asking if you object to tell me your name. I should like to introduce you to my daughter, who is very partial to Jessie Wiles and to Will Somers. But I can't venture to inflame her imagination by designating you as a prince in disguise."

"Mr. Travers, you express yourself with exquisite delicacy. But I am just starting in life, and I shrink from mortifying my father by associating my name with a signal failure. Suppose I were an anonymous contributor, say, to 'The Londoner,' and I had just brought that highly intellectual journal into discredit by a feeble attempt at a good-natured criticism or a generous sentiment, would that be the fitting occasion to throw off the mask, and parade myself to a mocking world as the imbecile violator of an established system? Should I not, in a moment so untoward, more than ever desire to merge my insignificant unit in the mysterious importance which the smallest Singular obtains when he makes himself a Plural, and speaks not as 'I,' but as 'We'? *We* are insensible to the charm of young ladies; *We* are not bribed by suppers; *We*, like the witches of Macbeth, have no name on earth; *We* are the greatest wisdom of the greatest number; *We* are so upon system; *We* salute you, Mr. Travers, and depart unassailable."

Here Kenelm rose, doffed and replaced his hat in majestic salutation, turned towards the entrance of the fernery and found himself suddenly face to face with George Belvoir, behind whom followed, with a throng of guests, the fair form of Cecilia. George Belvoir caught Kenelm by the hand, and exclaimed, "Chillingly! I thought I could not be mistaken."

"Chillingly!" echoed Leopold Travers from behind. "Are you the son of my old friend, Sir Peter?"

Thus discovered and environed, Kenelm did not lose his wonted presence of mind; he turned round to Leopold Travers, who was now close in his rear, and whispered, "If my father was your friend, do not disgrace his son. Do not say I am a failure. Deviate from your system, and let Will Somers succeed Mrs. Bawtrey." Then reverting his face to Mr. Belvoir, he said tranquilly, "Yes; we have met before."

"Cecilia," said Travers, now interposing, "I am happy to introduce to you as Mr. Chillingly, not only the son of an old friend of mine, not only the knight-errant of whose gallant conduct on behalf of your *protégée* Jessie Wiles we have heard so much, but the eloquent arguer who has conquered my better judgment in a matter on which I thought myself infallible. Tell Mr. Lethbridge that I accept Will Somers as a tenant for Mrs. Bawtrey's premises."

Kenelm grasped the Squire's hand cordially. "May it be in my power to do a kind thing to you, in spite of any system to the contrary!"

"Mr. Chillingly, give your arm to my daughter. You will not now object to join the dancers?"

CHAPTER V.

CECILIA stole a shy glance at Kenelm as the two emerged from the fernery into the open space of the lawn. His countenance pleased her. She thought she discovered much latent gentleness under the cold and mournful gravity of its expression; and attributing the silence he maintained to some painful sense of an awkward position in the abrupt betrayal of his incognito, sought with womanly tact to dispel his supposed embarrassment.

"You have chosen a delightful mode of seeing the country this lovely summer weather, Mr. Chillingly, I believe such pedestrian exercises are very common with University Students during the long vacation."

"Very common, though they generally wander in packs like wild dogs or Australian dingoes. It is only a tame dog that one finds on the road travelling by himself; and then, unless he behaves very quietly, it is ten to one that he is stoned as a mad dog."

"But I am afraid, from what I hear, that you have not been travelling very quietly."

"You are quite right, Miss Travers, and I am a sad dog if not a mad one. But pardon me, we are nearing the marquee; the band is striking up, and, alas! I am not a dancing dog."

He released Cecilia's arm, and bowed.

"Let us sit here a while, then," said she, motioning to a garden-bench. "I have no engagement for the next dance, and as I am a little tired, I shall be glad of a reprieve."

Kenelm sighed, and with the air of a martyr stretching himself on the rack, took his place beside the fairest girl in the county.

"You were at college with Mr. Belvoir?"

"I was."

"He was thought clever there?"

"I have not a doubt of it."

"You know he is canvassing our county for the next election. My father takes a warm interest in his success, and thinks he will be a useful member of Parliament."

"Of that I am certain. For the first five years he will be called pushing, noisy, and conceited, much sneered at by men of his own age, and coughed down on great occasions; for the five following years he will be considered a sensible man in committees, and a necessary feature in debate; at the end of those years he will be an under-secretary; in five years more he will be a Cabinet Minister, and the representative of an important section of opinions: he will be an irreproachable private character, and his wife will be seen wearing the family diamonds at all the great parties. She will take an interest in politics and theology; and if she die before him, her husband will show his sense of wedded happiness by choosing another lady, equally fitted to wear the family diamonds and to maintain the family consequence."

In spite of her laughter, Cecilia felt a certain awe at the solemnity of voice and manner with which Kenelm delivered these oracular sentences, and the whole prediction seemed strangely in unison with her own impressions of the character whose fate was thus shadowed out.

"Are you a fortune-teller, Mr. Chillingly?" she asked, falteringly, and after a pause.

"As good a one as any whose hand you could cross with a shilling."

"Will you tell me my fortune?"

"No; I never tell the fortunes of ladies, because your sex is credulous, and a lady might believe what I tell her. And when we believe such and such is to be our fate, we are too apt to work out our life into the verification of the belief. If Lady Macbeth had disbelieved in the witches, she would never have persuaded her lord to murder Duncan."

"But can you not predict me a more cheerful fortune than that tragical illustration of yours seems to threaten?"

"The future is never cheerful to those who look on the dark side of the question. Mr. Gray is too good a poet for people to read nowadays, otherwise I should refer you to his lines in the Ode to Eton College—

> 'See how all around us wait
> The ministers of human fate,
> And black Misfortune's baleful train.'

Meanwhile it is something to enjoy the present. We are young—we are listening to music—there is no cloud over the summer stars—our conscience is clear—our hearts untroubled; why look forward in search of happiness?—shall we ever be happier than we are at this moment?"

Here Mr. Travers came up. "We are going to supper in a few minutes," said he; "and before we lose sight of each other, Mr. Chillingly, I wish to impress on you the moral fact that one good turn deserves another. I have yielded to your wish, and now you must yield to mine. Come and stay a few days with me, and see your benevolent intentions carried out."

Kenelm paused. Now that he was discovered, why should he not pass a few days among his equals? Realities or shams might be studied with squires no less than with farmers; besides, he had taken a liking to Travers. That graceful *ci-devant* Wildair, with the slight form and the delicate face, was unlike rural squires in general. Kenelm paused, and then said, frankly—

"I accept your invitation. Would the middle of next week suit you?"

"The sooner the better. Why not to-morrow?"

"To-morrow I am pre-engaged to an excursion with Mr. Bowles. That may occupy two or three days, and meanwhile I must write home for other garments than those in which I am a sham."

"Come any day you like."

"Agreed."

"Agreed; and, hark! the supper-bell."

"Supper," said Kenelm, offering his arm to Miss Travers,—"supper is a word truly interesting, truly poetical. It associates itself with the entertainments of the ancients—with the Augustan age—with Horace and Mæcenas;—with the only elegant but too fleeting period of the modern world—with the nobles and wits of Paris, when Paris had wits and nobles;—with Molière and the warm-hearted Duke who is said to have been the original of Molière's Misanthrope;—with Madame de Sévigné and the Racine whom that inimitable letter-writer denied to be a poet;—with Swift and Bolingbroke—with Johnson, Goldsmith, and Garrick. Epochs are signalized by their eatings. I honour him who revives the Golden Age of suppers." So saying, his face brightened.

CHAPTER VI.

KENELM CHILLINGLY, ESQ., TO SIR PETER CHILLINGLY, BART., ETC., ETC.

"MY DEAR FATHER,—I am alive and unmarried. Providence has watched over me in these respects; but I have had narrow escapes. Hitherto I have not acquired much worldly wisdom in my travels. It is true that I have been paid two shillings as a day labourer, and, in fact, have fairly earned at least six shillings more; but against that additional claim I generously set off, as an equivalent, my board and lodging. On the other hand, I have spent forty-five pounds out of the fifty which I devoted to the purchase of experience. But I hope you will be a gainer by that investment. Send an order to Mr. William Somers, basket-maker, Graveleigh, ——shire, for the hampers and game-baskets you require, and I undertake to say that you will save twenty per cent. on that article (all expenses of carriage deducted), and do a good action into the bargain. You know, from long habit, what a good action is worth better than I do. I daresay you will be more pleased to learn, than I am to record, the fact, that I have been again decoyed into the society of ladies and gentlemen, and have accepted an invitation to pass a few days at Neesdale Park with Mr. Travers—christened Leopold—who calls you 'his old friend'—a term which I take for granted belongs to that class of poetic exaggeration in which the 'dears' and 'darlings' of conjugal intercourse may be categorized. Having for that visit no suitable garments in my knapsack, kindly tell Jenkes to forward me a portmanteauful of those which I habitually wore as Kenelm Chillingly, directed to me at 'Neesdale Park, near Beaverston.' Let me find it there on Wednesday.

"I leave this place to-morrow morning in company with a friend of the name of Bowles—no relation to the reverend gentleman of that name who held the doctrine that a poet should bore us to death with fiddle-faddle minutiæ of natural objects in preference to that study of the insignificant creature Man, in his relations to his species, to which Mr. Pope limited the range of his inferior muse; and who, practising as he preached, wrote some very nice verses, to which the Lake school and its successors are largely indebted. My Mr. Bowles has exercised his faculty upon Man, and has a powerful inborn gift in that line which only requires cultivation to render him a match for any one. His more masculine nature is at present much obscured by that passing cloud which, in conventional language, is called 'a Hopeless Attachment.' But I trust, in the course of our excursion, which is to be taken on foot, that this vapour may consolidate by motion, as some old-fashioned astronomers held that the nebula does consolidate into a matter-of-fact world. Is it Rochefoucauld who says that a man is never more likely to form a hopeful attachment for one than when his heart is softened by a hopeless attachment to another? May it be long, my dear father, before you condole with me on the first or congratulate me on the second.— Your affectionate son, KENELM.

"Direct to me at Mr. Travers's. Kindest love to my mother."

The answer to this letter is here subjoined as the most convenient place for its insertion, though of course it was not received till some days after the date of my next chapter.

SIR PETER CHILLINGLY, BART., TO KENELM CHILLINGLY, ESQ.

"MY DEAR BOY,—With this I despatch the portmanteau you require to the address that you give. I remember well Leopold Travers when he was in the Guards—a very handsome and a very wild young fellow. But he had much more sense than people gave him credit for, and frequented intellectual society; at least I met him very often at my friend Campion's, whose house was then the favourite rendezvous of distinguished persons. He had very winning manners, and one could not help taking an interest in him. I was very glad when I heard he had married and reformed. Here I beg to observe that a man who contracts a taste for low company may indeed often marry, but he seldom reforms when he does so. And, on the whole, I should be much pleased to hear that the experience which has cost you forty-five pounds had convinced you that you might be better employed than earning two, or even six shillings, as a day-labourer.

"I have not given your love to your mother, as you requested. In fact, you have placed me in a very false position towards that other author of your eccentric being. I could only guard you from the inquisition of the police and the notoriety of descriptive handbills by allowing my lady to suppose that you had gone abroad with the Duke of Clairville and his family. It is easy to tell a fib, but it is very difficult to untell it. However, as soon as you have made up your mind to resume your normal position among ladies and gentlemen, I should be greatly obliged if you would apprise me. I don't wish to keep a fib on my conscience a day longer than may be necessary to prevent the necessity of telling another.

"From what you say of Mr. Bowles's study of Man, and his inborn talent for that scientific investigation, I suppose that he is a professed Metaphysician, and I should be glad of his candid opinion upon the Primary Basis of Morals, a subject upon which I have for three years meditated the consideration of a critical paper. But having lately read a controversy thereon between two eminent philosophers, in which each accuses the other of not understanding him, I have resolved for the present to leave the Basis in its unsettled condition.

"You rather alarm me when you say you have had a narrow escape from marriage. Should you, in order to increase the experience you set out to acquire, decide on trying the effect of a Mrs. Chillingly upon your nervous system, it would be well to let me know a little beforehand, so that I might prepare your mother's mind for that event. Such household trifles are within her special province; and she would be much put out if a Mrs. Chillingly dropped on her unawares.

"This subject, however, is too serious to admit of a jest even between two persons who understand, so well as you and I do, the secret cipher by which each other's outward style of jest is to be gravely interpreted into the irony which says one thing and means another. My dear boy, you are very young—you are wandering about in a very strange manner—and may, no doubt, meet with many a pretty face by the way, with which you may fancy that you fall in love. You cannot think me a barbarous tyrant if I ask you to promise me, on your honour, that you will not propose to any young lady before you come first to me and submit the case to my examination and approval. You know me too well to suppose that I should unreasonably withhold my consent if convinced that your happiness was at stake. But while what a young man may fancy to be love is often a trivial incident in his life, marriage is the greatest event in it; if on one side it may involve his happiness, on the other side it may insure his misery. Dearest, best, and oddest of sons, give me the promise I ask, and you will free my breast from a terribly anxious thought which now sits on it like a nightmare.

"Your recommendation of a basket-maker comes opportunely. All such matters go through the bailiff's hands, and it was but the other day that Green was complaining of the high prices of the man he employed for hampers and game-baskets. Green shall write to your *protégé*.

"Keep me informed of your proceedings as much as your anomalous character will permit; so that nothing may diminish my confidence that the man who had the honour to be christened Kenelm will not disgrace his name, but acquire the distinction denied to a Peter.—Your affectionate father."

CHAPTER VII.

VILLAGERS lie abed on Sundays later than on workdays, and no shutter was unclosed in a window of the rural street through which Kenelm Chillingly and Tom Bowles went, side by side, in the still soft air of the Sabbath morn. Side by side they went on, crossing the pastoral glebe-lands, where the kine still drowsily reclined under the bowery shade of glinting chestnut leaves; and diving thence into a narrow lane or by-road, winding deep between lofty banks all tangled with convolvulus and wild-rose and honey-suckle.

They walked in silence, for Kenelm, after one or two vain attempts at conversation, had the tact to discover that his companion was in no mood for talk; and being himself one of those creatures whose minds glide easily into the dreamy monologue of reverie, he was not displeased to muse on undisturbed, drinking quietly into his heart the subdued joy of the summer morn, with the freshness of its sparkling dews, the wayward carol of its earliest birds, the serene quietude of its limpid breezy air. Only when they came to fresh turnings in the road that led towards the town to which they were bound, Tom Bowles stepped before his companion, indicating the way by a monosyllable or a gesture. Thus they journeyed for hours, till the sun attained power, and a little wayside inn near a hamlet invited Kenelm to the thought of rest and food.

"Tom," said he then, rousing from his reverie, "what do you say to breakfast?"

Answered Tom sullenly, "I am not hungry—but as you like."

"Thank you, then we will stop here a while. I find it difficult to believe that you are not hungry, for you are very strong, and there are two things which generally accompany great physical strength: the one is a keen appetite; the other is—though you may not suppose it, and it is not commonly known—a melancholic temperament."

"Eh!—a what?"

"A tendency to melancholy. Of course you have heard of Hercules—you know the saying 'as strong as Hercules'?"

"Yes—of course."

"Well, I was first led to the connection between strength, appetite, and melancholy, by reading in an old author, named Plutarch, that Hercules was among the most notable instances of melancholy temperament which the author was enabled to quote. That must have been the traditional notion of the Herculean constitution; and as for appetite, the appetite of Hercules was a standard joke of the comic writers. When I read that observation it set me thinking, being myself melancholic, and having an exceedingly good appetite. Sure enough, when I began to collect evidence, I found that the strongest men with whom I made acquaintance, including prize-fighters and Irish draymen, were disposed to look upon life more on the shady than the sunny side of the way; in short, they were melancholic. But the kindness of Providence allowed them to enjoy their meals, as you and I are about to do."

In the utterance of this extraordinary crotchet Kenelm had halted his steps; but now striding briskly forward he entered the little inn, and after a glance at its larder, ordered the whole contents to be brought out and placed within a honey-suckle arbour which he spied in the angle of a bowling-green at the rear of the house.

In addition to the ordinary condiments of loaf, and butter, and eggs, and milk, and tea, the board soon groaned beneath the weight of pigeon-pie, cold ribs of beef and shoulder of mutton, remains of a feast which the members of a monthly rustic club had held there the day before. Tom ate little at first; but example is contagious, and gradually he vied with his companion in the diminution of the solid viands before him. Then he called for brandy.

"No," said Kenelm. "No, Tom; you have promised me friendship, and that is not compatible with brandy. Brandy is the worst enemy a man like you can have; and would make you quarrel even with me. If you want a stimulus I allow you a pipe: I don't smoke myself, as a rule, but there have been times in my life when I required soothing, and then I have felt that a whiff of tobacco stills and softens one like the kiss of a little child. Bring this gentleman a pipe."

Tom grunted, but took to the pipe kindly, and in a few minutes, during which Kenelm left him in silence, a lowering furrow between his brows smoothed itself away.

Gradually he felt the sweetening influences of the day and the place, of the merry sunbeams at play amid the leaves of the arbour, of the frank perfume of the honeysuckle, of the warble of the birds before they sank into the taciturn repose of a summer noon.

It was with a reluctant sigh that he rose at last, when Kenelm said, "We have yet far to go, we must push on."

The landlady, indeed, had already given them a hint that she and the family wanted to go to church, and to shut up the house in their absence. Kenelm drew out his purse, but Tom did the same with a return of cloud on his brow, and Kenelm saw that he would be mortally offended if suffered to be treated as an inferior; so each paid his due share, and the two men resumed their wandering. This time it was along a by-path amid fields, which was a shorter cut than the lane they had previously followed, to the main road to Luscombe. They walked slowly till they came to a rustic footbridge which spanned a gloomy trout-stream, not noisy, but with a low, sweet murmur, doubtless the same stream beside which, many miles away, Kenelm had conversed with the minstrel. Just as they came to this bridge there floated to their ears the distant sound of the hamlet church bell.

"Now let us sit here a while and listen," said Kenelm, seating himself on the baluster of the bridge. "I see that you brought away your pipe from the inn, and provided yourself with tobacco: refill the pipe and listen."

Tom half smiled and obeyed.

"O friend," said Kenelm, earnestly, and after a long pause of thought, "do you not feel what a blessed thing it is in this mortal life to be ever and anon reminded that you have a soul?"

Tom, startled, withdrew the pipe from his lips, and muttered—
"Eh!"

Kenelm continued—

"You and I, Tom, are not so good as we ought to be—of that there is no doubt; and good people would say justly that we should now be within yon church itself rather than listening to its bell. Granted, my friend, granted; but still it is something to hear that bell, and to feel by the train of thought which began in our innocent childhood, when we said our prayers at the knees of a mother, that we were lifted beyond this visible Nature, beyond these fields, and woods, and waters, in which, fair though they be, you and I miss something, in which neither you nor I are as happy as the kine in the fields, as the birds on the bough, as the fishes in the water—lifted to a consciousness of a sense vouchsafed to you and to me, not vouchsafed to the kine, to the bird, and the fish—a sense to comprehend that Nature has a God, and Man has a life hereafter. The bell says that to you and to me. Were that bell a thousand times more musical it could not say that to beast, bird, and fish. Do you understand me, Tom?"

Tom remains silent for a minute, and then replies—"I never thought of it before; but as you put it, I understand."

"Nature never gives to a living thing capacities not practically meant for its benefit and use. If Nature gives to us capacities to believe that we have a Creator whom we never saw, of whom we have no direct proof, who is kind and good and tender beyond all that we know of kind and good and tender on earth, it is because the endowment of capacities to conceive such a Being must be for our benefit and use; it would not be for our benefit and use if it were a lie. Again, if Nature has given to us a capacity to receive the notion that we live again, no matter whether some of us refuse so to believe, and argue against it,—why, the very capacity to receive the idea (for unless we receive it we could not argue against it) proves that it is for our benefit and use; and if there were no such life hereafter, we should be governed and influenced, arrange our mode of life, and mature our civilization, by obedience to a lie, which Nature falsified herself in giving us the capacity to believe. You still understand me?"

"Yes; it bothers me a little, for you see I am not a parson's man; but I do understand."

"Then, my friend, study to apply—for it requires constant study—study to apply that which you understand to your own case. You are something more than Tom Bowles, the smith and doctor of horses; something more than the magnificent animal who rages for his mate, and fights every rival: the bull does that. You are a soul endowed with the capacity to receive the idea of a Creator so divinely wise and great and good that, though acting by the agency of general laws, He can accommodate them to all individual cases, so that—taking into account the life hereafter, which He grants to you the capacity to believe—all that troubles you now will be proved to you wise and great and good either in this life or the other. Lay that truth to your heart, friend, now—before the bell stops ringing; recall it every time you hear the church bell ring again. And oh, Tom, you have such a noble nature!——"

"I—I! don't jeer me—don't."

"Such a noble nature; for you can love so passionately, you can war so fiercely, and yet, when convinced that your love would be misery to her you love, can resign it; and yet, when beaten in your war, can so forgive your victor that you are walking in this solitude with him as a friend, knowing that you have but to drop a foot behind him in order to take his life in an unguarded moment; and rather than take his life, you would defend it against an army. Do you think I am so dull as not to see all that? and is not all that a noble nature?"

Tom Bowles covered his face with his hands, and his broad breast heaved.

"Well, then, to that noble nature I now trust. I myself have done little good in life. I may never do much; but let me think that I have not crossed your life in vain for you and for those whom your life can colour for good or for bad. As you are strong, be gentle; as you can love one, be kind to all; as you have so much that is grand as Man—that is, the highest of God's works on earth, —let all your acts attach your manhood to the idea of Him, to whom the voice of the bell appeals. Ah! the bell is hushed; but not your heart, Tom,—that speaks still."

Tom was weeping like a child.

CHAPTER VIII.

NOW when our two travellers resumed their journey, the relationship between them had undergone a change; nay, you might have said that their characters were also changed. For Tom found himself pouring out his turbulent heart to Kenelm, confiding to this philosophical scoffer at love all the passionate humanities of love—its hope, its anguish, its jealousy, its wrath—the all that links the gentlest of emotions to tragedy and terror. And Kenelm, listening tenderly, with softened eyes, uttered not one cynic word—nay, not one playful jest. He felt that the gravity of all he heard was too solemn for mockery, too deep even for comfort. True love of this sort was a thing he had never known, never wished to know, never thought he could know, but he sympathized in it not the less. Strange, indeed, how much we do sympathize, on the stage, for instance, or in a book, with passions that have never agitated ourselves. Had Kenelm jested, or reasoned, or preached, Tom would have shrunk at once into dreary silence; but Kenelm said nothing, save now and then, as he rested his arm, brother-like, on the strong man's shoulder, he murmured, "poor fellow!" So, then, when Tom had finished his confessions, he felt wondrously relieved and comforted. He had cleansed his bosom of the perilous stuff that weighed upon the heart.

Was this good result effected by Kenelm's artful diplomacy, or by that insight into human passions vouchsafed, unconsciously to himself, by gleams or in flashes, to this strange man who surveyed the objects and pursuits of his fellows with a yearning desire to share them, murmuring to himself, "I cannot—I do not stand in this world; like a ghost I glide beside it, and look on?"

Thus the two men continued their way slowly, amid soft pastures and yellowing corn-fields, out at length into the dusty thoroughfares of the main road. That gained, their talk insensibly changed its tone—it became more commonplace, and Kenelm permitted himself the licence of those crotchets by which he extracted a sort of quaint pleasantry out of commonplace itself; so that from time to time Tom was startled into the mirth of laughter. This big fellow had one very agreeable gift, which is only granted, I think, to men of genuine character and affectionate dispositions—a spontaneous and sweet laugh, manly and frank, but not boisterous, as you might have supposed it would be. But that sort of laugh had not before come from his lips, since the day on which his love for Jessie Wiles had made him at war with himself and the world.

The sun was setting when from the brow of a hill they beheld the spires of Luscombe, embedded amid the level meadows that stretched below, watered by the same stream that had wound along their more rural pathway, but which now expanded into stately width, and needed, to span it, a mighty bridge fit for the convenience of civilized traffic. The town seemed near, but it was full two miles off by road.

"There is a short cut across the fields beyond that stile, which leads straight to my uncle's house," said Tom; "and I daresay, sir, that you will be glad to escape the dirty suburb by which the road passes before we get into the town."

"A good thought, Tom. It is very odd that fine towns always are approached by dirty suburbs—a covert symbolical satire, perhaps,

G

on the ways to success in fine towns. Avarice or ambition go through very mean little streets before they gain the place which they jostle the crowd to win—in the Townhall or on 'Change. Happy the man who, like you, Tom, finds that there is a shorter and a cleaner and a pleasanter way to goal or to resting-place than that through the dirty suburbs!"

They met but few passengers on their path through the fields—a respectable, staid, elderly couple, who had the air of a Dissenting minister and his wife; a girl of fourteen leading a little boy seven years younger by the hand; a pair of lovers, evidently lovers at least to the eye of Tom Bowles—for, on regarding them as they passed unheeding him, he winced, and his face changed. Even after they had passed, Kenelm saw on the face that pain lingered there; the lips were tightly compressed, and their corners gloomily drawn down.

Just at this moment a dog rushed towards them with a short quick bark—a Pomeranian dog with pointed nose and pricked ears. It hushed its bark as it neared Kenelm, sniffed his trousers, and wagged its tail.

"By the sacred Nine," cried Kenelm, "thou art the dog with the tin tray! where is thy master?"

The dog seemed to understand the question, for it turned its head significantly, and Kenelm saw, seated under a lime-tree, at a good distance from the path, a man, with book in hand, evidently employed in sketching.

"Come this way," he said to Tom; "I recognize an acquaintance. You will like him." Tom desired no new acquaintance at that moment, but he followed Kenelm submissively.

CHAPTER IX.

"YOU see we are fated to meet again," said Kenelm, stretching himself at his ease beside the Wandering Minstrel, and motioning Tom to do the same. "But you seem to add the accomplishment of drawing to that of verse-making! You sketch from what you call Nature?"

"From what I call Nature! yes, sometimes."

"And do you not find in drawing, as in verse-making, the truth that I have before sought to din into your reluctant ears—viz., that Nature has no voice except that which man breathes into her out of his mind! I would lay a wager that the sketch you are now taking is rather an attempt to make her embody some thought of your own, than to present her outlines as they appear to any other observer. Permit me to judge for myself." And he bent over the sketch-book. It is often difficult for one who is not himself an artist nor a connoisseur, to judge whether the pencilled jottings in an impromptu sketch are by the hand of a professed master or a mere amateur. Kenelm was neither artist nor connoisseur, but the mere pencil-work seemed to him much what might be expected from any man with an accurate eye, who had taken a certain number of lessons from a good drawing-master. It was enough for him, however, that it furnished an illustration of his own theory. "I was right," he cried, triumphantly. "From this height there is a beautiful view, as it presents itself to me; a beautiful view of the town, its meadows, its river, harmonized by the sunset; for sunset, like gilding, unites conflicting colours, and softens them in uniting. But I see nothing of that view in your sketch. What I do see is to me mysterious."

"The view you suggest," said the minstrel, "is no doubt very fine, but it is for a Turner or a Claude to treat it. My grasp is not wide enough for such a landscape."

"I see indeed in your sketch but one figure, a child."

"Hist! there she stands. Hist! while I put in this last touch."

Kenelm strained his sight, and saw far off a solitary little girl, who was tossing something in the air (he could not distinguish what), and catching it as it fell. She seemed standing on the very verge of the upland, backed by rose-clouds gathering round the setting sun; below lay in confused outlines the great town. In the sketch those outlines seemed infinitely more confused, being only indicated by a few bold strokes; but the figure and face of the child were distinct and lovely. There was an ineffable sentiment in her solitude, there was a depth of quiet enjoyment in her mirthful play, and in her upturned eyes.

"But at that distance," asked Kenelm, when the wanderer had finished his last touch, and, after contemplating it, silently closed his book, and turned round with a genial smile—"but at that distance, how can you distinguish the girl's face? How can you discover that the dim object she has just thrown up and recaught is a ball made of flowers? Do you know the child?"

"I never saw her before this evening; but as I was seated here she was straying around me alone, weaving into chains some wildflowers which she had gathered by the hedgerows yonder, next the high-road; and as she strung them she was chanting to herself some pretty nursery rhymes. You can well understand that when I heard her thus chanting I became interested, and as she came near me I spoke to her, and we soon made friends. She told me she was an orphan, and brought up by a very old man distantly related to her, who had been in some small trade, and now lived in a crowded lane in the heart of the town. He was very kind to her, and being confined himself to the house by age or ailment, he sent her out to play in the fields on summer Sundays. She had no companions of her own age. She said she did not like the other little girls in the lane; and the only little girl she liked at school had a grander station in life, and was not allowed to play with her, so she came out to play alone; and as long as the sun shines and the flowers bloom, she says she never wants other society."

"Tom, do you hear that? As you will be residing in Luscombe, find out this strange little girl, and be kind to her, Tom, for my sake."

Tom put his large hand upon Kenelm's, making no other answer; but he looked hard at the minstrel, recognized the genial charm of his voice and face, and slid along the grass nearer to him.

The minstrel continued: "While the child was talking to me I mechanically took the flower-chains from her hand, and not thinking what I was about, gathered them up into a ball. Suddenly she saw what I had done, and instead of scolding me for spoiling her pretty chains, which I richly deserved, was delighted to find I had twisted them into a new plaything. She ran off with the ball, tossing it about till, excited with her own joy, she got to the brow of the hill, and I began my sketch."

"Is that charming face you have drawn like hers?"

"No; only in part. I was thinking of another face while I sketched, but it is not like that either; in fact, it is one of those patchworks which we call 'fancy heads,' and I meant it to be another version of a thought that I had just put into rhyme, when the child came across me."

"May we hear the rhyme?"

"I fear that if it did not bore yourself it would bore your friend."

"I am sure not. Tom, do you sing?"

"Well, I *have* sung," said Tom, hanging his head sheepishly, "and I should like to hear this gentleman."

"But I do not know these verses, just made, well enough to sing them; it is enough if I can recall them well enough to recite." Here the minstrel paused a minute or so as if for recollection, and then, in the clear sweet tones, and the rare purity of enunciation which characterized his utterance, whether in recital or song, gave to the following verses a touching and a varied expression which no one could discover in merely reading them.

THE FLOWER-GIRL BY THE CROSSING.

By the muddy crossing in the crowded streets
  Stands a little maid with her basket full of posies,
Proffering all who pass her choice of knitted sweets,
  Tempting Age with heart's-ease, courting Youth with roses.

  Age disdains the heart's-ease,
    Love rejects the roses;
  London life is busy—
    Who can stop for posies?

One man is too grave, another is too gay—
  This man has his hothouse, that man not a penny;
Flowerets too are common in the month of May,
  And the things most common least attract the many.

  Ill on London crossings
    Fares the sale of posies;
  Age disdains the heart's-ease,
    Youth rejects the roses.

When the verse-maker had done, he did not pause for approbation, nor look modestly down, as do most people who recite their own verses, but unaffectedly thinking much more of his art than his audience, hurried on somewhat disconsolately—

"I see with great grief that I am better at sketching than rhyming. Can you" (appealing to Kenelm) "even comprehend what I mean by the verses?"

KENELM—"Do you comprehend, Tom?"

TOM (in a whisper).—"No."

KENELM.—"I presume that by his flower-girl our friend means to represent not only Poetry, but a poetry like his own, which is not at all the sort of poetry now in fashion. I, however, expand his meaning, and by his flower-girl I understand any image of natural truth or beauty for which, when we are living the artificial life of crowded streets, we are too busy to give a penny."

"Take it as you please," said the minstrel, smiling and sighing at the same time; "but I have not expressed in words that which I did mean half so well as I have expressed it in my sketch-book."

"Ah! and how?" asked Kenelm.

"The image of my thought in the sketch, be it Poetry or whatever you prefer to call it, does not stand forlorn in the crowded streets—the child stands on the brow of the green hill, with the city stretched in confused fragments below, and, thoughtless of pennies and passers-by, she is playing with the flowers she has gathered—but in play casting them heavenward, and following them with heavenward eyes."

"Good!" muttered Kenelm—"good!" and then, after a long pause, he added, in a still lower mutter, "Pardon me that remark of mine the other day about a beefsteak. But own that I am right—what you call a sketch from Nature is but a sketch of your own thought."

CHAPTER X.

THE child with the flower-ball had vanished from the brow of the hill; sinking down amid the streets below, the rose-clouds had faded from the horizon; and night was closing round, as the three men entered the thick of the town. Tom pressed Kenelm to accompany him to his uncle's, promising him a hearty welcome and bed and board, but Kenelm declined. He entertained a strong persuasion that it would be better for the desired effect on Tom's mind that he should be left alone with his relations that night, but proposed that they should spend the next day together, and agreed to call at the veterinary surgeon's in the morning.

When Tom quitted them at his uncle's door, Kenelm said to the minstrel, "I suppose you are going to some inn—may I accompany you? We can sup together, and I should like to hear you talk upon poetry and Nature."

"You flatter me much; but I have friends in the town, with whom I lodge, and they are expecting me. Do you not observe that I have changed my dress? I am not known here as the 'Wandering Minstrel.'"

Kenelm glanced at the man's attire, and for the first time observed the change. It was still picturesque in its way, but it was such as gentlemen of the highest rank frequently wear in the country—the knickerbocker costume—very neat, very new, and complete, to the square-toed shoes with their latchets and buckles.

"I fear," said Kenelm, gravely, "that your change of dress betokens the neighbourhood of those pretty girls of whom you spoke in an earlier meeting. According to the Darwinian doctrine of selection, fine plumage goes far in deciding the preference of Jenny Wren and her sex, only we are told that fine-feathered birds are very seldom songsters as well. It is rather unfair to rivals when you unite both attractions."

The minstrel laughed. "There is but one girl in my friend's house—his niece; she is very plain, and only thirteen. But to me the society of women, whether ugly or pretty, is an absolute necessity; and I have been trudging without it for so many days that I can scarcely tell you how my thoughts seemed to shake off the dust of travel when I found myself again in the presence of——"

"Petticoat interest," interrupted Kenelm. "Take care of yourself. My poor friend with whom you found me is a grave warning against petticoat interest, from which I hope to profit. He is passing through a great sorrow; it might have been worse than sorrow. My friend is going to stay in this town. If you are staying here too, pray let him see something of you. It will do him a wondrous good if you can beguile him from this real life into the gardens of poet-land; but do not sing nor talk of love to him."

"I honour all lovers," said the minstrel, with real tenderness in his tone, "and would willingly serve to cheer or comfort your friend, if I could; but I am bound elsewhere, and must leave Luscombe, which I visit on business—money business—the day after to-morrow."

"So, too, must I. At least give us both some hours of your time to-morrow."

"Certainly; from twelve to sunset I shall be roving about—a mere idler. If you will both come with me, it will be a great pleasure to myself. Agreed! Well, then, I will call at your inn to-morrow at twelve; and I recommend for your inn the one facing us—The Golden Lamb. I have heard it recommended for the attributes of civil people and good fare."

Kenelm felt that he here received his *congé*, and well comprehended the fact that the minstrel, desiring to preserve the secret of his name, did not give the address of the family with whom he was a guest.

"But one word more," said Kenelm. "Your host or hostess, if resident here, can, no doubt, from your description of the little girl and the old man her protector, learn the child's address. If so, I should like my companion to make friends with her. Petticoat interest there at least will be innocent and safe. And I know nothing so likely to keep a big, passionate heart like Tom's, now aching with a horrible void, occupied and softened, and turned to directions pure and gentle, as an affectionate interest in a little child."

The minstrel changed colour—he even started.

"Sir, are you a wizard that you say that to me?"

"I am not a wizard, but I guess from your question that you have a little child of your own. So much the better; the child may keep you out of much mischief. Remember the little child. Good evening."

Kenelm crossed the threshold of the Golden Lamb, engaged his room, made his ablutions, ordered, and, with his usual zest, partook of his evening meal; and then, feeling the pressure of that melancholic temperament which he so strangely associated with Herculean constitutions, roused himself up, and seeking a distraction from thought, sauntered forth into the gaslit streets.

It was a large, handsome town—handsomer than Tor-Hadham, on account of its site in a valley surrounded by wooded hills, and watered by the fair stream whose windings we have seen as a brook —handsomer, also, because it boasted a fair cathedral, well cleared to the sight, and surrounded by venerable old houses, the residences of the clergy, or of the quiet lay gentry with mediæval tastes. The main street was thronged with passengers—some soberly returning home from the evening service—some, the younger, lingering in pleasant promenade with their sweethearts or families, or arm in arm with each other, and having the air of bachelors or maidens unattached. Through this street Kenelm passed with an inattentive eye. A turn to the right took him towards the cathedral and its surroundings. There all was solitary. The solitude pleased him, and he lingered long, gazing on the noble church lifting its spires and turrets into the deep blue starry air.

Musingly, then, he strayed on, entering a labyrinth of gloomy lanes, in which, though the shops were closed, many a door stood open, with men of the working class lolling against the threshold, idly smoking their pipes, or women seated on the door-steps gossiping, while noisy children were playing or quarrelling in the kennel. The whole did not present the indolent side of an English Sabbath in the pleasantest and rosiest point of view. Somewhat quickening his steps, he entered a broader street, attracted to it involuntarily by a bright light in the centre. On nearing the light he found that it shone forth from a gin-palace, of which the mahogany doors opened and shut momently, as customers went in and out. It was the handsomest building he had seen in his walk, next to that of the cathedral. "The new civilization *versus* the old," murmured Kenelm. As he so murmured, a hand was laid on his arm with a sort of timid impudence. He looked down and saw a young face, but it had survived the look of youth; it was worn and hard, and the bloom on it was not that of Nature's giving. "Are you kind to-night?" asked a husky voice.

"Kind!" said Kenelm, with mournful tones and softened eyes— "kind! Alas, my poor sister mortal! if pity be kindness, who can see you and not be kind?"

The girl released his arm, and he walked on. She stood some

moments gazing after him till out of sight, then she drew her hand suddenly across her eyes, and retracing her steps, was, in her turn, caught hold of by a rougher hand than hers, as she passed the gin-palace. She shook off the grasp with a passionate scorn, and went straight home. Home! is that the right word? Poor sister mortal!

CHAPTER XI.

AND now Kenelm found himself at the extremity of the town, and on the banks of the river. Small squalid houses still lined the bank for some way, till, nearing the bridge, they abruptly ceased, and he passed through a broad square again into the main street. On the other side of the street there was a row of villa-like mansions, with gardens stretching towards the river.

All around in the thoroughfare was silent and deserted. By this time the passengers had gone home. The scent of night-flowers from the villa-gardens came sweet on the starlit air. Kenelm paused to inhale it, and then lifting his eyes, hitherto downcast, as are the eyes of men in meditative moods, he beheld, on the balcony of the nearest villa, a group of well-dressed persons. The balcony was unusually wide and spacious. On it was a small round table, on which were placed wine and fruits. Three ladies were seated round the table on wire-work chairs, and on the side nearest to Kenelm, one man. In that man, now slightly turning his profile, as if to look towards the river, Kenelm recognized the minstrel. He was still in his picturesque knickerbocker dress, and his clear-cut features, with the clustering curls of hair, and Rubens-like hue and shape of beard, had more than their usual beauty, softened in the light of skies, to which the moon, just risen, added deeper and fuller radiance. The ladies were in evening dress, but Kenelm could not distinguish their faces, hidden behind the minstrel. He moved softly across the street, and took his stand behind a buttress in the low wall of the garden, from which he could have full view of the balcony, unseen himself. In this watch he had no other object than that of a vague pleasure. The whole grouping had in it a kind of scenic romance, and he stopped as one stops before a picture.

He then saw that of the three ladies one was old; another was a slight girl, of the age of twelve or thirteen; the third appeared to be somewhere about seven or eight and twenty. She was dressed with more elegance than the others. On her neck, only partially veiled by a thin scarf, there was the glitter of jewels; and, as she now turned her full face towards the moon, Kenelm saw that she was very handsome—a striking kind of beauty, calculated to fascinate a poet or an artist—not unlike Raffaele's Fornarina, dark, with warm tints.

Now there appeared at the open window a stout, burly, middle-aged gentleman, looking every inch of him a family man, a moneyed man, sleek and prosperous. He was bald, fresh-coloured, and with light whiskers.

"Holloa," he said, in an accent very slightly foreign, and with a loud clear voice, which Kenelm heard distinctly, "Is it not time for you to come in?"

"Don't be so tiresome, Fritz," said the handsome lady, half petulantly, half playfully, in the way ladies address the tiresome spouses they lord it over. "Your friend has been sulking the whole evening, and is only just beginning to be pleasant as the moon rises."

"The moon has a good effect on poets and other mad folks, I daresay," said the bald man, with a good-humoured laugh. "But I can't have my little niece laid up again just as she is on the mend —Annie, come in."

The girl obeyed reluctantly. The old lady rose too.

"Ah, mother, you are wise," said the bald man; "and a game at *euchre* is safer than poetizing in night air." He wound his arm round the old lady with a careful fondness, for she moved with some difficulty as if rather lame. "As for you two sentimentalists and moongazers, I give you ten minutes' law—not more, mind."

"Tyrant!" said the minstrel.

The balcony now held only two forms—the minstrel and the handsome lady. The window was closed, and partially veiled by muslin draperies, but Kenelm caught glimpses of the room within. He could see that the room, lit by a lamp on the centre table, and candles elsewhere, was decorated and fitted up with cost, and in a taste not English. He could see, for instance, that the ceiling was painted, and the walls were not papered, but painted in panels between arabesque pilasters.

"They are foreigners," thought Kenelm, "though the man does speak English so well. That accounts for playing *euchre* of a Sunday evening, as if there were no harm in it. *Euchre* is an American game. The man is called Fritz. Ah! I guess—Germans who have lived a good deal in America; and the verse-maker said he was at Luscombe on pecuniary business. Doubtless his host is a merchant, and the verse-maker in some commercial firm. That accounts for his concealment of name, and fear of its being known that he was addicted, in his holiday, to taste and habits so opposed to his calling."

While he was thus thinking, the lady had drawn her chair close to the minstrel, and was speaking to him with evident earnestness, but in tones too low for Kenelm to hear. Still it seemed to him, by her manner and by the man's look, as if she were speaking in some sort of reproach, which he sought to deprecate. Then he spoke, also in a whisper, and she averted her face for a moment— then she held out her hand, and the minstrel kissed it. Certainly, thus seen, the two might well be taken for lovers; and the soft night, the fragrance of the flowers, silence and solitude, stars and moonlight, all girt them as with an atmosphere of love. Presently the man rose and leaned over the balcony, propping his cheek on his hand, and gazing on the river. The lady rose too, and also leaned over the balustrade, her dark hair almost touching the auburn locks of her companion.

Kenelm sighed. Was it from envy, from pity, from fear? I know not; but he sighed.

After a brief pause, the lady said, still in low tones, but not too low this time to escape Kenelm's fine sense of hearing—

"Tell me those verses again. I must remember every word of them when you are gone."

The man shook his head gently, and answered, but inaudibly.

"Do," said the lady, "set them to music later; and the next time you come I will sing them. I have thought of a title for them."

"What?" asked the minstrel.

"Love's Quarrel."

The minstrel turned his head, and their eyes met, and, in meeting, lingered long. Then he moved away, and with face turned from her and towards the river, gave the melody of his wondrous voice to the following lines:—

LOVE'S QUARREL.

Standing by the river, gazing on the river,
  See it paved with starbeams; heaven is at our feet,
Now the wave is troubled, now the rushes quiver;
  Vanished is the starlight—it was a deceit.

Comes a little cloudlet 'twixt ourselves and heaven,
  And from all the river fades the silver track;
Put thine arms around me, whisper low, "Forgiven!"—
  See how on the river starlight settles back.

When he had finished, still with face turned aside, the lady did not, indeed, whisper "forgiven," nor put her arms around him; but, as if by irresistible impulse, she laid her hand lightly on his shoulder.

The minstrel started.

There came to his ear—he knew not from whence, from whom—"Mischief—mischief! Remember the little child!"

"Hush!" he said, staring round. "Did you not hear a voice?"

"Only yours," said the lady.

"It was our guardian angel's, Amalie. It came in time. We will go within."

CHAPTER XII.

THE next morning betimes, Kenelm visited Tom at his uncle's home. A comfortable and respectable home it was, like that of an owner in easy circumstances. The veterinary surgeon himself was intelligent, and apparently educated beyond the range of his calling; a childless widower, between sixty and seventy, living with a sister, an old maid. They were evidently much attached to Tom, and delighted by the hope of keeping him with them. Tom himself looked rather sad, but not sullen, and his face brightened wonderfully at first sight of Kenelm. That oddity made himself as pleasant and as much like other people as he could in conversing with the old widower and the old maid, and took leave, engaging Tom to be at his inn at half-past twelve, and spend the day with him and the minstrel. He then returned to the Golden Lamb, and waited there for his first visitant, the minstrel.

That votary of the muse arrived punctually at twelve o'clock. His countenance was less cheerful and sunny than usual. Kenelm made no allusion to the scene he had witnessed, nor did his visitor seem to suspect that Kenelm had witnessed it, or been the utterer of that warning voice.

KENELM.—"I have asked my friend Tom Bowles to come a little later, because I wished you to be of use to him, and in order to be so, I should suggest how :——"

THE MINSTREL.—"Pray do."

KENELM.—"You know that I am not a poet, and I do not have much reverence for verse-making, merely as a craft."

THE MINSTREL.—"Neither have I."

KENELM.—"But I have a great reverence for poetry as a priesthood. I felt that reverence for you when you sketched and talked priesthood last evening, and placed in my heart—I hope for ever while it beats—the image of the child on the sunlit hill, high above the abodes of men, tossing her flower-ball heavenward, and with heavenward eyes."

The singer's cheek coloured high, and his lip quivered; he was very sensitive to praise—most singers are.

Kenelm resumed, "I have been educated in the Realistic school, and with realism I am discontented, because in realism as a school there is no truth. It contains but a bit of truth, and that the coldest and hardest bit of it, and he who utters a bit of truth and suppresses the rest of it, tells a lie."

THE MINSTREL (slyly).—"Does the critic who says to me, 'Sing of beefsteak, because the appetite for food is a real want of daily life, and don't sing of art and glory and love, because in daily life a man may do without such ideas,'—tell a lie?"

KENELM.—"Thank you for that rebuke. I submit to it. No doubt I did tell a lie—that is, if I were quite in earnest in my recommendation; and if not in earnest, why——"

THE MINSTREL.—"You belied yourself."

KENELM.—"Very likely. I set out on my travels to escape from shams, and begin to discover that I am a sham *par excellence*. But I suddenly come across you, as a boy dulled by his syntax and his vulgar fractions suddenly comes across a pleasant poem or a picture-book, and feels his wits brighten up. I owe you much; you have done me a world of good."

"I cannot guess how."

"Possibly not, but you have shown me how the realism of Nature herself takes colour and life and soul when seen on the ideal or poetic side of it. It is not exactly the words that you say or sing that do me the good, but they awaken within me new trains of thought, which I seek to follow out. The best teacher is the one who suggests rather than dogmatizes, and inspires his listener with the wish to teach himself. Therefore, O singer! whatever be the worth in critical eyes of your songs, I am glad to remember that you would like to go through the world always singing."

"Pardon me; you forget that I added, 'if life were always young, and the seasons were always summer.'"

"I do not forget. But if youth and summer fade for you, you leave youth and summer behind you as you pass along—behind in hearts which mere realism would make always old, and counting their slothful beats under the gray of a sky without sun or stars; wherefore I pray you to consider how magnificent a mission the singer's is—to harmonize your life with your song, and toss your flowers, as your child does, heavenward, with heavenward eyes. Think only of this when you talk with my sorrowing friend, and you will do him good, as you have done me, without being able to guess how a seeker after the Beautiful, such as you, carries us along with him on his way; so that we, too, look out for beauty, and see it in the wildflowers to which we had been blind before."

Here Tom entered the little sanded parlour where this dialogue had been held, and the three men sallied forth, taking the shortest cut from the town into the fields and woodlands.

CHAPTER XIII.

WHETHER or not his spirits were raised by Kenelm's praise and exhortations, the minstrel that day talked with a charm that spell-bound Tom, and Kenelm was satisfied with brief remarks on his side tending to draw out the principal performer.

The talk was drawn from outward things, from natural objects—objects that interest children, and men who, like Tom Bowles, have been accustomed to view surroundings more with the heart's eye than the mind's eye. This rover about the country knew much of the habits of birds and beasts and insects, and told anecdotes of them with a mixture of humour and pathos, which fascinated Tom's attention, made him laugh heartily, and sometimes brought tears into his big blue eyes.

They dined at an inn by the wayside, and the dinner was mirthful; then they wended their way slowly back. By the declining daylight their talk grew somewhat graver, and Kenelm took more part in it. Tom listened mute—still fascinated. At length, as the town came in sight, they agreed to halt awhile, in a bosky nook soft with mosses and sweet with wild thyme.

There, as they lay stretched at their ease, the birds hymning vesper songs amid the boughs above, or dropping, noiseless and fearless, for their evening food on the swards around them, the wanderer said to Kenelm—"You tell me that you are no poet, yet I am sure you have a poet's perception; you must have written poetry?"

"Not I; as I before told you, only school verses in dead languages; but I found in my knapsack this morning a copy of some rhymes, made by a fellow-collegian, which I put into my pocket, meaning to read them to you both. They are not verses like yours, which evidently burst from you spontaneously, and are not imitated from any other poets. These verses were written by a Scotchman, and smack of imitation from the old ballad style. There is little to admire in the words themselves, but there is something in the idea which struck me as original, and impressed me sufficiently to keep a copy, and somehow or other it got into the leaves of one of the two books I carried with me from home."

"What are those books? Books of poetry both, I will venture to wager——"

"Wrong! Both metaphysical, and dry as a bone. Tom, light your pipe, and you, sir, lean more at ease on your elbow; I should warn you that the ballad is long. Patience!"

"Attention!" said the minstrel.

"Fire!" added Tom.

Kenelm began to read—and he read well—

LORD RONALD'S BRIDE.

Part I.

"Why gathers the crowd in the Market-place
  Ere the stars have yet left the sky?"
"For a holiday show and an act of grace—
  At the sunrise a witch shall die."

"What deed has she done to deserve that doom—
  Has she blighted the standing corn,
Or rifled for philtres a dead man's tomb,
  Or rid mothers of babes new-born?"

"Her pact with the Fiend was not thus revealed,
  She taught sinners the Word to hear;
The hungry she fed, and the sick she healed,
  And was held as a Saint last year.

"But a holy man, who at Rome had been,
  Had discovered, by book and bell,
That the marvels she wrought were through arts unclean,
  And the lies of the Prince of Hell.

"And our Mother the Church, for the dame was rich,
  And her husband was Lord of Clyde,
Would fain have been mild to this saint-like witch
  If her sins she had not denied.

"But hush, and come nearer to see the sight,
  Sheriff, halberds, and torchmen—look!
That's the witch, standing mute in her garb of white,
  By the priest with his bell and book."

So the witch was consumed on the sacred pyre,
  And the priest grew in power and pride,
And the witch left a son to succeed his sire
  In the halls and the lands of Clyde.

And the infant waxed comely and strong and brave,
  But his manhood had scarce begun,
When his vessel was launched on the northern wave,
  To the shores which are near the sun.

PART II.

Lord Ronald has come to his halls in Clyde
  With a bride of some unknown race:
Compared with the man who would kiss that bride
  Wallace wight were a coward base.

Her eyes had the glare of the mountain-cat
  When it springs on the hunter's spear;
At the head of the board when that lady sate
  Hungry men could not eat for fear.

And the tones of her voice had the deadly growl
  Of the bloodhound that scents its prey;
No storm was so dark as that lady's scowl
  Under tresses of wintry gray.

"Lord Ronald! men marry for love or gold,
  Mickle rich must have been thy bride!"
"Man's heart may be bought, woman's hand be sold,
  On the banks of our northern Clyde.

"My bride is, in sooth, mickle rich to me
  Though she brought not a groat in dower,
For her face, couldst thou see it as I do see,
  Is the fairest in hall or bower!"

Quoth the bishop one day to our lord the king,
  "Satan reigns on the Clyde alway,
And the taint in the blood of the witch doth cling
  To the child that she brought to-day.

"Lord Ronald hath come from the Paynim land
  With a bride that appals the sight;
Like his dam she hath moles on her dread right hand,
  And she turns to a snake at night.

"It is plain that a Scot who can blindly dote
  On the face of an Eastern ghoul,
And a ghoul who was worth not a silver groat,
  Is a Scot who has lost his soul.

"It were wise to have done with this demon tree
  Which has teemed with such cankered fruit:
Add the soil where it stands to my holy See,
  And consign to the flames its root."

"Holy man!" quoth King James, and he laughed, "we know
  That thy tongue never wags in vain,
But the Church cist is full, and the king's is low,
  And the Clyde is a fair domain.

"Yet a knight that's bewitched by a laidly fere
  Needs not much to dissolve the spell:
We will summon the bride and the bridegroom here,
  Be at hand with thy book and bell."

KENELM CHILLINGLY.

PART III.

Lord Ronald stood up in King James's court,
    And his dame by his dauntless side ;
The barons who came in the hopes of sport
    Shook with fright when they saw the bride.

The bishop, though armed with his bell and book,
    Grew as white as if turned to stone,
It was only our king who could face that look,
    But he spoke with a trembling tone :

"Lord Ronald, the knights of thy race and mine
    Should have mates in their own degree ;
What parentage, say, hath that bride of thine
    Who hath come from the far countree?

"And what was her dowry in gold or land,
    Or what was the charm, I pray,
That a comely young gallant should woo the hand
    Of the ladye we see to-day?"

And the lords would have laughed, but that awful dame
    Struck them dumb with her thunder-frown :
"Saucy king, did I utter my father's name,
    Thou wouldst kneel as his liegeman down.

"Though I brought to Lord Ronald nor lands nor gold,
    Nor the bloom of a fading cheek ;
Yet, were I a widow, both young and old
    Would my hand and my dowry seek.

"For the wish that he covets the most below,
    And would hide from the saints above,
Which he dares not to pray for in weal or woe,
    Is the dowry I bring my love.

"Let every man look in his heart and see
    What the wish he most lusts to win,
And then let him fasten his eyes on me
    While he thinks of his darling sin."

And every man,—bishop, and lord, and king,—
    Thought of that he most wished to win,
And, fixing his eye on that gruesome thing,
    He beheld his own darling sin.

No longer a ghoul in that face he saw,
    It was fair as a boy's first love ;
The voice which had curdled his veins with awe
    Was the coo of the woodland dove.

Each heart was on flame for the peerless dame
    At the price of the husband's life ;
Bright claymores flash out, and loud voices shout,
    "In thy widow shall be my wife."

Then darkness fell over the palace hall,
    More dark and more dark it fell,
And a death-groan boomed hoarse underneath the pall,
    And was drowned amid roar and yell.

When Light through the lattice-pane stole once more,
  It was gray as a wintry dawn,
And the bishop lay cold on the regal floor,
  With a stain on his robes of lawn.

Lord Ronald was standing beside the dead,
  In the scabbard he plunged his sword,
And with visage as wan as the corpse, he said,
  "Lo! my ladye hath kept her word.

"Now I leave her to others to woo and win,
  For no longer I find her fair;
Could I look on the face of my darling sin,
  I should see but a dead man's there.

"And the dowry she brought me is here returned,
  For the wish of my heart has died,
It is quenched in the blood of the priest who burned
  My sweet mother, the Saint of Clyde."

Lord Ronald strode over the stony floor,
  Not a hand was outstretched to stay;
Lord Ronald has passed through the gaping door,
  Not an eye ever traced his way.

And the ladye, left widowed, was prized above
  All the maidens in hall and bower,
Many bartered their lives for that ladye's love,
  And their souls for that ladye's dower.

God grant that the wish which I dare not pray
  Be not that which I lust to win,
And that ever I look with my first dismay
  On the face of my darling sin!

As he ceased, Kenelm's eye fell on Tom's face upturned to his own, with open lips, and intent stare, and paled cheeks, and a look of that higher sort of terror which belongs to awe. The man, then recovering himself, tried to speak, and attempted a sickly smile, but neither would do. He rose abruptly and walked away, crept under the shadow of a dark beech-tree, and stood there leaning against the trunk.

"What say you to the ballad?" asked Kenelm of the singer.

"It is not without power," answered he.

"Ay, of a certain kind."

The minstrel looked hard at Kenelm, and dropped his eyes, with a heightened glow on his cheek.

"The Scotch are a thoughtful race. The Scot who wrote this thing may have thought of a day when he saw beauty in the face of a darling sin; but if so, it is evident that his sight recovered from that glamoury. Shall we walk on? Come, Tom."

The minstrel left them at the entrance of the town, saying, "I regret that I cannot see more of either of you, as I quit Luscombe at daybreak. Here, by the by, I forgot to give it before, is the address you wanted."

KENELM.—"Of the little child. I am glad you remembered her."

The minstrel again looked hard at Kenelm, this time without dropping his eyes. Kenelm's expression of face was so simply quiet that it might be almost called vacant.

Kenelm and Tom continued to walk on towards the veterinary surgeon's house, for some minutes silently. Then Tom said in a whisper, "Did not you mean those rhymes to hit me—*here*," and he struck his breast.

"The rhymes were written long before I saw you, Tom; but it is well if their meaning strike us all. Of you, my friend, I have no fear now. Are you not already a changed man?"

"I feel as if I were going through a change," answered Tom, in slow, dreary accents. "In hearing you and that gentleman talk so much of things that I never thought of, I felt something in me—you will laugh when I tell you—something like a bird."

"Like a bird—good!—a bird has wings."

"Just so."

"And you felt wings that you were unconscious of before, fluttering and beating themselves as against the wires of a cage. You were true to your instincts then, my dear fellow-man—instincts of space and heaven. Courage!—the cage-door will open soon. And now, practically speaking, I give you this advice in parting: you have a quick and sensitive mind which you have allowed that strong body of yours to incarcerate and suppress. Give that mind fair play. Attend to the business of your calling diligently: the craving for regular work is the healthful appetite of mind; but in your spare hours cultivate the new ideas which your talk with men who have been accustomed to cultivate the mind more than the body, has sown within you. Belong to a book-club, and interest yourself in books. A wise man has said, 'Books widen the present by adding to it the past and the future.' Seek the company of educated men and educated women too; and when you are angry with another, reason with him—don't knock him down; and don't be knocked down yourself by an enemy much stronger than yourself— Drink. Do all this, and when I see you again you will be——"

"Stop, sir—you will see me again?"

"Yes, if we both live, I promise it."

"When?"

"You see, Tom, we have both of us something in our old selves which we must work off. You will work off your something by repose, and I must work off mine, if I can, by moving about. So I am on my travels. May we both have new selves better than the old selves, when we again shake hands. For your part try your best, dear Tom, and heaven prosper you."

"And heaven bless you!" cried Tom, fervently, with tears rolling unheeded from his bold blue eyes.

CHAPTER XIV.

THOUGH Kenelm left Luscombe on Tuesday morning, he did not appear at Neesdale Park till the Wednesday, a little before the dressing-bell for dinner. His adventures in the interim are not worth repeating. He had hoped he might fall in again with the minstrel, but he did not.

His portmanteau had arrived, and he heaved a sigh as he cased himself in a gentleman's evening dress, "Alas! I have soon got back again into my own skin."

There were several other guests in the house, though not a large party. They had been asked with an eye to the approaching election, consisting of squires and clergy from remoter parts of the county. Chief among the guests in rank and importance, and rendered by the occasion the central object of interest, was George Belvoir.

Kenelm bore his part in this society with a resignation that partook of repentance.

The first day he spoke very little, and was considered a very dull young man by the lady he took in to dinner. Mr. Travers in vain tried to draw him out. He had anticipated much amusement from the eccentricities of his guest, who had talked volubly enough in the fernery, and was sadly disappointed. "I feel," he whispered to Mrs. Campion, "like poor Lord Pomfret, who, charmed with Punch's lively conversation, bought him, and was greatly surprised that, when he had once brought him home, Punch would not talk."

"But your Punch listens," said Mrs. Campion, "and he observes."

George Belvoir, on the other hand, was universally declared to be very agreeable. Though not naturally jovial, he forced himself to appear so—laughing loud with the squires, and entering heartily with their wives and daughters into such topics as county-balls and croquet-parties; and when after dinner he had, Cato-like, 'warmed his virtue with wine,' the virtue came out very lustily in praise of good men—viz., men of his own party,—and anathema on bad men—viz., men of the other party.

Now and then he appealed to Kenelm, and Kenelm always returned the same answer, "There is much in what you say."

The first evening closed in the usual way in country-houses. There was some lounging under moonlight on the terrace before the house; then there was some singing by young lady amateurs, and a rubber of whist for the elders; then wine-and-water, hand-candlesticks, a smoking-room for those who smoked, and bed for those who did not.

In the course of the evening, Cecilia, partly in obedience to the duties of hostess, and partly from that compassion for shyness which kindly and high-bred persons entertain, had gone a little out of her way to allure Kenelm forth from the estranged solitude he had contrived to weave around him; in vain for the daughter as for the father. He replied to her with the quiet self-possession which should have convinced her that no man on earth was less entitled to indulgence for the gentlemanlike infirmity of shyness, and no man less needed the duties of any hostess for the augmentation of his comforts, or rather for his diminished sense of discomfort; but his replies were in monosyllables, and made with the air of a man who says in his heart, "If this creature would but leave me alone!"

Cecilia, for the first time in her life, was piqued, and, strange to say, began to feel more interest about this indifferent stranger than about the popular, animated, pleasant George Belvoir, whom she knew by womanly instinct was as much in love with her as he could be.

Cecilia Travers that night on retiring to rest told her maid, smilingly, that she was too tired to have her hair done; and yet, when the maid was dismissed, she looked at herself in the glass more gravely and more discontentedly than she had ever looked there before; and, tired though she was, stood at the window gazing into the moonlit night for a good hour after the maid had left her.

CHAPTER XV.

KENELM CHILLINGLY has now been several days a guest at Neesdale Park. He has recovered speech; the other guests have gone, including George Belvoir. Leopold Travers has taken a great fancy to Kenelm. Leopold was one of those men, not uncommon perhaps in England, who, with great mental energies, have a little book-knowledge, and when they come in contact with a book-reader who is not a pedant, feel a pleasant excitement in his society, a source of interest in comparing notes with him, a constant surprise in finding by what venerable authorities the deductions which their own mother-wit has drawn from life are supported; or by what cogent arguments, derived from books, those deductions are contravened or upset. Leopold Travers had in him that sense of humour which generally accompanies a strong practical understanding (no man, for instance, has more practical understanding than a Scot, and no man has a keener susceptibility to humour), and not only enjoyed Kenelm's odd way of expressing himself, but very often mistook Kenelm's irony for opinion spoken in earnest.

Since his early removal from the capital and his devotion to agricultural pursuits, it was so seldom that Leopold Travers met a man by whose conversation his mind was diverted to other subjects than those which were incidental to the commonplace routine of his life, that he found in Kenelm's views of men and things a source of novel amusement, and a stirring appeal to such metaphysical creeds of his own as had been formed unconsciously, and had long reposed unexamined in the recesses of an intellect shrewd and strong, but more accustomed to dictate than to argue. Kenelm, on his side, saw much in his host to like and to admire; but, reversing their relative positions in point of years, he conversed with Travers as with a mind younger than his own. Indeed, it was one of his crotchety theories that each generation is in substance mentally older than the generation preceding it, especially in all that relates to science; and, as he would say, "The study of life is a science, and not an art."

But Cecilia,—what impression did she create upon the young visitor? Was he alive to the charms of her rare beauty, to the grace of a mind sufficiently stored for commune with those who love to think and to imagine, and yet sufficiently feminine and playful to seize the sportive side of realities, and allow their proper place to the trifles which make the sum of human things? An impression she did make, and that impression was new to him and pleasing. Nay, sometimes in her presence, and sometimes when alone, he fell into abstracted consultations with himself, saying, "Kenelm Chillingly, now that thou hast got back into thy proper skin, dost thou not think that thou hadst better remain there? Couldst thou not be contented with thy lot as erring descendant of Adam, if thou couldst win for thy mate so faultless a descendant of Eve as now flits before thee?" But he could not abstract from himself any satisfactory answer to the questions he had addressed to himself.

Once he said abruptly to Travers, as, on their return from their rambles, they caught a glimpse of Cecilia's light form bending over the flower-beds on the lawn, "Do you admire Virgil?"

"To say truth I have not read Virgil since I was a boy; and, between you and me, I then thought him rather monotonous."

"Perhaps because his verse is so smooth in its beauty?"

"Probably. When one is very young one's taste is faulty; and if a poet is not faulty, we are apt to think he wants vivacity and fire."

"Thank you for your lucid explanation," answered Kenelm, adding musingly to himself, "I am afraid I should yawn very often if I were married to a Miss Virgil."

CHAPTER XVI.

THE house of Mr. Travers contained a considerable collection of family portraits, few of them well painted, but the Squire was evidently proud of such evidences of ancestry. They not only occupied a considerable space on the walls of the reception rooms, but swarmed into the principal sleeping chambers, and smiled or frowned on the beholder from dark passages and remote lobbies. One morning Cecilia, on her way to the China Closet, found Kenelm gazing very intently upon a female portrait consigned to one of these obscure receptacles by which through a back staircase he gained the only approach from the hall to his chamber.

"I don't pretend to be a good judge of paintings," said Kenelm, as Cecilia paused beside him; "but it strikes me that this picture is very much better than most of those to which places of honour are assigned in your collection. And the face itself is so lovely, that it would add an embellishment to the princeliest galleries."

"Yes," said Cecilia, with a half-sigh. "The face is lovely, and the portrait is considered one of Lely's rarest masterpieces. It used to hang over the chimney-piece in the drawing-room. My father had it placed here many years ago."

"Perhaps because he discovered it was not a family portrait?"

"On the contrary—because it grieves him to think it is a family portrait. Hush! I hear his footstep; don't speak of it to him; don't let him see you looking at it. The subject is very painful to him."

Here Cecilia vanished into the China Closet, and Kenelm turned off to his own room.

What sin committed by the original in the time of Charles II., but only discovered in the reign of Victoria, could have justified Leopold Travers in removing the most pleasing portrait in the house from the honoured place it had occupied, and banishing it to so obscure a recess? Kenelm said no more on the subject, and indeed an hour afterwards had dismissed it from his thoughts. The next day he rode out with Travers and Cecilia. Their way passed through quiet shady lanes without any purposed direction, when suddenly, at the spot where three of those lanes met on an angle of common ground, a lonely gray tower, in the midst of a wide space of grass land which looked as if it had once been a park, with huge boles of pollarded oak dotting the space here and there, rose before them.

"Cissy!" cried Travers, angrily reining in his horse and stopping short in a political discussion which he had forced upon Kenelm— "Cissy! How comes this! We have taken the wrong turn! No matter, I see there," pointing to the right, "the chimney-pots of old Mondell's homestead. He has not yet promised his vote to George Belvoir. I'll go and have a talk with him. Turn back, you and Mr. Chillingly—meet me at Terner's Green, and wait for me there till I come. I need not excuse myself to you, Chillingly. A vote is a vote." So saying, the Squire, whose ordinary riding-horse was an old hunter, halted, turned, and, no gate being visible, put the horse over a stiff fence and vanished in the direction of old Mondell's chimney-pots. Kenelm, scarcely hearing his host's instructions to Cecilia and excuses to himself, remained still and gazing on the old gray tower thus abruptly obtruded on his view.

Though no learned antiquarian like his father, Kenelm had a strange fascinating interest in all relics of the past; and old gray towers, where they are not church towers, are very rarely to be seen in England. All around the old gray tower spoke with an unutterable mournfulness of a past in ruins: you could see remains of some large Gothic building once attached to it, rising here and there in fragments of deeply-buttressed walls; you could see in a dry ditch, between high ridges, where there had been a fortified moat: nay, you could even see where once had been the bailey hill from which a baron of old had dispensed justice. Seldom indeed does the most acute of antiquarians discover that remnant of Norman times on lands still held by the oldest of Anglo-Norman families. Then, the wild nature of the demesne around; those ranges of sward, with those old giant oak-trunks, hollowed within and pollarded at top; all spoke, in unison with the gray tower, of a past as remote from the reign of Victoria as the Pyramids are from the sway of the Viceroy of Egypt.

"Let us turn back," said Miss Travers; "my father would not like me to stay here."

"Pardon me a moment. I wish my father were here; he would stay till sunset. But what is the history of that old tower?—a history it must have."

"Every home has a history—even a peasant's hut," said Cecilia. "But do pardon me if I ask you to comply with my father's request. I at least must turn back."

Thus commanded, Kenelm reluctantly withdrew his gaze from the ruin and regained Cecilia, who was already some paces in return down the lane.

"I am far from a very inquisitive man by temperament," said Kenelm, "so far as the affairs of the living are concerned. But I should not care to open a book if I had no interest in the past. Pray indulge my curiosity to learn something about that old tower. It could not look more melancholy and solitary if I had built it myself."

"Its most melancholy associations are with a very recent past," answered Cecilia. "The tower, in remote times, formed the keep of a castle belonging to the most ancient and once the most powerful family in these parts. The owners were barons who took active share in the Wars of the Roses. The last of them sided with Richard III., and after the battle of Bosworth the title was attainted, and the larger portion of the lands were confiscated. Loyalty to a Plantagenet was of course treason to a Tudor. But the regeneration of the family rested with their direct descendants, who had saved from the general wreck of their fortunes what may be called a good squire's estate—about, perhaps, the same rental as my father's, but of much larger acreage. These squires, however, were more looked up to in the county than the wealthiest peer. They were still by far the oldest family in the county; and traced in their pedigree alliances with the most illustrious houses in English history. In themselves too, for many generations, they were a high-spirited, hospitable, popular race, living unostentatiously on their income, and contented with their rank of squires. The castle—ruined by time and siege—they did not attempt to restore. They dwelt in a house near to it, built about Elizabeth's time, which you could not see, for it lies in a hollow behind the tower—a moderate-sized, picturesque, country gentleman's house. Our family intermarried with them. The portrait you saw was a daughter of their house. And very proud was any squire in the county of intermarriage with the Fletwodes."

"Fletwode—that was their name? I have a vague recollection of having heard the name connected with some disastrous—oh, but it can't be the same family—pray go on."

"I fear it is the same family. But I will finish the story as I have heard it. The property descended at last to one Bertram Fletwode, who, unfortunately, obtained the reputation of being a very clever man of business. There was some mining company in which, with other gentlemen in the county, he took great interest; invested largely in shares; became the head of the direction——"

"I see; and was, of course, ruined."

"No; worse than that, he became very rich; and, unhappily, became desirous of being richer still. I have heard that there was a great mania for speculations just about that time. He embarked in these, and prospered, till at last he was induced to invest a large share of the fortune thus acquired in the partnership of a bank, which enjoyed a high character. Up to that time he had retained popularity and esteem in the county; but the squires who shared in the adventures of the mining company, and knew little or nothing about other speculations in which his name did not appear, professed to be shocked at the idea of a Fletwode, of Fletwode, being ostensibly joined in partnership with a Jones, of Clapham, in a London bank."

"Slow folks, those country squires,—behind the progress of the age. Well?"

"I have heard that Bertram Fletwode was himself very reluctant to take this step, but was persuaded to do so by his son. This son, Alfred, was said to have still greater talents for business than the father, and had been not only associated with but consulted by him in all the later speculations which had proved so fortunate. Mrs. Campion knew Alfred Fletwode very well. She describes him as handsome, with quick, eager eyes; showy and imposing in his talk; immensely ambitious—more ambitious than avaricious,—collecting money less for its own sake than for that which it could give—rank and power. According to her it was the dearest wish of his heart to claim the old barony, but not before there could go with the barony a fortune adequate to the lustre of a title so ancient, and equal to the wealth of modern peers with higher nominal rank."

"A poor ambition at the best; of the two I should prefer that of a poet in a garret. But I am no judge. Thank heaven I have no ambition. Still, all ambition, all desire to rise, is interesting to him who is ignominiously contented if he does not fall. So the son had his way, and Fletwode joined company with Jones on the road to wealth and the peerage?—meanwhile, did the son marry? if so, of course the daughter of a duke or a millionaire. Tuft-hunting, or money-making, at the risk of degradation and the workhouse. Progress of the age!"

"No," replied Cecilia, smiling at this outburst, but smiling sadly, "Fletwode did not marry the daughter of a duke or a millionaire; but still his wife belonged to a noble family—very poor, but very proud. Perhaps he married from motives of ambition, though not of gain. Her father was of much political influence that might perhaps assist his claim to the barony. The mother, a woman of the world; enjoying a high social position and nearly related to a connection of ours—Lady Glenalvon."

"Lady Glenalvon, the dearest of my lady friends! You are connected with her?"

"Yes; Lord Glenalvon was my mother's uncle. But I wish to finish my story before my father joins us. Alfred Fletwode did not marry till long after the partnership in the bank. His father, at his desire, had bought up the whole business,—Mr. Jones having died. The bank was carried on in the names of Fletwode and Son. But the father had become merely a nominal or what I believe is called a 'sleeping' partner. He had long ceased to reside in the county. The old house was not grand enough for him. He had purchased a palatial residence in one of the home counties; lived there in great splendour; was a munificent patron of science and art; and in spite of his earlier addiction to business-like speculations he appears to have been a singularly accomplished, high-bred gentleman. Some years before his son's marriage, Mr. Fletwode had been afflicted with partial paralysis, and his medical attendant enjoined rigid abstention from business. From that time he never interfered with his son's management of the bank. He had an only daughter, much younger than Alfred. Lord Eagleton, my mother's brother, was engaged to be married to her. The wedding-day was fixed— when the world was startled by the news that the great firm of Fletwode and Son had stopped payment,—is that the right phrase?"

"I believe so."

"A great many people were ruined in that failure. The public indignation was very great. Of course all the Fletwode property went to the creditors. Old Mr. Fletwode was legally acquitted of all other offence than that of over-confidence in his son. Alfred was convicted of fraud—of forgery. I don't, of course, know the particulars,—they are very complicated. He was sentenced to a long term of servitude, but died the day he was condemned—

apparently by poison, which he had long secreted about his person. Now you can understand why my father, who is almost gratuitously sensitive on the point of honour, removed into a dark corner the portrait of Arabella Fletwode,—his own ancestress, but also the ancestress of a convicted felon,—you can understand why the whole subject is so painful to him. His wife's brother was to have married the felon's sister; and though, of course, that marriage was tacitly broken off by the terrible disgrace that had befallen the Fletwodes, yet I don't think my poor uncle ever recovered the blow to his hopes. He went abroad, and died in Madeira, of a slow decline."

"And the felon's sister, did she die too?"

"No; not that I know of. Mrs. Campion says that she saw in a newspaper the announcement of old Mr. Fletwode's death, and a paragraph to the effect that after that event Miss Fletwode had sailed from Liverpool for New York."

"Alfred Fletwode's wife went back, of course, to her family?"

"Alas! no,—poor thing! She had not been many months married when the bank broke; and among his friends her wretched husband appears to have forged the names of the trustees to her marriage settlement, and sold out the sums which would otherwise have served her as a competence. Her father, too, was a great sufferer by the bankruptcy, having by his son-in-law's advice placed a considerable portion of his moderate fortune in Alfred's hands for investment, all of which was involved in the general wreck. I am afraid he was a very hard-hearted man; at at events his poor daughter never returned to him. She died, I think, even before the death of Bertram Fletwode. The whole story is very dismal."

"Dismal indeed, but pregnant with salutary warnings to those who live in an age of progress. Here you see a family of fair fortune, living hospitably, beloved, revered, more looked up to by their neighbours than the wealthiest nobles—no family not proud to boast alliance with it. All at once, in the tranquil record of this happy race, appears that darling of the age, that hero of progress—a clever man of business. He be contented to live as his fathers! He be contented with such trifles as competence, respect, and love! Much too clever for that. The age is money-making—go with the age! He goes with the age. Born a gentleman only, he exalts himself into a trader. But at least he, it seems, if greedy, was not dishonest. He was born a gentleman, but his son was born a trader. The son is a still cleverer man of business; the son is consulted and trusted. Aha! He too goes with the age; to greed he links ambition. The trader's son wishes to return—what? to the rank of gentleman!

—gentleman! nonsense! everybody is a gentleman nowadays—to the title of Lord. How ends it all! Could I sit but for twelve hours in the innermost heart of that Alfred Fletwode—could I see how, step by step from his childhood, the dishonest son was avariciously led on by the honest father to depart from the old *vestigia* of Fletwodes of Fletwode—scorning The Enough to covet The More —gaining The More to sigh 'it is not The Enough'—I think I might show that the age lives in a house of glass, and had better not for its own sake throw stones on the felon!"

"Ah, but, Mr. Chillingly, surely this is a very rare exception in the general——"

"Rare!" interrupted Kenelm, who was excited to a warmth of passion which would have startled his most intimate friend—if indeed an intimate friend had ever been vouchsafed to him—" rare! nay, how common—I don't say to the extent of forgery and fraud, but to the extent of degradation and ruin—is the greed of a Little More to those who have The Enough; is the discontent with competence, respect, and love, when catching sight of a money-bag! How many well-descended county families, cursed with an heir who is called a clever man of business, have vanished from the soil. A company starts—the clever man joins it—one bright day. Pouf! the old estates and the old name are powder. Ascend higher. Take nobles whose ancestral titles ought to be to English ears like the sound of clarions, awakening the most slothful to the scorn of money-bags and the passion for renown. Lo! in that mocking dance of death called the Progress of the Age, one who did not find Enough in a sovereign's revenue, and seeks The Little More as a gambler on the turf by the advice of blacklegs! Lo! another, with lands wider than his greatest ancestors ever possessed, must still go in for The Little More, adding acre to acre, heaping debt upon debt! Lo! a third, whose name, borne by his ancestors, was once the terror of England's foes—the landlord of a hotel! A fourth— but why go on through the list? Another and another still succeeds —each on the Road to Ruin, each in the Age of Progress. Ah, Miss Travers! in the old time it was through the Temple of Honour that one passed to the Temple of Fortune. In this wise age the process is reversed. But here comes your father."

"A thousand pardons!" said Leopold Travers. "That numskull Mondell kept me so long with his old-fashioned Tory doubts whether liberal politics are favourable to agricultural prospects. But as he owes a round sum to a Whig lawyer I had to talk with his wife, a prudent woman; convinced her that his own agricultural prospects were safest on the Whig side of the question; and after kissing his baby and shaking his hand, booked his vote for George Belvoir—a plumper."

"I suppose," said Kenelm to himself, and with that candour which characterized him whenever he talked to himself, "that Travers has taken the right road to the Temple, not of Honour, but of honours, in every country, ancient or modern, which has adopted the system of popular suffrage.

CHAPTER XVII.

THE next day Mrs. Campion and Cecilia were seated under the verandah. They were both ostensibly employed on two several pieces of embroidery, one intended for a screen, the other for a sofa-cushion. But the mind of neither was on her work.

MRS. CAMPION.—"Has Mr. Chillingly said when he means to take leave?"

CECILIA.—"Not to me. How much my dear father enjoys his conversation!"

MRS. CAMPION.—"Cynicism and mockery were not so much the fashion among young men in your father's day as I suppose they are now, and therefore they seem new to Mr. Travers. To me they are not new, because I saw more of the old than the young when I lived in London, and cynicism and mockery are more natural to men who are leaving the world than to those who are entering it."

CECILIA.—"Dear Mrs. Campion, how bitter you are, and how unjust! You take much too literally the jesting way in which Mr. Chillingly expresses himself. There can be no cynicism in one who goes out of his way to make others happy."

MRS. CAMPION.—"You mean in the whim of making an ill-assorted marriage between a pretty village flirt and a sickly cripple, and settling a couple of peasants in a business for which they are wholly unfitted."

CECILIA.—"Jessie Wiles is not a flirt, and I am convinced that she will make Will Somers a very good wife, and that the shop will be a great success."

MRS. CAMPION.—"We shall see. Still, if Mr. Chillingly's talk belies his actions, he may be a good man, but he is a very affected one."

CECILIA.—"Have I not heard you say that there are persons so natural that they seem affected to those who do not understand them?"

Mrs. Campion raised her eyes to Cecilia's face, dropped them again over her work, and said, in grave undertones—

"Take care, Cecilia."

"Take care of what?"

"My dearest child, forgive me; but I do not like the warmth with which you defend Mr. Chillingly."

"Would not my father defend him still more warmly if he had heard you?"

"Men judge of men in their relations to men. I am a woman, and judge of men in their relations to women. I should tremble for the happiness of any woman who joined her fate with that of Kenelm Chillingly."

"My dear friend, I do not understand you to-day."

"Nay; I did not mean to be so solemn, my love. After all, it is nothing to us whom Mr. Chillingly may or may not marry. He is but a passing visitor, and, once gone, the chances are that we may not see him again for years."

Thus speaking, Mrs. Campion again raised her eyes from her work, stealing a sidelong glance at Cecilia; and her mother-like heart sank within her, on noticing how suddenly pale the girl had become, and how her lips quivered. Mrs. Campion had enough knowledge of life to feel aware that she had committed a grievous blunder. In that earliest stage of virgin affection, when a girl is unconscious of more than a certain vague interest in one man which distinguishes him from others in her thoughts,—if she hears him unjustly disparaged, if some warning against him is implied, if the probability that he will never be more to her than a passing acquaintance is forcibly obtruded on her,—suddenly that vague interest, which might otherwise have faded away with many another girlish fancy, becomes arrested, consolidated; the quick pang it occasions makes her involuntarily, and for the first time, question herself, and ask, "Do I love?" But when a girl of a nature so delicate as that of Cecilia Travers can ask herself the question, "Do I love?" her very modesty, her very shrinking from acknowledging that any power over her thoughts for weal or for woe can be acquired by a man, except through the sanction of that love which only becomes divine in her eyes when it is earnest and pure and self-devoted, makes her prematurely disposed to answer "yes." And when a girl of such a nature in her own heart answers "yes" to such a question, even if she deceive herself at the moment, she begins to cherish the deceit till the belief in her love becomes a reality. She has adopted a religion, false or true, and she would despise herself if she could be easily converted.

Mrs. Campion had so contrived that she had forced that question upon Cecilia, and she feared, by the girl's change of countenance, that the girl's heart had answered "yes."

CHAPTER XVIII.

WHILE the conversation just narrated took place, Kenelm had walked forth to pay a visit to Will Somers. All obstacles to Will's marriage were now cleared away; the transfer of lease for the shop had been signed, and the banns were to be published for the first time on the following Sunday. We need not say that Will was very happy. Kenelm then paid a visit to Mrs. Bowles, with whom he stayed an hour. On re-entering the Park, he saw Travers, walking slowly, with downcast eyes, and his hands clasped behind him (his habit when in thought). He did not observe Kenelm's approach till within a few feet of him, and he then greeted his guest in listless accents, unlike his usual cheerful tones.

"I have been visiting the man you have made so happy," said Kenelm.

"Who can that be?"

"Will Somers. Do you make so many people happy that your reminiscence of them is lost in their number?"

Travers smiled faintly, and shook his head.

Kenelm went on. "I have also seen Mrs. Bowles, and you will be pleased to hear that Tom is satisfied with his change of abode; there is no chance of his returning to Graveleigh; and Mrs. Bowles took very kindly to my suggestion that the little property you wish for should be sold to you, and in that case, she would remove to Luscombe to be near her son."

"I thank you much for your thought of me," said Travers, "and the affair shall be seen to at once, though the purchase is no longer important to me. I ought to have told you three days ago, but it slipped my memory, that a neighbouring squire, a young fellow just come into his property, has offered to exchange a capital farm, much nearer to my residence, for the lands I hold in Graveleigh, including Saunderson's farm and the cottages: they are quite at the outskirts of my estate, but run into his, and the exchange will be advantageous to both. Still I am glad that the neighbourhood should be thoroughly rid of a brute like Tom Bowles."

"You would not call him brute if you knew him; but I am sorry to hear that Will Somers will be under another landlord."

"It does not matter, since his tenure is secured for fourteen years."

"What sort of man is the new landlord?"

"I don't know much of him. He was in the army till his father died, and has only just made his appearance in the county. He has, however, already earned the character of being too fond of the other sex, and it is well that pretty Jessie is to be safely married."

Travers then relapsed into a moody silence from which Kenelm found it difficult to rouse him. At length the latter said, kindly—

"My dear Mr. Travers, do not think I take a liberty if I venture to guess that something has happened this morning which troubles or vexes you. When that is the case, it is often a relief to say what it is, even to a confidant so unable to advise or to comfort as myself."

"You are a good fellow, Chillingly, and I know not, at least in these parts, a man to whom I would unburthen myself more freely. I am put out, I confess; disappointed unreasonably, in a cherished wish, and," he added, with a slight laugh, "it always annoys me when I don't have my own way."

"So it does me."

"Don't you think that George Belvoir is a very fine young man?"

"Certainly."

"*I* call him handsome; he is steadier, too, than most men of his age, and of his command of money; and yet he does not want spirit nor knowledge of life. To every advantage of rank and fortune he adds the industry and the ambition which attain distinction in public life."

"Quite true. Is he going to withdraw from the election after all?"

"Good heavens, no!"

"Then how does he not let you have your own way?"

"It is not he," said Travers, peevishly; "it is Cecilia. Don't you understand that George is precisely the husband I would choose for her; and this morning came a very well-written manly letter from him, asking my permission to pay his addresses to her."

"But that is your own way so far."

"Yes, and here comes the balk. Of course I had to refer it to Cecilia, and she positively declines, and has no reasons to give; does not deny that George is good-looking and sensible, that he is a man of whose preference any girl might be proud; but she chooses to say she cannot love him, and when I ask why she cannot love

H

him, has no other answer than that 'she cannot say.' It is too provoking."

"It is provoking," answered Kenelm; "but then Love is the most dunderheaded of all the passions; it never will listen to reason. The very rudiments of logic are unknown to it. 'Love has no wherefore,' says one of those Latin poets who wrote love-verses called elegies—a name which we moderns appropriate to funeral dirges. For my own part, I can't understand how any one can be expected voluntarily to make up his mind to go out of his mind. And if Miss Travers cannot go out of her mind because George Belvoir does, you could not argue her into doing so if you talked till doomsday."

Travers smiled in spite of himself, but he answered gravely,—"Certainly, I would not wish Cissy to marry any man she disliked, but she does not dislike George—no girl could; and where that is the case, a girl so sensible, so affectionate, so well brought up, is sure to love, after marriage, a thoroughly kind and estimable man, especially when she has no previous attachment—which, of course, Cissy never had. In fact, though I do not wish to force my daughter's will, I am not yet disposed to give up my own. Do you understand?"

"Perfectly."

"I am the more inclined to a marriage so desirable in every way, because when Cissy comes out in London—which she has not yet done—she is sure to collect around her face and her presumptive inheritance all the handsome fortune-hunters and titled *vauriens;* and if in love there is no wherefore, how can I be sure that she may not fall in love with a scamp?"

"I think you may be sure of that," said Kenelm. "Miss Travers has too much mind."

"Yes, at present; but did you not say that in love people go out of their mind?"

"True! I forgot that."

"I am not then disposed to dismiss poor George's offer with a decided negative, and yet it would be unfair to mislead him by encouragement. In fact, I'll be hanged if I know how to reply."

"You think Miss Travers does not dislike George Belvoir, and if she saw more of him may like him better, and it would be good for her as well as for him not to put an end to that chance?"

"Exactly so."

"Why not then write: 'My dear George,—You have my best wishes, but my daughter does not seem disposed to marry at present. Let me consider your letter not written, and continue on the same terms as we were before.' Perhaps, as George knows Virgil, you might find your own schoolboy recollections of that poet useful here, and add, '*Varium et mutabile semper femina;*' hackneyed, but true."

"My dear Chillingly, your suggestion is capital. How the deuce at your age have you contrived to know the world so well?"

Kenelm answered in the pathetic tones so natural to his voice, "By being only a looker-on;—alas!"

Leopold Travers felt much relieved after he had written his reply to George. He had not been quite so ingenuous in his revelation to Chillingly as he may have seemed. Conscious, like all proud and fond fathers, of his daughter's attractions, he was not without some apprehension that Kenelm himself might entertain an ambition at variance with that of George Belvoir: if so, he deemed it well to put an end to such ambition while yet in time—partly because his interest was already pledged to George; partly because, in rank and fortune, George was the better match; partly because George was of the same political party as himself—while Sir Peter, and probably Sir Peter's heir, espoused the opposite side; and partly also because, with all his personal liking to Kenelm, Leopold Travers, as a very sensible, practical man of the world, was not sure that a baronet's heir who tramped the country on foot in the dress of a petty farmer, and indulged pugilistic propensities in martial encounters with stalwart farriers, was likely to make a safe husband and a comfortable son-in-law. Kenelm's words, and still more his manner, convinced Travers that any apprehensions of rivalry that he had previously conceived, were utterly groundless.

CHAPTER XIX.

THE same evening, after dinner (during that lovely summer month they dined at Neesdale Park at an unfashionably early hour), Kenelm, in company with Travers and Cecilia, ascended a gentle eminence at the back of the gardens, on which there were some picturesque ivy-grown ruins of an ancient priory, and commanding the best view of a glorious sunset and a subject landscape of vale and wood, rivulet and distant hills.

"Is the delight in scenery," said Kenelm, "really an acquired gift, as some philosophers tell us? is it true that young children and rude savages do not feel it—that the eye must be educated to comprehend its charm, and that the eye can be only educated through the mind?"

"I should think your philosophers are right," said Travers. "When I was a schoolboy, I thought no scenery was like the flat of a cricket ground; when I hunted at Melton, I thought that unpicturesque country more beautiful than Devonshire. It is only of late years that I feel a sensible pleasure in scenery for its own sake, apart from associations of custom or the uses to which we apply them."

"And what say you, Miss Travers?"

"I scarcely know what to say," answered Cecilia, musingly. "I can remember no time in my childhood when I did not feel delight in that which seemed to me beautiful in scenery, but I suspect that I very vaguely distinguished one kind of beauty from another. A common field with daisies and buttercups was beautiful to me then, and I doubt if I saw anything more beautiful in extensive landscapes."

"True," said Kenelm: "it is not in early childhood that we carry the sight into distance: as is the mind so is the eye; in early childhood the mind revels in the present, and the eye rejoices most in the things nearest to it. I don't think in childhood that we

"'Watched with wistful eyes the setting sun.'"

"Ah! what a world of thought in that word '*wistful*'!" murmured Cecilia, as her gaze riveted itself on the western heavens, towards which Kenelm had pointed as he spoke, where the enlarging orb rested half its disc on the rim of the horizon.

She had seated herself on a fragment of the ruin, backed by the hollows of a broken arch. The last rays of the sun lingered on her young face, and then lost themselves in the gloom of the arch behind. There was a silence for some minutes, during which the sun had sunk. Rosy clouds in thin flakes still floated, momently waning; and the eve-star stole forth steadfast, bright, and lonely— nay, lonely not now;—that sentinel has aroused a host.

Said a voice, "No sign of rain yet, Squire. What will become of the turnips?"

"Real life again! Who can escape it?" muttered Kenelm, as his eyes rested on the burly figure of the Squire's bailiff.

"Ha! North," said Travers, "what brings you here? No bad news, I hope."

"Indeed, yes, Squire. The Durham bull——"

"The Durham bull! What of him? You frighten me."

"Taken bad. Colic."

"Excuse me, Chillingly," cried Travers; "I must be off. A

most valuable animal, and no one I can trust to doctor him but myself."

"That's true enough," said the bailiff, admiringly. "There's not a veterinary in the county like the Squire."

Travers was already gone, and the panting bailiff had hard work to catch him up.

Kenelm seated himself beside Cecilia on the ruined fragment.

"How I envy your father!" said he.

"Why just at this moment? Because he knows how to doctor the bull?" said Cecilia, with a sweet low laugh.

"Well, that is something to envy. It is a pleasure to relieve from pain any of God's creatures—even a Durham bull."

"Indeed, yes. I am justly rebuked."

"On the contrary, you are to be justly praised. Your question suggested to me an amiable sentiment in place of the selfish one which was uppermost in my thoughts. I envied your father because he creates for himself so many objects of interest; because while he can appreciate the mere sensuous enjoyment of a landscape and a sunset, he can find mental excitement in turnip crops and bulls. Happy, Miss Travers, is the Practical Man."

"When my dear father was as young as you, Mr. Chillingly, I am sure that he had no more interest in turnips and bulls than you have. I do not doubt that some day you will be as practical as he is in that respect."

"Do you think so—sincerely?"

Cecilia made no answer.

Kenelm repeated the question.

"Sincerely, then, I do not know whether you will take interest in precisely the same things that interest my father; but there are other things than turnips and cattle which belong to what you call 'practical life,' and in these you will take interest, as you took it in the fortunes of Will Somers and Jessie Wiles."

"That was no practical interest. I got nothing by it. But even if that interest were practical—I mean productive, as cattle and turnip crops are—a succession of Somerses and Wileses is not to be hoped for. History never repeats itself."

"May I answer you, though very humbly?"

"Miss Travers, the wisest man that ever existed never was wise enough to know woman; but I think most men ordinarily wise will agree in this, that woman is by no means a humble creature, and that when she says she 'answers very humbly,' she does not mean what she says. Permit me to entreat you to answer very loftily."

Cecilia laughed and blushed. The laugh was musical; the blush was—what? Let any man, seated beside a girl like Cecilia at starry twilight, find the right epithet for that blush. I pass it by epithetless. But she answered, firmly though sweetly—

"Are there not things very practical, and affecting the happiness, not of one or two individuals, but of innumerable thousands, in which a man like Mr. Chillingly cannot fail to feel interest, long before he is my father's age?"

"Forgive me; you do not answer—you question. I imitate you, and ask what are those things as applicable to a man like Mr. Chillingly?"

Cecilia gathered herself up, as with the desire to express a great deal in short substance, and then said—

"In the expression of thought, literature; in the conduct of action, politics."

Kenelm Chillingly stared, dumfounded. I suppose the greatest enthusiast for Woman's Rights could not assert more reverentially than he did the cleverness of women; but among the things which the cleverness of women did not achieve, he had always placed "laconics." "No woman," he was wont to say, "ever invented an axiom or a proverb."

"Miss Travers," he said at last, "before we proceed farther, vouchsafe to tell me if that very terse reply of yours is spontaneous and original; or whether you have not borrowed it from some book which I have not chanced to read?"

Cecilia pondered honestly, and then said, "I don't think it is from any book; but I owe so many of my thoughts to Mrs. Campion, and she lived so much among clever men, that——"

"I see it all, and accept your definition, no matter whence it came. You think I might become an author or a politician. Did you ever read an essay by a living author called 'Motive Power?'"

"No."

"That essay is designed to intimate that without motive power a man, whatever his talents or his culture, does nothing practical. The mainsprings of motive power are Want and Ambition. They are absent from my mechanism. By the accident of birth I do not require bread and cheese; by the accident of temperament and of philosophical culture I care nothing about praise or blame. But without want of bread and cheese, and with a most stolid indifference to praise and blame, do you honestly think that a man will do anything practical in literature or politics? Ask Mrs. Campion."

"I will not ask her. Is the sense of duty nothing?"

"Alas! we interpret duty so variously. Of mere duty, as we commonly understand the word, I do not think I shall fail more than other men. But for the fair development of all the good that is in us, do you believe that we should adopt some line of conduct against which our whole heart rebels? Can you say to the clerk, 'Be a poet?' Can you say to the poet, 'Be a clerk?' It is no more to the happiness of a man's being to order him to take to one career when his whole heart is set on another, than it is to order him to marry one woman when it is to another woman that his heart will turn."

Cecilia here winced and looked away. Kenelm had more tact than most men of his age—that is, a keener perception of subjects to avoid; but then Kenelm had a wretched habit of forgetting the person he talked to and talking to himself. Utterly oblivious of George Belvoir, he was talking to himself now. Not then observing the effect his *mal-à-propos* dogma had produced on his listener, he went on—"Happiness is a word very lightly used. It may mean little—it may mean much. By the word happiness I would signify, not the momentary joy of a child who gets a plaything, but the lasting harmony between our inclinations and our objects; and without that harmony we are a discord to ourselves, we are incompletions, we are failures. Yet there are plenty of advisers who say to us, 'It is a duty to be a discord.' I deny it."

Here Cecilia rose and said in a low voice, "It is getting late. We must go homeward."

They descended the green eminence slowly, and at first in silence. The bats, emerging from the ivied ruins they left behind, flitted and skimmed before them, chasing the insects of the night. A moth, escaping from its pursuer, alighted on Cecilia's breast, as if for refuge.

"The bats are practical," said Kenelm: "they are hungry, and their motive power to-night is strong. Their interest is in the insects they chase. They have no interest in the stars; but the stars lure the moth."

Cecilia drew her slight scarf over the moth, so that it might not fly off and become a prey to the bats. "Yet," said she, "the moth is practical too."

"Ay, just now, since it has found an asylum from the danger that threatened it in its course towards the stars."

Cecilia felt the beating of her heart, upon which lay the moth concealed. Did she think that a deeper and more tender meaning than they outwardly expressed was couched in these words? If so, she erred. They now neared the garden gate, and Kenelm paused as he opened it. "See," he said, "the moon has just risen over those dark firs, making the still night stiller. Is it not strange that we mortals, placed amid perpetual agitation and tumult and strife, as if our natural element, conceive a sense of holiness in the images antagonistic to our real life—I mean in images of repose? I feel at the moment as if I suddenly were made better, now that heaven and earth have suddenly become yet more tranquil. I am now conscious of a purer and sweeter moral than either I or you drew from the insect you have sheltered. I must come to the poets to express it—

> 'The desire of the moth for the star,
> Of the night for the morrow;
> *The devotion to something afar
> From the sphere of our sorrow.*'

Oh, that something afar! that something afar! never to be reached on this earth—never, never!"

There was such a wail in that cry from the man's heart that Cecilia could not resist the impulse of a divine compassion. She laid her hand on his, and looked on the dark mildness of his upward face with eyes that heaven meant to be wells of comfort to grieving man. At the light touch of that hand Kenelm started, looked down, and met those soothing eyes.

"I am happy to tell you that I have saved my Durham," cried out Mr. Travers from the other side of the gate.

CHAPTER XX.

AS Kenelm that night retired to his own room, he paused on the landing-place opposite to the portrait which Mr. Travers had consigned to that desolate exile. This daughter of a race dishonoured in its extinction might well have been the glory of the house she had entered as a bride. The countenance was singularly beautiful, and of a character of beauty eminently patrician; there was in its expression a gentleness and modesty not often found in the female portraits of Sir Peter Lely; and in the eyes and in the smile a wonderful aspect of innocent happiness.

"What a speaking homily," soliloquized Kenelm, addressing the picture, "against the ambition thy fair descendant would awake in me, art thou, O lovely image! For generations thy beauty lived in this canvas, a thing of joy, the pride of the race it adorned. Owner after owner said to admiring guests, 'Yes, a fine portrait, by Lely; she was my ancestress—a Fletwode of Fletwode.' Now, lest guests should remember that a Fletwode married a Travers, thou art thrust out of sight; not even Lely's art can make thee of value, can redeem thine innocent self from disgrace. And the last of the Fletwodes, doubtless the most ambitious of all—the most bent on restoring and regilding the old lordly name—dies a felon; the infamy of one living man so large that it can blot out the honour of the dead." He turned his eyes from the smile of the portrait, entered his own room, and, seating himself by the writing-table, drew blotting-book and note-paper towards him, took up the pen, and instead of writing fell into deep reverie. There was a slight frown on his brow, on which frowns were rare. He was very angry with himself.

"Kenelm," he said, entering into his customary dialogue with that self, "it becomes you, forsooth, to moralize about the honour of races which have no affinity with you. Son of Sir Peter Chillingly, look at home. Are you quite sure that you have not said or done or looked a something that may bring trouble to the hearth on which you are received as guest? What right had you to be moaning forth your egotisms, not remembering that your words fell on compassionate ears, and that such words, heard at moonlight by a girl whose heart they move to pity, may have dangers for her peace. Shame on you, Kenelm! shame! knowing too what her father's wish is; and knowing too that you have not the excuse of desiring to win that fair creature for yourself. What do you mean, Kenelm? I don't hear you; speak out. Oh, 'that I am a vain coxcomb to fancy that she could take a fancy to me'—well, perhaps I am; I hope so earnestly; and, at all events, there has been and shall be no time for much mischief. We are off to-morrow, Kenelm; bestir yourself and pack up, write your letters, and then 'put out the light—put out *the* light!'"

But this converser with himself did not immediately set to work, as agreed upon by that twofold one. He rose and walked restlessly to and fro the floor, stopping ever and anon to look at the pictures on the walls.

Several of the worst painted of the family portraits had been consigned to the room tenanted by Kenelm, which, though both the oldest and largest bedchamber in the house, was always appropriated to a bachelor male guest, partly because it was without dressing-room, remote, and only approached by the small back staircase, to the landing-place of which Arabella had been banished in disgrace; and partly because it had the reputation of being haunted, and ladies are more alarmed by that superstition than men are supposed to be. The portraits on which Kenelm now paused to gaze were of various dates, from the reign of Elizabeth to that of George III., none of them by eminent artists, and none of them the effigies of ancestors who had left names in history—in short, such portraits as are often seen in the country houses of well-born squires. One family type of feature or expression pervaded most of these portraits—features clear-cut and hardy, expression open and honest. And though not one of those dead men had been famous, each of them had contributed his unostentatious share, in his own simple way, to the movements of his time. That worthy in ruff and corselet had manned his own ship at his own cost against the Armada; never had been repaid by the thrifty Burleigh the expenses which had harassed him and diminished his patrimony; never had been even knighted. That gentleman with short straight hair, which overhung his forehead, leaning on his sword with one hand, and a book open in the other hand, had served as representative of his county town in the Long Parliament, fought under Cromwell at Marston Moor, and resisting the Protector when he removed the 'bauble,' was one of the patriots incarcerated in "Hell hole." He, too, had diminished his patrimony, maintaining two troopers and two horses at his own charge, and "Hell hole" was all he got in return. A third, with a sleeker expression of countenance, and a large wig, flourishing in the quiet times of Charles II., had only been a justice of the peace, but his alert look showed that he had been a very active one. He had neither increased nor diminished his ancestral fortune. A fourth, in the costume of William III.'s reign, had somewhat added to the patrimony by becoming a lawyer. He must have been a successful one. He is inscribed "Serjeant at law." A fifth, a lieutenant in the army, was killed at Blenheim; his portrait was that of a very young and handsome man, taken the year before his death. His wife's portrait is placed in the drawing-room because it was painted by Kneller. She was handsome too, and married again a nobleman, whose portrait, of course, was not in the family collection. Here there was a gap in chronological arrangement, the lieutenant's heir being an infant; but in the time of George II. another Travers appeared as the governor of a West India colony. His son took part in a very different movement of the age. He is represented old, venerable, with white hair, and underneath his effigy is inscribed, "Follower of Wesley." His successor completes the collection. He is in naval uniform; he is in full length, and one of his legs is a wooden one. He is Captain, R.N., and inscribed, "Fought under Nelson at Trafalgar." That portrait would have found more dignified place in the reception-rooms if the face had not been forbiddingly ugly, and the picture itself a villainous daub.

"I see," said Kenelm, stopping short, "why Cecilia Travers has been reared to talk of duty as a practical interest in life. These men of a former time seem to have lived to discharge a duty, and not to follow the progress of the age in the chase of a money-bag—except perhaps one, but then to be sure he was a lawyer. Kenelm, rouse up and listen to me; whatever we are, whether active or indolent, is not my favourite maxim a just and a true one—viz., 'A good man does good by living'? But, for that, he must be a harmony and not a discord. Kenelm, you lazy dog, we must pack up."

Kenelm then refilled his portmanteau, and labelled and directed it to Exmundham, after which he wrote these three notes:—

Note 1.

TO THE MARCHIONESS OF GLENALVON.

"My dear Friend and Monitress,—I have left your last letter a month unanswered. I could not reply to your congratulations on the event of my attaining the age of twenty-one. That event is a conventional sham, and you know how I abhor shams and conventions. The truth is, that I am either much younger than twenty-one or much older. As to all designs on my peace in standing for our county at the next election, I wished to defeat them, and I have done so; and now I have commenced a course of travel. I had intended on starting to confine it to my native country. Intentions are mutable. I am going abroad. You shall hear of my whereabout. I write this from the house of Leopold Travers, who, I understand from his fair daughter, is a connection of yours;—a man to be highly esteemed and cordially liked.

"No, in spite of all your flattering predictions, I shall never be anything in this life more distinguished than what I am now. Lady Glenalvon allows me to sign myself her grateful friend, K. C."

Note 2.

"Dear Cousin Mivers,—I am going abroad. I may want money; for, in order to rouse motive power within me, I mean to want money if I can. When I was a boy of sixteen you offered me money to write attacks upon veteran authors for 'The Londoner.' Will you give me money now for a similar display of that grand New Idea of our generation—viz., that the less a man knows of a subject the better he understands it? I am about to travel into countries which I have never seen, and among races I have never known. My arbitrary judgments on both will be invaluable to 'The Londoner' from a Special Correspondent who shares your respect for the anonymous, and whose name is never to be divulged. Direct your answer by return to me, *poste restante*, Calais.—Yours truly, K. C."

Note 3.

"MY DEAR FATHER,—I found your letter here, whence I depart to-morrow. Excuse haste. I go abroad, and shall write to you from Calais.

"I admire Leopold Travers very much. After all, how much of self-balance there is in a true English gentleman! Toss him up and down where you will, and he always alights on his feet—a gentleman. He has one child, a daughter named Cecilia—handsome enough to allure into wedlock any mortal whom Decimus Roach had not convinced that in celibacy lay the right 'Approach to the Angels.' Moreover, she is a girl whom one can talk with. Even you could talk with her. Travers wishes her to marry a very respectable, good-looking, promising gentleman, in every way 'suitable,' as they say. And if she does, she will rival that pink and perfection of polished womanhood, Lady Glenalvon. I send you back my portmanteau. I have pretty well exhausted my experience-money, but have not yet encroached on my monthly allowance. I mean still to live upon that, eking it out, if necessary, by the sweat of my brow—or brains. But if any case requiring extra funds should occur—a case in which that extra would do such real good to another that I feel *you* would do it—why, I must draw a cheque on your bankers. But understand that is your expense, not mine, and it is *you* who are to be repaid in heaven. Dear father, how I do love and honour you every day more and more! Promise you not to propose to any young lady till I come first to you for consent!—oh, my dear father, how could you doubt it? how doubt that I could not be happy with any wife whom you could not love as a daughter? Accept that promise as sacred. But I wish you had asked me something in which obedience was not much too facile to be a test of duty. I could not have obeyed you more cheerfully if you had asked me to promise never to propose to any young lady at all. Had you asked me to promise that I would renounce the dignity of reason for the frenzy of love, or the freedom of man for the servitude of husband, then I might have sought to achieve the impossible; but I should have died in the effort!—and thou wouldst have known that remorse which haunts the bed of the tyrant.—Your affectionate son,

"K. C."

CHAPTER XXI.

THE next morning Kenelm surprised the party at breakfast by appearing in the coarse habiliments in which he had first made his host's acquaintance. He did not glance towards Cecilia when he announced his departure; but, his eye resting on Mrs. Campion, he smiled, perhaps a little sadly, at seeing her countenance brighten up and hearing her give a short sigh of relief. Travers tried hard to induce him to stay a few days longer, but Kenelm was firm. "The summer is wearing away," said he, "and I have far to go before the flowers fade and the snows fall. On the third night from this I shall sleep on foreign soil."

"You are going abroad, then?" asked Mrs. Campion.

"Yes."

"A sudden resolution, Mr. Chillingly. The other day you talked of visiting the Scotch lakes."

"True; but on reflection, they will be crowded with holiday tourists, many of whom I shall probably know. Abroad I shall be free, for I shall be unknown."

"I suppose you will be back for the hunting season," said Travers.

"I think not. I do not hunt foxes."

"Probably we shall at all events meet in London," said Travers. "I think, after long rustication, that a season or two in the bustling capital may be a salutary change for mind as well as for body! and it is time that Cecilia were presented and her court-dress specially commemorated in the columns of the 'Morning Post.'"

Cecilia was seemingly too busied behind the tea-urn to heed this reference to her *début*.

"I shall miss you terribly," cried Travers, a few moments afterwards, and with a hearty emphasis. "I declare that you have quite unsettled me. Your quaint sayings will be ringing in my ears long after you are gone."

There was a rustle as of a woman's dress in sudden change of movement behind the tea-urn.

"Cissy," said Mrs. Campion, "are we ever to have our tea?"

"I beg pardon," answered a voice behind the urn. "I hear Pompey" (the Skye terrier) "whining on the lawn. They have shut him out. I will be back presently."

Cecilia rose and was gone. Mrs. Campion took her place at the tea-urn.

"It is quite absurd of Cissy to be so fond of that hideous dog," said Travers, petulantly.

"Its hideousness is its beauty," returned Mrs. Campion, laughing. "Mr. Belvoir selected it for her as having the longest back and the shortest legs of any dog he could find in Scotland."

"Ah, George gave it to her; I forgot that," said Travers, laughing pleasantly.

It was some minutes before Miss Travers returned with the Skye terrier, and she seemed to have recovered her spirits in regaining that ornamental accession to the party—talking very quickly and gaily, and with flushed cheeks, like a young person excited by her own overflow of mirth.

But when, half an hour afterwards, Kenelm took leave of her and Mrs. Campion at the hall-door, the flush was gone, her lips were tightly compressed, and her parting words were not audible. Then, as his figure (side by side with her father, who accompanied his guest to the lodge) swiftly passed across the lawn and vanished amid the trees beyond, Mrs. Campion wound a mother-like arm around her waist and kissed her. Cecilia shivered and turned her face to her friend smiling; but such a smile,—one of those smiles that seem brimful of tears.

"Thank you, dear," she said, meekly; and gliding away towards the flower-garden, lingered a while by the gate which Kenelm had opened the night before. Then she went with languid steps up the green slopes towards the ruined priory.

BOOK IV.

CHAPTER I.

IT is somewhat more than a year and a half since Kenelm Chillingly left England, and the scene now is in London, during that earlier and more sociable season which precedes the Easter holidays—season in which the charm of intellectual companionship is not yet withered away in the heated atmosphere of crowded rooms—season in which parties are small, and conversation extends beyond the interchange of commonplace with one's next neighbour at a dinner-table—season in which you have a fair chance of finding your warmest friends not absorbed by the superior claims of their chilliest acquaintances.

There was what is called a conversazione at the house of one of those Whig noblemen who yet retain the graceful art of bringing agreeable people together, and collecting round them the true aristocracy, which combines letters and art and science with hereditary rank and political distinction—that art which was the happy secret of the Lansdownes and Hollands of the last generation. Lord Beaumanoir was himself a genial, well-read man, a good judge of art, and a pleasant talker. He had a charming wife, devoted to him and to her children, but with enough love of general approbation to make herself as popular in the fashionable world as if she sought in its gaieties a refuge from the dulness of domestic life.

Amongst the guests at the Beaumanoirs this evening were two men, seated apart in a small room, and conversing familiarly. The one might be about fifty-four; he was tall, strongly built, but not corpulent, somewhat bald, with black eyebrows, dark eyes, bright and keen, mobile lips, round which there played a shrewd and sometimes sarcastic smile.

This gentleman, the Right Hon. Gerard Danvers, was a very influential member of Parliament. He had, when young for English public life, attained to high office; but—partly from a great distaste to the drudgery of administration; partly from a pride of temperament, which unfitted him for the subordination that a Cabinet owes to its chief; partly, also, from a not uncommon kind of epicurean philosophy, at once joyous and cynical, which sought the pleasures of life and held very cheap its honours—he had obstinately declined to re-enter office, and only spoke on rare occasions. On such occasions he carried great weight, and, by the brief expression of his opinions, commanded more votes than many an orator infinitely more eloquent. Despite his want of ambition, he was fond of power in his own way—power over the people who *had* power; and, in the love of political intrigue, he found an amusement for an intellect very subtle and very active. At this moment he was bent on a new combination among the leaders of different sections in the same party by which certain veterans were to retire, and certain younger men to be admitted into the Administration. It was an amiable feature in his character that he had a sympathy with the young, and had helped to bring into Parliament, as well as into office, some of the ablest of a generation later than his own. He gave them sensible counsel, was pleased when they succeeded, and encouraged them when they failed—always provided that they had stuff enough in them to redeem the failure; if not, he gently dropped them from his intimacy, but maintained sufficiently familiar terms with them to be pretty sure that he could influence their votes whenever he so desired.

The gentleman with whom he was now conversing was young, about five-and-twenty—not yet in Parliament, but with an intense desire to obtain a seat in it, and with one of those reputations which a youth carries away from school and college, justified, not by honours purely academical, but by an impression of ability and power created on the minds of his contemporaries, and endorsed by his elders. He had done little at the university beyond taking a fair degree—except acquiring at the Debating Society the fame of an exceedingly ready and adroit speaker. On quitting college he had written one or two political articles in a quarterly review which created a sensation; and though belonging to no profession, and having but a small yet independent income, society was very civil to him, as to a man who would some day or other attain a position in which he could damage his enemies and serve his friends. Something in this young man's countenance and bearing tended to favour the credit given to his ability and his promise. In his countenance there was no beauty; in his bearing no elegance. But in that countenance there was vigour—there was energy—there was audacity. A forehead wide but low, protuberant in those organs over the brow which indicate the qualities fitted for perception and judgment— qualities for everyday life; eyes of the clear English blue, small, somewhat sunken, vigilant, sagacious, penetrating; a long straight upper lip, significant of resolute purpose; a mouth in which a student of physiognomy would have detected a dangerous charm.

The smile was captivating, but it was artificial, surrounded by dimples, and displaying teeth white, small, strong, but divided from each other. The expression of that smile would have been frank and candid to all who failed to notice that it was not in harmony with the brooding forehead and the steely eye—that it seemed to stand distinct from the rest of the face, like a feature that had learned its part. There was that physical power in the back of the head which belongs to men who make their way in life—combative and destructive. All gladiators have it; so have great debaters and great reformers—that is, reformers who can destroy, but not necessarily reconstruct. So, too, in the bearing of the man there was a hardy self-confidence, much too simple and unaffected for his worst enemy to call it self-conceit. It was the bearing of one who knew how to maintain personal dignity without seeming to care about it. Never servile to the great, never arrogant to the little; so little over-refined that it was never vulgar,—a popular bearing.

The room in which these gentlemen were seated was separated from the general suite of apartments by a lobby off the landing-place, and served for Lady Beaumanoir's boudoir. Very pretty it was, but simply furnished, with chintz draperies. The walls were adorned with drawings in water-colours, and precious specimens of china on fanciful Parian brackets. At one corner, by a window that looked southward and opened on a spacious balcony, glazed in and filled with flowers, stood one of those high trellised screens, first invented, I believe, in Vienna, and along which ivy is so trained as to form an arbour.

The recess thus constructed, and which was completely out of sight from the rest of the room, was the hostess's favourite writing nook. The two men I have described were seated near the screen, and had certainly no suspicion that any one could be behind it.

"Yes," said Mr. Danvers, from an ottoman niched in another recess of the room, "I think there will be an opening at Saxboro' soon; Milroy wants a colonial Government; and if we can reconstruct the Cabinet as I propose, he would get one. Saxboro' would thus be vacant. But, my dear fellow, Saxboro' is a place to be wooed through love, and only won through money. It demands liberalism from a candidate—two kinds of liberalism seldom united; the liberalism in opinion which is natural enough to a very poor man, and the liberalism in expenditure which is scarcely to be obtained except from a very rich one. You may compute the cost of Saxboro' at £3000 to get in, and about £2000 more to defend your seat against a petition—the defeated candidate nearly always petitions. £5000 is a large sum; and the worst of it is, that the extreme opinions to which the member for Saxboro' must pledge himself are a drawback to an official career. Violent politicians are not the best raw material out of which to manufacture fortunate placemen."

"The opinions do not so much matter; the expense does. I cannot afford £5000, or even £3000."

"Would not Sir Peter assist? He has, you say, only one son; and if anything happen to that son, you are the next heir."

"My father quarrelled with Sir Peter, and harassed him by an imprudent and ungracious litigation. I scarcely think I could apply to him for money to obtain a seat in Parliament upon the democratic side of the question; for though I know little of his politics, I take it for granted that a country gentleman of old family and £10,000 a-year cannot well be a democrat."

"Then I presume you would not be a democrat if, by the death of your cousin, you became heir to the Chillinglys."

"I am not sure what I might be in that case. There are times when a democrat of ancient lineage and good estates could take a very high place amongst the aristocracy."

"Humph! my dear Gordon, *vous irez loin.*"

"I hope to do so. Measuring myself against the men of my own day, I do not see many who should outstrip me."

"What sort of a fellow is your cousin Kenelm? I met him once or twice when he was very young, and reading with Welby in London. People then said that he was very clever; he struck me as very odd."

"I never saw him; but from all I hear, whether he be clever or whether he be odd, he is not likely to do anything in life—a dreamer."

"Writes poetry perhaps?"

"Capable of it, I dare say."

Just then some other guests came into the room, amongst them a lady of an appearance at once singularly distinguished and singularly prepossessing, rather above the common height, and with a certain indescribable nobility of air and presence. Lady Glenalvon was one of the queens of the London world, and no queen of that world was ever less worldly or more queen-like. Side by side with the lady was Mr. Chillingly Mivers. Gordon and Mivers interchanged friendly nods, and the former sauntered away and was soon lost amid a crowd of other young men, with whom, as he could converse well and lightly on things which interested them, he was rather a favourite, though he was not an intimate associate. Mr. Danvers retired into a corner of the adjoining lobby, where he favoured the French ambassador with his views on the state of Europe and the reconstruction of Cabinets in general.

"But," said Lady Glenalvon to Chillingly Mivers, "are you quite sure that my old young friend Kenelm is here? Since you told me so, I have looked everywhere for him in vain. I should so much like to see him again."

"I certainly caught a glimpse of him half an hour ago; but before I could escape from a geologist, who was boring me about the Silurian system, Kenelm had vanished."

"Perhaps it was his ghost!"

"Well, we certainly live in the most credulous and superstitious age upon record; and so many people tell me that they converse with the dead under the table, that it seems impertinent in me to say that I don't believe in ghosts."

"Tell me some of those incomprehensible stories about table-rapping," said Lady Glenalvon. "There is a charming snug recess here behind the screen."

Scarcely had she entered the recess than she drew back with a start and an exclamation of amaze. Seated at the table within the recess, his chin resting on his hand, and his face cast down in abstracted reverie, was a young man. So still was his attitude, so calmly mournful the expression of his face, so estranged did he seem from all the motley but brilliant assemblage which circled around the solitude he had made for himself, that he might well have been deemed one of those visitants from another world whose secrets the intruder had wished to learn. Of that intruder's presence he was evidently unconscious. Recovering her surprise, she stole up to him, placed her hand on his shoulder, and uttered his name in a low gentle voice. At that sound Kenelm Chillingly looked up.

"Do you not remember me?" asked Lady Glenalvon. Before he could answer, Mivers, who had followed the Marchioness into the recess, interposed.

"My dear Kenelm, how are you? When did you come to London? Why have you not called on me; and what on earth are you hiding yourself for?"

Kenelm had now recovered the self-possession which he rarely lost long in the presence of others. He returned cordially his kinsman's greeting, and kissed with his wonted chivalrous grace the fair hand which the lady withdrew from his shoulder and extended to his pressure. "Remember you!" he said to Lady Glenalvon, with the kindliest expression of his soft dark eyes; "I am not so far advanced towards the noon of life as to forget the sunshine that brightened its morning. My dear Mivers, your questions are easily answered. I arrived in England two weeks ago, stayed at Exmundham till this morning, to-day dined with Lord Thetford, whose acquaintance I made abroad, and was persuaded by him to come here and be introduced to his father and mother, the Beaumanoirs. After I had undergone that ceremony, the sight of so many strange faces frightened me into shyness. Entering this room at a moment when it was quite deserted, I resolved to turn hermit behind the screen."

"Why, you must have seen your cousin Gordon as you came into the room."

"But you forget I don't know him by sight. However, there was no one in the room when I entered; a little later some others came in, for I heard a faint buzz, like that of persons talking in a whisper. However, I was no eavesdropper, as a person behind a screen is on the dramatic stage."

This was true. Even had Gordon and Danvers talked in a louder tone, Kenelm had been too absorbed in his own thoughts to have heard a word of their conversation.

"You ought to know young Gordon; he is a very clever fellow, and has an ambition to enter Parliament. I hope no old family quarrel between his bear of a father and dear Sir Peter will make you object to meet him."

"Sir Peter is the most forgiving of men, but he would scarcely forgive me if I declined to meet a cousin who had never offended him."

"Well said. Come and meet Gordon at breakfast to-morrow— ten o'clock. I am still in the old rooms."

While the kinsmen thus conversed, Lady Glenalvon had seated herself on the couch beside Kenelm, and was quietly observing his countenance. Now she spoke: "My dear Mr. Mivers, you will have many opportunities of talking with Kenelm; do not grudge me five minutes' talk with him now."

"I leave your ladyship alone in your hermitage. How all the men in this assembly will envy the hermit!"

CHAPTER II.

"I AM glad to see you once more in the world," said Lady Glenalvon, "and I trust that you are now prepared to take that part in it, which ought to be no mean one if you do justice to your talents and your nature."

KENELM.—"When you go to the theatre, and see one of the pieces which appear now to be the fashion, which would you rather be—an actor or a looker-on?"

LADY GLENALVON.—"My dear young friend, your question saddens me." (After a pause.)—"But though I used a stage metaphor when I expressed my hope that you would take no mean part in the world, the world is not really a theatre. Life admits of no lookers-on. Speak to me frankly, as you used to do. Your face retains its old melancholy expression. Are you not happy?"

KENELM.—"Happy, as mortals go, I ought to be. I do not think I am unhappy. If my temper be melancholic, melancholy has a happiness of its own. Milton shows that there are as many charms in life to be found on the Penseroso side of it as there are on the Allegro."

LADY GLENALVON.—"Kenelm, you saved the life of my poor son, and when, later, he was taken from me, I felt as if he had commended you to my care. When at the age of sixteen, with a boy's years and a man's heart, you came to London, did I not try to be to you almost as a mother? and did you not often tell me that you could confide to me the secrets of your heart more readily than to any other?"

"You were to me," said Kenelm, with emotion, "that most precious and sustaining good genius which a youth can find at the threshold of life—a woman gently wise, kindly sympathizing, shaming him by the spectacle of her own purity from all grosser errors, elevating him from mean tastes and objects by the exquisite, ineffable loftiness of soul which is only found in the noblest order of womanhood. Come, I will open my heart to you still. I fear it is more wayward than ever. It still feels estranged from the companionship and pursuits natural to my age and station. However, I have been seeking to brace and harden my nature, for the practical ends of life, by travel and adventure, chiefly among rougher varieties of mankind than we meet in drawing-rooms. Now, in compliance with the duty I owe to my dear father's wishes, I come back to these circles, which under your auspices I entered in boyhood, and which even then seemed to me so inane and artificial. Take a part in the world of these circles; such is your wish. My answer is brief. I have been doing my best to acquire a motive power, and I have not succeeded. I see nothing that I care to strive for, nothing that I care to gain. The very times in which we live are to me as to Hamlet—out of joint; and I am not born like Hamlet to set them right. Ah! if I could look on society through the spectacles with which the poor hidalgo in 'Gil Blas' looked on his meagre board—spectacles by which cherries appeared the size of peaches, and tomtits as large as turkeys! The imagination which is necessary to ambition is a great magnifier."

"I have known more than one man, now very eminent, very active, who at your age felt the same estrangement from the practical pursuits of others."

"And what reconciled those men to such pursuits?"

"That diminished sense of individual personality, that unconscious fusion of one's own being into other existences, which belong to home and marriage."

"I don't object to home, but I do to marriage."

"Depend on it there is no home for man where there is no woman."

"Prettily said. In that case I resign the home."

"Do you mean seriously to tell me that you never see the woman you could love enough to make her your wife, and never enter any home that you do not quit with a touch of envy at the happiness of married life?"

"Seriously, I never see such a woman; seriously, I never enter such a home."

"Patience, then; your time will come, and I hope it is at hand. Listen to me. It was only yesterday that I felt an indescribable longing to see you again—to know your address that I might write to you; for yesterday, when a certain young lady left my house, after a week's visit, I said, this girl would make a perfect wife, and, above all, the exact wife to suit Kenelm Chillingly."

"Kenelm Chillingly is very glad to hear that this young lady has left your house."

"But she has not left London—she is here to-night. She only stayed with me till her father came to town, and the house he had taken for the season was vacant; those events happened yesterday."

"Fortunate events for me: they permit me to call on you without danger."

"Have you no curiosity to know, at least, who and what is the young lady who appears to me so well suited to you?"

"No curiosity, but a vague sensation of alarm."

"Well, I cannot talk pleasantly with you while you are in this irritating mood, and it is time to quit the hermitage. Come, there are many persons here with some of whom you should renew old acquaintance, and to some of whom I should like to make you known."

"I am prepared to follow Lady Glenalvon wherever she deigns to lead me—except to the altar with another."

CHAPTER III.

THE rooms were now full—not overcrowded, but full—and it was rarely even in that house that so many distinguished persons were collected together. A young man thus honoured by so *grande* a *dame* as Lady Glenalvon, could not but be cordially welcomed by all to whom she presented him, Ministers and Parliamentary leaders, ball-givers and beauties in vogue—even authors and artists; and there was something in Kenelm Chillingly, in his striking countenance and figure, in that calm ease of manner natural to his indifference to effect, which seemed to justify the favour shown to him by the brilliant princess of fashion, and mark him out for general observation.

That first evening of his reintroduction into the polite world was a success which few young men of his years achieve. He produced a sensation. Just as the rooms were thinning, Lady Glenalvon whispered to Kenelm—

"Come this way—there is one person I must reintroduce you to—thank me for it hereafter."

Kenelm followed the Marchioness, and found himself face to face with Cecilia Travers. She was leaning on her father's arm, looking very handsome, and her beauty was heightened by the blush which overspread her cheeks as Kenelm Chillingly approached.

Travers greeted him with great cordiality; and Lady Glenalvon asking him to escort her to the refreshment-room, Kenelm had no option but to offer his arm to Cecilia.

Kenelm felt somewhat embarrassed. "Have you been long in town, Miss Travers?"

"A little more than a week, but we only settled into our house yesterday."

"Ah, indeed! were you then the young lady who——" He stopped short, and his face grew gentler and graver in its expression.

"The young lady who—what?" asked Cecilia, with a smile.

"Who has been staying with Lady Glenalvon?"

"Yes; did she tell you?"

"She did not mention your name, but praised that young lady so justly that I ought to have guessed it."

Cecilia made some not very audible answer, and on entering the refreshment-room other young men gathered round her, and Lady Glenalvon and Kenelm remained silent in the midst of a general small-talk. When Travers, after giving his address to Kenelm, and, of course, pressing him to call, left the house with Cecilia, Kenelm said to Lady Glenalvon, musingly, "So that is the young lady in whom I was to see my fate : you knew that we had met before?"

"Yes, she told me when and where. Besides, it is not two years since you wrote to me from her father's house. Do you forget?"

"Ah," said Kenelm, so abstractedly that he seemed to be dreaming, "no man with his eyes open rushes on his fate; when he does so, his sight is gone. Love is blind. They say the blind are very happy, yet I never met a blind man who would not recover his sight if he could."

CHAPTER IV.

MR. CHILLINGLY MIVERS never gave a dinner at his own rooms. When he did give a dinner it was at Greenwich or Richmond. But he gave breakfast-parties pretty often, and they were considered pleasant. He had handsome bachelor apartments in Grosvenor Street, daintily furnished, with a prevalent air of exquisite neatness. A good library stored with books of reference, and adorned with presentation copies from authors of the day, very beautifully bound. Though the room served for the study of the professed man of letters, it had none of the untidy litter which generally characterizes the study of one whose vocation it is to deal with books and papers. Even the implements for writing were not apparent, except when required. They lay concealed in a vast cylinder bureau, French made, and French polished. Within that bureau were numerous pigeon-holes and secret drawers, and a profound well with a separate patent lock. In the well were deposited the articles intended for publication in 'The Londoner'—proof-sheets, &c.; pigeon-holes were devoted to ordinary correspondence; secret drawers to confidential notes, and outlines of biographies of eminent men now living, but intended to be completed for publication the day after their death.

No man wrote such funeral compositions with a livelier pen than that of Chillingly Mivers; and the large and miscellaneous circle of his visiting acquaintances allowed him to ascertain, whether by authoritative report or by personal observation, the signs of mortal disease in the illustrious friends whose dinners he accepted, and whose failing pulses he instinctively felt in returning the pressure of their hands, so that he was often able to put the finishing-stroke to their obituary memorials, days, weeks, even months, before their fate took the public by surprise. That cylinder bureau was in harmony with the secrecy in which this remarkable man shrouded the productions of his brain. In his literary life Mivers had no "I ;" there he was ever the inscrutable, mysterious "We." He was only "I" when you met him in the world, and called him Mivers.

Adjoining the library on one side was a small dining or rather breakfast-room, hung with valuable pictures—presents from living painters. Many of these painters had been severely handled by Mr. Mivers in his existence as "We,"—not always in 'The Londoner.' His most pungent criticisms were often contributed to other intellectual journals, conducted by members of the same intellectual clique. Painters knew not how contemptuously "We" had treated them when they met Mr. Mivers. His "I" was so complimentary that they sent him a tribute of their gratitude.

On the other side was his drawing-room, also enriched by many gifts, chiefly from fair hands—embroidered cushions and table-covers, bits of Sèvres or old Chelsea, elegant knick-knacks of all kinds. Fashionable authoresses paid great court to Mr. Mivers ; and in the course of his life as a single man, he had other female adorers besides fashionable authoresses.

Mr. Mivers had already returned from his early constitutional walk in the Park, and was now seated by the cylinder *sécrétaire* with a mild-looking man, who was one of the most merciless contributors to 'The Londoner,' and no unimportant councillor in the oligarchy of the clique that went by the name of the "Intellectuals."

"Well," said Mivers, languidly, "I can't even get through the book ; it is as dull as the country in November. But, as you justly say, the writer is an 'Intellectual,' and a clique would be anything but intellectual if it did not support its members. Review the book yourself—mind and make the dulness of it the signal proof of its merit. Say—'To the ordinary class of readers this exquisite work may appear less brilliant than the flippant smartness of'—any other author you like to name ; 'but to the well-educated and intelligent every line is pregnant with,' &c., &c. By the way, when we come by and by to review the exhibition at Burlington House, there is one painter whom we must try our best to crush. I have not seen his pictures myself, but he is a new man, and our friend, who has seen him, is terribly jealous of him, and says that if the good judges do not put him down at once, the villainous taste of the public will set him up as a prodigy. A low-lived fellow too, I hear. There is the name of the man and the subject of the pictures. See to it when the time comes. Meanwhile, prepare the way for onslaught on the pictures by occasional sneers at the painter." Mr. Mivers here took out of his cylinder a confidential note from the jealous rival and handed it to his mild-looking *confrère;* then rising, he said, "I fear we must suspend business till to-morrow; I expect two young cousins to breakfast."

As soon as the mild-looking man was gone, Mr. Mivers sauntered to his drawing-room window, amiably offering a lump of sugar to a canary-bird sent him as a present the day before, and who, in the gilded cage which made part of the present, scanned him suspiciously, and refused the sugar.

Time had remained very gentle in its dealings with Chillingly Mivers. He scarcely looked a day older than when he was first presented to the reader on the birth of his kinsman Kenelm. He was reaping the fruit of his own sage maxims. Free from whiskers and safe in wig, there was no sign of gray—no suspicion of dye. Superiority to passion, abnegation of sorrow, indulgence of amusement, avoidance of excess, had kept away the crow's-feet, preserved the elasticity of his frame and the unflushed clearness of his gentlemanlike complexion. The door opened, and a well-dressed valet, who had lived long enough with Mivers to grow very much like him, announced Mr. Chillingly Gordon.

"Good morning," said Mivers; "I was much pleased to see you talking so long and so familiarly with Danvers: others, of course, observed it, and it added a step to your career. It does you great good to be seen in a drawing-room talking apart with a Somebody. But may I ask if the talk itself was satisfactory?"

"Not at all: Danvers throws cold water on the notion of Saxboro', and does not even hint that his party will help me to any other opening. Party has few openings at its disposal now-a-days for any young man. The schoolmaster being abroad has swept away the school for statesmen as he has swept away the school for actors —an evil, and an evil of a far graver consequence to the destinies of the nation than any good likely to be got from the system that succeeded it."

"But it is of no use railing against things that can't be helped. If I were you, I would postpone all ambition of Parliament, and read for the bar."

"The advice is sound, but too unpalatable to be taken. I am resolved to find a seat in the House, and where there is a will there is a way."

"I am not so sure of that."

"But I am."

"Judging by what your contemporaries at the University tell me of your speeches at the Debating Society, you were not then an ultra-Radical. But it is only an ultra-Radical who has a chance of success at Saxboro'."

"I am no fanatic in politics. There is much to be said on all sides—*cæteris paribus*, I prefer the winning side to the losing: nothing succeeds like success."

"Ay, but in politics there is always reaction. The winning side one day may be the losing side another. The losing side represents a minority, and a minority is sure to comprise more intellect than a majority: in the long-run intellect will force its way, get a majority and then lose it, because with a majority it will become stupid."

"Cousin Mivers, does not the history of the world show you that a single individual can upset all theories as to the comparative wisdom of the few or the many? Take the wisest few you can find, and one man of genius not a tithe so wise crushes them into powder. But then that man of genius, though he despises the many, must make use of them. That done, he rules them. Don't you see how in free countries political destinations resolve themselves into individual impersonations? At a general election it is one name around which electors rally. The candidate may enlarge as much as he pleases on political principles, but all his talk will not win him votes enough for success, unless he says, 'I go with Mr. A.,' the Minister, or with Mr. Z., the chief of the Opposition. It was not the Tories who beat the Whigs when Mr. Pitt dissolved Parliament. It was Mr. Pitt who beat Mr. Fox, with whom in general political principles—slave-trade, Roman Catholic emancipation, Parliamentary reform—he certainly agreed much more than he did with any man in his own Cabinet."

"Take care, my young cousin," cried Mivers, in accents of alarm; "don't set up for a man of genius. Genius is the worst quality a public man can have now-a-days—nobody heeds it, and everybody is jealous of it."

"Pardon me, you mistake; my remark was purely objective, and intended as a reply to your argument. I prefer at present to go with the many because it is the winning side. If we then want a man of genius to keep it the winning side, by subjugating its partisans to his will, he will be sure to come. The few will drive him to us, for the few are always the enemies of the one man of genius. It is they who distrust—it is they who are jealous—not the many. You have allowed your judgment, usually so clear, to be somewhat dimmed by your experience as a critic. The critics are the *few*. They have infinitely more culture than the many. But when a man of real genius appears and asserts himself, the critics are seldom such fair judges of him as the many are. If he be not one of their oligarchical clique, they either abuse, or disparage, or affect to ignore him; though a time at last comes when, having gained the many, the critics acknowledge him. But the difference between the man of action and the author is this, that the author rarely finds this acknowledgment till he is dead, and it is necessary to the man of action to enforce it while he is alive. But enough of this speculation: you ask me to meet Kenelm—is he not coming?"

"Yes, but I did not ask him till ten o'clock. I asked you at half-past nine, because I wished to hear about Danvers and Saxboro', and also to prepare you somewhat for your introduction to your cousin. I must be brief as to the last, for it is only five minutes to the hour, and he is a man likely to be punctual. Kenelm is in all ways your opposite. I don't know whether he is cleverer or less clever—there is no scale of measurement between you; but he is wholly void of ambition, and might possibly assist yours. He can do what he likes with Sir Peter; and considering how your poor father—a worthy man, but cantankerous—harassed and persecuted Sir Peter, because Kenelm came between the estate and you, it is probable that Sir Peter bears you a grudge, though Kenelm declares him incapable of it; and it would be well if you could annul that grudge in the father by conciliating the goodwill of the son."

"I should be glad so to annul it: but what is Kenelm's weak side?—the turf? the hunting-field? women? poetry? One can only conciliate a man by getting on his weak side."

"Hist! I see him from the windows. Kenelm's weak side was, when I knew him some years ago, and I rather fancy it still is——"

"Well, make haste! I hear his ring at your door-bell."

"A passionate longing to find ideal truth in real life."

"Ah!" said Gordon, "as I thought—a mere dreamer."

CHAPTER V.

KENELM entered the room. The young cousins were introduced, shook hands, receded a step, and gazed at each other. It is scarcely possible to conceive a greater contrast outwardly than that between the two Chillingly representatives of the rising generation. Each was silently impressed by the sense of that contrast. Each felt that the contrast implied antagonism, and that if they two met in the same arena it must be as rival combatants; still, by some mysterious intuition each felt a certain respect for the other, each divined in the other a power that he could not fairly estimate, but against which his own power would be strongly tasked to contend. So might exchange looks a thorough-bred deer-hound and a half-bred mastiff: the bystander could scarcely doubt which was the nobler animal, but he might hesitate which to bet on, if the two came to deadly quarrel. Meanwhile the thorough-bred deer-hound and the half-bred mastiff sniffed at each other in polite salutation. Gordon was the first to give tongue.

"I have long wished to know you personally," said he, throwing into his voice and manner that delicate kind of deference which a well-born cadet owes to the destined head of his house. "I cannot conceive how I missed you last night at Lady Beaumanoir's, where Mivers tells me he met you; but I left early."

Here Mivers led the way to the breakfast-room, and there seated, the host became the principal talker, running with lively glibness over the principal topics of the day—the last scandal, the last new book, the reform of the army, the reform of the turf, the critical state of Spain, and the *début* of an Italian singer. He seemed an embodied Journal, including the Leading Article, the Law Reports, Foreign Intelligence, the Court Circular, down to the Births, Deaths, and Marriages. Gordon from time to time interrupted this flow of soul with brief, trenchant remarks, which evinced his own knowledge of the subjects treated, and a habit of looking on all subjects connected with the pursuits and business of mankind from a high ground appropriated to himself, and through the medium of that blue glass which conveys a wintry aspect to summer landscapes. Kenelm said little, but listened attentively.

The conversation arrested its discursive nature, to settle upon a political chief—the highest in fame and station of that party to which Mivers professed—not to belong, he belonged to himself alone—but to appropinquate. Mivers spoke of this chief with the greatest distrust, and in a spirit of general depreciation. Gordon acquiesced in the distrust and the depreciation, adding—"But he is master of the position, and must, of course, be supported through thick and thin for the present."

"Yes, for the present," said Mivers; "one has no option. But you will see some clever articles in 'The Londoner' towards the close of the session, which will damage him greatly, by praising him in the wrong place, and deepening the alarm of important followers—an alarm now at work, though suppressed."

Here Kenelm asked, in humble tones, "Why Gordon thought that a Minister he considered so untrustworthy and dangerous must, for the present, be supported through thick and thin."

"Because at present a member elected so to support him, would lose his seat if he did not : needs must when the devil drives."

KENELM.—"When the devil drives, I should have thought it better to resign one's seat on the coach; perhaps one might be of some use, out of it, in helping to put on the drag."

MIVERS.—"Cleverly said, Kenelm. But, metaphor apart, Gordon is right: a young politician must go with his party; a veteran journalist like myself is more independent. So long as the journalist blames everybody, he will have plenty of readers."

Kenelm made no reply, and Gordon changed the conversation from men to measures. He spoke of some Bills before Parliament with remarkable ability, evincing much knowledge of the subject, much critical acuteness, illustrating their defects, and proving the danger of their ultimate consequences.

Kenelm was greatly struck with the vigour of this cold, clear mind, and owned to himself that the House of Commons was a fitting place for its development.

"But," said Mivers, "would you not be obliged to defend these Bills if you were member for Saxboro'?"

"Before I answer your question, answer me this. Dangerous as the Bills are, is it not necessary that they shall pass? Have not the public so resolved?"

"There can be no doubt of that."

"Then the member for Saxboro' cannot be strong enough to go against the public."

"Progress of the age!" said Kenelm, musingly. "Do you think the class of gentlemen will long last in England?"

"What do you call gentlemen? The aristocracy by birth?—the *gentilhommes?*"

"Nay, I suppose no laws can take away a man's ancestors, and a class of well-born men is not to be exterminated. But a mere class of well-born men—without duties, responsibilities, or sentiment of that which becomes good birth in devotion to country or individual honour—does no good to a nation. It is a misfortune which statesmen of democratic creed ought to recognize, that the class of the well-born cannot be destroyed—it must remain as it remained in Rome and remains in France, after all efforts to extirpate it, as the most dangerous class of citizens when you deprive it of the attributes which made it the most serviceable. I am not speaking of that class ; I speak of that unclassified order peculiar to

England, which, no doubt, forming itself originally from the ideal standard of honour and truth supposed to be maintained by the *gentilhommes*, or well-born, no longer requires pedigrees and acres to confer upon its members the designation of gentlemen ; and when I hear a 'gentleman' say that he has no option but to think one thing and say another, at whatever risk to his country, I feel as if in the progress of the age the class of gentlemen was about to be superseded by some finer development of species."

Therewith Kenelm rose, and would have taken his departure, if Gordon had not seized his hand and detained him.

"My dear cousin, if I may so call you," he said, with the frank manner which was usual to him, and which suited well the bold expression of his face and the clear ring of his voice—"I am one of those who, from an over-dislike to sentimentality and cant, often make those not intimately acquainted with them think worse of their principles than they deserve. It may be quite true that a man who goes with his party dislikes the measures he feels bound to support, and says so openly when among friends and relations, yet that man is not therefore devoid of loyalty and honour ; and I trust, when you know me better, you will not think it likely I should derogate from that class of gentlemen to which we both belong."

"Pardon me if I seemed rude," answered Kenelm ; "ascribe it to my ignorance of the necessities of public life. It struck me that where a politician thought a thing evil, he ought not to support it as good. But I dare say I am mistaken."

"Entirely mistaken," said Mivers, "and for this reason : in politics formerly there was a direct choice between good and evil. That rarely exists now. Men of high education having to choose whether to accept or reject a measure forced upon their option by constituent bodies of very low education, are called upon to weigh evil against evil!—the evil of accepting or the evil of rejecting ; and if they resolve on the first, it is as the lesser evil of the two."

"Your definition is perfect," said Gordon, "and I am contented to rest on it my excuse for what my cousin deems insincerity."

"I suppose that is real life," said Kenelm, with his mournful smile.

"Of course it is," said Mivers.

"Every day I live," sighed Kenelm, "still more confirms my conviction that real life is a phantasmal sham. How absurd it is in philosophers to deny the existence of apparitions ! what apparitions we, living men, must seem to the ghosts !

"'The spirits of the wise
Sit in the clouds and mock us.'"

CHAPTER VI.

CHILLINGLY GORDON did not fail to confirm his acquaintance with Kenelm. He very often looked in upon him of a morning, sometimes joined him in his afternoon rides, introduced him to men of his own set who were mostly busy members of Parliament, rising barristers, or political journalists, but not without a proportion of brilliant idlers—club men, sporting men, men of fashion, rank, and fortune. He did so with a purpose, for these persons spoke well of him—spoke well not only of his talents, but of his honourable character. His general nickname amongst them was "HONEST GORDON." Kenelm at first thought this *sobriquet* must be ironical; not a bit of it. It was given to him on account of the candour and boldness with which he expressed opinions embodying that sort of cynicism which is vulgarly called "the absence of humbug." The man was certainly no hypocrite; he affected no beliefs which he did not entertain. And he had very few beliefs in anything, except the first half of the adage, "Every man for himself,—and God for us all."

But whatever Chillingly Gordon's theoretical disbeliefs in things which make the current creed of the virtuous, there was nothing in his conduct which evinced predilection for vices: he was strictly upright in all his dealings, and in delicate matters of honour was a favourite umpire amongst his coevals. Though so frankly ambitious, no one could accuse him of attempting to climb on the shoulders of patrons. There was nothing servile in his nature, and though he was perfectly prepared to bribe electors if necessary, no money could have bought himself. His one master-passion was the desire of power. He sneered at patriotism as a worn-out prejudice, at philanthropy as a sentimental catch-word. He did not want to serve his country, but to rule it. He did not want to raise mankind, but to rise himself. He was therefore unscrupulous, unprincipled, as hungerers after power for itself too often are; yet still if he got power he would probably use it well, from the clearness and strength of his mental perceptions. The impression he made on Kenelm may be seen in the following letter:—

TO SIR PETER CHILLINGLY, BART., ETC.

"MY DEAR FATHER,—You and my dear mother will be pleased to hear that London continues very polite to me: that 'arida nutrix leonum' enrols me among the pet class of lions which ladies of fashion admit into the society of their lap-dogs. It is somewhere about six years since I was allowed to gaze on this peep-show through the loopholes of Mr. Welby's retreat. It appears to me, perhaps erroneously, that even within that short space of time the tone of 'society' is perceptibly changed. That the change is for the better is an assertion I leave to those who belong to the *progressista* party.

"I don't think nearly so many young ladies six years ago painted their eyelids and dyed their hair: a few of them there might be, imitators of the slang invented by school-boys and circulated through the medium of small novelists; they might use such expressions as 'stunning,' 'cheek,' 'awfully jolly,' &c. But now I find a great many who have advanced to a slang beyond that of verbal expressions,—a slang of mind, a slang of sentiment, a slang in which very little seems left of the woman, and nothing at all of the lady.

"Newspaper essayists assert that the young men of the day are to blame for this; that the young men like it; and the fair husband-anglers dress their flies in the colours most likely to attract a nibble. Whether this excuse be the true one I cannot pretend to judge. But it strikes me that the men about my own age who affect to be fast are a more languid race than the men from ten to twenty years older, whom they regard as *slow*. The habit of dram-drinking in the morning is a very new idea, an idea greatly in fashion at the moment. Adonis calls for a 'pick-me-up' before he has strength enough to answer a *billet-doux* from Venus. Adonis has not the strength to get nobly drunk, but his delicate constitution requires stimulants, and he is always tippling.

"The men of high birth or renown for social success, belonging, my dear father, to your time, are still distinguished by an air of good-breeding, by a style of conversation more or less polished and not without evidences of literary culture, from men of the same rank in my generation, who appear to pride themselves on respecting nobody and knowing nothing, not even grammar. Still we are assured that the world goes on steadily improving. *That* new idea is in full vigour.

"Society in the concrete has become wonderfully conceited as to its own progressive excellencies, and the individuals who form the concrete entertain the same complacent opinion of themselves. There are, of course, even in my brief and imperfect experience, many exceptions to what appear to me the prevalent characteristics of the rising generation in 'society.' Of these exceptions I must content myself with naming the most remarkable. *Place aux dames*, the first I name is Cecilia Travers. She and her father are now in town, and I meet them frequently. I can conceive no civilized era in the world which a woman like Cecilia Travers would not grace and adorn, because she is essentially the type of woman as man likes to imagine woman—viz., on the fairest side of the womanly character. And I say 'woman' rather than girl, because among 'Girls of the Period' Cecilia Travers cannot be classed. You might call her damsel, virgin, maiden, but you could no more call her girl than you could call a well-born French demoiselle '*fille*.' She is handsome enough to please the eye of any man, however fastidious, but not that kind of beauty which dazzles all men too much to fascinate one man; for—speaking, thank heaven, from mere theory —I apprehend that the love for woman has in it a strong sense of property; that one requires to individualize one's possession as being wholly one's own, and not a possession which all the public are invited to admire. I can readily understand how a rich man, who has what is called a show place, in which the splendid rooms and the stately gardens are open to all inspectors, so that he has no privacy in his own demesnes, runs away to a pretty cottage which he has all to himself, and of which he can say, '*This* is Home—*this* is all mine.'

"But there are some kinds of beauty which are eminently show places—which the public think they have as much a right to admire as the owner has; and the show place itself would be dull, and perhaps fall out of repair, if the public could be excluded from the sight of it.

"The beauty of Cecilia Travers is not that of a show place. There is a feeling of safety in her. If Desdemona had been like her, Othello would not have been jealous. But then Cecilia would not have deceived her father—nor I think have told a blackamoor that she wished 'Heaven had made her such a man.' Her mind harmonizes with her person—it is a companionable mind. Her talents are not showy, but, take them altogether, they form a pleasant whole: she has good sense enough in the practical affairs of life, and enough of that ineffable womanly gift called tact to counteract the effects of whimsical natures like mine, and yet enough sense of the humoristic views of life not to take too literally all that a whimsical man like myself may say. As to temper, one never knows what a woman's temper is—till one puts her out of it. But I imagine hers, in its normal state, to be serene, and disposed to be cheerful. Now, my dear father, if you were not one of the cleverest of men you would infer from this eulogistic mention of Cecilia Travers that I was in love with her. But you no doubt will detect the truth, that a man in love with a woman does not weigh her merits with so steady a hand as that which guides this steel pen. I am not in love with Cecilia Travers. I wish I were. When Lady Glenalvon, who remains wonderfully kind to me, says, day after day, 'Cecilia Travers would make you a perfect wife,' I have no answer to give, but I don't feel the least inclined to ask Cecilia Travers if she would waste her perfection on one who so coldly concedes it.

"I find that she persisted in rejecting the man whom her father wished her to marry, and that he has consoled himself by marrying somebody else. No doubt other suitors as worthy will soon present themselves.

"Oh, dearest of all my friends—sole friend whom I regard as a confidant—shall I ever be in love? and if not, why not? Sometimes I feel as if, with love as with ambition, it is because I have some impossible ideal in each, that I must always remain indifferent to the sort of love and the sort of ambition which are within my reach. I have an idea that if I did love, I should love as intensely as Romeo, and that thought inspires me with vague forebodings of terror; and if I did find an object to arouse my ambition, I could be as earnest in its pursuit as—whom shall I name?—Cæsar or Cato? I like Cato's ambition the better of the two. But people now-a-days call ambition an impracticable crotchet, if it be invested on the losing side. Cato would have saved Rome from the mob and the dictator; but Rome could not be saved, and Cato falls on his own sword. Had we a Cato now, the verdict at a coroner's inquest would be, 'suicide while in a state of unsound mind;' and the verdict would have been proved by his senseless resistance to a mob and a dictator! Talking of ambition, I come to the other exception to the youth of the day—I have named a *demoiselle*, I now name a *damoiseau*. Imagine a man of about five-and-twenty, and who is morally about fifty years older than a healthy man of sixty, —imagine him with the brain of age and the flower of youth—with a heart absorbed into the brain, and giving warm blood to frigid ideas—a man who sneers at everything I call lofty, yet would do nothing that *he* thinks mean—to whom vice and virtue are as indifferent as they were to the Æsthetics of Goethe—who would never jeopardize his career as a practical reasoner by an imprudent virtue, and never sully his reputation by a degrading vice. Imagine this man with an intellect keen, strong, ready, unscrupulous, dauntless— all cleverness and no genius. Imagine this man, and then do not be astonished when I tell you he is a Chillingly.

"The Chillingly race culminates in him, and becomes Chillinglyest. In fact, it seems to me that we live in a day precisely suited to the Chillingly idiosyncrasies. During the ten centuries or more that our race has held local habitation and a name, it has been as airy nothings. Its representatives lived in hot-blooded times, and were compelled to skulk in still water with their emblematic Daces. But the times now, my dear father, are so cold-blooded that you can't be too cold-blooded to prosper. What could Chillingly Mivers have been in an age when people cared twopence-halfpenny about their religious creeds, and their political parties deemed their cause was sacred, and their leaders were heroes? Chillingly Mivers would not have found five subscribers to 'The Londoner.' But now 'The Londoner' is the favourite organ of the intellectual public; it sneers away all the foundations of the social system, without an attempt at reconstruction; and every new journal set up, if it keep its head above water, models itself on 'The Londoner.' Chillingly Mivers is a great man, and the most potent writer of the age, though nobody knows what he has written. Chillingly Gordon is a still more notable instance of the rise of the Chillingly worth in the modern market.

"There is a general impression in the most authoritative circles that Chillingly Gordon will have high rank in the van of the coming men. His confidence in himself is so thorough that it infects all with whom he comes into contact—myself included.

"He said to me the other day, with a *sang-froid* worthy of the iciest Chillingly, 'I mean to be Prime Minister of England—it is only a question of time.' Now, if Chillingly Gordon is to be Prime Minister, it will be because the increasing cold of our moral and social atmosphere will exactly suit the development of his talents.

"He is the man above all others to argue down the declaimers of old-fashioned sentimentalities, love of country, care for its position among nations, zeal for its honour, pride in its renown. (Oh, if you could hear him philosophically and logically sneer away the word 'prestige!') Such notions are fast being classified as 'bosh.' And when that classification is complete—when England has no colonies to defend, no navy to pay for, no interest in the affairs of other nations, and has attained to the happy condition of Holland, —then Chillingly Gordon will be her Prime Minister.

"Yet while, if ever I am stung into political action, it will be by abnegation of the Chillingly attributes, and in opposition, however hopeless, to Chillingly Gordon, I feel that this man cannot be suppressed and ought to have fair play; his ambition will be infinitely more dangerous if it become soured by delay. I propose, my dear father, that you should have the honour of laying this clever kinsman under an obligation, and enabling him to enter Parliament. In our last conversation at Exmundham, you told me of the frank resentment of Gordon *père*, when my coming into the world shut him out from the Exmundham inheritance; you confided in me your intention at that time to lay by yearly a sum that might ultimately serve as a provision for Gordon *fils*, and as some compensation for the loss of his expectations when you realized your hope of an heir; you told me also how this generous intention on your part had been frustrated by a natural indignation at the elder Gordon's conduct in his harassing and costly litigation and by the addition you had been tempted to make to the estate in a purchase which added to its acreage, but at a rate of interest which diminished your own income, and precluded the possibility of further savings. Now, chancing to meet your lawyer, Mr. Vining, the other day, I learned from him that it had been long a wish which your delicacy prevented your naming to me, that I, to whom the fee-simple descends, should join with you in cutting off the entail and resettling the estate. He showed me what an advantage this would be to the property, because it would leave your hands free for many improvements in which I heartily go with the progress of the age, for which, as merely tenant for life, you could not raise the money except upon ruinous terms; new cottages for labourers, new buildings for tenants; the consolidation of some old mortgages and charges on the rent-roll, &c. And allow me to add that I should like to make a large increase to the jointure of my dear mother. Vining says, too, that there is a part of the outlying land which, as being near a town, could be sold to considerable profit if the estate were resettled.

"Let us hasten to complete the necessary deeds, and so obtain the £20,000 required for the realization of your noble, and let me add, your just desire to do something for Chillingly Gordon. In the new deeds of settlement we could insure the power of willing the estate as we pleased, and I am strongly against devising it to Chillingly Gordon. It may be a crotchet of mine, but one which I think you share, that the owner of English soil should have a son's love for the native land, and Gordon will never have that. I think, too, that it will be best for his own career, and for the establishment of a frank understanding between us and himself, that he should be fairly told that he would not be benefited in the event of our deaths. Twenty thousand pounds given to him now would be a greater boon to him than ten times the sum twenty years later. With that at his command, he can enter Parliament, and have an income, added to what he now possesses, if modest, still sufficient to make him independent of a Minister's patronage.

"Pray humour me, my dearest father, in the proposition I venture to submit to you.—Your affectionate son,   KENELM."

FROM SIR PETER CHILLINGLY TO KENELM CHILLINGLY.

"MY DEAR BOY,—You are not worthy to be a Chillingly; you are decidedly warm-blooded: never was a load lifted off a man's mind with a gentler hand. Yes, I have wished to cut off the entail and resettle the property; but as it was eminently to my advantage to do so, I shrank from asking it, though eventually it would be almost as much to your own advantage. What with the purchase I made of the Faircleuch lands—which I could only effect by money borrowed at high interest on my personal security, and paid off by yearly instalments, eating largely into income—and the old mortgages, &c., I own I have been pinched of late years. But what rejoices me the most is the power to make homes for our honest labourers more comfortable, and nearer to their work, which last is the chief point, for the old cottages in themselves are not bad; the misfortune is, when you build an extra room for the children, the silly people let it out to a lodger.

"My dear boy, I am very much touched by your wish to increase your mother's jointure—a very proper wish, independently of filial feeling, for she brought to the estate a very pretty fortune, which the trustees consented to my investing in land; and though the land completed our ring-fence, it does not bring in two per cent., and the conditions of the entail limited the right of jointure to an amount below that which a widowed Lady Chillingly may fairly expect.

"I care more about the provision on these points than I do for the interests of old Chillingly Gordon's son. I had meant to behave very handsomely to the father; and when the return for behaving handsomely is being put into Chancery—A Worm Will Turn. Nevertheless, I agree with you that a son should not be punished for his father's faults; and if the sacrifice of £20,000 makes you and myself feel that we are better Christians and truer gentlemen, we shall buy that feeling very cheaply."

Sir Peter then proceeded, half jestingly, half seriously, to combat Kenelm's declaration that he was not in love with Cecilia Travers; and, urging the advantages of marriage with one whom Kenelm allowed would be a perfect wife, astutely remarked, that unless Kenelm had a son of his own, it did not seem to him quite just to the next of kin to will the property from him, upon no better plea than the want of love for his native country. "He would love his country fast enough if he had 10,000 acres in it."

Kenelm shook his head when he came to this sentence.

"Is even, then, love for one's country but cupboard-love after all?" said he; and he postponed finishing the perusal of his father's letter.

CHAPTER VII.

KENELM CHILLINGLY did not exaggerate the social position he had acquired when he classed himself amongst the lions of the fashionable world. I dare not count the number of three-cornered notes showered upon him by the fine ladies who grow romantic upon any kind of celebrity; or the carefully-sealed envelopes, containing letters from fair anonymas, who asked if he had a heart, and would be in such a place in the Park at such an hour. What there was in Kenelm Chillingly that should make him thus favoured, especially by the fair sex, it would be difficult to say, unless it was the twofold reputation of being unlike other people, and of being unaffectedly indifferent to the gain of any reputation at all. He might, had he so pleased, have easily established a proof that the prevalent though vague belief in his talents was not altogether unjustified. For the articles he had sent from abroad to 'The Londoner,' and by which his travelling expenses were defrayed, had been stamped by that sort of originality in tone and treatment which rarely fails to excite curiosity as to the author, and meets with more general praise than perhaps it deserves.

But Mivers was true to his contract to preserve inviolable the incognito of the author, and Kenelm regarded with profound contempt the articles themselves, and the readers who praised them.

Just as misanthropy with some persons grows out of benevolence disappointed, so there are certain natures—and Kenelm Chillingly's was perhaps one of them—in which indifferentism grows out of earnestness baffled.

He had promised himself pleasure in renewing acquaintance with his old tutor, Mr. Welby—pleasure in refreshing his own taste for metaphysics and casuistry and criticism. But that accomplished professor of realism had retired from philosophy altogether, and was now enjoying a holiday for life in the business of a public office. A Minister in favour of whom, when in opposition, Mr. Welby, in a moment of whim, wrote some very able articles in a leading journal, had, on acceding to power, presented the realist with one of those few good things still left to Ministerial patronage —a place worth about £1200 a-year. His mornings thus engaged in routine work, Mr. Welby enjoyed his evenings in a convivial way.

"*Inveni portum,*" he said to Kenelm; "I plunge into no troubled waters now. But come and dine with me to-morrow, *tête-à-tête.* My wife is at St. Leonard's with my youngest born for the benefit of sea-air." Kenelm accepted the invitation.

The dinner would have contented a Brillat-Savarin—it was faultless; and the claret was that rare nectar, the Lafitte of 1848.

"I never share this," said Welby, "with more than one friend at a time."

Kenelm sought to engage his host in discussion on certain new works in vogue, and which were composed according to purely realistic canons of criticism. "The more realistic these books pretend to be, the less real they are," said Kenelm. "I am half inclined to think that the whole school you so systematically sought to build up is a mistake, and that realism in art is a thing impossible."

"I dare say you are right. I took up that school in earnest because I was in a passion with pretenders to the Idealistic school; and whatever one takes up in earnest is generally a mistake, especially if one is in a passion. I was not in earnest and I was not in a passion when I wrote those articles to which I am indebted for my office." Mr. Welby here luxuriously stretched his limbs, and lifting his glass to his lips voluptuously inhaled its *bouquet.*

"You sadden me," returned Kenelm. "It is a melancholy thing to find that one's mind was influenced in youth by a teacher who mocks at his own teachings."

Welby shrugged his shoulders. "Life consists in the alternate process of learning and unlearning; but it is often wiser to unlearn than to learn. For the rest, as I have ceased to be a critic, I care little whether I was wrong or right when I played that part. I think I am right now as a placeman. Let the world go its own way, provided the world lets you live upon it. I drain my wine to the lees, and cut down hope to the brief span of life. Reject realism in art if you please, and accept realism in conduct. For the first time in my life I am comfortable: my mind having worn out its walking-shoes, is now enjoying the luxury of slippers. Who can deny the realism of comfort?"

"Has a man a right," Kenelm said to himself, as he entered his brougham, "to employ all the brilliancy of a rare wit—all the acquisitions of as rare a scholarship—to the scaring of the young generation out of the safe old roads which youth left to itself would take—old roads skirted by romantic rivers and bowery trees—directing them into new paths on long sandy flats, and then, when they are faint and footsore, to tell them that he cares not a pin whether they have worn out their shoes in right paths or wrong paths, for that he has attained the *summum bonum* of philosophy in the comfort of easy slippers?"

Before he could answer the question he thus put to himself, his brougham stopped at the door of the Minister whom Welby had contributed to bring into power.

That night there was a crowded muster of the fashionable world at the great man's house. It happened to be a very critical moment for the Minister. The fate of his cabinet depended on the result of a motion about to be made the following week in the House of Commons. The great man stood at the entrance of the apartments to receive his guests, and among the guests were the framers of the hostile motion and the leaders of the Opposition. His smile was not less gracious to them than to his dearest friends and stanchest supporters.

"I suppose this is realism," said Kenelm to himself; "but it is not truth, and it is not comfort." Leaning against the wall near the doorway, he contemplated with grave interest the striking countenance of his distinguished host. He detected beneath that courteous smile and that urbane manner the signs of care. The eye was absent, the cheek pinched, the brow furrowed. Kenelm turned away his looks, and glanced over the animated countenances of the idle loungers along commoner thoroughfares in life. Their eyes were not absent, their brows were not furrowed; their minds seemed quite at home in exchanging nothings. Interest many of them had in the approaching struggle, but it was much such an interest as betters of small sums may have on the Derby day—just enough to give piquancy to the race; nothing to make gain a great joy, or loss a keen anguish.

"Our host is looking ill," said Mivers, accosting Kenelm. "I detect symptoms of suppressed gout. You know my aphorism, 'nothing so gouty as ambition,' especially Parliamentary ambition."

"You are not one of those friends who press on my choice of life that source of disease; allow me to thank you."

"Your thanks are misplaced. I strongly advise you to devote yourself to a political career."

"Despite the gout?"

"Despite the gout. If you could take the world as I do, my advice might be different. But your mind is overcrowded with doubts and fantasies and crotchets, and you have no choice but to give them vent in active life."

"You had something to do in making me what I am—an idler; something to answer for as to my doubts, fantasies, and crotchets. It was by your recommendation that I was placed under the tuition of Mr. Welby, and at that critical age in which the bent of the twig forms the shape of the tree."

"And I pride myself on that counsel. I repeat the reasons for which I gave it: it is an incalculable advantage for a young man to start in life thoroughly initiated into the New Ideas which will more or less influence his generation. Welby was the ablest representative of these ideas. It is a wondrous good fortune when the propagandist of the New Ideas is something more than a bookish philosopher—when he is a thorough 'man of the world,' and is what we emphatically call 'practical.' Yes, you owe me much that I secured to you such tuition, and saved you from twaddle and sentiment, the poetry of Wordsworth and the muscular Christianity of cousin John."

"What you say that you saved me from might have done me more good than all you conferred on me. I suspect that when education succeeds in placing an old head upon young shoulders, the combination is not healthful—it clogs the blood and slackens the pulse. However, I must not be ungrateful; you meant kindly. Yes, I suppose Welby is practical; he has no belief, and he has got a place. But our host, I presume, is also practical; his place is a much higher one than Welby's, and yet he surely is not without belief?"

"He was born before the new ideas came into practical force; but in proportion as they have done so, his beliefs have necessarily disappeared. I don't suppose that he believes in much now, except the two propositions; firstly, that if he accept the new ideas, he will have power and keep it, and if he does not accept them, power is out of the question; and secondly, that if the new ideas are to prevail, he is the best man to direct them safely,—beliefs quite enough for a Minister. No wise Minister should have more."

"Does he not believe that the motion he is to resist next week is a bad one?"

"A bad one of course, in its consequences, for if it succeed it will upset him; a good one in itself I am sure he must think it, for he would bring it on himself if he were in opposition."

"I see that Pope's definition is still true, 'Party is the madness of the many for the gain of the few.'"

"No, it is not true. Madness is a wrong word applied to the many; the many are sane enough—they know their own objects, and they make use of the intellect of the few in order to gain their objects. In each party it is the many that control the few who nominally lead them. A man becomes Prime Minister because he seems to the many of his party the fittest person to carry out their views. If he presume to differ from these views, they put him into a moral pillory, and pelt him with their dirtiest stones and their rottenest eggs."

"Then the maxim should be reversed, and party is rather the madness of the few for the gain of the many?"

"Of the two, that is the more correct definition."

"Let me keep my senses and decline to be one of the few."

Kenelm moved away from his cousin's side, and entering one of the less crowded rooms, saw Cecilia Travers seated there in a recess with Lady Glenalvon. He joined them, and after a brief interchange of a few commonplaces, Lady Glenalvon quitted her post to accost a foreign ambassadress, and Kenelm sank into the chair she vacated.

It was a relief to his eye to contemplate Cecilia's candid brow; to his ear to hearken to the soft voice that had no artificial tones, and uttered no cynical witticisms.

"Don't you think it strange," said Kenelm, "that we English should so mould all our habits as to make even what we call pleasure as little pleasurable as possible? We are now in the beginning of June, the fresh outburst of summer, when every day in the country is a delight to eye and ear, and we say, 'the season for hot rooms is beginning.' We alone of civilized races spend our summer in a capital, and cling to the country when the trees are leafless and the brooks frozen."

"Certainly that is a mistake; but I love the country in all seasons, even in winter."

"Provided the country house is full of London people?"

"No; that is rather a drawback. I never want companions in the country."

"True; I should have remembered that you differ from young ladies in general, and make companions of books. They are always more conversible in the country than they are in town; or rather, we listen there to them with less distracted attention. Ha! do I not recognize yonder the fair whiskers of George Belvoir? Who is the lady leaning on his arm?"

"Don't you know?—Lady Emily Belvoir, his wife."

"Ah! I was told that he had married. The lady is handsome. She will become the family diamonds. Does she read Blue-books?"

"I will ask her if you wish."

"Nay, it is scarcely worth while. During my rambles abroad, I saw but few English newspapers. I did, however, learn that George had won his election. Has he yet spoken in Parliament?"

"Yes; he moved the answer to the address this session, and

was much complimented on the excellent tone and taste of his speech. He spoke again a few weeks afterwards, I fear not so successfully."

"Coughed down?"

"Something like it."

"Do him good; he will recover the cough, and fulfil my prophecy of his success."

"Have you done with poor George for the present? If so, allow me to ask whether you have quite forgotten Will Somers and Jessie Wiles?"

"Forgotten them! no."

"But you have never asked after them?"

"I took it for granted that they were as happy as could be expected. Pray assure me that they are."

"I trust so now; but they have had trouble, and have left Graveleigh."

"Trouble! left Graveleigh! You make me uneasy. Pray explain."

"They had not been three months married and installed in the home they owed to you, when poor Will was seized with a rheumatic fever. He was confined to his bed for many weeks; and when at last he could move from it, was so weak as to be still unable to do any work. During his illness Jessie had no heart and little leisure to attend to the shop. Of course I—that is, my dear father—gave them all necessary assistance; but——"

"I understand; they were reduced to objects of charity. Brute that I am, never to have thought of the duties I owed to the couple I had brought together. But pray go on."

"You are aware that just before you left us my father received a proposal to exchange his property at Graveleigh for some lands more desirable to him?"

"I remember. He closed with that offer."

"Yes; Captain Stavers, the new landlord of Graveleigh, seems to be a very bad man; and though he could not turn the Somerses out of the cottage so long as they paid rent—which we took care they did pay—yet out of a very wicked spite he set up a rival shop in one of his other cottages in the village, and it became impossible for these poor young people to get a livelihood at Graveleigh."

"What excuse for spite against so harmless a young couple could Captain Stavers find or invent?"

Cecilia looked down and coloured. "It was a revengeful feeling against Jessie."

"Ah! I comprehend."

"But they have now left the village, and are happily settled elsewhere. Will has recovered his health, and they are prospering—much more than they could ever have done at Graveleigh."

"In that change you were their benefactress, Miss Travers?" said Kenelm, in a more tender voice and with a softer eye than he had ever before evinced towards the heiress.

"No, it is not I whom they have to thank and bless."

"Who, then, is it? Your father?"

"No. Do not question me; I am bound not to say. They do not themselves know; they rather believe that their gratitude is due to you."

"To me! Am I to be for ever a sham in spite of myself? My dear Miss Travers, it is essential to my honour that I should undeceive this credulous pair; where can I find them?"

"I must not say; but I will ask permission of their concealed benefactor, and send you their address."

A touch was laid on Kenelm's arm, and a voice whispered—"May I ask you to present me to Miss Travers?"

"Miss Travers," said Kenelm, "I entreat you to add to the list of your acquaintances a cousin of mine—Mr. Chillingly Gordon."

While Gordon addressed to Cecilia the well-bred conventionalisms with which acquaintance in London drawing-rooms usually commences, Kenelm, obedient to a sign from Lady Glenalvon, who had just re-entered the room, quitted his seat, and joined the Marchioness.

"Is not that young man whom you left talking with Miss Travers your clever cousin Gordon?"

"The same."

"She is listening to him with great attention. How his face brightens up as he talks! He is positively handsome, thus animated."

"Yes, I could fancy him a dangerous wooer. He has wit, and liveliness, and audacity; he could be very much in love with a great fortune, and talk to the owner of it with a fervour rarely exhibited by a Chillingly. Well, it is no affair of mine."

"It ought to be."

"Alas and alas! that 'ought to be;' what depths of sorrowful meaning lie within that simple phrase! How happy would be our lives, how grand our actions, how pure our souls, if all could be with us as it ought to be!"

CHAPTER VIII.

WE often form cordial intimacies in the confined society of a country house, or a quiet watering-place, or a small Continental town, which fade away into remote acquaintanceship in the mighty vortex of London life, neither party being to blame for the estrangement. It was so with Leopold Travers and Kenelm Chillingly. Travers, as we have seen, had felt a powerful charm in the converse of the young stranger, so in contrast with the routine of the rural companionships to which his alert intellect had for many years circumscribed its range. But, on reappearing in London the season before Kenelm again met him, he had renewed old friendships with men of his own standing,—officers in the regiment of which he had once been a popular ornament, some of them still unmarried, a few of them like himself, widowed; others who had been his rivals in fashion, and were still pleasant idlers about town; and it rarely happens in a metropolis that we have intimate friendships with those of another generation, unless there be some common tie in the cultivation of art and letters, or the action of kindred sympathies in the party strife of politics. Therefore Travers and Kenelm had had little familiar communication with each other since they first met at the Beaumanoirs'. Now and then they found themselves at the same crowded assemblies, and interchanged nods and salutations. But their habits were different. The houses at which they were intimate were not the same; neither did they frequent the same clubs. Kenelm's chief bodily exercise was still that of long and early rambles into rural suburbs; Leopold's was that of a late ride in the Row. Of the two, Leopold was much more the man of pleasure. Once restored to metropolitan life, a temper constitutionally eager, ardent, and convivial, took kindly, as in earlier youth, to its light range of enjoyments.

Had the intercourse between the two men been as frankly familiar as it had been at Neesdale Park, Kenelm would probably have seen much more of Cecilia at her own home; and the admiration and esteem with which she already inspired him might have ripened into much warmer feeling, had he thus been brought into clearer comprehension of the soft and womanly heart, and its tender predisposition towards himself.

He had said somewhat vaguely in his letter to Sir Peter, that "sometimes he felt as if his indifference to love, as to ambition, was because he had some impossible ideal in each." Taking that conjecture to task, he could not honestly persuade himself that he had formed any ideal of woman and wife with which the reality of Cecilia Travers was at war. On the contrary, the more he thought over the characteristics of Cecilia, the more they seemed to correspond to any ideal that had floated before him in the twilight of dreamy reverie, and yet he knew that he was not in love with her, that his heart did not respond to his reason. And mournfully he resigned himself to the conviction that nowhere in this planet, from the normal pursuits of whose inhabitants he felt so estranged, was there waiting for him the smiling playmate, the earnest helpmate. As this conviction strengthened, so an increased weariness of the artificial life of the metropolis, and of all its objects and amusements, turned his thoughts with an intense yearning towards the Bohemian freedom and fresh excitements of his foot ramblings. He often thought with envy of the wandering minstrel, and wondered whether, if he again traversed the same range of country, he might encounter again that vagrant singer.

CHAPTER IX.

IT is nearly a week since Kenelm had met Cecilia, and he is sitting in his rooms with Lord Thetford at that hour of three in the afternoon which is found the most difficult to dispose of by idlers about town. Amongst young men of his own age and class with whom Kenelm assorted in the fashionable world, perhaps the one whom he liked the best, and of whom he saw the most, was this young heir of the Beaumanoirs; and though Lord Thetford has nothing to do with the direct stream of my story, it is worth pausing a few minutes to sketch an outline of one of the best whom the last generation has produced for a part that, owing to accidents of birth and fortune, young men like Lord Thetford must play on that stage from which the curtain is not yet drawn up. Destined to be the head of a family that unites with princely possessions and an historical name a keen though honourable ambition for political power, Lord Thetford has been carefully educated, especially in the new ideas of his time. His father, though a man of no ordinary talents, has never taken a prominent part in public life. He desires his eldest son to do so. The Beaumanoirs have been Whigs from the time of William III. They have shared the good and the ill fortunes of a party which, whether we side with it or not, no politician who dreads extremes in the government of a State so pre-eminently artificial that a prevalent extreme at either end of the balance would be fatal to equilibrium, can desire to become extinct or feeble so long as a constitutional monarchy exists in England. From the reign of George I. to the death of George IV., the Beaumanoirs were in the ascendant. Visit their family portrait gallery, and you must admire the eminence of a house which, during that interval of less than a century, contributed so many men to the service of the State or the adornment of the Court—so many Ministers, Ambassadors, Generals, Lord Chamberlains, and Masters of the Horse. When the younger Pitt beat the great Whig Houses, the Beaumanoirs vanish into comparative obscurity; they re-emerge with the accession of William IV., and once more produce bulwarks of the State and ornaments of the Crown. The present Lord of Beaumanoir, *poco curante* in politics though he be, has at least held high offices at Court; and, as a matter of course, he is Lord Lieutenant of his county, as well as Knight of the Garter. He is a man whom the chiefs of his party have been accustomed to consult on critical questions. He gives his opinions confidentially and modestly, and when they are rejected never takes offence. He thinks that a time is coming when the head of the Beaumanoirs should descend into the lists and fight hand-to-hand with any Hodge or Hobson in the cause of his country for the benefit of the Whigs. Too lazy or too old to do this himself, he says to his son, "You must do it: without effort of mine the thing may last my life. It needs effort of yours that the thing may last through your own."

Lord Thetford cheerfully responds to the paternal admonition. He curbs his natural inclinations, which are neither inelegant nor unmanly; for, on the one side, he is very fond of music and painting, an accomplished amateur, and deemed a sound connoisseur in both; and, on the other side, he has a passion for all field sports, and especially for hunting. He allows no such attractions to interfere with diligent attention to the business of the House of Commons. He serves in Committees, he takes the chair at public meetings on sanitary questions, or projects for social improvement, and acquits himself well therein. He has not yet spoken in debate, but he has been only two years in Parliament, and he takes his father's wise advice not to speak till the third. But he is not without weight among the well-born youth of the party, and has in him the stuff out of which, when it becomes seasoned, the Corinthian capitals of a Cabinet may be very effectively carved. In his own heart he is convinced that his party are going too far and too fast; but with that party he goes on light-heartedly, and would continue to do so if they went to Erebus. But he would prefer their going the other way. For the rest, a pleasant bright-eyed young fellow, with vivid animal spirits; and, in the holiday moments of reprieve from public duty he brings sunshine into draggling hunting-fields, and a fresh breeze into heated ball-rooms.

"My dear fellow," said Lord Thetford, as he threw aside his cigar, "I quite understand that you bore yourself—you have nothing else to do."

"What can I do?"

"Work."

"Work!"

"Yes, you are clever enough to feel that you have a mind; and mind is a restless inmate of body—it craves occupation of some sort, and regular occupation too; it needs its daily constitutional exercise. Do you give your mind that?"

"I am sure I don't know, but my mind is always busying itself about something or other."

"In a desultory way—with no fixed object."

"True."

"Write a book, and then it will have its constitutional."

"Nay, my mind is always writing a book (though it may not publish one), always jotting down impressions, or inventing incidents, or investigating characters; and between you and me, I do not think that I do bore myself so much as I did formerly. Other people bore me more than they did."

"Because you will not create an object in common with other people: come into Parliament, side with a party, and you have that object."

"Do you mean seriously to tell me that you are not bored in the House of Commons?"

"With the speakers very often, yes; but with the strife between the speakers, no. The House of Commons life has a peculiar excitement scarcely understood out of it; but you may conceive its charm when you observe that a man who has once been in the thick of it, feels forlorn and shelved if he lose his seat, and even repines when the accident of birth transfers him to the serener air of the Upper House. Try that life, Chillingly."

"I might if I were an ultra-Radical, a Republican, a Communist, a Socialist, and wished to upset everything existing, for then the strife would at least be a very earnest one."

"But could not you be equally in earnest against those revolutionary gentlemen?"

"Are you and your leaders in earnest against them? They don't appear to me so."

Thetford was silent for a minute. "Well, if you doubt the principles of my side, go with the other side. For my part, I and many of our party would be glad to see the Conservatives stronger."

"I have no doubt they would. No sensible man likes to be carried off his legs by the rush of the crowd behind him; and a crowd is less headlong when it sees a strong force arrayed against it in front. But it seems to me that, at present, Conservatism can but be what it now is—a party that may combine for resistance, and will not combine for inventive construction. We are living in an age in which the process of unsettlement is going blindly at work, as if impelled by a Nemesis as blind as itself. New ideas come beating in surf and surge against those which former reasoners had considered as fixed banks and breakwaters; and the new ideas are so mutable, so fickle, that those which were considered novel ten years ago are deemed obsolete to-day, and the new ones of to-day will in their turn be obsolete to-morrow. And, in a sort of fatalism, you see statesmen yielding way to these successive mockeries of experiment—for they are experiments against experience—and saying to each other with a shrug of the shoulders, 'Bismillah, it must be so; the country will have it, even though it sends the country to the dogs.' I don't feel sure that the country will not go there the sooner, if you can only strengthen the Conservative element enough to set it up in office, with the certainty of knocking it down again. Alas! I am too dispassionate a looker-on to be fit for a partisan; would I were not. Address yourself to my cousin Gordon."

"Ay, Chillingly Gordon is a coming man, and has all the earnestness you find absent in party and in yourself."

"You call him earnest?"

"Thoroughly, in the pursuit of one object—the advancement of Chillingly Gordon. If he get into the House of Commons, and succeed there, I hope he will never become my leader; for if he thought Christianity in the way of his promotion, he would bring in a bill for its abolition."

"In that case would he still be your leader?"

"My dear Kenelm, you don't know what is the spirit of party, and how easily it makes excuses for any act of its leader. Of course, if Gordon brought in a bill for the abolition of Christianity, it would be on the plea that the abolition was good for the Christians, and his followers would cheer that enlightened sentiment."

"Ah," said Kenelm, with a sigh, "I own myself the dullest of blockheads; for instead of tempting me into the field of party politics, your talk leaves me in stolid amaze that you do not take to your heels, where honour can only be saved by flight."

"Pooh! my dear Chillingly, we cannot run away from the age in which we live—we must accept its conditions and make the best of them; and if the House of Commons be nothing else, it is a famous debating society and a capital club. Think over it. I must leave you now. I am going to see a picture at the Exhibition which has been most truculently criticised in 'The Londoner,' but which I am assured, on good authority, is a work of remarkable merit. I can't bear to see a man snarled and sneered down, no doubt by jealous rivals, who have their influence in journals, so I shall judge of the picture for myself. If it be really as good as I am told, I shall talk about it to everybody I meet—and in matters of art I fancy my word goes for something. Study art, my dear Kenelm. No gentleman's education is complete if he don't know a good picture from a bad one. After the Exhibition I shall just have time for a canter round the Park before the debate of the session, which begins to-night."

With a light step the young man quitted the room, humming an air from the 'Figaro' as he descended the stairs. From the window Kenelm watched him swinging himself with careless grace into his saddle and riding briskly down the street—in form and face and bearing, a very model of young, high-born, high-bred manhood. "The Venetians," muttered Kenelm, "decapitated Marino Faliero for conspiring against his own order—the nobles. The Venetians loved their institutions, and had faith in them. Is there such love and such faith among the English?"

As he thus soliloquized he heard a shrilling sort of squeak; and a showman stationed before his window the stage on which Punch satirises the laws and moralities of the world, "kills the beadle and defies the devil."

CHAPTER X.

KENELM turned from the sight of Punch and Punch's friend the cur, as his servant, entering, said, "A person from the country, who would not give his name, asked to see him."

Thinking it might be some message from his father, Kenelm ordered the stranger to be admitted, and in another minute there entered a young man of handsome countenance and powerful frame, in whom, after a surprised stare, Kenelm recognized Tom Bowles. Difficult indeed would have been that recognition to an unobservant beholder: no trace was left of the sullen bully or the village farrier;

the expression of the face was mild and intelligent—more bashful than hardy; the brute strength of the form had lost its former clumsiness, the simple dress was that of a gentleman—to use an expressive idiom, the whole man was wonderfully "toned down."

"I am afraid, sir, I am taking a liberty," said Tom, rather nervously, twiddling his hat between his fingers.

"I should be a greater friend to liberty than I am if it were always taken in the same way," said Kenelm, with a touch of his saturnine humour; but then yielding at once to the warmer impulse of his nature, he grasped his old antagonist's hand and exclaimed, "My dear Tom, you are so welcome. I am so glad to see you. Sit down, man—sit down; make yourself at home."

"I did not know you were back in England, sir, till within the last few days; for you did say that when you came back I should see or hear from you," and there was a tone of reproach in the last words.

"I am to blame, forgive me," said Kenelm, remorsefully. "But how did you find me out? you did not, then, I think, even know my name. That, however, it was easy enough to discover; but who gave you my address in this lodging?"

"Well, sir, it was Miss Travers; and she bade me come to you. Otherwise, as you did not send for me, it was scarcely my place to call uninvited."

"But, my dear Tom, I never dreamed that you were in London. One don't ask a man whom one supposes to be more than a hundred miles off to pay one an afternoon call. You are still with your uncle, I presume? and I need not ask if all thrives well with you—you look a prosperous man, every inch of you, from crown to toe."

"Yes," said Tom; "thank you kindly, sir, I am doing well in the way of business, and my uncle is to give me up the whole concern at Christmas."

While Tom thus spoke Kenelm had summoned his servant, and ordered up such refreshments as could be found in the larder of a bachelor in lodgings. "And what brings you to town, Tom?"

"Miss Travers wrote to me about a little business which she was good enough to manage for me, and said you wished to know about it; and so, after turning it over in my mind for a few days, I resolved to come to town: indeed," added Tom, heartily, "I did wish to see your face again."

"But you talk riddles. What business of yours could Miss Travers imagine I wished to know about?"

Tom coloured high, and looked very embarrassed. Luckily the

servant here entering with the refreshment-tray, allowed him time to recover himself. Kenelm helped him to a liberal slice of cold pigeon-pie, pressed wine on him, and did not renew the subject till he thought his guest's tongue was likely to be more freely set loose; then he said, laying a friendly hand on Tom's shoulders, "I have been thinking over what passed between me and Miss Travers. I wished to have the new address of Will Somers; she promised to write to his benefactor to ask permission to give it. You are that benefactor?"

"Don't say benefactor, sir. I will tell you how it came about if you will let me. You see, I sold my little place at Graveleigh to the new Squire, and when mother removed to Luscombe to be near me, she told me how poor Jessie had been annoyed by Captain Stavers, who seems to think his purchase included the young women on the property along with the standing timber; and I was half afraid that she had given some cause for his persecution, for you know she has a blink of those soft eyes of hers that might charm a wise man out of his skin, and put a fool there instead."

"But I hope she has done with those blinks since her marriage."

"Well, and I honestly think she has. It is certain she did not encourage Captain Stavers, for I went over to Graveleigh myself on the sly, and lodged concealed with one of the cottagers who owed me a kindness; and one day, as I was at watch, I saw the Captain peering over the stile which divides Holmwood from the glebe—you remember Holmwood?"

"I can't say I do."

"The footway from the village to Squire Travers's goes through the wood, which is a few hundred yards at the back of Will Somers's orchard. Presently the Captain drew himself suddenly back from the stile, and disappeared among the trees, and then I saw Jessie coming from the orchard with a basket over her arm, and walking quick towards the wood. Then, sir, my heart sank. I felt sure she was going to meet the Captain. However, I crept along the hedgerow, hiding myself, and got into the wood almost as soon as Jessie got there, by another way. Under the cover of the brushwood I stole on till I saw the Captain come out from the copse on the other side of the path, and plant himself just before Jessie. Then I saw at once I had wronged her. She had not expected to see him, for she hastily turned back, and began to run homeward; but he caught her up, and seized her by the arm. I could not hear what he said, but I heard her voice quite sharp with fright and anger. And then he suddenly seized her round the waist, and she screamed, and I sprang forward——"

"And thrashed the Captain?"

"No, I did not," said Tom; "I had made a vow to myself that I never would be violent again if I could help it. So I took him with one hand by the cuff of the neck, and with the other by the waist-band, and just pitched him on a bramble-bush—quite mildly. He soon picked himself up, for he is a dapper little chap, and became very blustering and abusive. But I kept my temper, and said civilly, 'Little gentleman, hard words break no bones; but if ever you molest Mrs. Somers again, I will carry you into her orchard, souse you into the duck-pond there, and call all the villagers to see you scramble out of it again; and I will do it now if you are not off. I dare say you have heard of my name—I am Tom Bowles.' Upon that his face, which was before very red, grew very white, and muttering something I did not hear, he walked away.

"Jessie—I mean Mrs. Somers—seemed at first as much frightened at me as she had been at the Captain; and though I offered to walk with her to Miss Travers's, where she was going with a basket which the young lady had ordered, she refused, and went back home. I felt hurt, and returned to my uncle's the same evening; and it was not for months that I heard the Captain had been spiteful enough to set up an opposition shop, and that poor Will had been taken ill, and his wife was confined about the same time, and the talk was that they were in distress, and might have to be sold up.

"When I heard all this, I thought that after all it was my rough tongue that had so angered the Captain and been the cause of his spite, and so it was my duty to make it up to poor Will and his wife. I did not know how to set about mending matters, but I thought I'd go and talk to Miss Travers; and if ever there was a kind heart in a girl's breast, hers is one."

"You are right there, I guess. What did Miss Travers say?"

"Nay; I hardly know what she did say, but she set me thinking, and it struck me that Jessie—Mrs. Somers—had better move to a distance, and out of the Captain's reach, and that Will would do better in a less out-of-the-way place. And then, by good luck, I read in the newspaper that a stationery and fancy-work business, with a circulating library, was to be sold on moderate terms at Moleswich, the other side of London. So I took the train and went to the place, and thought the shop would just suit these young folks, and not be too much work for either; then I went to Miss Travers, and I had a lot of money lying by me from the sale of the old forge and premises, which I did not know what to do with; and so, to cut short a long story, I bought the business, and Will and his wife are settled at Moleswich, thriving and happy, I hope, sir."

Tom's voice quivered at the last words, and he turned aside quickly, passing his hand over his eyes.

Kenelm was greatly moved.

"And they don't know what you did for them?"

"To be sure not. I don't think Will would have let himself be beholden to me. Ah! the lad has a spirit of his own, and Jessie— Mrs. Somers—would have felt pained and humbled that I should even think of such a thing. Miss Travers managed it all. They take the money as a loan which is to be paid by instalments. They have sent Miss Travers more than one instalment already, so I know they are doing well."

"A loan from Miss Travers?"

"No; Miss Travers wanted to have a share in it, but I begged her not. It made me happy to do what I did all myself; and Miss Travers felt for me and did not press. They perhaps think it is Squire Travers (though he is not a man who would like to say it, for fear it should bring applicants on him), or some other gentleman who takes an interest in them."

"I always said you were a grand fellow, Tom. But you are grander still than I thought you."

"If there be any good in me, I owe it to you, sir. Think what a drunken, violent brute I was when I first met you. Those walks with you, and I may say that other gentleman's talk, and then that long kind letter I had from you, not signed in your name, and written from abroad—all these changed me, as the child is changed at nurse."

"You have evidently read a good deal since we parted."

"Yes; I belong to our young men's library and institute; and when of an evening I get hold of a book, especially a pleasant story book, I don't care for other company."

"Have you never seen any other girl you could care for, and wish to marry?"

"Ah, sir," answered Tom, "a man does not go so mad for a girl as I did for Jessie Wiles, and when it is all over, and he has come to his senses, put his heart into joint again as easily as if it were only a broken leg. I don't say that I may not live to love and to marry another woman—it is my wish to do so. But I know that I shall love Jessie to my dying day; but not sinfully, sir—not sinfully. I would not wrong her by a thought."

There was a long pause.

At last Kenelm said—"You promised to be kind to that little girl with the flower-ball; what has become of her?"

"She is quite well, thank you, sir. My aunt has taken a great fancy to her, and so has my mother. She comes to them very often of an evening, and brings her work with her. A quick, intelligent little thing, and full of pretty thoughts. On Sundays, if the weather is fine, we stroll out together in the fields."

"She has been a comfort to you, Tom."

"Oh yes."

"And loves you?"

"I am sure she does; an affectionate, grateful child."

"She will be a woman, soon, Tom, and may love you as a woman then."

Tom looked indignant and rather scornful at that suggestion, and hastened to revert to the subject more immediately at his heart.

"Miss Travers said you would like to call on Will Somers and his wife; will you? Moleswich is not far from London, you know."

"Certainly, I will call."

"I do hope you will find them happy; and if so, perhaps you will kindly let me know; and—and—I wonder whether Jessie's child is like her? It is a boy—somehow or other I would rather it had been a girl."

"I will write you full particulars. But why not come with me?"

"No, I don't think I could do that, just at present. It unsettled me sadly when I did again see her sweet face at Graveleigh, and she was still afraid of me too!—that was a sharp pang."

"She ought to know what you have done for her, and will."

"On no account, sir; promise me that. I should feel mean if I humbled them—that way."

"I understand, though I will not as yet make you any positive promise. Meanwhile, if you are staying in town, lodge with me; my landlady can find you a room."

"Thank you heartily, sir; but I go back by the evening train; and, bless me! how late it is now! I must wish you good-bye. I have some commissions to do for my aunt, and I must buy a new doll for Susey."

"Susey is the name of the little girl with the flower-ball?"

"Yes. I must run off now; I feel quite light at heart seeing you again and finding that you receive me still so kindly, as if we were equals."

"Ah, Tom, I wish I was your equal—nay, half as noble as heaven has made you!"

Tom laughed incredulously, and went his way.

"This mischievous passion of love," said Kenelm to himself, "has its good side, it seems, after all. If it was nearly making a wild beast of that brave fellow—nay, worse than wild beast, a homicide doomed to the gibbet—so, on the other hand, what a refined, delicate, chivalrous nature of gentleman it has developed out of the stormy elements of its first madness. Yes, I will go and look at this new-married couple. I dare say they are already snarling and spitting at each other like cat and dog. Moleswich is within reach of a walk."

BOOK V.

CHAPTER I.

TWO days after the interview recorded in the last chapter of the previous Book, Travers, chancing to call at Kenelm's lodgings, was told by his servant that Mr. Chillingly had left London, alone, and had given no orders as to forwarding letters. The servant did not know where he had gone, or when he would return.

Travers repeated this news incidentally to Cecilia, and she felt somewhat hurt that he had not written her a line respecting Tom's visit. She, however, guessed that he had gone to see the Somerses, and would return to town in a day or so. But weeks passed, the season drew to its close, and of Kenelm Chillingly she saw or heard nothing: he had wholly vanished from the London world. He had but written a line to his servant, ordering him to repair to Exmundham and await him there, and enclosing him a check to pay outstanding bills.

We must now follow the devious steps of the strange being who has grown into the hero of this story. He had left his apartment at daybreak long before his servant was up, with his knapsack, and a small portmanteau, into which he had thrust—besides such additional articles of dress as he thought he might possibly require, and which his knapsack could not contain—a few of his favourite books. Driving with these in a hack-cab to the Vauxhall station, he directed the portmanteau to be forwarded to Moleswich, and flinging the knapsack on his shoulders, walked slowly along the drowsy suburbs that stretched far into the landscape, before, breathing more freely, he found some evidences of rural culture on either side of the highroad. It was not, however, till he had left the roofs and trees of pleasant Richmond far behind him that he began to feel he was out of reach of the metropolitan disquieting influences. Finding at a little inn, where he stopped to breakfast, that there was a path along fields, and in sight of the river, through which he could gain the place of his destination, he then quitted the highroad, and traversing one of the loveliest districts in one of our loveliest counties, he reached Moleswich about noon.

CHAPTER II.

ON entering the main street of the pretty town, the name of Somers, in gilt capitals, was sufficiently conspicuous over the door of a very imposing shop. It boasted two plate-glass windows, at one of which were tastefully exhibited various articles of fine stationery, embroidery patterns, &c.; at the other, no less tastefully, sundry specimens of ornamental basket-work.

Kenelm crossed the threshold and recognized behind the counter —fair as ever, but with an expression of face more staid, and a figure more rounded and matron-like—his old friend Jessie. There were two or three customers before her, between whom she was dividing her attention. While a handsome young lady, seated, was saying, in a somewhat loud, but cheery and pleasant voice, "Do not mind me, Mrs. Somers—I can wait," Jessie's quick eye darted towards the stranger, but too rapidly to distinguish his features, which, indeed, he turned away, and began to examine the baskets.

In a minute or so the other customers were served and had departed. And the voice of the lady was again heard—"Now, Mrs. Somers, I want to see your picture-books and toys. I am giving a little children's party this afternoon, and I want to make them as happy as possible."

"Somewhere or other on this planet, or before my Monad was whisked away to it, I have heard that voice," muttered Kenelm. While Jessie was alertly bringing forth her toys and picture-books, she said, "I am sorry to keep you waiting, sir; but if it is the baskets you come about, I can call my husband."

"Do," said Kenelm.

"William—William," cried Mrs. Somers; and after a delay long enough to allow him to slip on his jacket, William Somers emerged from the back parlour.

His face had lost its old trace of suffering and ill health; it was still somewhat pale, and retained its expression of intellectual refinement.

"How you have improved in your art!" said Kenelm, heartily.

William started, and recognized Kenelm at once. He sprang

forward and took Kenelm's outstretched hand in both his own, and, in a voice between laughing and crying, exclaimed—"Jessie, Jessie, it is he!—he whom we pray for every night. God bless you!—God bless and make you as happy as He permitted you to make me!"

Before this little speech was faltered out, Jessie was by her husband's side, and she added, in a lower voice, but tremulous with deep feeling—"And me too!"

"By your leave, Will," said Kenelm, and he saluted Jessie's white forehead with a kiss that could not have been kindlier or colder if it had been her grandfather's.

Meanwhile the lady had risen noiselessly and unobserved, and stealing up to Kenelm, looked him full in the face.

"You have another friend here, sir, who has also some cause to thank you——"

"I thought I remembered your voice," said Kenelm, looking puzzled. "But pardon me if I cannot recall your features. Where have we met before?"

"Give me your arm when we go out, and I will bring myself to your recollection. But no: I must not hurry you away now. I will call again in half an hour. Mrs. Somers, meanwhile put up the things I have selected. I will take them away with me when I come back from the vicarage, where I have left the pony-carriage." So, with a parting nod and smile to Kenelm, she turned away, and left him bewildered.

"But who is that lady, Will?"

"A Mrs. Braefield. She is a new-comer."

"She may well be that, Will," said Jessie, smiling, "for she has only been married six months."

"And what was her name before she married?"

"I am sure I don't know, sir. It is only three months since we came here, and she has been very kind to us, and an excellent customer. Everybody likes her. Mr. Braefield is a city gentleman, and very rich; and they live in the finest house in the place, and see a great deal of company."

"Well, I am no wiser than I was before," said Kenelm. "People who ask questions very seldom are."

"And how did you find us out, sir?" said Jessie. "Oh! I guess," she added, with an arch glance and smile. "Of course, you have seen Miss Travers, and she told you."

"You are right. I first learned your change of residence from her, and thought I would come and see you, and be introduced to the baby—a boy, I understand? Like you, Will?"

"No, sir—the picture of Jessie."

"Nonsense, Will; it is you all over, even to its little hands."

"And your good mother, Will, how did you leave her?"

"Oh, sir!" cried Jessie, reproachfully; "do you think we could have the heart to leave mother—so lone and rheumatic too? She is tending baby, now—always does while I am in the shop."

Here Kenelm followed the young couple into the parlour, where, seated by the window, they found old Mrs. Somers reading the Bible and rocking the baby, who slept peacefully in its cradle.

"Will," said Kenelm, bending his dark face over the infant, "I will tell you a pretty thought of a foreign poet's, which has been thus badly translated:—

"'Blest babe, a boundless world this bed so narrow seems to thee;
Grow man, and narrower than this bed the boundless world shall be.'"[1]

"I don't think that is true, sir," said Will, simply; "for a happy home is a world wide enough for any man."

Tears started into Jessie's eyes; she bent down and kissed—not the baby—but the cradle. "Will made it." She added, blushing, "I mean the cradle, sir."

Time flew past while Kenelm talked with Will and the old mother, for Jessie was soon summoned back to the shop; and Kenelm was startled when he found the half-hour's grace allowed to him was over, and Jessie put her head in at the door and said, "Mrs. Braefield is waiting for you."

"Good-bye, Will; I shall come and see you again soon; and my mother gives me a commission to buy I don't know how many specimens of your craft."

CHAPTER III.

A SMART pony-phaeton, with a box for a driver in livery equally smart, stood at the shop-door.

"Now, Mr. Chillingly," said Mrs. Braefield, "it is my turn to run away with you; get in!"

"Eh!" murmured Kenelm, gazing at her with large dreamy eyes. "Is it possible?"

"Quite possible; get in. Coachman, home! Yes, Mr. Chillingly, you meet again that giddy creature whom you threatened to thrash; it would have served her right. I ought to feel so ashamed

[1] Schiller.

to recall myself to your recollection, and yet I am not a bit ashamed. I am proud to show you that I have turned out a steady, respectable woman, and, my husband tells me, a good wife."

"You have only been six months married, I hear," said Kenelm, dryly. "I hope your husband will say the same six years hence."

"He will say the same sixty years hence, if we live as long."

"How old is he now?"

"Thirty-eight."

"When a man wants only two years of his hundredth, he probably had learned to know his own mind; but then, in most cases, very little mind is left to him to know."

"Don't be satirical, sir; and don't talk as if you were railing at marriage, when you have just left as happy a young couple as the sun ever shone upon; and owing,—for Mrs. Somers has told me all about her marriage—owing their happiness to you."

"Their happiness to me! not in the least. I helped them to marry, and in spite of marriage, they helped each other to be happy."

"You are still unmarried yourself?"

"Yes, thank Heaven!"

"And are you happy?"

"No; I can't make myself happy—myself is a discontented brute."

"Then why do you say 'thank Heaven'?"

"Because it is a comfort to think I am not making somebody else unhappy."

"Do you believe that if you loved a wife who loved you, you should make her unhappy?"

"I am sure I don't know; but I have not seen a woman whom I could love as a wife. And we need not push our inquiries further. What has become of that ill-treated gray cob?"

"He was quite well, thank you, when I last heard of him."

"And the uncle who would have inflicted me upon you, if you had not so gallantly defended yourself?"

"He is living where he did live, and has married his housekeeper. He felt a delicate scruple against taking that step till I was married myself, and out of the way."

Here Mrs. Braefield, beginning to speak very hurriedly, as women who seek to disguise emotion often do, informed Kenelm how unhappy she had felt for weeks after, having found an asylum with her aunt—how she had been stung by remorse and oppressed by a sense of humiliation at the thought of her folly and the odious recollection of Mr. Compton—how she had declared to herself that she would never marry any one now—never! How Mr. Braefield happened to be on a visit in the neighbourhood, and saw her at church—how he had sought an introduction to her—and how at first she rather disliked him than not; but he was so good and so kind, and when at last he proposed—and she had frankly told him all about her girlish flight and infatuation—how generously he had thanked her for a candour which had placed her as high in his esteem as she had been before in his love. "And from that moment," said Mrs. Braefield, passionately, "my whole heart leapt to him. And now you know all. And here we are at the Lodge."

The pony-phaeton went with great speed up a broad gravel-drive, bordered with rare evergreens, and stopped at a handsome house with a portico in front, and a long conservatory at the garden side— one of those houses which belong to "city gentlemen," and often contain more comfort and exhibit more luxury than many a stately manorial mansion.

Mrs. Braefield evidently felt some pride as she led Kenelm through the handsome hall, paved with Malvern tiles and adorned with Scagliola columns, and into a drawing-room furnished with much taste, and opening on a spacious flower-garden.

"But where is Mr. Braefield?" asked Kenelm.

"Oh, he has taken the rail to his office; but he will be back long before dinner, and of course you dine with us."

"You're very hospitable, but——"

"No buts: I will take no excuse. Don't fear that you shall have only mutton-chops and a rice pudding; and besides, I have a children's party coming at two o'clock, and there will be all sorts of fun. You are fond of children, I am sure?"

"I rather think I am not. But I have never clearly ascertained my own inclinations upon that subject."

"Well, you shall have ample opportunity to do so to-day. And oh! I promise you the sight of the loveliest face that you can picture to yourself when you think of your future wife."

"My future wife, I hope, is not yet born," said Kenelm, wearily, and with much effort suppressing a yawn. "But, at all events, I will stay till after two o'clock; for two o'clock, I presume, means luncheon."

Mrs. Braefield laughed.—"You retain your appetite?"

"Most single men do, provided they don't fall in love and become doubled up."

At this abominable attempt at a pun, Mrs. Braefield disdained to laugh; but turning away from its perpetrator she took off her hat and gloves and passed her hands lightly over her forehead, as if to smooth back some vagrant tress in locks already sufficiently sheen and trim. She was not quite so pretty in female attire as she had appeared in boy's dress, nor did she look quite as young. In all other respects she was wonderfully improved. There was a serener, a more settled intelligence in her frank bright eyes, a milder expression in the play of her parted lips. Kenelm gazed at her with pleased admiration. And as now, turning from the glass, she encountered his look, a deeper colour came into the clear delicacy of her cheeks, and the frank eyes moistened. She came up to him as he sate, and took his hand in both hers, pressing it warmly, "Ah, Mr. Chillingly," she said, with impulsive tremulous tones, "look round, look round this happy peaceful home!—the life so free from a care, the husband whom I so love and honour; all the blessings that I might have so recklessly lost for ever had I not met with you, had I been punished as I deserved. How often I thought of your words, that 'you would be proud of my friendship when we met again!' What strength they gave me in my hours of humbled self-reproach!" Her voice here died away as if in the effort to suppress a sob.

She released his hand, and before he could answer, passed quickly through the open sash into the garden.

CHAPTER IV.

THE children have come,—some thirty of them, pretty as English children generally are, happy in the joy of the summer sunshine, and the flower lawns, and the feast under cover of an awning suspended between chestnut-trees, and carpeted with sward.

No doubt Kenelm held his own at the banquet, and did his best to increase the general gaiety, for whenever he spoke the children listened eagerly, and when he had done they laughed mirthfully.

"The fair face I promised you," whispered Mrs. Braefield, "is not here yet. I have a little note from the young lady to say that Mrs. Cameron does not feel very well this morning, but hopes to recover sufficiently to come later in the afternoon."

"And pray who is Mrs. Cameron?"

"Ah! I forgot that you are a stranger to the place. Mrs. Cameron is the aunt with whom Lily resides. Is it not a pretty name, Lily?"

"Very! emblematic of a spinster that does not spin, with a white head and a thin stalk."

"Then the name belies my Lily, as you will see."

The children now finished their feast, and betook themselves to dancing in an alley smoothed for a croquet-ground, and to the sound of a violin played by the old grandfather of one of the party. While Mrs. Braefield was busying herself with forming the dance, Kenelm seized the occasion to escape from a young nymph of the age of twelve who had sat next him at the banquet, and taken so great a fancy to him that he began to fear she would vow never to forsake his side, and stole away undetected.

There are times when the mirth of others only saddens us, especially the mirth of children with high spirits, that jar on our own quiet mood. Gliding through a dense shrubbery, in which, though the lilacs were faded, the laburnum still retained here and there the waning gold of its clusters, Kenelm came into a recess which bounded his steps and invited him to repose. It was a circle, so formed artificially by slight trellises, to which clung parasite roses heavy with leaves and flowers. In the midst played a tiny fountain with a silvery murmuring sound; at the background, dominating the place, rose the crests of stately trees, on which the sunlight shimmered, but which rampired out all horizon beyond. Even as in life do the great dominant passions—love, ambition, desire of power, or gold, or fame, or knowledge—form the proud background to the brief-lived flowerets of our youth, lift our eyes beyond the smile of their bloom, catch the glint of a loftier sunbeam, and yet, and yet, exclude our sight from the lengths and the widths of the space which extends behind and beyond them.

Kenelm threw himself on the turf beside the fountain. From afar came the whoop and the laugh of the children in their sports or their dance. At the distance their joy did not sadden him—he marvelled why; and thus, in musing reverie, thought to explain the why to himself.

"The poet," so ran his lazy thinking, "has told us that 'distance lends enchantment to the view,' and thus compares to the charm of distance the illusion of hope. But the poet narrows the scope of his own illustration. Distance lends enchantment to the ear as well as to the sight; nor to these bodily senses alone. Memory no less than hope owes its charm to 'the far away.'

"I cannot imagine myself again a child when I am in the midst of yon noisy children. But as their noise reaches me here, subdued and mellowed, and knowing, thank Heaven! that the urchins are not within reach of me, I could readily dream myself back into childhood, and into sympathy with the lost playfields of school.

"So surely it must be with grief: how different the terrible agony for a beloved one just gone from earth, to the soft regret for one

K

who disappeared into heaven years ago! So with the art of poetry: how imperatively, when it deals with the great emotions of tragedy, it must remove the actors from us, in proportion as the emotions are to elevate, and the tragedy is to please us by the tears it draws! Imagine our shock if a poet were to place on the stage some wise gentleman with whom we dined yesterday, and who was discovered to have killed his father and married his mother. But when Œdipus commits those unhappy mistakes nobody is shocked. Oxford in the nineteenth century is a long way off from Thebes 3000 or 4000 years ago.

"And," continued Kenelm, plunging deeper into the maze of metaphysical criticism, "even where the poet deals with persons and things close upon our daily sight—if he would give them poetic charm he must resort to a sort of moral or psychological distance; the nearer they are to us in external circumstance, the farther they must be in some internal peculiarities. Werter and Clarissa Harlowe are described as contemporaries of their artistic creation, and with the minutest details of an apparent realism; yet they are at once removed from our daily lives by their idiosyncrasies and their fates. We know that while Werter and Clarissa are so near to us in much that we sympathize with them as friends and kinsfolk, they are yet as much remote from us in the poetic and idealized side of their natures as if they belonged to the age of Homer; and this it is that invests with charm the very pain which their fate inflicts on us. Thus, I suppose, it must be in love. If the love we feel is to have the glamour of poetry, it must be love for some one morally at a distance from our ordinary habitual selves; in short, differing from us in attributes which, however near we draw to the possessor, we can never approach, never blend, in attributes of our own; so that there is something in the loved one that always remains an ideal—a mystery—'a sun-bright summit mingling with the sky!'"

Herewith the soliloquist's musings slided vaguely into mere reverie. He closed his eyes drowsily, not asleep, nor yet quite awake: as sometimes in bright summer days when we recline on the grass we do close our eyes, and yet dimly recognize a golden light bathing the drowsy lids; and athwart that light images come and go like dreams, though we know that we are not dreaming.

CHAPTER V.

FROM this state, half comatose, half unconscious, Kenelm was roused slowly, reluctantly. Something struck softly on his cheek—again a little less softly; he opened his eyes—they fell first upon two tiny rosebuds, which, on striking his face, had fallen on his breast; and then looking up, he saw before him, in an opening of the trellised circle, a female child's laughing face. Her hand was still uplifted charged with another rosebud, but behind the child's figure, looking over her shoulder and holding back the menacing arm, was a face as innocent but lovelier far—the face of a girl in her first youth, framed round with the blossoms that festooned the trellis. How the face became the flowers! It seemed the fairy spirit of them.

Kenelm started and rose to his feet. The child, the one whom he had so ungallantly escaped from, ran towards him through a wicket in the circle. Her companion disappeared.

"Is it you?" said Kenelm to the child—"you who pelted me so cruelly? Ungrateful creature! Did I not give you the best strawberries in the dish and all my own cream?"

"But why did you run away and hide yourself when you ought to be dancing with me?" replied the young lady, evading, with the instinct of her sex, all answer to the reproach she had deserved.

"I did not run away, and it is clear that I did not mean to hide myself since you so easily found me out. But who was the young lady with you? I suspect she pelted me too, for *she* seems to have run away to hide herself."

"No, she did not pelt you; she wanted to stop me, and you would have had another rosebud—oh, so much bigger!—if she had not held back my arm. Don't you know her—don't you know Lily?"

"No; so that is Lily? You shall introduce me to her."

By this time they had passed out of the circle through the little wicket opposite the path by which Kenelm had entered, and opening at once on the lawn. Here at some distance the children were grouped, some reclined on the grass, some walking to and fro, in the interval of the dance.

In the space between the group and the trellis, Lily was walking alone and quickly. The child left Kenelm's side and ran after her friend, soon overtook, but did not succeed in arresting her steps. Lily did not pause till she had reached the grassy ball-room, and here all the children came round her and shut out her delicate form from Kenelm's sight.

Before he had reached the place, Mrs. Braefield met him.

"Lily is come!"

"I know it—I have seen her."

"Is not she beautiful?"

"I must see more of her if I am to answer critically; but before you introduce me, may I be permitted to ask who and what is Lily?"

Mrs. Braefield paused a moment before she answered, and yet the answer was brief enough not to need much consideration. "She is a Miss Mordaunt, an orphan; and, as I before told you, resides with her aunt, Mrs. Cameron, a widow. They have the prettiest cottage you ever saw on the banks of the river, or rather rivulet, about a mile from this place. Mrs. Cameron is a very good, simple-hearted woman. As to Lily, I can praise her beauty only with safe conscience, for as yet she is a mere child—her mind quite unformed."

"Did you ever meet any man, much less any woman, whose mind was formed?" muttered Kenelm. "I am sure mine is not, and never will be on this earth."

Mrs. Braefield did not hear this low-voiced observation. She was looking about for Lily; and perceiving her at last as the children who surrounded her were dispersing to renew the dance, she took Kenelm's arm, led him to the young lady, and a formal introduction took place.

Formal as it could be on those sunlit swards, amidst the joy of summer and the laugh of children. In such scene and such circumstance, formality does not last long. I know not how it was, but in a very few minutes Kenelm and Lily had ceased to be strangers to each other. They found themselves seated apart from the rest of the merry-makers, on the bank shadowed by lime-trees; the man listening with downcast eyes, the girl with mobile shifting glances now on earth now on heaven, and talking freely, gaily—like the babble of a happy stream, with a silvery dulcet voice, and a sparkle of rippling smiles.

No doubt this is a reversal of the formalities of well-bred life, and conventional narrating thereof. According to them, no doubt, it is for the man to talk and the maid to listen; but I state the facts as they were, honestly. And Lily knew no more of the formalities of drawing-room life than a skylark fresh from its nest knows of the song-teacher and the cage. She was still so much of a child. Mrs. Braefield was right—her mind was still so unformed.

What she did talk about in that first talk between them that could make the meditative Kenelm listen so mutely, so intently, I know not, at least I could not jot it down on paper. I fear it was very egotistical, as the talk of children generally is—about herself and her aunt, and her home and her friends—all her friends seemed children like herself, though younger—Clemmy the chief of them. Clemmy was the one who had taken a fancy to Kenelm. And amidst all this ingenuous prattle there came flashes of a quick intellect, a lively fancy—nay, even a poetry of expression or of sentiment. It might be the talk of a child, but certainly not of a silly child.

But as soon as the dance was over, the little ones again gathered round Lily. Evidently she was the prime favourite of them all; and as her companion had now become tired of dancing, new sports were proposed, and Lily was carried off to " Prisoner's Base."

"I am very happy to make your acquaintance, Mr. Chillingly," said a frank, pleasant voice; and a well-dressed, good-looking man held out his hand to Kenelm.

"My husband," said Mrs. Braefield, with a certain pride in her look.

Kenelm responded cordially to the civilities of the master of the house, who had just returned from his city office, and left all its cares behind him. You had only to look at him to see that he was prosperous, and deserved to be so. There were in his countenance the signs of strong sense, of good-humour—above all, of an active energetic temperament. A man of broad smooth forehead, keen hazel eyes, firm lips and jaw; with a happy contentment in himself, his house, the world in general, mantling over his genial smile, and out-spoken in the metallic ring of his voice.

"You will stay and dine with us, of course," said Mr. Braefield; "and unless you want very much to be in town to-night, I hope you will take a bed here."

Kenelm hesitated.

"Do stay at least till to-morrow," said Mrs. Braefield. Kenelm hesitated still; and while hesitating his eye rested on Lily, leaning on the arm of a middle-aged lady, and approaching the hostess—evidently to take leave.

"I cannot resist so tempting an invitation," said Kenelm, and he fell back a little behind Lily and her companion.

"Thank you much for so pleasant a day," said Mrs. Cameron to the hostess. "Lily has enjoyed herself extremely. I only regret we could not come earlier."

"If you are walking home," said Mr. Braefield, "let me accompany you. I want to speak to your gardener about his heart's-ease—it is much finer than mine."

"If so," said Kenelm to Lily, "may I come too? Of all flowers that grow, heart's-ease is the one I most prize."

A few minutes afterwards Kenelm was walking by the side of Lily along the banks of a little stream, tributary to the Thames— Mrs. Cameron and Mr. Braefield in advance, for the path only held two abreast.

Suddenly Lily left his side, allured by a rare butterfly—I think it is called the Emperor of Morocco—that was sunning its yellow wings upon a group of wild reeds. She succeeded in capturing this wanderer in her straw hat, over which she drew her sun-veil. After this notable capture she returned demurely to Kenelm's side.

"Do you collect insects?" said that philosopher, as much surprised as it was his nature to be at anything.

"Only butterflies," answered Lily; "they are not insects, you know; they are souls."

"Emblems of souls you mean—at least, so the Greeks prettily represented them to be."

"No, real souls—the souls of infants that die in their cradles unbaptized; and if they are taken care of, and not eaten by birds, and live a year, then they pass into fairies."

"It is a very poetical idea, Miss Mordaunt, and founded on evidence quite as rational as other assertions of the metamorphosis of one creature into another. Perhaps you can do what the philosophers cannot—tell me how you learned a new idea to be an incontestible fact?"

"I don't know," replied Lily, looking very much puzzled; "perhaps I learned it in a book, or perhaps I dreamed it."

"You could not make a wiser answer if you were a philosopher. But you talk of taking care of butterflies; how do you do that? Do you impale them on pins stuck into a glass case?"

"Impale them! How can you talk so cruelly? You deserve to be pinched by the fairies."

"I am afraid," thought Kenelm, compassionately, "that my companion has no mind to be formed; what is euphoniously called 'an innocent.'"

He shook his head and remained silent.

Lily resumed—

"I will show you my collection when we get home—they seem so happy. I am sure there are some of them who know me—they will feed from my hand. I have only had one die since I began to collect them last summer."

"Then you have kept them a year; they ought to have turned into fairies."

"I suppose many of them have. Of course I let out all those that had been with me twelve months—they don't turn to fairies in the cage, you know. Now I have only those I caught this year, or last autumn; the prettiest don't appear till the autumn."

The girl here bent her uncovered head over the straw hat, her tresses shadowing it, and uttered loving words to the prisoner. Then again she looked up and around her, and abruptly stopped, and exclaimed—

"How can people live in towns—how can people say they are ever dull in the country? Look," she continued, gravely and earnestly— "look at that tall pine-tree, with its long branch sweeping over the water; see how, as the breeze catches it, it changes its shadow, and how the shadow changes the play of the sunlight on the brook:—

'Wave your tops, ye pines;
With every plant, in sign of worship wave.'

What an interchange of music there must be between Nature and a poet!"

Kenelm was startled. This "an innocent"!—this a girl who had no mind to be formed! In that presence he could not be cynical; could not speak of Nature as a mechanism, a lying humbug; as he had done to the man poet. He replied gravely—

"The Creator has gifted the whole universe with language, but few are the hearts that can interpret it. Happy those to whom it is no foreign tongue, acquired imperfectly with care and pain, but rather a native language, learned unconsciously from the lips of the great mother. To them the butterfly's wing may well buoy into heaven a fairy's soul!"

When he had thus said Lily turned, and for the first time attentively looked into his dark soft eyes; then instinctively she laid her light hand on his arm, and said in a low voice, "Talk on—talk thus; I like to hear you."

But Kenelm did not talk on. They had now arrived at the garden-gate of Mrs. Cameron's cottage, and the elder persons in advance paused at the gate and walked with them to the house.

It was a long, low, irregular cottage, without pretention to architectural beauty, yet exceedingly picturesque—a flower-garden, large, but in proportion to the house, with parterres in which the colours were exquisitely assorted, sloping to the grassy margin of the rivulet, where the stream expanded into a lake-like basin, narrowed at either end by locks, from which with gentle sound flowed shallow waterfalls. By the banks was a rustic seat, half overshadowed by the drooping boughs of a vast willow.

The inside of the house was in harmony with the exterior—cottage-like, but with an unmistakable air of refinement about the rooms, even in the little entrance-hall, which was painted in Pompeian frescoes.

"Come and see my butterfly-cage," said Lily, whisperingly.

Kenelm followed her through the window that opened on the garden; and at one end of a small conservatory, or rather, greenhouse, was the habitation of these singular favourites. It was as large as a small room; three sides of it formed by minute wirework, with occasional draperies of muslin or other slight material, and covered at intervals, sometimes within, sometimes without, by dainty creepers; a tiny cistern in the centre, from which upsprang a sparkling jet. Lily cautiously lifted a sash-door and glided in, closing it behind her. Her entrance set in movement a multitude of gossamer wings, some fluttering round her, some more boldly settling on her hair or dress. Kenelm thought she had not vainly boasted when she said that some of the creatures had learned to know her. She relieved the Emperor of Morocco from her hat; it circled round her fearlessly, and then vanished amidst the leaves of the creepers. Lily opened the door and came out.

"I have heard of a philosopher who tamed a wasp," said Kenelm, "but never before of a young lady who tamed butterflies."

"No," said Lily, proudly; "I believe I am the first who attempted it. I don't think I should have attempted it if I had been told that others had succeeded before me. Not that I have succeeded quite. No matter; if they don't love me, I love them."

They re-entered the drawing-room, and Mrs. Cameron addressed Kenelm.

"Do you know much of this part of the country, Mr. Chillingly?"

"It is quite new to me, and more rural than many districts further from London."

"That is the good fortune of most of our home counties," said Mr. Braefield; "they escape the smoke and din of manufacturing towns, and agricultural science has not demolished their leafy hedgerows. The walks through our green lanes are as much bordered with convolvulus and honeysuckle as they were when Izaak Walton sauntered through them to angle in that stream!"

"Does tradition say that he angled in that stream? I thought his haunts were rather on the other side of London."

"Possibly; I am not learned in Walton or in his art, but there is an old summer-house, on the other side of the lock yonder, on which is carved the name of Izaak Walton, but whether by his own hand or another's who shall say? Has Mr. Melville been here lately, Mrs. Cameron?"

"No, not for several months."

"He has had a glorious success this year. We may hope that at last his genius is acknowledged by the world. I meant to buy his picture, but I was not in time—a Manchester man was before me."

"Who is Mr. Melville? any relation to you?" whispered Kenelm to Lily.

"Relation—I scarcely know. Yes, I suppose so, because he is my guardian. But if he were the nearest relation on earth, I could not love him more," said Lily, with impulsive eagerness, her cheeks flushing, her eyes filling with tears.

"And he is an artist—a painter?" asked Kenelm.

"Oh yes; no one paints such beautiful pictures—no one so clever, no one so kind."

Kenelm strove to recollect if he had ever heard the name of Melville as a painter, but in vain. Kenelm, however, knew but little of painters—they were not in his way; and he owned to himself, very humbly, that there might be many a living painter of eminent renown whose name and works would be strange to him.

He glanced round the wall,—Lily interpreted his look. "There are no pictures of his here," said she; "there is one in my own room. I will show it you when you come again."

"And now," said Mr. Braefield, rising, "I must just have a word with your gardener, and then go home. We dine earlier here than in London, Mr. Chillingly."

As the two gentlemen, after taking leave, re-entered the hall, Lily followed them and said to Kenelm, "What time will you come to-morrow to see the picture?"

Kenelm averted his head, and then replied, not with his wonted courtesy, but briefly and brusquely—

"I fear I cannot call to-morrow. I shall be far away by sunrise."

Lily made no answer, but turned back into the room.

Mr. Braefield found the gardener watering a flower-border, conferred with him about the heart's-ease, and then joined Kenelm, who had halted a few yards beyond the garden-gate.

"A pretty little place that," said Mr. Braefield, with a sort of lordly compassion, as became the owner of Braefieldville, "What I call quaint."

"Yes, quaint," echoed Kenelm abstractedly.

"It is always the case with houses enlarged by degrees. I have heard my poor mother say that when Melville or Mrs. Cameron first bought it, it was little better than a mere labourer's cottage, with a field attached to it. And two or three years afterwards a room or so more was built, and a bit of the field taken in for a garden; and then by degrees the whole part now inhabited by the family was built, leaving only the old cottage as a scullery and wash-house; and the whole field was turned into the garden, as you see. But whether it was Melville's money or the aunt's that did it, I don't know. More likely the aunt's. I don't see what interest Melville has in the place; he does not go there often, I fancy—it is not his home."

"Mr. Melville, it seems, is a painter, and, from what I heard you say, a successful one."

"I fancy he had little success before this year. But surely you saw his pictures at the Exhibition?"

"I am ashamed to say I have not been to the Exhibition."

"You surprise me. However, Melville had three pictures there —all very good; but the one I wished to buy made much more sensation than the others, and has suddenly lifted him from obscurity into fame."

"He appears to be a relation of Miss Mordaunt's, but so distant a one, that she could not even tell me what grade of cousinship he could claim."

"Nor can I. He is her guardian, I know. The relationship, if any, must, as you say, be very distant; for Melville is of humble extraction, while any one can see that Mrs. Cameron is a thorough gentlewoman, and Lily Mordaunt is her sister's child. I have heard my mother say that it was Melville, then a very young man, who bought the cottage, perhaps with Mrs. Cameron's money; saying it was for a widowed lady, whose husband had left her with very small means. And when Mrs. Cameron arrived with Lily, then a mere infant, she was in deep mourning, and a very young woman herself—pretty, too. If Melville had been a frequent visitor then, of course there would have been scandal; but he very seldom came, and when he did, he lodged in a cottage, Cromwell Lodge, on the other side of the brook; now and then bringing with him a fellow-lodger—some other young artist, I suppose, for the sake of angling. So there could be no cause for scandal, and nothing can be more blameless than poor Mrs. Cameron's life. My mother, who then resided at Braefieldville, took a great fancy to both Lily and her aunt, and when by degrees the cottage grew into a genteel sort of place, the few gentry in the neighbourhood followed my mother's example and were very kind to Mrs. Cameron, so that she has now her place in the society about here, and is much liked."

"And Mr. Melville?—does he still very seldom come here?"

"To say truth, he has not been at all since I settled at Braefieldville. The place was left to my mother for her life, and I was not much there during her occupation. In fact, I was then a junior partner in our firm, and conducted the branch business in New York, coming over to England for my holiday once a year or so. When my mother died, there was much to arrange before I could settle personally in England, and I did not come to settle at Braefieldville till I married. I did see Melville on one of my visits to the place some years ago; but, between ourselves, he is not the sort of person whose intimate acquaintance one would wish to court. My mother told me he was an idle, dissipated man, and I have heard from others that he was very unsteady. Mr. ———, the great painter, told me that he was a loose fish; and I suppose his habits were against his getting on, till this year, when, perhaps by a lucky accident, he has painted a picture that raises him to the top of the tree. But is not Miss Lily wondrously nice to look at? What a pity her education has been so much neglected!"

"Has it?"

"Have not you discovered that already? She has not had even a music-master, though my wife says she has a good ear, and can sing prettily enough. As for reading, I don't think she has read anything but fairy tales and poetry, and such silly stuff. However, she is very young yet; and now that her guardian can sell his pictures, it is to be hoped that he will do more justice to his ward. Painters and actors are not so regular in their private lives as we plain men are, and great allowance is to be made for them; still, every one is bound to do his duty. I am sure you agree with me?"

"Certainly," said Kenelm, with an emphasis which startled the merchant. "That is an admirable maxim of yours: it seems a commonplace, yet how often, when it is put into our heads, it strikes as a novelty. A duty may be a very difficult thing, a very disagreeable thing, and, what is strange, it is often a very invisible thing. It is present—close before us, and yet we don't see it; somebody shouts its name in our ears, 'Duty,' and straight it towers before us a grim giant. Pardon me if I leave you—I can't stay to dine. Duty summons me elsewhere. Make my excuses to Mrs. Braefield."

Before Mr. Braefield could recover his self-possession, Kenelm had vaulted over a stile and was gone.

CHAPTER VI.

KENELM walked into the shop kept by the Somers's, and found Jessie still at the counter. "Give me back my knapsack. Thank you," he said, flinging the knapsack across his shoulders. "Now, do me a favour. A portmanteau of mine ought to be at the station. Send for it, and keep it till I give further directions. I think of going to Oxford for a day or two. Mrs. Somers, one more word with you. Think, answer frankly, are you, as you said this morning, thoroughly happy, and yet married to the man you loved?"

"Oh, so happy!"

"And wish for nothing beyond? Do not wish Will to be other than he is?"

"God forbid! You frighten me, sir."

"Frighten you! Be it so. Every one who is happy should be frightened, lest happiness fly away. Do your best to chain it, and you will, for you attach Duty to Happiness; and," muttered Kenelm, as he turned from the shop, "Duty is sometimes not a rose-coloured tie, but a heavy iron-hued clog."

He strode on through the street towards the sign-post with "To Oxford" inscribed thereon. And whether he spoke literally of the knapsack, or metaphorically of duty, he murmured, as he strode—

"A pedlar's pack that bows the bearer down."

CHAPTER VII.

KENELM might have reached Oxford that night, for he was a rapid and untirable pedestrian; but he halted a little after the moon rose, and laid himself down to rest beneath a new-mown haystack, not very far from the highroad.

He did not sleep. Meditatingly propped on his elbow, he said to himself—

"It is long since I have wondered at nothing. I wonder now: can this be love—really love—unmistakably love? Pooh! it is impossible; the very last person in the world to be in love with. Let us reason upon it—you, myself, and I. To begin with—face! What is face? In a few years the most beautiful face may be very plain. Take the Venus at Florence. Animate her; see her ten years after; a chignon, front teeth (blue or artificially white), mottled complexion, double chin—all that sort of plump prettiness goes into double chin. Face, bah! What man of sense—what pupil of Welby, the realist—can fall in love with a face? and even if I were simpleton enough to do so, pretty faces are as common as daisies. Cecilia Travers has more regular features; Jessie Wiles a richer colouring. I was not in love with them—not a bit of it. Myself, you have nothing to say there. Well, then, mind? Talk of mind, indeed! a creature whose favourite companionship is that of butterflies, and who tells me that butterflies are the souls of infants unbaptized. What an article for 'The Londoner,' on the culture of young women. What a girl for Miss Garrett and Miss Emily Faithful! Put aside Mind as we have done Face. What rests?—the Frenchman's ideal of happy marriage? congenial circumstance of birth, fortune, tastes, habits. Worse still. Myself, answer honestly, are you not floored?"

Whereon "Myself" took up the parable and answered—"O thou fool! why wert thou so ineffably blest in one presence? Why, in quitting that presence, did Duty become so grim? Why dost thou address to me those inept pedantic questionings, under the light of yon moon, which has suddenly ceased to be to thy thoughts an astronomical body, and has become, for ever and for ever, identified in thy heart's dreams with romance and poesy and first love? Why, instead of gazing on that uncomfortable orb, art thou not quickening thy steps towards a cozy inn and a good supper at Oxford? Kenelm, my friend, thou art in for it. No disguising the fact—thou art in love!"

"I'll be hanged if I am," said the Second in the Dualism of Kenelm's mind; and therewith he shifted his knapsack into a pillow, turned his eyes from the moon, and still could not sleep. The face of Lily still haunted his eyes—the voice of Lily still rang in his ears.

Oh, my reader! dost thou here ask me to tell thee what Lily was like?—was she dark, was she fair, was she tall, was she short. Never shalt thou learn these secrets from me. Imagine to thyself the being to which thine whole of life, body and mind and soul, moved irresistibly as the needle to the pole. Let her be tall or short, dark or fair, she is that which out of all womankind has suddenly become the one woman for thee. Fortunate art thou, my reader, if thou chance to have heard the popular song of "My Queen" sung by the one lady who alone can sing it with expression worthy the verse of the poetess and the music of the composition, by the sister of the exquisite songstress. But if thou hast not heard the verse thus sung, to an accompaniment thus composed, still the words themselves are, or ought to be, familiar to thee, if thou art, as I take for granted, a lover of the true lyrical muse. Recall then the words supposed to be uttered by him who knows himself destined to do homage to one he has not yet beheld:—

> "She is standing somewhere—she I shall honour,
>   She that I wait for, my queen, my queen;
> Whether her hair be golden or raven,
>   Whether her eyes be hazel or blue,
> I know not now, it will be engraven
>   Some day hence as my loveliest hue.
> She may be humble or proud, my lady,
>   Or that sweet calm which is just between;
> But whenever she comes, she will find me ready
>   To do her homage, my queen, my queen."

Was it possible that the cruel boy-god "who sharpens his arrows on the whetstone of the human heart" had found the moment to avenge himself for the neglect of his altars and the scorn of his power! Must that redoubted knight-errant, the hero of this tale, despite The Three Fishes on his charmed shield, at last veil the crest and bow the knee, and murmur to himself, "She has come, my queen!"

CHAPTER VIII.

THE next morning Kenelm arrived at Oxford—"Verum secretumque Mouseion."

If there be a place in this busy island which may distract the passions of youth from love to scholarship, to Ritualism, to mediæval associations, to that sort of poetical sentiment or poetical fanaticism which a Mivers and a Welby and an advocate of the Realistic School would hold in contempt—certainly that place is Oxford. Home, nevertheless, of great thinkers and great actors in the practical world.

The vacation had not yet commenced, but the commencement was near at hand. Kenelm thought he could recognize the leading men by their slower walk and more abstracted expression of countenance. Among the fellows was the eminent author of that book which had so powerfully fascinated the earlier adolescence of Kenelm Chillingly, and who had himself been subject to the fascination of a yet stronger spirit. The Rev. Decimus Roach had been ever an intense and reverent admirer of John Henry Newman—an admirer, I mean, of the pure and lofty character of the man, quite apart from sympathy with his doctrines. But although Roach remained an unconverted Protestant of orthodox, if High Church, creed, yet there was one tenet he did hold in common with the author of the 'Apologia.' He ranked celibacy among the virtues most dear to Heaven. In that eloquent treatise, 'The Approach to the Angels,' he not only maintained that the state of single blessedness was strictly incumbent on every member of a Christian priesthood, but to be commended to the adoption of every conscientious layman.

It was the desire to confer with this eminent theologian that had induced Kenelm to direct his steps to Oxford.

Mr. Roach was a friend of Welby's, at whose house, when a pupil, Kenelm had once or twice met him, and been even more charmed by his conversation than by his treatise. Kenelm called on Mr. Roach, who received him very graciously, and not being a tutor or examiner, placed his time at Kenelm's disposal; took him the round of the colleges and the Bodleian; invited him to dine in his college-hall; and after dinner led him into his own rooms, and gave him an excellent bottle of Chateau Margeaux.

Mr. Roach was somewhere about fifty—a good-looking man, and evidently thought himself so, for he wore his hair long behind and parted in the middle; which is not done by men who form modest estimates of their personal appearance.

Kenelm was not long in drawing out his host on the subject to which that profound thinker had devoted so much meditation.

"I can scarcely convey to you," said Kenelm, "the intense admiration with which I have studied your noble work, 'Approach to the Angels.' It produced a great effect on me in the age between boyhood and youth. But of late some doubts on the universal application of your doctrine have crept into my mind."

"Ay, indeed?" said Mr. Roach, with an expression of interest in his face.

"And I come to you for their solution."

Mr. Roach turned away his head, and pushed the bottle to Kenelm.

"I am quite willing to concede," resumed the heir of the Chillinglys, "that a priesthood should stand apart from the distracting cares of a family, and pure from all carnal affections."

"Hem, hem," grunted Mr. Roach, taking his knee on his lap and caressing it.

"I go farther," continued Kenelm, "and supposing with you that the Confessional has all the importance, whether in its monitory or its cheering effects upon repentant sinners, which is attached to it by the Roman Catholics, and that it ought to be no less cultivated by the Reformed Church, it seems to me essential that the Confessor should have no better half to whom it can be even suspected he may, in an unguarded moment, hint at the frailties of one of her female acquaintances."

"I pushed that argument too far," murmured Roach.

"Not a bit of it. Celibacy in the Confessor stands or falls with the Confessional. Your argument there is as sound as a bell. But when it comes to the layman, I think I detect a difference."

Mr. Roach shook his head, and replied stoutly, "No; if celibacy be incumbent on the one, it is equally incumbent on the other. I say 'if.'"

"Permit me to deny that assertion. Do not fear that I shall insult your understanding by the popular platitude—viz., that if celibacy were universal, in a very few years the human race would be extinct. As you have justly observed, in answer to that fallacy, 'It is the duty of each human soul to strive towards the highest perfection of the spiritual state for itself, and leave the fate of the human race to the care of the Creator.' If celibacy be necessary to spiritual perfection, how do we know but that it may be the purpose and decree of the All Wise that the human race, having attained to that perfection, should disappear from earth? Universal celibacy would thus be the euthanasia of mankind. On the other hand, if the Creator decided that the human race, having culminated to this crowning but barren flower of perfection, should nevertheless continue to increase and multiply upon earth, have you not victoriously exclaimed, 'Presumptuous mortal! how canst thou presume to limit the resources of the Almighty? Would it not be easy for Him to continue some other mode, unexposed to trouble and sin and passion, as in the nuptials of the vegetable world, by which the generations will be renewed? Can we suppose that the angels—the immortal companies of Heaven—are not hourly increasing in number, and extending their population throughout infinity? and yet in heaven there is no marrying nor giving in marriage.'—All this, clothed by you in words which my memory only serves me to quote imperfectly—all this I unhesitatingly concede."

Mr. Roach rose and brought another bottle of the Chateau Margeaux from his cellaret, filled Kenelm's glass, reseated himself, and took the other knee into his lap to caress.

"But," resumed Kenelm, "my doubt is this."

"Ah!" cried Mr. Roach, "let us hear the doubt."

"In the first place, is celibacy essential to the highest state of spiritual perfection? and, in the second place, if it were, are mortals, as at present constituted, capable of that culmination?"

"Very well put," said Mr. Roach, and he tossed off his glass with more cheerful aspect than he had hitherto exhibited.

"You see," said Kenelm, "we are compelled in this, as in other questions of philosophy, to resort to the inductive process, and draw our theories from the facts within our cognizance. Now, looking round the world, is it the fact that old maids and old bachelors are so much more spiritually advanced than married folks? Do they pass their time, like an Indian dervish, in serene contemplation of divine excellence and beatitude? Are they not quite as worldly in their own way as persons who have been married as often as the Wife of Bath, and generally speaking, more selfish, more frivolous, and more spiteful? I am sure I don't wish to speak uncharitably against old maids and old bachelors. I have three aunts who are old maids, and fine specimens of the genus; but I am sure they would all three have been more agreeable companions, and quite as spiritually gifted, if they had been happily married, and were caressing their children instead of lap-dogs. So, too, I have an old bachelor-cousin, Chillingly Mivers, whom you know. As clever as a man can be. But, Lord bless you! as to being wrapped in spiritual meditation, he could not be more devoted to the things of earth if he had married as many wives as Solomon, and had as many children as Priam. Finally, have not half the mistakes in the world arisen from a separation between the spiritual and the moral nature of man? Is it not, after all, through his dealings with his fellow-men that man makes his safest 'approach to the angels'? And is not the moral system a very muscular system? Does it not require for healthful vigour plenty of continued exercise, and does it not get that exercise naturally, by the relationships of family, with all the wider collateral struggles with life which the care of family necessitates?

"I put these questions to you with the humblest diffidence. I expect to hear such answers as will thoroughly convince my reason, and I shall be delighted if so. For at the root of the controversy lies the passion of love. And love must be a very disquieting troublesome emotion, and has led many heroes and sages into wonderful weaknesses and follies."

"Gently, gently, Mr. Chillingly; don't exaggerate. Love, no doubt, is—ahem—a disquieting passion. Still, every emotion that changes life from a stagnant pool into the freshness and play of a running stream is disquieting to the pool. Not only love and its fellow-passions—such as ambition—but the exercise of the reasoning faculty, which is always at work in changing our ideas, is very disquieting. Love, Mr. Chillingly, has its good side as well as its bad. Pass the bottle."

KENELM (passing the bottle).—"Yes, yes; you are quite right in putting the adversary's case strongly before you demolish it—all good rhetoricians do that. Pardon me if I am up to that trick in argument. Assume that I know all that can be said in favour of the abnegation of common-sense, euphoniously called 'love,' and proceed to the demolition of the case."

THE REV. DECIMUS ROACH (hesitatingly).—"The demolition of the case? humph! The passions are ingrafted in the human system as part and parcel of it, and are not to be demolished so easily as you seem to think. Love, taken rationally and morally by a man of good education and sound principles, is—is——"

KENELM.—"Well, is what?"

THE REV. DECIMUS ROACH.—"A—a—a—thing not to be despised. Like the sun, it is the great colourist of life, Mr. Chillingly. And you are so right—the moral system does require daily exercise. What can give that exercise to a solitary man, when he arrives at the practical age in which he cannot sit for six hours at a stretch musing on the divine essence; and rheumatism or other ailments forbid his adventure into the wilds of Africa as a missionary? At that age, Nature, which will be heard, Mr. Chillingly, demands her rights. A sympathizing female companion by one's side; innocent little children climbing one's knee,—lovely, bewitching picture! Who can be Goth enough to rub it out, who fanatic enough to paint over it the image of a St. Simon sitting alone on a pillar! Take another glass. You don't drink enough, Mr. Chillingly."

"I have drunk enough," replied Kenelm, in a sullen voice, "to think I see double. I imagined that before me sate the austere adversary of the insanity of love and the miseries of wedlock. Now, I fancy I listen to a puling sentimentalist uttering the platitudes which the other Decimus Roach had already refuted. Certainly either I see double, or you amuse yourself with mocking my appeal to your wisdom."

"Not so, Mr. Chillingly. But the fact is, that when I wrote that book of which you speak, I was young, and youth is enthusiastic and one-sided. Now, with the same disdain of the excesses to which love may hurry weak intellects, I recognize its benignant effects when taken, as I before said, rationally—taken rationally, my young friend. At that period of life when the judgment is matured, the soothing companionship of an amiable female cannot but cheer the mind, and prevent that morose hoar-frost into which solitude is chilled and made rigid by increasing years. In short, Mr. Chillingly, having convinced myself that I erred in the opinion once too rashly put forth, I owe it to Truth, I owe it to Mankind, to make my conversion known to the world. And I am about next month to enter into the matrimonial state with a young lady who——."

"Say no more, say no more, Mr. Roach. It must be a painful subject to you. Let us drop it."

"It is not a painful subject at all!" exclaimed Mr. Roach, with warmth. "I look forward to the fulfilment of my duty with the pleasure which a well-trained mind always ought to feel in recanting a fallacious doctrine. But you do me the justice to understand that of course I do not take this step I propose—for my personal satisfaction. No, sir, it is the value of my example to others, which purifies my motives and animates my soul."

After this concluding and noble sentence, the conversation drooped. Host and guest both felt they had had enough of each other. Kenelm soon rose to depart.

Mr. Roach, on taking leave of him at the door, said, with marked emphasis—

"Not for my personal satisfaction—remember that. Whenever you hear my conversion discussed in the world, say that from my own lips you heard these words—NOT FOR MY PERSONAL SATISFACTION. No! My kind regards to Welby—a married man himself, and a father; *he* will understand me."

CHAPTER IX.

ON quitting Oxford, Kenelm wandered for several days about the country, advancing to no definite goal, meeting with no noticeable adventure. At last he found himself mechanically retracing his steps. A magnetic influence he could not resist drew him back towards the grassy meads and the sparkling rill of Moleswich.

"There must be," said he to himself, "a mental, like an optical, illusion. In the last, we fancy we have seen a spectre. If we dare not face the apparition—dare not attempt to touch it—run superstitiously away from it—what happens? We shall believe to our dying day that it was not an illusion—that it was a spectre—and so we may be crazed for life. But if we manfully walk up to the

Phantom, stretch our hands to seize it, lo! it fades into thin air, the cheat of our eyesight is dispelled, and we shall never be ghost-ridden again. So it must be with this mental illusion of mine. I see an image strange to my experience—it seems to me, at that first sight, clothed with a supernatural charm; like an unreasoning coward, I run away from it. It continues to haunt me; I cannot shut out its apparition. It pursues me by day alike in the haunts of men—alike in the solitudes of nature; it visits me by night in my dreams. I begin to say this must be a real visitant from another world—it must be love—the love of which I read in the Poets, as in the Poets I read of witchcraft and ghosts. Surely I must approach that apparition as a philosopher like Sir David Brewster would approach the black cat seated on a hearth-rug, which he tells us that some lady of his acquaintance constantly saw till she went into a world into which black cats are not held to be admitted. The more I think of it the less it appears to me possible that I can be really in love with a wild, half-educated, anomalous creature, merely because the apparition of her face haunts me. With perfect safety, therefore, I can approach that creature; in proportion as I see more of her, the illusion will vanish. I will go back to Moleswich manfully."

Thus said Kenelm to himself, and himself answered—

"Go; for thou canst not help it. Thinkest thou that Daces can escape the net that has meshed a Roach? No—

'Come it will, the day decreed by fate,'

when thou must succumb to the 'nature which will be heard.' Better succumb now, and with a good grace, than resist till thou hast reached thy fiftieth year, and then make a rational choice not for thy personal satisfaction."

Whereupon Kenelm answered to himself, indignantly, "Pooh! thou flippant. My *alter ego,* thou knowest not what thou art talking about! It is not a question of nature; it is a question of the supernatural—an illusion—a phantom!"

Thus Kenelm and himself continued to quarrel with each other; and the more they quarrelled, the nearer they approached to the haunted spot in which had been seen, and fled from the fatal apparition of first love.

BOOK VI.

CHAPTER I.

SIR PETER had not heard from Kenelm since a letter informing him that his son had left town on an excursion, which would probably be short, though it might last a few weeks; and the good Baronet now resolved to go to London himself, take his chance of Kenelm's return, and if still absent, at least learn from Mivers and others how far that very eccentric planet had contrived to steer a regular course amidst the fixed stars of the metropolitan system. He had other reasons for his journey. He wished to make the acquaintance of Gordon Chillingly before handing him over the £20,000 which Kenelm had released in that resettlement of estates, the necessary deeds of which the young heir had signed before quitting London for Moleswich. Sir Peter wished still more to see Cecilia Travers, in whom Kenelm's accounts of her had inspired a very strong interest.

The day after his arrival in town Sir Peter breakfasted with Mivers.

"Upon my word you are very comfortable here," said Sir Peter, glancing at the well-appointed table, and round the well-furnished rooms.

"Naturally so—there is no one to prevent my being comfortable. I am not married:—taste that omelette."

"Some men declare they never knew comfort till they were married, cousin Mivers."

"Some men are reflecting bodies, and catch a pallid gleam from the comfort which a wife concentres on herself. With a fortune so modest and secure, what comforts, possessed by me now, would not a Mrs. Chillingly Mivers ravish from my hold and appropriate to herself! Instead of these pleasant rooms, where should I be lodged? In a dingy den looking on a backyard, excluded from the sun by day, and vocal with cats by night; while Mrs. Mivers luxuriated in two drawing-rooms with southern aspect and perhaps a boudoir. My brougham would be torn from my uses and monopolized by 'the angel of my hearth,' clouded in her crinoline and halved by her chignon. No! if ever I marry—and I never deprive myself of the civilities and needlework which single ladies waste upon me, by saying I shall not marry—it will be when women have fully established their rights; for then, men may have a chance of vindicating their own. Then if there are two drawing-rooms in the house, I shall take one, if not, we will toss up who shall have the back parlour; if we keep a brougham, it will be exclusively mine three days in the week; if Mrs. M. wants £200 a-year for her wardrobe, she must be contented with one, the other half will belong to my personal decoration; if I am oppressed by proof sheets and printers' devils, half of the oppression falls to her lot, while I take my holiday on the croquet ground at Wimbledon. Yes, when the present wrongs of women are exchanged for equality with men—I will cheerfully marry; and to do the thing generous, I will not oppose Mrs. M.'s voting in the vestry or for Parliament. I will give her my own votes with pleasure."

"I fear, my dear cousin, that you have infected Kenelm with your selfish ideas on the nuptial state. He does not seem inclined to marry—Eh?"

"Not that I know of."

"What sort of girl is Cecilia Travers?"

"One of those superior girls who are not likely to tower into that terrible giantess called 'a superior woman.' A handsome, well-educated, sensible young lady. Not spoilt by being an heiress—in fine, just the sort of girl whom you could desire to fix on for a daughter-in-law."

"And you don't think Kenelm has a fancy for her?"

"Honestly speaking—I do not."

"Any counter-attraction? There are some things in which sons do not confide in their fathers. You have never heard that Kenelm has been a little wild?"

"Wild he is, as the noble savage who ran in woods," said cousin Mivers.

"You frighten me!"

"Before the noble savage ran across the squaws, and was wise enough to run away from them. Kenelm has run away now, somewhere."

"Yes, he does not tell me where, nor do they know at his lodgings. A heap of notes on his table and no directions where they are to be forwarded. On the whole, however, he has held his own in London society—Eh?"

"Certainly! he has been more courted than most young men, and perhaps more talked of. Oddities generally are."

"You own he has talents above the average? Do you not think he will make a figure in the world some day, and discharge that debt to the literary stores or the political interests of his country, which alas, I and my predecessors, the other Sir Peters, failed to do; and for which I hailed his birth, and gave him the name of Kenelm?"

"Upon my word," answered Mivers—who had now finished his breakfast, retreated to an easy chair, and taken from the chimney-piece one of his famous trabucos,—"upon my word, I can't guess; if some great reverse of fortune befell him, and he had to work for his livelihood, or if some other direful calamity gave a shock to his nervous system and jolted it into a fussy fidgety direction, I dare say he might make a splash in that current of life which bears men on to the grave. But you see he wants, as he himself very truly says, the two stimulants to definite action—poverty and vanity."

"Surely there have been great men who were neither poor nor vain?"

"I doubt it. But vanity is a ruling motive that takes many forms and many aliases—call it ambition, call it love of fame, still its substance is the same—the desire of applause carried into fussiness of action."

"There may be the desire for abstract truth without care for applause."

"Certainly. A philosopher on a desert island may amuse himself by meditating on the distinction between light and heat. But if on returning to the world, he publish the result of his meditations, vanity steps in, and desires to be applauded."

"Nonsense, cousin Mivers, he may rather desire to be of use and benefit to mankind. You don't deny that there is such a thing as philanthropy."

"I don't deny that there is such a thing as humbug. And whenever I meet a man who has the face to tell me, that he is taking a great deal of trouble, and putting himself very much out of his way, for a philanthropical object, without the slightest idea of reward either in praise or pence, I know that I have a humbug before me—a dangerous humbug—a swindling humbug—a fellow with his pocket full of villainous prospectuses and appeals to subscribers."

"Pooh, pooh; leave off that affectation of cynicism; you are not a bad-hearted fellow—you must love mankind—you must have an interest in the welfare of posterity."

"Love mankind? Interest in posterity? Bless my soul, cousin Peter, I hope you have no prospectuses in *your* pockets; no schemes for draining the Pontine Marshes out of pure love to mankind; no propositions for doubling the income tax, as a reserve fund for posterity, should our coalfields fail three thousand years hence. Love of mankind! Rubbish! This comes of living in the country."

"But you do love the human race—you do care for the generations that are to come."

"I! Not a bit of it. On the contrary, I rather dislike the human race, taking it altogether, and including the Australian bushmen; and I don't believe any man who tells me that he would grieve half as much if ten millions of human beings were swallowed up by an earthquake at a considerable distance from his own residence, say Abyssinia, as he would for a rise in his butcher's bills. As to posterity, who would consent to have a month's fit of the gout or tic-douloureux in order that in the fourth thousand year, A.D., posterity should enjoy a perfect system of sewage."

Sir Peter, who had recently been afflicted by a very sharp attack of neuralgia, shook his head, but was too conscientious not to keep silence.

"To turn the subject," said Mivers, relighting the cigar which he had laid aside while delivering himself of his amiable opinions, "I think you would do well, while in town, to call on your old friend Travers, and be introduced to Cecilia. If you think as favourably of her as I do, why not ask father and daughter to pay you a visit at Exmundham? Girls think more about a man when they see the place which he can offer to them as a home, and Exmundham is an attractive place to girls—picturesque and romantic."

"A very good idea," cried Sir Peter, heartily. "And I want also to make the acquaintance of Chillingly Gordon. Give me his address."

"Here is his card on the chimney-piece, take it; you will always find him at home till two o'clock. He is too sensible to waste the forenoon in riding out in Hyde Park with young ladies."

"Give me your frank opinion of that young kinsman. Kenelm tells me that he is clever and ambitious."

"Kenelm speaks truly. He is not a man who will talk stuff about love of mankind and posterity. He is of our day, with large keen wide-awake eyes, that look only on such portions of mankind as can be of use to him—and do not spoil their sight by poring through cracked telescopes, to catch a glimpse of posterity. Gordon is a man to be a Chancellor of the Exchequer, perhaps a Prime Minister."

"And old Gordon's son is cleverer than my boy—than the namesake of Kenelm Digby!" and Sir Peter sighed.

"I did not say that. I am cleverer than Chillingly Gordon, and the proof of it is that I am too clever to wish to be Prime Minister— very disagreeable office—hard work—irregular hours for meals— much abuse and confirmed dyspepsia."

Sir Peter went away rather downhearted. He found Chillingly Gordon at home in a lodging in Jermyn Street. Though prepossessed against him by all he had heard, Sir Peter was soon propitiated in his favour. Gordon had a frank man-of-the-world way with him, and much too fine a tact to utter any sentiments likely to displease an old-fashioned country gentleman, and a relation who might possibly be of service in his career. He touched briefly, and with apparent feeling, on the unhappy litigation commenced by his father; spoke with affectionate praise of Kenelm; and with a discriminating good-nature of Mivers, as a man who, to parody the epigram on Charles II.,

"Never says a kindly thing
And never does a harsh one."

Then he drew Sir Peter on to talk of the country and agricultural prospects. Learned that among his objects in visiting town, was the wish to inspect a patented hydraulic ram that might be very useful for his farmyard, which was ill supplied with water. Startled the Baronet by evincing some practical knowledge of mechanics; insisted on accompanying him to the city to inspect the ram; did so, and approved the purchase; took him next to see a new American reaping-machine, and did not part with him till he had obtained Sir Peter's promise to dine with him at the Garrick; an invitation peculiarly agreeable to Sir Peter, who had a natural curiosity to see some of the more recently distinguished frequenters of that social club. As, on quitting Gordon, Sir Peter took his way to the house of Leopold Travers, his thoughts turned with much kindliness towards his young kinsman. "Mivers and Kenelm," quoth he to himself, "gave me an unfavourable impression of this lad; they represent him as worldly, self-seeking, and so forth. But Mivers takes such cynical views of character, and Kenelm is too eccentric to judge fairly of a sensible man of the world. At all events, it is not like an egotist to put himself out of his way to be so civil to an old fellow like me. A young man about town must have pleasanter modes of passing his day than inspecting hydraulic rams and reaping-machines. Clever they allow him to be. Yes, decidedly clever— and not offensively clever—practical."

Sir Peter found Travers in the dining-room with his daughter, Mrs. Campion, and Lady Glenalvon. Travers was one of those men rare in middle age, who are more often to be found in their drawing-room than in their private study; he was fond of female society; and perhaps it was this predilection which contributed to preserve in him the charm of good breeding and winning manners. The two men had not met for many years; not indeed since Travers was at the zenith of his career of fashion, and Sir Peter was one of those pleasant *dilettanti* and half humoristic conversationalists who become popular and courted diners-out.

Sir Peter had originally been a moderate Whig because his father had been one before him, but he left the Whig party with the Duke of Richmond, Mr. Stanley (afterwards Lord Derby), and others, when it seemed to him that that party had ceased to be moderate.

Leopold Travers had, as a youth in the Guards, been a high Tory, but, siding with Sir Robert Peel on the repeal of the Corn Laws, remained with the Peelites after the bulk of the Tory party had renounced the guidance of their former chief, and now went with these Peelites in whatever direction the progress of the age might impel their strides in advance of Whigs and in defiance of Tories.

However, it is not the politics of these two gentlemen that are in question now. As I have just said, they had not met for many years. Travers was very little changed. Sir Peter recognized him at a glance; Sir Peter was much changed, and Travers hesitated before, on hearing his name announced, he felt quite sure that it was the right Sir Peter towards whom he advanced, and to whom he extended his cordial hand. Travers preserved the colour of his hair and the neat proportions of his figure, and was as scrupulously well dressed as in his dandy days. Sir Peter, originally very thin and with fair locks and dreamy blue eyes, had now become rather portly, at least towards the middle of him—very gray—had long ago taken to spectacles—his dress, too, was very old-fashioned, and made by a country tailor. He looked quite as much a gentleman as Travers did; quite perhaps as healthy, allowing for difference of years; quite as likely to last his time. But between them was the difference of the nervous temperament and the lymphatic. Travers, with less brain than Sir Peter, had kept his brain constantly active; Sir Peter had allowed his brain to dawdle over old books and lazy delight in letting the hours slip by. Therefore Travers still looked young— alert—up to his day, up to anything; while Sir Peter, entering that drawing-room, seemed a sort of Rip van Winkle who had slept through the past generation, and looked on the present with eyes yet drowsy. Still, in those rare moments when he was thoroughly roused up, there would have been found in Sir Peter a glow of heart, nay, even a vigour of thought, much more expressive than the constitutional alertness that characterized Leopold Travers, of the attributes we most love and admire in the young.

"My dear Sir Peter, is it you? I am so glad to see you again," said Travers. "What an age since we met, and how condescendingly kind you were then to me; silly fop that I was! But bygones are bygones; come to the present. Let me introduce to you, first, my valued friend, Mrs. Campion, whose distinguished husband you remember. Ah, what pleasant meetings we had at his house! And next, that young lady of whom she takes motherly charge; my daughter Cecilia. Lady Glenalvon, your wife's friend, of course needs no introduction, time stands still with her."

Sir Peter lowered his spectacles, which in reality he only wanted for books in small print, and gazed attentively on the three ladies—at each gaze a bow. But while his eyes were still lingeringly fixed on Cecilia, Lady Glenalvon advanced, naturally in right of rank and the claim of old acquaintance, the first of the three to greet him.

"Alas, my dear Sir Peter! time does not stand still for any of us; but what matter, if it leaves pleasant footprints! When I see you again, my youth comes before me. My early friend, Caroline Brotherton, now Lady Chillingly; our girlish walks with each other; wreaths and ball-dresses the practical topic; prospective husbands, the dream at a distance. Come and sit here: tell me all about Caroline."

Sir Peter, who had little to say about Caroline that could possibly interest anybody but himself, nevertheless took his seat beside Lady Glenalvon, and, as in duty bound, made the most flattering account of his She Baronet which experience or invention would allow. All the while, however, his thoughts were on Kenelm, and his eyes on Cecilia.

Cecilia resumes some mysterious piece of lady's work—no matter what—perhaps embroidery for a music-stool, perhaps a pair of slippers for her father (which, being rather vain of his feet and knowing they looked best in plain morocco, he will certainly never wear). Cecilia appears absorbed in her occupation; but her eyes and her thoughts are on Sir Peter. Why, my lady reader may guess. And oh, so flatteringly, so lovingly fixed! She thinks he has a most charming, intelligent, benignant countenance. She admires even his old-fashioned frock-coat, high neckcloth, and strapped trousers. She venerates his gray hairs, pure of dye. She tries to find a close resemblance between that fair, blue-eyed, plumpish, elderly gentleman and the lean, dark-eyed, saturnine, lofty Kenelm; she detects the likeness which nobody else would. She begins to love Sir Peter, though he has not said a word to her.

Ah! on this, a word for what it is worth to you, my young readers. You, sir, wishing to marry a girl who is to be deeply, lastingly in love with you, and a thoroughly good wife practically, consider well how she takes to your parents—how she attaches to them an inexpressible sentiment, a disinterested reverence—even should you but dimly recognize the sentiment, or feel the reverence, how if between you and your parents some little cause of coldness arise, she will charm you back to honour your father and your mother, even though they are not particularly genial to her—well, if you win that sort of girl as your wife, think you have got a treasure. You have won a woman to whom Heaven has given the two best attributes—intense feeling of love, intense sense of duty. What, my dear lady reader, I say of one sex, I say of another, though in a less degree; because a girl who marries becomes of her husband's family, and the man does not become of his wife's. Still I distrust the depth of any man's love to a woman, if he does not feel a great degree of tenderness (and forbearance where differences arise) for her parents. But the wife must not so put them in the foreground as to make the husband think he is cast into the cold of the shadow. Pardon this intolerable length of digression, dear reader—it is not altogether a digression, for it belongs to my tale that you should clearly understand the sort of girl that is personified in Cecilia Travers.

"What has become of Kenelm?" asks Lady Glenalvon.

"I wish I could tell you," answers Sir Peter. "He wrote me word that he was going forth on rambles into 'fresh woods and pastures new,' perhaps for some weeks. I have not had a word from him since."

"You make me uneasy," said Lady Glenalvon. "I hope nothing can have happened to him—he cannot have fallen ill."

Cecilia stops her work, and looks up wistfully.

"Make your mind easy," said Travers with a laugh; "I am in his secret. He has challenged the champion of England, and gone into the country to train."

"Very likely," said Sir Peter, quietly; "I should not be in the least surprised, should you, Miss Travers?"

"I think it more probable that Mr. Chillingly is doing some kindness to others which he wishes to keep concealed."

Sir Peter was pleased with this reply, and drew his chair nearer to Cecilia's. Lady Glenalvon, charmed to bring those two together, soon rose and took leave.

Sir Peter remained nearly an hour talking chiefly with Cecilia, who won her way into his heart with extraordinary ease; and he did not quit the house till he had engaged her father, Mrs. Campion, and herself to pay him a week's visit at Exmundham, towards the end of the London season, which was fast approaching.

Having obtained this promise, Sir Peter went away, and ten minutes after Mr. Gordon Chillingly entered the drawing-room. He had already established a visiting acquaintance with the Traverses. Travers had taken a liking to him. Mrs. Campion found him an extremely well-informed, unaffected young man, very superior to young men in general. Cecilia was cordially polite to Kenelm's cousin.

Altogether that was a very happy day for Sir Peter. He enjoyed greatly his dinner at the Garrick, where he met some old acquaintances, and was presented to some new "celebrities." He observed that Gordon stood well with these eminent persons. Though as yet undistinguished himself, they treated him with a certain respect, as well as with evident liking. The most eminent of them, at least the one with the most solidly-established reputation, said in Sir Peter's ear, "You may be proud of your nephew, Gordon!"

"He is not my nephew, only the son of a very distant cousin."

"Sorry for that. But he will shed lustre on kinsfolk, however distant. Clever fellow, yet popular; rare combination—sure to rise."

Sir Peter suppressed a gulp in the throat. "Ah, if some one as eminent had spoken thus of Kenelm!"

But he was too generous to allow that half-envious sentiment to last more than a moment. Why should he not be proud of any member of the family who could irradiate the antique obscurity of the Chillingly race? And how agreeable this clever young man made himself to Sir Peter!

The next day Gordon insisted on accompanying him to see the latest acquisitions in the British Museum, and various other exhibitions, and went at night to the Prince of Wales's Theatre, where Sir Peter was infinitely delighted with an admirable little comedy by Mr. Robertson, admirably placed on the stage by Maria Wilton. The day after, when Gordon called on him at his hotel, he cleared his throat, and thus plunged at once into the communication he had hitherto delayed.

"Gordon, my boy, I owe you a debt, and I am now, thanks to Kenelm, able to pay it."

Gordon gave a little start of surprise, but remained silent.

"I told your father, shortly after Kenelm was born, that I meant to give up my London house, and lay by £1000 a-year for you, in compensation for your chance of succeeding to Exmundham should I have died childless. Well, your father did not seem to think much of that promise, and went to law with me about certain unquestionable rights of mine. How so clever a man could have made such a mistake, would puzzle me, if I did not remember that he had a quarrelsome temper. Temper is a thing that often dominates cleverness—an uncontrollable thing; and allowances must be made for it. Not being of a quarrelsome temper myself (the Chillinglys are a placid race), I did not make the allowance for your father's differing, and (for a Chillingly) abnormal, constitution. The language and the tone of his letter respecting it nettled me. I did not see why, thus treated, I should pinch myself to lay by a thousand a-year. Facilities for buying a property most desirable for the possessor of Exmundham presented themselves. I bought it with borrowed money, and though I gave up the house in London, I did not lay by the thousand a-year."

"My dear Sir Peter, I have always regretted that my poor father was misled—perhaps out of too paternal a care for my supposed interests—into that unhappy and fruitless litigation, after which no one could doubt that any generous intentions on your part would be finally abandoned. It has been a grateful surprise to me that I have been so kindly and cordially received into the family by Kenelm and yourself. Pray oblige me by dropping all reference to pecuniary matters—the idea of compensation to a very distant relative for the loss of expectations he had no right to form, is too absurd, for me at least, ever to entertain."

"But I am absurd enough to entertain it—though you express yourself in a very high-minded way. To come to the point, Kenelm is of age, and we have cut off the entail. The estate of course remains absolutely with Kenelm to dispose of, as it did before, and we must take it for granted that he will marry; at all events he cannot fall into your poor father's error; but whatever Kenelm hereafter does with his property, it is nothing to you, and is not to be counted upon. Even the title dies with Kenelm if he has no son. On resettling the estate, however, sums of money have been released which, as I stated before, enable me to discharge the debt which, Kenelm heartily agrees with me, is due to you. £20,000 are now lying at my bankers' to be transferred to yours; meanwhile, if you will call on my solicitor, Mr. Vining, Lincoln's-inn, you can see the new deed, and give to him your receipt for the £20,000 for which he holds my cheque. Stop—stop—stop—I will not hear a word—no thanks, they are not due."

Here Gordon, who had during this speech uttered various brief exclamations, which Sir Peter did not heed, caught hold of his kinsman's hand, and, despite of all struggles, pressed his lips on it. "I must thank you, I must give some vent to my emotions," cried Gordon. "This sum, great in itself, is far more to me than you can imagine—it opens my career—it assures my future."

"So Kenelm tells me; he said that sum would be more use to you now than ten times the amount twenty years hence."

"So it will—it will. And Kenelm consents to this sacrifice?"

"Consents—urges it!"

Gordon turned away his face, and Sir Peter resumed: "You want to get into Parliament; very natural ambition for a clever young fellow. I don't presume to dictate politics to you. I hear you are what is called a liberal; a man may be a liberal, I suppose, without being a Jacobin."

"I hope so, indeed. For my part I am anything but a violent man."

"Violent, no! Who ever heard of a violent Chillingly? But I was reading in the newspaper to-day a speech addressed to some populous audience, in which the orator was for dividing all the land and all the capital belonging to other people among the working class, calmly and quietly, without any violence, and deprecating violence; but saying, perhaps very truly, that the people to be robbed might not like it, and might offer violence; in which case woe betide them—it was they who would be guilty of violence—and they must take the consequences if they resisted the reasonable propositions of himself and his friends! That, I suppose, is among the new ideas with which Kenelm is more familiar than I am. Do you entertain those new ideas?"

"Certainly not—I despise the fools who do."

"And you will not abet revolutionary measures if you get into Parliament?"

"My dear Sir Peter—I fear you have heard very false reports of my opinions if you put such questions. Listen," and therewith Gordon launched into dissertations very clever, very subtle, which committed him to nothing, beyond the wisdom of guiding popular opinion into right directions; what might be right directions he did not define, he left Sir Peter to guess them. Sir Peter did guess them, as Gordon meant he should, to be the directions which he, Sir Peter, thought right; and he was satisfied.

That subject disposed of, Gordon said, with much apparent feeling, "May I ask you to complete the favours you have lavished on me. I have never seen Exmundham, and the home of the race from which I sprang has a deep interest for me. Will you allow me to spend a few days with you, and under the shade of your own trees take lessons in political science from one who has evidently reflected on it profoundly?"

"Profoundly—no—a little—a little, as a mere bystander," said Sir Peter, modestly, but much flattered. "Come, my dear boy, by all means; you will have a hearty welcome. By the bye, Travers and his handsome daughter promised to visit me in about a fortnight, why not come at the same time?"

A sudden flash lit up the young man's countenance. "I shall be so delighted," he cried. "I am but slightly acquainted with Mr. Travers, but I like him much, and Mrs. Campion is so well informed."

"And what say you to the girl?"

"The girl, Miss Travers. Oh, she is very well in her way. But I don't talk with young ladies more than I can help."

"Then you are like your cousin Kenelm?"

"I wish I were like him in other things."

"No, one such oddity in a family is quite enough. But though I would not have you change to a Kenelm, I would not change Kenelm for the most perfect model of a son that the world can exhibit." Delivering himself of this burst of parental fondness, Sir Peter shook hands with Gordon, and walked off to Mivers, who was to give him luncheon, and then accompany him to the station. Sir Peter was to return to Exmundham by the afternoon express.

Left alone, Gordon indulged in one of those luxurious guesses into the future which form the happiest moments in youth, when so ambitious as his. The sum Sir Peter placed at his disposal would insure his entrance into Parliament. He counted with confidence on early successes there. He extended the scope of his views. With such successes he might calculate with certainty on a brilliant marriage, augmenting his fortune, and confirming his position. He had previously fixed his thoughts on Cecilia Travers—I will do him the justice to say not from mercenary motives alone, but not certainly with the impetuous ardour of youthful love. He thought her exactly fitted to be the wife of an eminent public man, in person, acquirement, dignified yet popular manners. He esteemed her, he liked her, and then her fortune would add solidity to his position. In fact, he had that sort of rational attachment to Cecilia which wise men, like Lord Bacon and Montaigne, would commend to another wise man seeking a wife. What opportunities of awaking in herself a similar, perhaps a warmer, attachment the visit to Exmundham would afford! He had learned when he had called on the Traverses that they were going thither, and hence that burst of family sentiment which had procured the invitation to himself.

But he must be cautious, he must not prematurely awaken Travers' suspicions. He was not as yet a match that the squire

could approve of for his heiress. And, though he was ignorant of
Sir Peter's designs on that young lady, he was much too prudent to
confide his own to a kinsman, of whose discretion he had strong
misgivings. It was enough for him at present that way was opened
for his own resolute energies. And cheerfully, though musingly, he
weighed its obstacles, and divined its goal, as he paced his floor
with bended head and restless strides, now quick, now slow.

Sir Peter, in the meanwhile, found a very good luncheon prepared
for him at Mivers's rooms, which he had all to himself, for his host
never "spoilt his dinner and insulted his breakfast" by that intermediate meal. He remained at his desk writing brief notes of
business, or of pleasure, while Sir Peter did justice to lamb cutlets
and grilled chicken. But he looked up from his task, with raised
eyebrows, when Sir Peter, after a somewhat discursive account of
his visit to the Traverses, his admiration of Cecilia, and the adroit-
ness with which, acting on his cousin's hint, he had engaged the
family to spend a few days at Exmundham, added, "And, by the
bye, I have asked young Gordon to meet them."

"To meet them; meet Mr. and Miss Travers! you have? I
thought you wished Kenelm to marry Cecilia. I was mistaken, you
meant Gordon!"

"Gordon," exclaimed Sir Peter, dropping his knife and fork.
" Nonsense, you don't suppose that Miss Travers prefers him to
Kenelm, or that he has the presumption to fancy that her father
would sanction his addresses."

"I indulge in no suppositions of the sort. I content myself with
thinking that Gordon is clever, insinuating, young; and it is a very
good chance of bettering himself that you have thrown in his way.
However, it is no affair of mine; and though on the whole I like
Kenelm better than Gordon, still I like Gordon very well, and I
have an interest in following his career which I can't say I have
in conjecturing what may be Kenelm's—more likely no career at all."

"Mivers, you delight in provoking me; you do say such uncomfortable things. But, in the first place, Gordon spoke rather
slightingly of Miss Travers."

"Ah, indeed; that's a bad sign," muttered Mivers.

Sir Peter did not hear him, and went on.

"And, besides, I feel pretty sure that the dear girl has already
a regard for Kenelm which allows no room for a rival. However,
I shall not forget your hint, but keep a sharp look-out; and if I
see the young man wants to be too sweet on Cecilia, I shall cut
short his visit."

"Give yourself no trouble in the matter; it will do no good.

Marriages are made in heaven. Heaven's will be done. If I can get away I will run down to you for a day or two. Perhaps in that case you can ask Lady Glenalvon. I like her, and she likes Kenelm. Have you finished? I see the brougham is at the door, and we have to call at your hotel to take up your carpet-bag."

Mivers was deliberately sealing his notes while he thus spoke. He now rang for his servant, gave orders for their delivery, and then followed Sir Peter downstairs and into the brougham. Not a word would he say more about Gordon, and Sir Peter shrank from telling him about the £20,000. Chillingly Mivers was perhaps the last person to whom Sir Peter would be tempted to parade an act of generosity. Mivers might not unfrequently do a generous act himself, provided it was not divulged; but he had always a sneer for the generosity of others.

CHAPTER II.

WANDERING back towards Moleswich, Kenelm found himself a little before sunset on the banks of the garrulous brook, almost opposite to the house inhabited by Lily Mordaunt. He stood long and silently by the grassy margin, his dark shadow falling over the stream, broken into fragments by the eddy and strife of waves, fresh from their leap down the neighbouring waterfall. His eyes rested on the house and the garden lawn in the front. The upper windows were open. "I wonder which is hers," he said to himself. At last he caught a glimpse of the gardener, bending over a flower-border with his watering-pot, and then moving slowly through the little shrubbery, no doubt to his own cottage. Now the lawn was solitary, save that a couple of thrushes dropped suddenly on the sward.

"Good evening, sir," said a voice. "A capital spot for trout this."

Kenelm turned his head, and beheld on the footpath, just behind him, a respectable elderly man, apparently of the class of a small retail tradesman, with a fishing-rod in his hand and a basket belted to his side.

"For trout," replied Kenelm; "I dare say. A strangely attractive spot indeed."

"Are you an angler, sir, if I may make bold to inquire?" asked the elderly man, somewhat perhaps puzzled as to the rank of the stranger; noticing, on the one hand, his dress and his mien, on the other, slung to his shoulders, the worn and shabby knapsack which Kenelm had carried, at home and abroad, the preceding year.

"Aye, I am an angler."

"Then this is the best place in the whole stream. Look, sir, there is Izaak Walton's summer-house; and further down you see that white, neat-looking house. Well, that is my house, sir, and I have an apartment which I let to gentlemen anglers. It is generally occupied throughout the summer months. I expect every day to have a letter to engage it, but it is vacant now. A very nice apartment, sir,—sitting-room and bedroom."

"*Descende cœlo, et dic age tibia,*" said Kenelm.

"Sir!" said the elderly man.

"I beg you ten thousand pardons. I have had the misfortune to have been at the university, and to have learned a little Latin, which sometimes comes back very inopportunely. But, speaking in plain English, what I meant to say is this: I invoked the Muse to descend from Heaven and bring with her—the original says a fife, but I meant—a fishing-rod. I should think your apartment would suit me exactly; pray show it to me."

"With the greatest pleasure," said the elderly man. "The Muse need not bring a fishing-rod! we have all sorts of tackle at your service, and a boat too, if you care for that. The stream hereabouts is so shallow and narrow that a boat is of little use till you get farther down."

"I don't want to get farther down; but should I want to get to the opposite bank, without wading across, would the boat take me, or is there a bridge?"

"The boat can take you. It is a flat-bottomed punt, and there is a bridge too for foot passengers, just opposite my house; and between this and Moleswich, where the stream widens, there is a ferry. The stone bridge for traffic is at the farther end of the town."

"Good. Let us go at once to your house."

The two men walked on.

"By the bye," said Kenelm as they walked, "do you know much of the family who inhabit the pretty cottage on the opposite side, which we have just left behind?"

"Mrs. Cameron's. Yes, of course, a very good lady; and Mr. Melville, the painter. I am sure I ought to know, for he has often lodged with me when he came to visit Mrs. Cameron. He recommends my apartments to his friends, and they are my best lodgers. I like painters, sir, though I don't know much about paintings. They are pleasant gentlemen, and easily contented with my humble roof and fare."

"You are quite right. I don't know much about paintings myself, but I am inclined to believe that painters, judging not from what I have seen of them, for I have not a single acquaintance among them personally, but from what I have read of their lives, are, as a general rule, not only pleasant but noble gentlemen. They form within themselves desires to beautify or exalt commonplace things, and they can only accomplish their desires by a constant study of what is beautiful and what is exalted. A man constantly so engaged ought to be a very noble gentleman, even though he may be the son of a shoeblack. And living in a higher world than we do, I can conceive that he is, as you say, very well contented with humble roof and fare in the world we inhabit."

"Exactly, sir; I see—I see now, though you put it in a way that never struck me before."

"And yet," said Kenelm, looking benignly at the speaker, "you seem to me a well-educated and intelligent man; reflective on things in general, without being unmindful of your interests in particular, especially when you have lodgings to let. Do not be offended. That sort of man is not perhaps born to be a painter, but I respect him highly. The world, sir, requires the vast majority of its inhabitants to live in it—to live by it. 'Each for himself, and God for us all.' The greatest happiness of the greatest number is best secured by a prudent consideration for Number One."

Somewhat to Kenelm's surprise (allowing that he had now learned enough of life to be occasionally surprised) the elderly man here made a dead halt, stretched out his hand cordially, and cried, "Hear, hear! I see that, like me, you are a decided democrat."

"Democrat! Pray, may I ask, not why you are one—that would be a liberty, and democrats resent any liberty taken with themselves —but why you suppose I am?"

"You spoke of the greatest happiness of the greatest number. That is a democratic sentiment surely! Besides, did not you say, sir, that painters — painters, sir, painters, even if they were the sons of shoeblacks, were the true gentlemen—the true noblemen?"

"I did not say that exactly, to the disparagement of other gentlemen and nobles. But if I did, what then?"

"Sir, I agree with you. I despise rank, I despise dukes, and earls, and aristocrats. 'An honest man's the noblest work of God.' Some poet says that. I think Shakespeare. Wonderful man, Shakespeare. A tradesman's son—butcher, I believe. Eh! My uncle was a butcher, and might have been an alderman. I go along with you heartily, heartily. I am a democrat, every inch of me.

Shake hands, sir—shake hands; we are all equals. 'Each for himself, and God for us all.'"

"I have no objection to shake hands," said Kenelm; "but don't let me owe your condescension to false pretences. Though we are all equal before the law, except the rich man, who has little chance of justice as against a poor man when submitted to an English jury, yet I utterly deny that any two men you select can be equals. One must beat the other in something, and when one man beats another, democracy ceases and aristocracy begins."

"Aristocracy! I don't see that. What do you mean by aristocracy?"

"The ascendancy of the better man. In a rude State the better man is the stronger; in a corrupt State, perhaps the more roguish; in modern republics the jobbers get the money and the lawyers get the power. In well-ordered States alone aristocracy appears at its genuine worth: the better man in birth, because respect for ancestry secures a higher standard of honour; the better man in wealth, because of the immense uses to enterprise, energy, and the fine arts, which rich men must be if they follow their natural inclinations; the better man in character, the better man in ability, for reasons too obvious to define; and these two last will beat the others in the government of the State, if the State be flourishing and free. All these four classes of better men constitute true aristocracy; and when a better government than a true aristocracy shall be devised by the wit of man, we shall not be far off from the Millennium and the reign of saints. But here we are at the house—yours, is it not? I like the look of it extremely."

The elderly man now entered the little porch over which clambered honeysuckle and ivy intertwined, and ushered Kenelm into a pleasant parlour, with a bay window, and an equally pleasant bedroom behind it.

"Will it do, sir?"

"Perfectly. I take it from this moment. My knapsack contains all I shall need for the night. There is a portmanteau of mine at Mr. Somers' shop, which can be sent here in the morning."

"But we have not settled about the terms," said the elderly man, beginning to feel rather doubtful whether he ought thus to have installed in his home a stalwart pedestrian of whom he knew nothing, and who, though talking glibly enough on other things, had preserved an ominous silence on the subject of payment.

"Terms—true, name them."

"Including board?"

"Certainly. Chameleons live on air, Democrats on wind-bags. I have a more vulgar appetite, and require mutton."

"Meat is very dear now-a-days," said the elderly man, "and I am afraid, for board and lodging, I cannot charge you less than £3 3s.—say £3 a-week. My lodgers usually pay a week in advance."

"Agreed," said Kenelm, extracting three sovereigns from his purse. "I have dined already—I want nothing more this evening; let me detain you no further. Be kind enough to shut the door after you."

When he was alone, Kenelm seated himself in the recess of the bay window, against the casement, and looked forth intently. Yes —he was right—he could see from thence the home of Lily. Not, indeed, more than a white gleam of the house through the interstices of trees and shrubs—but the gentle lawn sloping to the brook, with the gentle willow at the end dipping its boughs into the water, and shutting out all view beyond itself by its bower of tender leaves. The young man bent his face on his hands and mused dreamily: the evening deepened, the stars came forth, the rays of the moon now peered aslant through the arching dips of the willow, silvering their way as they stole to the waves below.

"Shall I bring lights, sir? or do you prefer a lamp or candles?" asked a voice behind—the voice of the elderly man's wife. "Do you like the shutters closed?"

The questions startled the dreamer. They seemed mocking his own old mockings on the romance of love. Lamp or candles, practical lights for prosaic eyes, and shutters closed against moon and stars!

"Thank you, ma'am, not yet," he said; and rising quietly, he placed his hand on the window-sill, swung himself through the open casement, and passed slowly along the margin of the rivulet, by a path checkered alternately with shade and starlight; the moon yet more slowly rising above the willows, and lengthening its track along the wavelets.

CHAPTER III.

THOUGH Kenelm did not think it necessary at present to report to his parents, or his London acquaintances, his recent movements and his present resting-place, it never entered into his head to lurk *perdu* in the immediate vicinity of Lily's house, and seek opportunities of meeting her clandestinely.

He walked to Mrs. Braefield's the next morning, found her at home, and said in rather a more off-hand manner than was habitual to him, "I have hired a lodging in your neighbourhood, on the banks of the brook, for the sake of its trout-fishing. So you will allow me to call on you sometimes, and one of these days I hope you will give me the dinner that I so unceremoniously rejected some days ago. I was then summoned away suddenly, much against my will."

"Yes; my husband said that you shot off from him with a wild exclamation about duty."

"Quite true; my reason, and I may say my conscience, were greatly perplexed upon a matter extremely important and altogether new to me. I went to Oxford—the place above all others in which questions of reason and conscience are most deeply considered, and perhaps least satisfactorily solved. Relieved in my mind by my visit to a distinguished ornament of that university, I felt I might indulge in a summer holiday, and here I am."

"Ah! I understand. You had religious doubts—thought perhaps of turning Roman Catholic. I hope you are not going to do so?"

"My doubts were not necessarily of a religious nature. Pagans have entertained them."

"Whatever they were I am pleased to see they did not prevent your return," said Mrs. Braefield, graciously. "But where have you found a lodging—why not have come to us? My husband would have been scarcely less glad than myself to receive you."

"You say that so sincerely, and so cordially, that to answer by a brief 'I thank you' seems rigid and heartless. But there are times in life when one yearns to be alone—to commune with one's own heart, and, if possible, be still; I am in one of those moody times. Bear with me."

Mrs. Braefield looked at him with affectionate, kindly interest. She had gone before him through the solitary load of young romance. She remembered her dreamy, dangerous girlhood, when she, too, had yearned to be alone.

"Bear with you—yes, indeed. I wish, Mr. Chillingly, that I were your sister, and that you would confide in me. Something troubles you."

"Troubles me—no. My thoughts are happy ones, and they may sometimes perplex me, but they do not trouble." Kenelm said this very softly; and in the warmer light of his musing eyes, the sweeter play of his tranquil smile, there was an expression which did not belie his words.

"You have not told me where you have found a lodging," said Mrs. Braefield, somewhat abruptly.

"Did I not?" replied Kenelm, with an unconscious start, as from an abstracted reverie. "With no undistinguished host, I presume, for when I asked him this morning for the right address of his cottage, in order to direct such luggage as I have to be sent there, he gave me his card with a grand air, saying, 'I am pretty well known at Moleswich, by and beyond it.' I have not yet looked at his card. Oh, here it is—'Algernon Sidney Gale Jones, Cromwell Lodge'—you laugh. What do you know of him?"

"I wish my husband were here; he would tell you more about him. Mr. Jones is quite a character."

"So I perceive."

"A great radical—very talkative and troublesome at the vestry; but our vicar, Mr. Emlyn, says there is no real harm in him—that his bark is worse than his bite—and that his republican or radical notions must be laid to the door of his godfathers! In addition to his name of Jones, he was unhappily christened Gale; Gale Jones being a noted radical orator at the time of his birth. And I suppose Algernon Sidney was prefixed to Gale in order to devote the new-born more emphatically to republican principles."

"Naturally, therefore, Algernon Sidney Gale Jones baptizes his house Cromwell Lodge, seeing that Algernon Sidney held the Protectorate in especial abhorrence, and that the original Gale Jones, if an honest radical, must have done the same, considering what rough usage the advocates of Parliamentary Reform met with at the hands of his Highness. But we must be indulgent to men who have been unfortunately christened before they had any choice of the names that were to rule their fate. I myself should have been less whimsical had I not been named after a Kenelm who believed in sympathetic powders. Apart from his political doctrines, I like my landlord—he keeps his wife in excellent order. She seems frightened at the sound of her own footsteps, and glides to and fro, a pallid image of submissive womanhood in list slippers."

"Great recommendations certainly, and Cromwell Lodge is very prettily situated. By the bye, it is very near Mrs. Cameron's."

"Now I think of it, so it is," said Kenelm, innocently.

Ah! my friend Kenelm, enemy of shams, and truth-teller *par excellence*, what hast thou come to! How are the mighty fallen! "Since you say you will dine with us, suppose we fix the day after to-morrow, and I will ask Mrs. Cameron and Lily."

"The day after to-morrow—I shall be delighted."

"An early hour?"

"The earlier the better."

"Is six o'clock too early?"

"Too early—certainly not—on the contrary——Good-day—I must now go to Mrs. Somers, she has charge of my portmanteau."

Then Kenelm rose.

"Poor dear Lily!" said Mrs. Braefield; "I wish she were less of a child."

Kenelm reseated himself.

"Is she a child? I don't think she is actually a child."

"Not in years; she is between seventeen and eighteen; but my husband says that she is too childish to talk to, and always tells me to take her off his hands; he would rather talk with Mrs. Cameron."

"Indeed!"

"Still I find something in her."

"Indeed!"

"Not exactly childish, nor quite womanish."

"What then?"

"I can't exactly define. But you know what Mr. Melville and Mrs. Cameron call her as a pet name?"

"No."

"Fairy! Fairies have no age; fairy is neither child nor woman."

"Fairy. She is called Fairy by those who know her best? Fairy!"

"And she believes in fairies."

"Does she?—so do I. Pardon me, I must be off. The day after to-morrow—six o'clock."

"Wait one moment," said Elsie, going to her writing-table. "Since you pass Grasmere on your way home, will you kindly leave this note?"

"I thought Grasmere was a lake in the north?"

"Yes; but Mr. Melville chose to call the cottage by the name of the lake. I think the first picture he ever sold was a view of Wordsworth's house there. Here is my note to ask Mrs. Cameron to meet you; but if you object to be my messenger——"

"Object! my dear Mrs. Braefield. As you say, I pass close by the cottage."

CHAPTER IV.

KENELM went with somewhat rapid pace from Mrs. Braefield's to the shop in the High Street, kept by Will Somers. Jessie was behind the counter, which was thronged with customers. Kenelm gave her a brief direction about his portmanteau, and then passed into the back parlour where her husband was employed on his baskets—with the baby's cradle in the corner, and its grandmother rocking it mechanically, as she read a wonderful missionary tract full of tales of miraculous conversions: into what sort of Christians we will not pause to inquire.

"And so you are happy, Will?" said Kenelm, seating himself between the basket-maker and the infant; the dear old mother beside him, reading the tract which linked her dreams of life eternal with life just opening in the cradle that she rocked. He not happy! How he pitied the man who could ask such a question.

"Happy, sir! I should think so, indeed. There is not a night on which Jessie and I, and mother too, do not pray that some day or other you may be as happy. By and bye the baby will learn to pray 'God bless papa, and mamma, and grandmamma, and Mr. Chillingly.'"

"There is some one else much more deserving of prayers than I, though needing them less. You will know some day—pass it by now. To return to the point; you are happy; if I asked you why, would not you say, 'Because I have married the girl I love, and have never repented'?"

"Well, sir, that is about it; though, begging your pardon, I think it could be put more prettily somehow."

"You are right there. But perhaps love and happiness never yet found any words that could fitly express them. Good-bye, for the present."

Ah! if it were as mere materialists, or as many middle-aged or elderly folks, who if materialists, are so without knowing it, unreflectingly say, "The main element of happiness is bodily or animal health and strength," that question which Chillingly put would appear a very unmeaning or a very insulting one addressed to a pale cripple, who, however improved of late in health, would still be sickly and ailing all his life,—put, too, by a man of the rarest conformation of physical powers that nature can adapt to physical enjoyment—a man who, since the age in which memory commences, had never known what it was to be unwell, who could scarcely understand you if you talked of a finger-ache, and whom those refinements of mental culture which multiply the delights of the senses had endowed with the most exquisite conceptions of such happiness as mere nature and its instincts can give! But Will did not think the question unmeaning or insulting. He, the poor cripple, felt a vast superiority on the scale of joyous being over the young Hercules, well born, cultured, and wealthy, who could know so little of happiness as to ask the crippled basket-maker if he were happy —he, blessed husband and father!

CHAPTER V.

LILY was seated on the grass under a chestnut-tree on the lawn. A white cat, not long emerged from kittenhood, curled itself by her side. On her lap was an open volume, which she was reading with the greatest delight.

Mrs. Cameron came from the house, looked round, perceived the girl, and approached; and either she moved so gently, or Lily was so absorbed in her book, that the latter was not aware of her presence till she felt a light hand on her shoulder, and, looking up, recognized her aunt's gentle face.

"Ah! Fairy, Fairy, that silly book, when you ought to be at your French verbs. What will your guardian say when he comes and finds you have so wasted time?"

"He will say that fairies never waste their time; and he will scold you for saying so." Therewith Lily threw down the book, sprang up to her feet, wound her arm round Mrs. Cameron's neck, and kissed her fondly. "There! is *that* wasting time? I love you so, aunty. In a day like this I think I love everybody and everything!" As she said this, she drew up her lithe form, looked into the blue sky, and with parted lips seemed to drink in air and sunshine. Then she woke up the dozing cat, and began chasing it round the lawn.

Mrs. Cameron stood still, regarding her with moistened eyes. Just at that moment Kenelm entered through the garden gate. He, too, stood still, his eyes fixed on the undulating movements of Fairy's exquisite form. She had arrested her favourite, and was now at play with it, shaking off her straw hat, and drawing the ribbon attached to it tantalizingly along the smooth grass. Her rich hair thus released and dishevelled by the exercise, fell partly over her face in wavy ringlets; and her musical laugh and words of sportive endearment, sounded on Kenelm's ear more joyously than the trill of the sky-lark, more sweetly than the coo of the ring-dove.

He approached towards Mrs. Cameron. Lily turned suddenly and saw him. Instinctively she smoothed back her loosened tresses, replaced the straw hat, and came up demurely to his side just as he had accosted her aunt.

"Pardon my intrusion, Mrs. Cameron. I am the bearer of this note from Mrs. Braefield." While the aunt read the note, he turned to the niece.

"You promised to show me the picture, Miss Mordaunt."

"But that was a long time ago."

"Too long to expect a lady's promise to be kept?"

Lily seemed to ponder that question, and hesitated before she answered.

"I will show you the picture. I don't think I ever broke a promise yet, but I shall be more careful how I make one in future."

"Why so?"

"Because you did not value mine when I made it, and that hurt me." Lily lifted up her head with a bewitching stateliness, and added gravely, "I was offended."

"Mrs. Braefield is very kind," said Mrs. Cameron; "she asks us to dine the day after to-morrow. You would like to go, Lily?"

"All grown-up people, I suppose? No, thank you, dear aunt. You go alone, I would rather stay at home. May I have little Clemmy to play with? She will bring Juba, and Blanche is very partial to Juba, though she does scratch him."

"Very well, my dear, you shall have your playmate, and I go by myself."

Kenelm stood aghast. "You will not go, Miss Mordaunt; Mrs. Braefield will be so disappointed. And if you don't go, whom shall I have to talk to? I don't like grown-up people better than you do."

"You are going?"

"Certainly."

"And if I go you will talk to me? I am afraid of Mr. Braefield. He is so wise."

"I will save you from him, and will not utter a grain of wisdom."

"Aunty, I will go."

Here Lily made a bound and caught up Blanche, who, taking her kisses resignedly, stared with evident curiosity upon Kenelm.

Here a bell within the house rung the announcement of luncheon.

Mrs. Cameron invited Kenelm to partake of that meal. He felt as Romulus might have felt when first invited to taste the ambrosia of the gods. Yet certainly that luncheon was not such as might have pleased Kenelm Chillingly in the early days of The Temperance Hotel. But somehow or other of late he had lost appetite; and on this occasion a very modest share of a very slender dish of chicken fricasseed, and a few cherries daintily arranged on vine leaves, which Lily selected for him, contented him—as probably a very little ambrosia contented Romulus while feasting his eyes on Hebe.

Luncheon over, while Mrs. Cameron wrote her reply to Elsie, Kenelm was conducted by Lily into her own *own* room, in vulgar parlance her *boudoir*, though it did not look as if any one ever *bouder*'d there. It was exquisitely pretty—pretty not as a woman's, but a child's dream of the own own room she would like to have—wondrously neat and cool, and pure-looking! a trellis paper, the trellis gay with roses and wood-bine, and birds and butterflies; draperies of muslin, festooned with dainty tassels and ribbons; a dwarf bookcase, that seemed well stored, at least as to bindings; a dainty little writing-table in French *marqueterie*—looking too fresh and spotless to have known hard service. The casement was open, and in keeping with the trellis paper; woodbine and roses from without encroached on the window-sides, gently stirred by the faint summer breeze, and wafted sweet odours into the little room. Kenelm went to the window, and glanced on the view beyond. "I was right," he said to himself; "I divined it." But though he spoke in a low inward whisper, Lily, who had watched his movements in surprise, overheard.

"You divined it. Divined what?"

"Nothing, nothing; I was but talking to myself."

"Tell me what you divined—I insist upon it!" and Fairy petulantly stamped her tiny foot on the floor.

"Do you? Then I obey. I have taken a lodging for a short time on the other side of the brook—Cromwell Lodge—and seeing your house as I passed, I divined that your room was in this part of it. How soft here is the view of the water! Ah! yonder is Izaak Walton's summer-house."

"Don't talk about Izaak Walton, or I shall quarrel with you, as I did with Lion when he wanted me to like that cruel book."

"Who is Lion?"

"Lion—of course, my guardian. I called him Lion when I was a little child. It was on seeing in one of his books a print of a lion playing with a little child."

"Ah! I know the design well," said Kenelm, with a slight sigh.

"It is from an antique Greek gem. It is not the lion that plays with the child, it is the child that masters the lion, and the Greeks called the child 'Love.'"

This idea seemed beyond Lily's perfect comprehension. She paused before she answered, with the *naïveté* of a child six years old—

"I see now why I mastered Blanche, who will not make friends with any one else—I love Blanche. Ah, that reminds me—come and look at the picture."

She went to the wall over the writing-table, drew a silk curtain aside from a small painting in a dainty velvet framework, and pointing to it, cried with triumph—"Look there! is it not beautiful?"

Kenelm had been prepared to see a landscape, or a group, or anything but what he did see—it was the portrait of Blanche when a kitten.

Little elevated though the subject was, it was treated with graceful fancy. The kitten had evidently ceased from playing with the cotton reel that lay between her paws, and was fixing her gaze intent on a bullfinch that had lighted on a spray within her reach.

"You understand," said Lily, placing her hand on his arm, and drawing him towards what she thought the best light for the picture; "it is Blanche's first sight of a bird. Look well at her face; don't you see a sudden surprise—half joy, half fear? She ceases to play with the reel. Her intellect—or, as Mr. Braefield would say, 'her instinct'—is for the first time aroused. From that moment Blanche was no longer a mere kitten. And it required, oh, the most careful education, to teach her not to kill the poor little birds. She never does now, but I had such trouble with her."

"I cannot say honestly that I do see all that you do in the picture; but it seems to me very simply painted, and was, no doubt, a striking likeness of Blanche at that early age."

"So it was. Lion drew the first sketch from life with his pencil; and when he saw how pleased I was with it—he was so good—he put it on canvas, and let me sit by him while he painted it. Then he took it away, and brought it back finished and framed as you see, last May, a present for my birthday."

"You were born in May—with the flowers."

"The best of all the flowers are born before May—violets."

"But they are born in the shade, and cling to it. Surely, as a child of May, you love the sun!"

"I love the sun—it is never too bright nor too warm for me. But I don't think that, though born in May, I was born in sunlight. I feel more like my own native self when I creep into the shade and sit down alone. I can weep then."

As she thus shyly ended, the character of her whole countenance was changed—its infantine mirthfulness was gone; a grave, thoughtful, even a sad, expression settled on the tender eyes and the tremulous lips.

Kenelm was so touched that words failed him, and there was silence for some moments between the two. At length Kenelm said, slowly—

"You say your own native self. Do you, then, feel, as I often do, that there is a second, possibly a *native*, self, deep hid beneath the self—not merely what we show to the world in common (that may be merely a mask)—but the self that we ordinarily accept even when in solitude as our own; an inner innermost self; oh, so different and so rarely coming forth from its hiding-place; asserting its right of sovereignty, and putting out the other self, as the sun puts out a star?"

Had Kenelm thus spoken to a clever man of the world—to a Chillingly Mivers—to a Chillingly Gordon—they certainly would not have understood him. But to such men he never would have thus spoken. He had a vague hope that this childlike girl, despite so much of childlike talk, would understand him; and she did at once.

Advancing close to him, again laying her hand on his arm, and looking up towards his bended face with startled wondering eyes, no longer sad, yet not mirthful—

"How true! You have felt that too? Where *is* that innermost self, so deep down—so deep; yet when it does come forth, so much higher—higher—immeasurably higher than one's everyday self? It does not tame the butterflies—it longs to get to the stars. And then—and then—ah, how soon it fades back again! You have felt that. Does it not puzzle you?"

"Very much."

"Are there no wise books about it that help to explain?"

"No wise books in my very limited reading even hint at the puzzle. I fancy that it is one of those insoluble questions that rest between the infant and his Maker. Mind and soul are not the same things, and what you and I call 'wise men' are always confounding the two——"

Fortunately for all parties—especially the reader; for Kenelm had here got on the back of one of his most cherished hobbies—the distinction between psychology and metaphysics—soul and mind scientifically or logically considered—Mrs. Cameron here entered the room and asked him how he liked the picture.

"Very much. I am no great judge of the art. But it pleased me at once, and now that Miss Mordaunt has interpreted the intention of the painter, I admire it yet more."

"Lily chooses to interpret his intention in her own way, and insists that Blanche's expression of countenance conveys an idea of her capacity to restrain her destructive instinct, and be taught to believe that it is wrong to kill birds for mere sport. For food she need not kill them, seeing that Lily takes care that she has plenty to eat. But I don't think that Mr. Melville had the slightest suspicion that he had indicated that capacity in his picture."

"He must have done so, whether he suspected it or not," said Lily, positively; "otherwise he would not be truthful."

"Why not truthful?" asked Kenelm.

"Don't you see? If you were called upon to describe truthfully the character of any little child, would you only speak of such naughty impulses as all children have in common, and not even hint at the capacity to be made better?"

"Admirably put!" said Kenelm. "There is no doubt that a much fiercer animal than a cat—a tiger, for instance, or a conquering hero—may be taught to live on the kindest possible terms with the creatures on which it was its natural instinct to prey."

"Yes—yes; hear that, aunty! You remember the Happy Family that we saw, eight years ago, at Moleswich fair, with a cat not half so nice as Blanche allowing a mouse to bite her ear? Well, then, would Lion not have been shamefully false to Blanche if Lion had not——"

Lily paused and looked half shyly, half archly, at Kenelm, then added, in slow, deep-drawn tones—"given a glimpse of her innermost self?"

"Innermost self!" repeated Mrs. Cameron, perplexed and laughing gently.

Lily stole nearer to Kenelm and whispered—

"Is not one's innermost self one's best self?"

Kenelm smiled approvingly. The fairy was rapidly deepening her spell upon him. If Lily had been his sister, his betrothed, his wife, how fondly he would have kissed her! She had expressed a thought over which he had often inaudibly brooded, and she had clothed it with all the charm of her own infantine fancy and womanlike tenderness! Goethe has said somewhere, or is reported to have said, "There is something in every man's heart, that, if you knew it, would make you hate him." What Goethe said, still more what Goethe is reported to have said, is never to be taken quite literally. No comprehensive genius—genius at once poet and thinker—ever can be so taken. The sun shines on a dunghill. But the sun has no predilection for a dunghill. It only comprehends a dunghill as it does a rose. Still Kenelm had always regarded that loose ray from Goethe's prodigal orb with an abhorrence most unphilosophical for a philosopher so young as generally to take upon oath any words of so great a master. Kenelm thought that the root of all private benevolence, of all enlightened advance in social reform, lay in the adverse theorem—that in every man's nature there lies a something that, could we get at it, cleanse it, polish it, render it visibly clear to our eyes, would make us love him. And in this spontaneous, uncultured sympathy with the results of so many laborious struggles of his own scholastic intellect against the dogma of the German giant, he felt as if he had found a younger—true, but oh, how much more subduing, because so much younger—sister of his own man's soul. Then came, so strongly, the sense of her sympathy with his own strange innermost self which a man will never feel more than once in his life with a daughter of Eve, that he dared not trust himself to speak. He somewhat hurried his leave-taking.

Passing in the rear of the garden towards the bridge which led to his lodging, he found on the opposite bank, at the other end of the bridge, Mr. Algernon Sidney Gale Jones peacefully angling for trout.

"Will you not try the stream to-day, sir? Take my rod."

Kenelm remembered that Lily had called Izaak Walton's book "a cruel one," and shaking his head gently, went his way into the house. There he seated himself silently by the window, and looked towards the grassy lawn and the dipping willows, and the gleam of the white walls through the girdling trees, as he had looked the eve before.

"Ah!" he murmured at last, "if, as I hold, a man but tolerably good does good unconsciously merely by the act of living—if he can no more traverse his way from the cradle to the grave, without letting fall, as he passes, the germs of strength, fertility, and beauty, than can a reckless wind or a vagrant bird, which, where it passes, leaves behind it the oak, the cornsheaf, or the flower—ah, if that be so, how tenfold the good must be, if the man find the gentler and purer duplicate of his own being in that mysterious, undefinable union which Shakespeares and day-labourers equally agree to call love; which Newton never recognizes, and which Descartes (his only rival in the realms of thought at once severe and imaginative) reduces into links of early association, explaining that he loved women who squinted because, when he was a boy, a girl with that infirmity squinted at him from the other side of his father's garden-wall! Ah! be this union between man and woman what it may; if it be really love—

really the bond which embraces the innermost and bettermost self of both—how, daily, hourly, momently, should we bless God for having made it so easy to be happy and to be good!"

CHAPTER VI.

THE dinner-party at Mr. Braefield's was not quite so small as Kenelm had anticipated. When the merchant heard from his wife that Kenelm was coming, he thought it would be but civil to the young gentleman to invite a few other persons to meet him.

"You see, my dear," he said to Elsie, "Mrs. Cameron is a very good, simple sort of woman, but not particularly amusing; and Lily, though a pretty girl, is so exceedingly childish. We owe much, my sweet Elsie, to this Mr. Chillingly"—here there was a deep tone of feeling in his voice and look—"and we must make it as pleasant for him as we can. I will bring down my friend Sir Thomas, and you ask Mr. Emlyn and his wife. Sir Thomas is a very sensible man, and Emlyn a very learned one. So Mr. Chillingly will find people worth talking to. By the bye, when I go to town I will send down a haunch of venison from Groves'."

So when Kenelm arrived, a little before six o'clock, he found in the drawing-room the Rev. Charles Emlyn, vicar of Moleswich proper, with his spouse, and a portly middle-aged man, to whom, as Sir Thomas Pratt, Kenelm was introduced. Sir Thomas was an eminent city banker. The ceremonies of introduction over, Kenelm stole to Elsie's side.

"I thought I was to meet Mrs. Cameron. I don't see her."

"She will be here presently. It looks as if it might rain, and I have sent the carriage for her and Lily. Ah, here they are!"

Mrs. Cameron entered, clothed in black silk. She always wore black; and behind her came Lily, in the spotless colour that became her name; no ornament, save a slender gold chain to which was appended a simple locket, and a single blush rose in her hair. She looked wonderfully lovely; and with that loveliness there was a certain nameless air of distinction, possibly owing to the delicacy of form and colouring; possibly to a certain grace of carriage, which was not without a something of pride.

Mr. Braefield, who was a very punctual man, made a sign to his servant, and in another moment or so dinner was announced. Sir Thomas, of course, took in the hostess; Mr. Braefield, the vicar's wife (she was a dean's daughter); Kenelm, Mrs. Cameron; and the vicar, Lily.

On seating themselves at the table Kenelm was on the left-hand, next to the hostess, and separated from Lily by Mrs. Cameron and Mr. Emlyn; and when the vicar had said grace, Lily glanced behind his back and her aunt's at Kenelm (who did the same thing), making at him what the French call a *moue*. The pledge to her had been broken. She was between two men very much grown up—the vicar and the host. Kenelm returned the *moue* with a mournful smile and an involuntary shrug.

All were silent till, after his soup and his first glass of sherry, Sir Thomas began—

"I think, Mr. Chillingly, we have met before, though I had not the honour then of making your acquaintance." Sir Thomas paused before he added, "Not long ago; the last State ball at Buckingham Palace."

Kenelm bent his head acquiescingly. He had been at that ball.

"You were talking with a very charming woman—a friend of mine—Lady Glenalvon."

(Sir Thomas was Lady Glenalvon's banker.)

"I remember perfectly," said Kenelm. "We were seated in the picture gallery. You came to speak to Lady Glenalvon, and I yielded to you my place on the settee."

"Quite true; and I think you joined a young lady—very handsome—the great heiress, Miss Travers."

Kenelm again bowed, and turning away as politely as he could, addressed himself to Mrs. Cameron. Sir Thomas, satisfied that he had impressed on his audience the facts of his friendship with Lady Glenalvon and his attendance at the court ball, now directed his conversational powers towards the vicar, who, utterly foiled in the attempt to draw out Lily, met the baronet's advances with the ardour of a talker too long suppressed. Kenelm continued, unmolested, to ripen his acquaintance with Mrs. Cameron. She did not, however, seem to lend a very attentive ear to his preliminary commonplace remarks about scenery or weather, but at his first pause, said,

"Sir Thomas spoke about a Miss Travers: is she related to a gentleman who was once in the Guards—Leopold Travers?"

"She is his daughter. Did you ever know Leopold Travers?"

"I have heard him mentioned by friends of mine long ago—long ago," replied Mrs. Cameron with a sort of weary languor, not unwonted, in her voice and manner; and then, as if dismissing the bygone reminiscence from her thoughts, changed the subject.

"Lily tells me, Mr. Chillingly, that you said you were staying at Mr. Jones's, Cromwell Lodge. I hope you are made comfortable there."

"Very. The situation is singularly pleasant."

"Yes, it is considered the prettiest spot on the brookside, and used to be a favourite resort for anglers; but the trout, I believe, are growing scarce; at least, now that the fishing in the Thames is improved, poor Mr. Jones complains that his old lodgers desert him. Of course you took the rooms for the sake of the fishing. I hope the sport may be better than it is said to be."

"It is of little consequence to me; I do not care much about fishing; and since Miss Mordaunt calls the book which first enticed me to take to it 'a cruel one,' I feel as if the trout had become as sacred as crocodiles were to the ancient Egyptians."

"Lily is a foolish child on such matters. She cannot bear the thought of giving pain to any dumb creature; and just before our garden there are a few trout which she has tamed. They feed out of her hand; she is always afraid they will wander away and get caught."

"But Mr. Melville is an angler?"

"Several years ago he would sometimes pretend to fish, but I believe it was rather an excuse for lying on the grass and reading 'the cruel book,' or perhaps, rather, for sketching. But now he is seldom here till autumn, when it grows too cold for such amusement."

Here Sir Thomas's voice was so loudly raised that it stopped the conversation between Kenelm and Mrs. Cameron. He had got into some question of politics on which he and the vicar did not agree, and the discussion threatened to become warm, when Mrs. Braefield, with a woman's true tact, broached a new topic, in which Sir Thomas was immediately interested, relating to the construction of a conservatory for orchids that he meditated adding to his country-house, and in which frequent appeal was made to Mrs. Cameron, who was considered an accomplished florist, and who seemed at some time or other in her life to have acquired a very intimate acquaintance with the costly family of orchids.

When the ladies retired Kenelm found himself seated next to Mr. Emlyn, who astounded him by a complimentary quotation from one of his own Latin prize poems at the university, hoped he would make some stay at Moleswich, told him of the principal places in the neighbourhood worth visiting, and offered him the run of his library, which he flattered himself was rather rich, both in the best editions of Greek and Latin classics and in early English literature. Kenelm was much pleased with the scholarly vicar, especially when

Mr. Emlyn began to speak about Mrs. Cameron and Lily. Of the first he said, "She is one of those women in whom Quiet is so predominant that it is long before one can know what undercurrents of good feeling flow beneath the unruffled surface. I wish, however, she was a little more active in the management and education of her niece—a girl in whom I feel a very anxious interest, and whom I doubt if Mrs. Cameron understands. Perhaps, however, only a poet, and a very peculiar sort of poet, can understand her: Lily Mordaunt is herself a poem."

"I like your definition of her," said Kenelm. "There is certainly something about her which differs much from the prose of common life."

"You probably know Wordsworth's lines:

> '. . . and she shall lean her ear
> In many a secret place
> Where rivulets dance their wayward round,
> And beauty, born of murmuring sound,
> Shall pass into her face.'

They are lines that many critics have found unintelligible; but Lily seems like the living key to them."

Kenelm's dark face lighted up, but he made no answer.

"Only," continued Mr. Emlyn, "how a girl of that sort, left wholly to herself, untrained, undisciplined, is to grow up into the practical uses of womanhood, is a question that perplexes and saddens me."

"Any more wine?" asked the host, closing a conversation on commercial matters with Sir Thomas. "No?—shall we join the ladies?"

CHAPTER VII.

THE drawing-room was deserted; the ladies were in the garden. As Kenelm and Mr. Emlyn walked side by side towards the group (Sir Thomas and Mr. Braefield following at a little distance), the former asked, somewhat abruptly, "What sort of man is Miss Cameron's guardian, Mr. Melville?"

"I can scarcely answer that question. I see little of him when he comes here. Formerly, he used to run down pretty often with a harum-scarum set of young fellows, quartered at Cromwell Lodge—Grasmere had no accommodation for them—students in the

Academy, I suppose. For some years he has not brought those persons, and when he does come himself it is but for a few days. He has the reputation of being very wild."

Further conversation was here stopped. The two men, while they thus talked, had been diverging from the straight way across the lawn towards the ladies, turning into sequestered paths through the shrubbery; now they emerged into the open sward, just before a table, on which coffee was served, and round which all the rest of the party were gathered.

"I hope, Mr. Emlyn," said Elsie's cheery voice, "that you have dissuaded Mr. Chillingly from turning Papist. I am sure you have taken time enough to do so."

Mr. Emlyn, Protestant every inch of him, slightly recoiled from Kenelm's side. "Do you meditate turning——" He could not conclude the sentence.

"Be not alarmed, my dear sir. I did but own to Mrs. Braefield that I had paid a visit to Oxford in order to confer with a learned man on a question that puzzled me, and as abstract as that feminine pastime, theology, is nowadays. I cannot convince Mrs. Braefield that Oxford admits other puzzles in life than those which amuse the ladies." Here Kenelm dropped into a chair by the side of Lily.

Lily half-turned her back to him.

"Have I offended again?"

Lily shrugged her shoulders slightly and would not answer.

"I suspect, Miss Mordaunt, that among your good qualities, nature has omitted one; the bettermost self within you should replace it."

Lily here abruptly turned to him her front face—the light of the skies was becoming dim, but the evening star shone upon it.

"How! what do you mean?"

"Am I to answer politely or truthfully?"

"Truthfully! Oh, truthfully! What is life without truth?"

"Even though one believes in fairies?"

"Fairies are truthful, in a certain way. But you are not truthful. You were not thinking of fairies when you——"

"When I what?"

"Found fault with me!"

"I am not sure of that. But I will translate to you my thoughts, so far as I can read them myself, and to do so I will resort to the fairies. Let us suppose that a fairy has placed her changeling into the cradle of a mortal; that into the cradle she drops all manner of fairy gifts, which are not bestowed on mere mortals; but that one mortal attribute she forgets. The changeling grows up, she charms those around her; they humour, and pet, and spoil her. But there arises a moment in which the omission of the one mortal gift is felt by her admirers and friends. Guess what that is."

Lily pondered. "I see what you mean; the reverse of truthfulness, politeness."

"No, not exactly that, though politeness slides into it unawares; it is a very humble quality, a very unpoetic quality; a quality that many dull people possess; and yet without it no fairy can fascinate mortals, when on the face of the fairy settles the first wrinkle. Can you not guess it now?"

"No; you vex me, you provoke me;" and Lily stamped her foot petulantly, as in Kenelm's presence she had stamped it once before. "Speak plainly, I insist."

"Miss Mordaunt, excuse me, I dare not," said Kenelm, rising with a sort of bow one makes to the Queen; and he crossed over to Mrs. Braefield.

Lily remained, still pouting fiercely.

Sir Thomas took the chair Kenelm had vacated.

CHAPTER VIII.

THE hour for parting came. Of all the guests, Sir Thomas alone stayed at the house a guest for the night. Mr. and Mrs. Emlyn had their own carriage. Mrs. Braefield's carriage came to the door for Mrs. Cameron and Lily.

Said Lily, impatiently and discourteously, "Who would not rather walk on such a night?" and she whispered to her aunt.

Mrs. Cameron, listening to the whisper, and obedient to every whim of Lily's, said, "You are too considerate, dear Mrs. Braefield, Lily prefers walking home; there is no chance of rain now."

Kenelm followed the steps of the aunt and niece, and soon overtook them on the brookside.

"A charming night, Mr. Chillingly," said Mrs. Cameron.

"An English summer night; nothing like it in such parts of the world as I have visited. But, alas! of English summer nights there are but few."

"You have travelled much abroad?"

"Much—no, a little; chiefly on foot."

Lily hitherto had not said a word, and had been walking with downcast head. Now she looked up and said, in the mildest and most conciliatory of human voices—

"You have been abroad;" then, with an acquiescence in the manners of the world which to him she had never yet manifested, she added his name, "Mr. Chillingly," and went on, more familiarly. "What a breadth of meaning the word 'abroad' conveys! Away, afar from one's self, from one's everyday life. How I envy you! you have been abroad: so has Lion "—(Here drawing herself up)—" I mean my guardian, Mr. Melville."

"Certainly, I have been abroad; but afar from myself—never. It is an old saying—all old sayings are true, most new sayings are false—a man carries his native soil at the sole of his foot."

Here the path somewhat narrowed. Mrs. Cameron went on first, Kenelm and Lily behind; she, of course, on the dry path, he on the dewy grass.

She stopped him. "You are walking in the wet, and with those thin shoes." Lily moved instinctively away from the dry path.

Homely though that speech of Lily's be, and absurd as said by a fragile girl to a gladiator like Kenelm, it lit up a whole world of womanhood — it showed all that undiscoverable land which was hidden to the learned Mr. Emlyn, all that land which an uncomprehended girl seizes and reigns over when she becomes wife and mother.

At that homely speech, and that impulsive movement, Kenelm halted, in a sort of dreaming maze. He turned timidly—"Can you forgive me for my rude words? I presumed to find fault with you."

"And so justly. I have been thinking over all you said, and I feel you were so right; only I still do not quite understand what you meant by the quality for mortals which the fairy did not give to her changeling."

"If I did not dare say it before, I should still less dare to say it now."

"Do." There was no longer the stamp of the foot, no longer the flash from her eyes, no longer the wilfulness which said "I insist;"—"Do," soothingly, sweetly, imploringly.

Thus pushed to it, Kenelm plucked up courage, and not trusting himself to look at Lily, answered brusquely—

"The quality desirable for men, but more essential to women in proportion as they are fairy-like, though the tritest thing possible, is good temper."

Lily made a sudden bound from his side, and joined her aunt, walking through the wet grass.

When they reached the garden-gate Kenelm advanced and opened it. Lily passed him by haughtily; they gained the cottage-door.

"I don't ask you in at this hour," said Mrs. Cameron. "It would be but a false compliment."

Kenelm bowed and retreated. Lily left her aunt's side, and came towards him, extending her hand.

"I shall consider your words, Mr. Chillingly," she said, with a strangely majestic air. "At present I think you are not right. I am not ill-tempered; but——" here she paused, and then added with a loftiness of mien which, had she not been so exquisitely pretty, would have been rudeness—"in any case I forgive you."

CHAPTER IX.

THERE were a good many pretty villas in the outskirts of Moleswich, and the owners of them were generally well off, and yet there was little of what is called visiting society—owing, perhaps, to the fact that there not being among these proprietors any persons belonging to what is commonly called "the aristocratic class," there was a vast deal of aristocratic pretension. The family of Mr. A——, who had enriched himself as a stock-jobber, turned up its nose at the family of Mr. B——, who had enriched himself still more as a linen draper, while the family of Mr. B—— showed a very cold shoulder to the family of Mr. C——, who had become richer than either of them as a pawnbroker, and whose wife wore diamonds, but dropped her h's. England would be a community so aristocratic that there would be no living in it, if one could exterminate what is now called "aristocracy." The Braefields were the only persons who really drew together the antagonistic atoms of the Moleswich society, partly because they were acknowledged to be the first persons there, in right not only of old settlement (the Braefields had held Braefieldville for four generations), but of the wealth derived from those departments of commercial enterprise which are recognized as the highest, and of an establishment considered to be the most elegant in the neighbourhood; principally because Elsie, while exceedingly genial and cheerful in temper, had a certain power of will (as her runaway folly had manifested), and when she got people together compelled them to be civil to each other. She had commenced this gracious career by inaugurating children's parties, and when the children became friends the parents necessarily grew closer together. Still her task had only recently begun, and its effects were not in full operation. Thus, though it became known at Moleswich that a young gentleman, the heir to a baronetcy and a high estate, was sojourning at Cromwell Lodge, no overtures were made to him on the part of the A's, B's, and C's. The vicar, who called on Kenelm the day after the dinner at Braefieldville, explained to him the social conditions of the place. "You understand," said he, "that it will be from no want of courtesy on the part of my neighbours if they do not offer you any relief from the pleasures of solitude. It will be simply because they are shy, not because they are uncivil. And it is this consideration that makes me, at the risk of seeming too forward, entreat you to look into the vicarage any morning or evening on which you feel tired of your own company—suppose you drink tea with us this evening—you will find a young lady whose heart you have already won."

"Whose heart I have won!" faltered Kenelm, and the warm blood rushed to his cheek.

"But," continued the vicar, smiling, "she has no matrimonial designs on you at present. She is only twelve years old—my little girl Clemmy."

"Clemmy!—she is your daughter. I did not know that. I very gratefully accept your invitation."

"I must not keep you longer from your amusement. The sky is just clouded enough for sport. What fly do you use?"

"To say truth, I doubt if the stream has much to tempt me in the way of its trout, and I prefer rambling about the lanes and by-paths to

'The noiseless angler's solitary stand.'

I am an indefatigable walker, and the home scenery round the place has many charms for me. Besides," added Kenelm, feeling conscious that he ought to find some more plausible excuse than the charms of home scenery for locating himself long in Cromwell Lodge—"besides—I intend to devote myself a good deal to reading. I have been very idle of late, and the solitude of this place must be favourable to study."

"You are not intended, I presume, for any of the learned professions?"

"The learned professions," replied Kenelm, "is an invidious form of speech that we are doing our best to eradicate from the language. All professions nowadays are to have much about the same amount of learning. The learning of the military profession is to be levelled upwards—the learning of the scholastic to be levelled downwards. Cabinet ministers sneer at the uses of Greek and Latin. And even such masculine studies as Law and Medicine are to be adapted to the measurements of taste and propriety in colleges for young ladies. No, I am not intended for any profession;

but still an ignorant man like myself may not be the worse for a little book-reading now and then."

"You seem to be badly provided with books here," said the vicar, glancing round the room, in which, on a table in the corner, lay half-a-dozen old-looking volumes, evidently belonging not to the lodger but the landlord. "But, as I before said, my library is at your service. What branch of reading do you prefer?"

Kenelm was, and looked, puzzled. But after a pause he answered:

"The more remote it be from the present day, the better for me. You said your collection was rich in medieval literature. But the Middle Ages are so copied by the modern Goths, that I might as well read translations of Chaucer, or take lodgings in Wardour Street. If you have any books about the manners and habits of those who, according to the newest idea in science, were our semi-human progenitors in the transition state between a marine animal and a gorilla, I should be very much edified by the loan."

"Alas," said Mr. Emlyn, laughing, "no such books have been left to us."

"No such books? You must be mistaken. There must be plenty of them somewhere. I grant all the wonderful powers of invention bestowed on the creators of poetic romance; still not the sovereign masters in that realm of literature—not Scott, not Cervantes, not Goethe, not even Shakespeare—could have presumed to rebuild the past without such materials as they found in the books that record it. And though I, no less cheerfully, grant that we have now living among us a creator of poetic romance immeasurably more inventive than they—appealing to our credulity in portents the most monstrous, with a charm of style the most conversationally familiar—still I cannot conceive that even that unrivalled romance-writer can so bewitch our understandings as to make us believe, that, if Miss Mordaunt's cat dislikes to wet her feet, it is probably because in the pre-historic age her ancestors lived in the dry country of Egypt; or that when some lofty orator, a Pitt or a Gladstone, rebuts with a polished smile which reveals his canine teeth the rude assault of an opponent, he betrays his descent from a 'semi-human progenitor' who was accustomed to snap at his enemy. Surely—surely there must be some books still extant written by philosophers before the birth of Adam, in which there is authority, even though but in mythic fable, for such poetic inventions. Surely—surely some early chroniclers must depose that they saw, saw with their own eyes, the great gorillas who scratched off their hairy coverings to please the eyes of the young ladies of their species, and that they noted the gradual metamorphosis of one animal into another. For, if you tell me that this illustrious romance-writer is but a cautious man of science, and that we must accept his inventions according to the sober laws of evidence and fact, there is not the most incredible ghost-story which does not better satisfy the common-sense of a sceptic. However, if you have no such books, lend me the most unphilosophical you possess—on magic, for instance—the philosopher's stone——"

"I have some of them," said the vicar, laughing, "you shall choose for yourself."

"If you are going homeward, let me accompany you part of the way—I don't yet know where the church and the vicarage are, and I ought to know before I come in the evening."

Kenelm and the vicar walked side by side, very sociably, across the bridge and on the side of the rivulet on which stood Mrs. Cameron's cottage. As they skirted the garden pale at the rear of the cottage, Kenelm suddenly stopped in the middle of some sentence which had interested Mr. Emlyn, and as suddenly arrested his steps on the turf that bordered the lane. A little before him stood an old peasant woman, with whom Lily, on the opposite side of the garden pale, was conversing. Mr. Emlyn did not at first see what Kenelm saw; turning round rather to gaze on his companion, surprised by his abrupt halt and silence. The girl put a small basket into the old woman's hand, who then dropped a low curtsey, and uttered low a "God bless you." Low though it was, Kenelm overheard it, and said abstractedly to Mr. Emlyn, "Is there a greater link between this life and the next than God's blessing on the young, breathed from the lips of the old?"

CHAPTER X.

"AND how is your goodman, Mrs. Haley?" said the vicar, who had now reached the spot on which the old woman stood—with Lily's fair face still bended down to her—while Kenelm slowly followed him.

"Thank you kindly, sir, he is better—out of his bed now. The young lady has done him a power of good——"

"Hush!" said Lily, colouring. "Make haste home now; you must not keep him waiting for his dinner."

The old woman again curtseyed, and went off at a brisk pace.

"Do you know, Mr. Chillingly," said Mr. Emlyn, "that Miss

Mordaunt is the best doctor in the place? Though if she goes on making so many cures she will find the number of her patients rather burthensome."

"It was only the other day," said Lily, "that you scolded me for the best cure I have yet made."

"I?—Oh! I remember; you led that silly child Madge to believe that there was a fairy charm in the arrowroot you sent her. Own you deserved a scolding there."

"No, I did not. I dress the arrowroot, and am I not Fairy? I have just got such a pretty note from Clemmy, Mr. Emlyn, asking me to come up this evening and see her new magic-lantern. Will you tell her to expect me? And—mind—no scolding."

"And all magic?" said Mr. Emlyn; "be it so."

Lily and Kenelm had not hitherto exchanged a word. She had replied with a grave inclination of her head to his silent bow. But now she turned to him shyly and said, "I suppose you have been fishing all the morning?"

"No; the fishes hereabout are under the protection of a Fairy—whom I dare not displease."

Lily's face brightened, and she extended her hand to him over the palings. "Good day; I hear aunty's voice—those dreadful French verbs!"

She disappeared among the shrubs, amid which they heard the trill of her fresh young voice singing to herself.

"That child has a heart of gold," said Mr. Emlyn, as the two men walked on. "I did not exaggerate when I said she was the best doctor in the place. I believe the poor really do believe that she is a Fairy. Of course we send from the vicarage to our ailing parishioners who require it food and wine; but it never seems to do them the good that her little dishes made by her own tiny hands do; and I don't know if you noticed the basket that old woman took away—Miss Lily taught Will Somers to make the prettiest little baskets; and she puts her jellies or other savouries into dainty porcelain gallipots nicely fitting into the baskets, which she trims with ribbons. It is the look of the thing that tempts the appetite of the invalids, and certainly the child may well be called Fairy at present; but I wish Mrs. Cameron would attend a little more strictly to her education. She can't be a Fairy for ever."

Kenelm sighed, but made no answer.

Mr. Emlyn then turned the conversation to erudite subjects, and so they came in sight of the town, when the vicar stopped and pointed towards the church, of which the spire rose a little to the left, with two aged yew-trees half-shadowing the burial-ground, and in the rear a glimpse of the vicarage seen amid the shrubs of its garden ground.

"You will know your way now," said the vicar; "excuse me if I quit you, I have a few visits to make; among others, to poor Haley, husband to the old woman you saw. I read to him a chapter in the Bible every day; yet still I fancy that he believes in fairy charms."

"Better believe too much, than too little," said Kenelm; and he turned aside into the village, and spent half-an-hour with Will, looking at the pretty baskets Lily had taught Will to make. Then, as he went slowly homeward, he turned aside into the churchyard.

The church, built in the thirteenth century, was not large, but it probably sufficed for its congregation, since it betrayed no signs of modern addition; restoration or repair it needed not. The centuries had but mellowed the tints of its solid walls, as little injured by the huge ivy stems that shot forth their aspiring leaves to the very summit of the stately tower, as by the slender roses which had been trained to climb up a foot or so of the massive buttresses. The site of the burial-ground was unusually picturesque: sheltered towards the north by a rising ground clothed with woods, sloping down at the south towards the glebe pasture-grounds through which ran the brooklet, sufficiently near for its brawling gurgle to be heard on a still day. Kenelm sat himself on an antique tomb, which was evidently appropriated to some one of higher than common rank in bygone days, but on which the sculpture was wholly obliterated.

The stillness and solitude of the place had their charm for his meditative temperament; and he remained there long, forgetful of time, and scarcely hearing the boom of the clock that warned him of its lapse.

When suddenly, a shadow—the shadow of a human form—fell on the grass on which his eyes dreamily rested. He looked up with a start, and beheld Lily standing before him mute and still. Her image was so present in his thoughts at the moment that he felt a thrill of awe, as if the thoughts had conjured up her apparition. She was the first to speak.

"You here, too?" she said very softly, almost whisperingly.

"Too!" echoed Kenelm, rising; "too! 'Tis no wonder that I, a stranger to the place, should find my steps attracted towards its most venerable building. Even the most careless traveller, halting at some remote abodes of the living, turns aside to gaze on the burial-ground of the dead. But my surprise is that you, Miss Mordaunt, should be attracted towards the same spot."

"It is my favourite spot," said Lily, "and always has been. I have sat many an hour on that tombstone. It is strange to think that no one knows who sleeps beneath it. The 'Guide Book to Moleswich,' though it gives the history of the church from the reign in which it was first built, can only venture a guess that this tomb, the grandest and oldest in the burial-ground, is tenanted by some member of a family named Montfichet, that was once very powerful in the county, and has become extinct since the reign of Henry VI. But," added Lily, "there is not a letter of the name Montfichet left. I found out more than any one else has done—I learned black-letter on purpose; look here," and she pointed to a small spot in which the moss had been removed. "Do you see those figures, are they not XVIII? and look again, in what was once the line above the figures, ELE. It must have been an Eleanor, who died at the age of eighteen——"

"I rather think it more probable that the figures refer to the date of the death, 1318 perhaps; and so far as I can decipher black-letter, which is more in my father's line than mine, I think it is A L, not E L, and that it seems as if there had been a letter between L and the second E, which is now effaced. The tomb itself is not likely to belong to any powerful family then resident at the place. Their monuments, according to usage, would have been within the church; probably in their own mortuary chapel."

"Don't try to destroy my fancy," said Lily, shaking her head; "you cannot succeed, I know *her* history too well. She was young, and some one loved her, and built over her the finest tomb he could afford; and see how long the epitaph must have been! how much it must have spoken in her praise, and of his grief. And then he went his way, and the tomb was neglected, and her fate forgotten."

"My dear Miss Mordaunt, this is indeed a wild romance to spin out of so slender a thread. But even if true, there is no reason to think that a life is forgotten though a tomb be neglected."

"Perhaps not," said Lily, thoughtfully. "But when I am dead, if I can look down, I think it would please me to see my grave not neglected by those who had loved me once."

She moved from him as she said this, and went to a little mound that seemed not long since raised; there was a simple cross at the head and a narrow border of flowers round it. Lily knelt beside the flowers and pulled out a stray weed. Then she rose, and said to Kenelm, who had followed, and now stood beside her—

"She was the little grandchild of poor old Mrs. Hales. I could not cure her, though I tried hard : she was so fond of me, and died in my arms. No, let me not say 'died'—surely there is no such thing as dying. 'Tis but a change of life—

'Less than the void between two waves of air,
The space between existence and a soul.'"

"Whose lines are those?" asked Kenelm.

"I don't know; I learnt them from Lion. Don't you believe them to be true?"

"Yes! But the truth does not render the thought of quitting this scene of life for another more pleasing to most of us. See how soft and gentle and bright is all that living summer land beyond; let us find subject for talk from that, not from the graveyard on which we stand."

"But is there not a summer land fairer than that we see now; and which we do see, as in a dream, best when we take subjects of talk from the graveyard?" Without waiting for a reply, Lily went on: "I planted these flowers; Mr. Emlyn was angry with me; he said it was 'Popish.' But he had not the heart to have them taken up; I come here very often to see to them. Do you think it wrong? Poor little Nell! she was so fond of flowers. And the Eleanor in the great tomb, she too perhaps knew some one who called her Nell; but there are no flowers round her tomb. Poor Eleanor!"

She took the nosegay she wore on her bosom, and as she repassed the tomb laid it on the mouldering stone.

CHAPTER XI.

THEY quitted the burial-ground, taking their way to Grasmere. Kenelm walked by Lily's side; not a word passed between them till they came in sight of the cottage.

Then Lily stopped abruptly, and lifting towards him her charming face, said—

"I told you I would think over what you said to me last night. I have done so, and feel I can thank you honestly. You were very kind; I never before thought that I had a bad temper, no one ever told me so. But I see now what you mean—sometimes I feel very quickly, and then I show it. But how did I show it to you, Mr. Chillingly?"

"Did you not turn your back to me when I seated myself next you in Mrs. Braefield's garden, vouchsafing me no reply when I asked if I had offended?"

Lily's face became bathed in blushes, and her voice faltered, as she answered—

"I was not offended, I was not in a bad temper then; it was worse than that."

"Worse—what could it possibly be?"

"I am afraid it was envy."

"Envy of what—of whom?"

"I don't know how to explain; after all, I fear aunty is right, and the fairy tales put very silly, very naughty thoughts into one's head. When Cinderella's sisters went to the king's ball, and Cinderella was left alone, did not she long to go too? Did not she envy her sisters?"

"Ah! I understand now—Sir Charles spoke of the Court Ball."

"And you were there talking with handsome ladies—and—oh! I was so foolish and felt sore."

"You, who when we first met wondered how people who could live in the country preferred to live in towns, do then sometimes contradict yourself, and sigh for the great world that lies beyond these quiet water banks. You feel that you have youth and beauty, and wish to be admired!"

"It is not that exactly," said Lily, with a perplexed look in her ingenuous countenance, "and in my better moments, when the 'bettermost self' comes forth, I know that I am not made for the great world you speak of. But you see——" Here she paused again, and as they had now entered the garden, dropped wearily on a bench beside the path. Kenelm seated himself there too, waiting for her to finish her broken sentence.

"You see," she continued, looking down embarrassed, and describing vague circles on the gravel with her fairy-like foot, "that at home, ever since I can remember, they have treated me as if,—well as if I were—what shall I say?—the child of one of your great ladies. Even Lion, who is so noble, so grand, seemed to think when I was a mere infant that I was a little queen; once when I told a fib he did not scold me, but I never saw him look so sad and so angry as when he said, 'never again forget that you are a lady.' And, but I tire you——"

"Tire me, indeed! go on."

"No, I have said enough to explain why I have at times proud thoughts, and vain thoughts; and why, for instance, I said to myself: 'Perhaps my place of right is among those fine ladies whom he'—but it is all over now." She rose hastily with a pretty laugh, and bounded towards Mrs. Cameron, who was walking slowly along the lawn with a book in her hand.

CHAPTER XII.

IT was a very merry party at the vicarage that evening. Lily had not been prepared to meet Kenelm there, and her face brightened wonderfully as at her entrance he turned from the bookshelves to which Mr. Emlyn was directing his attention. But instead of meeting his advance, she darted off to the lawn, where Clemmy and several other children greeted her with a joyous shout.

"Not acquainted with Macleane's 'Juvenal'?" said the reverend scholar; "you will be greatly pleased with it—here it is—a posthumous work, edited by George Long. I can lend you Munro's Lucretius, '69. Aha! we have some scholars yet to pit against the Germans."

"I am heartily glad to hear it," said Kenelm. "It will be a long time before they will ever wish to rival us in that game which Miss Clemmy is now forming on the lawn, and in which England has recently acquired a European reputation."

"I don't take you. What game?"

"Puss in the Corner. With your leave I will look out and see whether it be a winning game for puss—in the long-run." Kenelm joined the children, amidst whom Lily seemed not the least childlike. Resisting all overtures from Clemmy to join in their play, he seated himself on a sloping bank at a little distance—an idle looker-on. His eye followed Lily's nimble movements, his ear drank in the music of her joyous laugh. Could that be the same girl whom he had seen tending the flower-bed amid the gravestones? Mrs. Emlyn came across the lawn and joined him, seating herself also on the bank. Mrs. Emlyn was an exceedingly clever woman; nevertheless she was not formidable—on the contrary, pleasing; and though the ladies in the neighbourhood said 'she talked like a book,' the easy gentleness of her voice carried off that offence.

"I suppose, Mr. Chillingly," said she, "I ought to apologize for my husband's invitation to what must seem to you so frivolous an entertainment as a child's party. But when Mr. Emlyn asked you to come to us this evening, he was not aware that Clemmy had also invited her young friends. He had looked forward to a rational conversation with you on his own favourite studies."

"It is not so long since I left school, but that I prefer a half holiday to lessons, even from a tutor so pleasant as Mr. Emlyn—

'Ah, happy years—once more who would not be a boy!'"

"Nay," said Mrs. Emlyn with a grave smile. "Who that had started so fairly as Mr. Chillingly in the career of man would wish to go back and resume a place among boys?"

"But, my dear Mrs. Emlyn, the line I quoted was wrung from the heart of a man who had already outstripped all rivals in the raceground he had chosen, and who at that moment was in the very Maytime of youth and of fame. And if such a man at such an epoch in his career could sigh to 'be once more a boy,' it must have been when he was thinking of the boy's half holiday, and recoiling from the taskwork he was condemned to learn as man."

"The line you quote is, I think, from Childe Harold, and surely you would not apply to mankind in general the sentiment of a poet so peculiarly self-reflecting (if I may use that expression), and in whom sentiment is often so morbid."

"You are right, Mrs. Emlyn," said Kenelm ingenuously. "Still a boy's half holiday is a very happy thing; and among mankind in general there must be many who would be glad to have it back again. Mr. Emlyn himself I should think."

"Mr. Emlyn has his half holiday now. Do you not see him standing just outside the window? Do you not hear him laughing? He is a child again in the mirth of his children. I hope you will stay some time in the neighbourhood; I am sure you and he will like each other. And it is such a rare delight to him to get a scholar like yourself to talk to."

"Pardon me I am not a scholar—a very noble title that, and not to be given to a lazy trifler on the surface of book-lore like myself."

"You are too modest. My husband has a copy of your Cambridge prize verses, and says 'the Latinity of them is quite beautiful.' I quote his very words."

"Latin verse-making is a mere knack, little more than a proof that one had an elegant scholar for one's tutor, as I certainly had. But it is by special grace that a real scholar can send forth another real scholar, and a Kennedy produce a Munro. But to return to the more interesting question of half holidays; I declare that Clemmy is leading off your husband in triumph. He is actually going to be Puss in the Corner."

"When you know more of Charles—I mean my husband—you will discover that his whole life is more or less of a holiday. Perhaps because he is not what you accuse yourself of being—he is not lazy; he never wishes to be a boy once more; and taskwork itself is holiday to him. He enjoys shutting himself up in his study and reading —he enjoys a walk with the children—he enjoys visiting the poor— he enjoys his duties as a clergyman. And though I am not always contented for him, though I think he should have had those honours in his profession which have been lavished on men with less ability and less learning, yet he is never discontented himself. Shall I tell you his secret?"

"Do."

"He is a *Thanks-giving Man.* You, too, must have much to thank God for, Mr. Chillingly; and in thanksgiving to God does there not blend usefulness to man, and such sense of pastime in the usefulness as makes each day a holiday?"

Kenelm looked up into the quiet face of this obscure pastor's wife with a startled expression in his own.

"I see, ma'am," said he, "that you have devoted much thought to the study of the æsthetical philosophy as expounded by German thinkers, whom it is rather difficult to understand."

"I, Mr. Chillingly—good gracious. No! What do you mean by your æsthetical philosophy?"

"According to æsthetics, I believe man arrives at his highest state of moral excellence when labour and duty lose all the harshness of effort—when they become the impulse and habit of life; when, as the essential attributes of the beautiful, they are, like beauty, enjoyed as pleasure; and thus, as you expressed, each day becomes a holiday. A lovely doctrine, not perhaps so lofty as that of the Stoics, but more bewitching. Only, very few of us can practically merge our cares and our worries into so serene an atmosphere."

"Some do so without knowing anything of æsthetics and with no pretence to be Stoics; but, then, they are Christians."

"There are some such Christians, no doubt, but they are rarely to be met with. Take Christendom altogether, and it appears to comprise the most agitated population in the world; the population in which there is the greatest grumbling as to the quantity of labour to be done, the loudest complaints that duty instead of a pleasure is a very hard and disagreeable struggle, and in which holidays are fewest and the moral atmosphere least serene. Perhaps," added Kenelm, with a deeper shade of thought on his brow, "it is this perpetual consciousness of struggle; this difficulty in merging toil into ease, or stern duty into placid enjoyment; this refusal to ascend for one's self into the calm of an air aloof from the cloud which darkens, and the hailstorm which beats upon, the fellow-men we leave below,—that makes the troubled life of Christendom dearer to heaven, and more conducive to heaven's design in rendering earth the wrestling ground and not the resting-place of man, than is that of the Brahmin, ever seeking to abstract himself from the Christian's conflicts of action and desire, and to carry into its extremest practice the æsthetic theory, of basking undisturbed in the contemplation of the most absolute beauty human thought can reflect from its idea of divine good!"

Whatever Mrs. Emlyn might have said in reply was interrupted by the rush of the children towards her; they were tired of play, and eager for tea and the magic lantern.

CHAPTER XIII.

THE room is duly obscured and the white sheet attached to the wall; the children are seated, hushed, and awe-stricken. And Kenelm is placed next to Lily.

The tritest things in our mortal experience are among the most mysterious. There is more mystery in the growth of a blade of grass than there is in the wizard's mirror or the feats of a spirit medium. Most of us have known the attraction that draws one human being to another, and makes it so exquisite a happiness to sit quiet and mute by another's side; which stills for the moment the busiest thoughts in our brain, the most turbulent desires in our heart, and renders us but conscious of a present ineffable bliss. Most of us have known that. But who has ever been satisfied with any metaphysical account of its why or wherefore? We can but say it is love, and love at that earlier section of its history which has not yet escaped from romance: but by what process that other person has become singled out of the whole universe to attain such special power over one, is a problem that, though many have attempted to solve it, has never attained to solution. In the dim light of the room Kenelm could only distinguish the outlines of Lily's delicate face, but at each new surprise in the show, the face intuitively turned to his, and once, when the terrible image of a sheeted ghost, pursuing a guilty man, passed along the wall, she drew closer to him in her childish fright, and by an involuntary innocent movement laid her hand on his. He detained it tenderly, but, alas! it was withdrawn the next moment; the ghost was succeeded by a couple of dancing dogs. And Lily's ready laugh —partly at the dogs, partly at her own previous alarm—vexed Kenelm's ear. He wished there had been a succession of ghosts, each more appalling than the last.

The entertainment was over, and after a slight refreshment of cakes and wine-and-water the party broke up; the children-visitors went away attended by servant-maids who had come for them. Mrs. Cameron and Lily were to walk home on foot.

"It is a lovely night, Mrs. Cameron," said Mr. Emlyn, "and I will attend you to your gate."

"Permit me also," said Kenelm.

"Ay," said the vicar, "it is your own way to Cromwell Lodge."

The path led them through the churchyard as the nearest approach to the brookside. The moonbeams shimmered through the yew-trees and rested on the old tomb—playing, as it were, round the flowers which Lily's hand had, that day, dropped upon its stone. She was walking beside Kenelm—the elder two a few paces in front.

"How silly I was," said she, "to be so frightened at the false ghost! I don't think a real one would frighten me, at least if seen here, in this loving moonlight, and on God's ground!"

"Ghosts, were they permitted to appear except in a magic-lantern, could not harm the innocent. And I wonder why the idea of their apparition should always have been associated with such phantasies of horror, especially by sinless children, who have the least reason to dread them."

"Oh, that is true," cried Lily; "but even when we are grown up there must be times in which we should so long to see a ghost, and feel what a comfort, what a joy it would be."

"I understand you. If some one very dear to us had vanished from our life; if we felt the anguish of the separation so intensely as to efface the thought that life, as you said so well, 'never dies;' well, yes, then I can conceive that the mourner would yearn to have a glimpse of the vanished one, were it but to ask the sole and only question he could desire to put: 'Art thou happy? May I hope that we shall meet again, never to part—never!'"

Kenelm's voice trembled as he spoke, tears stood in his eyes. A melancholy—vague, unaccountable, overpowering—passed across his heart, as the shadow of some dark-winged bird passes over a quiet stream.

"You have never yet felt this?" asked Lily doubtingly, in a soft voice, full of tender pity, stopping short and looking into his face.

"I? No. I have never yet lost one whom I so loved and so yearned to see again. I was but thinking that such losses may befall us all ere we too vanish out of sight."

"Lily!" called forth Mrs. Cameron, halting at the gate of the burial-ground.

"Yes, auntie?"

"Mr. Emlyn wants to know how far you have got in 'Numa Pompilius.' Come and answer for yourself."

"Oh, those tiresome grown-up people!" whispered Lily, petulantly, to Kenelm. "I do like Mr. Emlyn; he is one of the very best of men. But still he is grown-up, and his 'Numa Pompilius' is so stupid."

"My first French lesson-book. No, it is not stupid. Read on. It has hints of the prettiest fairy tale I know, and of the fairy in especial who bewitched my fancies as a boy."

By this time they had gained the gate of the burial-ground.

"What fairy tale? what fairy?" asked Lily, speaking quickly.

"She was a fairy, though in heathen language she is called a nymph—Egeria. She was the link between men and gods to him she loved; she belongs to the race of Gods. True; she, too, may vanish, but she can never die."

"Well, Miss Lily," said the vicar, "and how far in the book I lent you—'Numa Pompilius.'"

"Ask me this day next week."

"I will; but mind you are to translate as you go on. I must see the translation."

"Very well. I will do my best," answered Lily meekly.

Lily now walked by the vicar's side, and Kenelm by Mrs. Cameron's, till they reached Grasmere.

"I will go on with you to the bridge, Mr. Chillingly," said the vicar, when the ladies had disappeared within their garden.

"We had little time to look over my books, and, by the bye, I hope you at least took the 'Juvenal.'"

"No, Mr. Emlyn; who can quit your house with an inclination for satire? I must come some morning and select a volume from those works which give pleasant views of life and bequeath favourable impressions of mankind. Your wife, with whom I have had an interesting conversation upon the principles of æsthetical philosophy——"

"My wife—Charlotte! She knows nothing about æsthetical philosophy."

"She calls it by another name, but she understands it well enough to illustrate the principles by example. She tells me that labour and duty are so taken up by you

'In den heitern Regionen
Wo die reinen Formen wohnen,'

that they become joy and beauty—is it so?"

"I am sure that Charlotte never said anything half so poetical. But, in plain words, the days pass with me very happily. I should be ungrateful if I were not happy. Heaven has bestowed on me so many sources of love—wife, children, books, and the calling which, when one quits one's own threshold, carries love along with it into the world beyond. A small world in itself—only a parish—but then my calling links it with infinity."

"I see; it is from the sources of love that you draw the supplies for happiness."

"Surely; without love one may be good, but one could scarcely be happy. No one can dream of a heaven except as the abode of love. What writer is it who says, 'How well the human heart was understood by him who first called God by the name of Father?'"

"I do not remember, but it is beautifully said. You evidently do not subscribe to the arguments in Decimus Roach's 'Approach to the Angels.'"

"Ah, Mr. Chillingly! your words teach me how lacerated a man's happiness may be if he does not keep the claws of vanity closely pared. I actually feel a keen pang when you speak to me of that eloquent panegyric on celibacy, ignorant that the only thing I ever published which I fancied was not without esteem by intellectual readers is a Reply to 'The Approach to the Angels'—a youthful book, written in the first year of my marriage. But it obtained success: I have just revised the tenth edition of it."

"That is the book I will select from your library. You will be pleased to hear that Mr. Roach, whom I saw at Oxford a few days ago, recants his opinions, and, at the age of fifty, is about to be married—he begs me to add, 'not for his own personal satisfaction.'"

"Going to be married!—Decimus Roach! I thought my Reply would convince him at last."

"I shall look to your Reply to remove some lingering doubts in my own mind."

"Doubts in favour of celibacy?"

"Well, if not for laymen, perhaps for a priesthood."

"The most forcible part of my Reply is on that head: read it attentively. I think that, of all sections of mankind, the clergy are those to whom, not only for their own sakes, but for the sake of the community, marriage should be most commended. Why, sir," continued the vicar, warming up into oratorical enthusiasm, "are you not aware that there are no homes in England from which men who have served and adorned their country have issued forth in such prodigal numbers as those of the clergy of our Church? What other class can produce a list so crowded with eminent names as we can boast in the sons we have reared and sent forth into the world? How many statesmen, soldiers, sailors, lawyers, physicians, authors, men of science, have been the sons of us village pastors? Naturally

—for with us they receive careful education; they acquire of necessity the simple tastes and disciplined habits which lead to industry and perseverance; and, for the most part, they carry with them throughout life a purer moral code, a more systematic reverence for things and thoughts religious associated with their earliest images of affection and respect, than can be expected from the sons of laymen, whose parents are wholly temporal and worldly. Sir, I maintain that this is a cogent argument, to be considered well by the nation, not only in favour of a married clergy—for, on that score, a million of Roaches could not convert public opinion in this country—but in favour of the Church, the Established Church, which has been so fertile a nursery of illustrious laymen; and I have often thought that one main and undetected cause of the lower tone of morality, public and private, of the greater corruption of manners, of the more prevalent scorn of religion which we see, for instance, in a country so civilized as France, is, that its clergy can train no sons to carry into the contests of earth the steadfast belief in accountability to Heaven."

"I thank you with a full heart," said Kenelm. "I shall ponder well over all that you have so earnestly said. I am already disposed to give up all lingering crotchets as to a bachelor clergy; but, as a layman, I fear that I shall never attain to the purified philanthropy of Mr. Decimus Roach, and, if ever I do marry, it will be very much for my personal satisfaction."

Mr. Emlyn laughed good-humouredly, and, as they had now reached the bridge, shook hands with Kenelm, and walked homewards, along the brook-side and through the burial-ground, with the alert step and the uplifted head of a man who has joy in life and admits of no fear in death.

CHAPTER XIV.

FOR the next two weeks or so Kenelm and Lily met, not indeed so often as the reader might suppose, but still frequently; five times at Mrs. Braefield's, once again at the Vicarage, and twice when Kenelm had called at Grasmere; and, being invited to stay to tea at one of those visits, he stayed the whole evening. Kenelm was more and more fascinated in proportion as he saw more and more of a creature so exquisitely strange to his experience. She was to him not only a poem, but a poem in the Sibylline Books—enigmatical, perplexing conjecture, and somehow or other mysteriously blending its interest with visions of the future.

Lily was indeed an enchanting combination of opposites rarely blended into harmony. Her ignorance of much that girls know before they number half her years, was so relieved by candid, innocent simplicity; so adorned by pretty fancies and sweet beliefs; and so contrasted and lit up by gleams of a knowledge that the young ladies we call well educated seldom exhibit — knowledge derived from quick observation of external nature, and impressionable susceptibility to its varying and subtle beauties. This knowledge had been perhaps first instilled, and subsequently nourished, by such poetry as she had not only learned by heart, but taken up as inseparable from the healthful circulation of her thoughts; not the poetry of our own day—most young ladies know enough of that—but selected fragments from the verse of old, most of them from poets now little read by the young of either sex, poets dear to spirits like Coleridge or Charles Lamb. None of them, however, so dear to her as the solemn melodies of Milton. Much of such poetry she had never read in books; it had been taught her in childhood by her guardian the painter. And with all this imperfect, desultory culture, there was such dainty refinement in her every look and gesture, and such deep woman-tenderness of heart. Since Kenelm had commended 'Numa Pompilius' to her study, she had taken very lovingly to that old-fashioned romance, and was fond of talking to him about Egeria as of a creature who had really existed.

But what was the effect that he—the first man of years correspondent to her own with whom she had ever familiarly conversed— what was the effect that Kenelm Chillingly produced on the mind and the heart of Lily?

This was, after all, the question that puzzled him the most—not without reason: it might have puzzled the shrewdest bystander. The artless candour with which she manifested her liking to him was at variance with the ordinary character of maiden love; it seemed more the fondness of a child for a favourite brother. And it was this uncertainty that, in his own thoughts, justified Kenelm for lingering on, and believing that it was necessary to win, or at least to learn more of, her secret heart before he could venture to disclose his own. He did not flatter himself with the pleasing fear that he might be endangering her happiness; it was only his own that was risked. Then, in all those meetings, all those conversations to themselves, there had passed none of the words which commit our destiny to the will of another. If in the man's eyes love would force its way, Lily's frank, innocent gaze chilled it back again to its inward cell. Joyously as she would spring forward to meet him, there was no tell-tale blush on her cheek, no self-betraying tremor in her clear, sweet-toned voice. No; there had not yet been a moment when he could say to himself, "She loves me." Often he said to himself, "She knows not yet what love is."

In the intervals of time not passed in Lily's society, Kenelm would take long rambles with Mr. Emlyn, or saunter into Mrs. Braefield's drawing-room. For the former he conceived a more cordial sentiment of friendship than he entertained for any man of his own age—a friendship that admitted the noble elements of admiration and respect.

Charles Emlyn was one of those characters in which the colours appear pale unless the light be brought very close to them, and then each tint seems to change into a warmer and richer one. The manner which, at first, you would call merely gentle, becomes unaffectedly genial; the mind you at first might term inert, though well-informed, you now acknowledge to be full of disciplined vigour. Emlyn was not, however, without his little amiable foibles; and it was, perhaps, these that made him lovable. He was a great believer in human goodness, and very easily imposed upon by cunning appeals to "his well-known benevolence." He was disposed to overrate the excellence of all that he once took to his heart. He thought he had the best wife in the world, the best children, the best servants, the best beehive, the best pony, and the best house-dog. His parish was the most virtuous, his church the most picturesque, his vicarage the prettiest, certainly, in the whole shire—perhaps, in the whole kingdom. Probably it was this philosophy of optimism which contributed to lift him into the serene realm of æsthetic joy.

He was not without his dislikes as well as likings. Though a liberal Churchman towards Protestant dissenters, he cherished the *odium theologicum* for all that savoured of Popery. Perhaps there was another cause for this besides the purely theological one. Early in life a young sister of his had been, to use his phrase, "secretly entrapped" into conversion to the Roman Catholic faith, and had since entered a convent. His affections had been deeply wounded by this loss to the range of them. Mr. Emlyn had also his little infirmities of self-esteem, rather than of vanity. Though he had seen very little of any world beyond that of his parish, he piqued himself on his knowledge of human nature and of practical affairs in general. Certainly no man had read more about them, especially in the books of the ancient classics. Perhaps it was owing to this that he so little understood Lily—a character to which the ancient classics afforded no counterpart nor clue; and perhaps it was this also that made Lily think him "so terribly grown up." Thus, despite his mild good-nature, she did not get on very well with him.

The society of this amiable scholar pleased Kenelm the more, because the scholar evidently had not the remotest idea that Kenelm's sojourn at Cromwell Lodge was influenced by the vicinity to Grasmere. Mr. Emlyn was sure that he knew human nature, and practical affairs in general, too well to suppose that the heir to a rich baronet could dream of taking for wife a girl without fortune or rank, the orphan ward of a low-born artist only just struggling into reputation; or, indeed, that a Cambridge prizeman, who had evidently read much on grave and dry subjects, and who had no less evidently seen a great deal of polished society, could find any other attraction in a very imperfectly-educated girl, who tamed butterflies and knew no more than they did of fashionable life, than Mr. Emlyn himself felt in the presence of a pretty wayward innocent child—the companion and friend of his Clemmy.

Mrs. Braefield was more discerning; but she had a good deal of tact, and did not as yet scare Kenelm away from her house by letting him see how much she had discerned. She would not even tell her husband, who, absent from the place on most mornings, was too absorbed in the cares of his own business to interest himself much in the affairs of others.

Now Elsie, being still of a romantic turn of mind, had taken it into her head that Lily Mordaunt, if not actually the princess to be found in poetic dramas whose rank was for awhile kept concealed, was yet one of the higher-born daughters of the ancient race whose name she bore, and in that respect no derogatory alliance for Kenelm Chillingly. A conclusion she had arrived at from no better evidence than the well-bred appearance and manners of the aunt, and the exquisite delicacy of the niece's form and features, with the undefinable air of distinction which accompanied even her most careless and sportive moments. But Mrs. Braefield also had the wit to discover that under the infantine ways and phantasies of this almost self-taught girl, there lay, as yet undeveloped, the elements of a beautiful womanhood. So that altogether, from the very day she first re-encountered Kenelm, Elsie's thought had been that Lily was the wife to suit him. Once conceiving that idea, her natural strength of will made her resolve on giving all facilities to carry it out silently and unobtrusively, and therefore skilfully.

"I am so glad to think," she said one day, when Kenelm had joined her walk through the pleasant shrubberies in her garden ground, "that you have made such friends with Mr. Emlyn. Though all hereabouts like him so much for his goodness, there are few who can appreciate his learning. To you it must be a surprise as well as pleasure to find, in this quiet humdrum place, a companion so clever and well-informed; it compensates for your disappointment in discovering that our brook yields such bad sport."

"Don't disparage the brook; it yields the pleasantest banks on which to lie down under old pollard oaks at noon, or over which to saunter at morn and eve. Where those charms are absent even a salmon could not please. Yes; I rejoice to have made friends with Mr. Emlyn. I have learned a great deal from him, and am often asking myself whether I shall ever make peace with my conscience by putting what I have learned into practice."

"May I ask what special branch of learning is that?"

"I scarcely know how to define it. Suppose we call it 'Worthwhileism.' Among the New Ideas which I was recommended to study as those that must govern my generation, the Not-worth-while Idea holds a very high rank; and being myself naturally of calm and equable constitution, that new idea made the basis of my philosophical system. But since I have become intimate with Charles Emlyn I think there is a great deal to be said in favour of Worthwhileism, old idea though it be. I see a man who, with very commonplace materials for interest or amusement at his command, continues to be always interested or generally amused; I ask myself why and how? And it seems to me as if the cause started from fixed beliefs which settle his relations with God and man, and that settlement he will not allow any speculations to disturb. Be those beliefs questionable or not by others, at least they are such as cannot displease a Deity, and cannot fail to be kindly and useful to fellowmortals. Then he plants these beliefs on the soil of a happy and genial home, which tends to confirm and strengthen and call them into daily practice; and when he goes forth from home, even to the farthest verge of the circle that surrounds it, he carries with him the home influences of kindliness and use. Possibly my line of life may be drawn to the verge of a wider circle than his; but so much the better for interest and amusement, if it can be drawn from the same centre—namely, fixed beliefs daily warmed into vital action in the sunshine of a congenial home."

Mrs. Braefield listened to this speech with pleased attention, and as it came to its close, the name of Lily trembled on her tongue, for she divined that when he spoke of home Lily was in his thoughts; but she checked the impulse, and replied by a generalized platitude.

"Certainly the first thing in life is to secure a happy and congenial home. It must be a terrible trial for the best of us if we marry without love."

"Terrible, indeed, if the one loves and the other does not."

"That can scarcely be your case, Mr. Chillingly, for I am sure you could not marry where you did not love; and do not think I flatter you when I say that a man far less gifted than you can scarcely fail to be loved by the woman he woos and wins."

Kenelm, in this respect one of the modestest of human beings, shook his head doubtingly, and was about to reply in self-disparagement, when, lifting his eyes and looking round, he halted mute and still as if rooted to the spot. They had entered the trellised circle through the roses of which he had first caught sight of the young face that had haunted him ever since.

"Ah!" he said abruptly; "I cannot stay longer here, dreaming away the work-day hours in a fairy ring. I am going to town to-day by the next train."

"You are coming back?"

"Of course—this evening. I left no address at my lodgings in London. There must be a large accumulation of letters—some, no doubt, from my father and mother. I am only going for them. Good-bye. How kindly you have listened to me!"

"Shall we fix a day next week for seeing the remains of the old Roman villa? I will ask Mrs. Cameron and her niece to be of the party."

"Any day you please," said Kenelm, joyfully.

CHAPTER XV.

KENELM did indeed find a huge pile of letters and notes on reaching his forsaken apartment in Mayfair—many of them merely invitations for days long past, none of them of interest except two from Sir Peter, three from his mother, and one from Tom Bowles.

Sir Peter's were short. In the first he gently scolded Kenelm for going away without communicating any address; and stated the acquaintance he had formed with Gordon, the favourable impression that young gentleman had made on him, the transfer of the £20,000, and the invitation given to Gordon, the Traverses, and Lady Glenalvon. The second, dated much later, noted the arrival of his invited guests, dwelt with warmth unusual to Sir Peter on the attractions of Cecilia, and took occasion to refer, not the less emphatically because as it were incidentally, to the sacred promise which Kenelm had given him never to propose to a young lady until the case had been submitted to the examination and received the consent of Sir Peter. "Come to Exmundham, and if I do not give my consent to propose to Cecilia Travers, hold me a tyrant and rebel."

Lady Chillingly's letters were much longer. They dwelt more complainingly on his persistence in eccentric habits—so exceedingly unlike other people, quitting London at the very height of the season, going without even a servant nobody knew where—she did not wish to wound his feelings; but still these were not the ways natural to a young gentleman of station. If he had no respect for himself, he ought to have some consideration for his parents, especially his poor mother. She then proceeded to comment on the elegant manners of Leopold Travers, and the good sense and pleasant conversation of Chillingly Gordon, a young man of whom any mother might be proud. From that subject she diverged to mildly querulous references to family matters. Parson John had expressed himself very rudely to Mr. Chillingly Gordon upon some book by a foreigner—Comte, or Count, or some such name—in which, so far as she could pretend to judge, Mr. Gordon had uttered some very benevolent sentiments about humanity, which, in the most insolent manner, Parson John had denounced as an attack on religion. But really Parson John was too High Church for her. Having thus disposed of Parson John, she indulged some ladylike wailings on the singular costume of the three Miss Chillinglys. They had been asked by Sir Peter, unknown to her—so like him—to meet their guests; to meet Lady Glenalvon and Miss Travers, whose dress was so perfect (here she described their dress)—and they came in pea-green with pelerines of mock blonde, and Miss Sally with corkscrew ringlets and a wreath of jessamine, "which no girl after eighteen would venture to wear."

"But, my dear," added her ladyship, "your poor father's family are certainly great oddities. I have more to put up with than any one knows. I do my best to carry it off. I know my duties, and will do them."

Family grievances thus duly recorded and lamented, Lady Chillingly returned to her guests.

Evidently unconscious of her husband's designs on Cecilia, she dismissed her briefly: "A very handsome young lady, though rather too blonde for her taste, and certainly with an air *distingué*." Lastly, she enlarged on the extreme pleasure she felt on meeting again *the* friend of her youth, Lady Glenalvon.

"Not at all spoilt by the education of the great world, which, alas! obedient to the duties of wife and mother, however little my sacrifices are appreciated, I have long since relinquished. Lady Glenalvon suggests turning that hideous old moat into a fernery—a great improvement. Of course your poor father makes objections."

Tom's letter was written on black-edged paper, and ran thus:—

"DEAR SIR,—Since I had the honour to see you in London I have had a sad loss—my poor uncle is no more. He died very suddenly after a hearty supper. One doctor says it was apoplexy, another valvular disease of the heart. He has left me his heir, after providing for his sister—no one had an idea that he had saved so much money. I am quite a rich man now. And I shall leave the veterinary business, which of late—since I took to reading, as you kindly advised—is not much to my liking. The principal corn-merchant here has offered to take me into partnership; and, from what I can see, it will be a very good thing, and a great rise in life. But, sir, I can't settle to it at present—I can't settle, as I would wish, to anything. I know you will not laugh at me when I say I have a strange longing to travel for a while. I have been reading books of travels, and they get into my head more than any other books. But I don't think I could leave the country with a contented heart, till I have had just another look at you know whom—just to see her, and know she is happy. I am sure I could shake hands with Will, and kiss her little one without a wrong thought. What do you say to that, dear sir? You promised to write to me about her. But I have not heard from you. Susy, the little girl with the flower-ball, has had a loss too—the poor old man she lived with died within a few days of my dear uncle's decease. Mother moved here, as I think you know, when the forge at Graveleigh was sold; and she is going to take Susy to live with her. She is quite fond of Susy. Pray let me hear from you soon, and do, dear sir, give me your advice about travelling—and about Her. You see I should like Her to think of me more kindly when I am in distant parts.

"I remain, dear sir,
"Your grateful servant,
"T. BOWLES."

"P.S.—Miss Travers has sent me Will's last remittance. There is very little owed me now; so they must be thriving. I hope she is not overworked."

On returning by the train that evening Kenelm went to the house of Will Somers. The shop was already closed, but he was admitted by a trusty servant-maid to the parlour, where he found them all at supper, except indeed the baby, who had long since retired to the cradle, and the cradle had been removed up-stairs. Will and Jessie were very proud when Kenelm invited himself to share their repast, which, though simple, was by no means a bad one. When the meal was over and the supper things removed, Kenelm drew his chair near to the glass door which led into a little garden very neatly kept —for it was Will's pride to attend to it—before he sat down to his more professional work. The door was open, and admitted the coolness of the starlit air and the fragrance of the sleeping flowers.

"You have a pleasant home here, Mrs. Somers."

"We have, indeed, and know how to bless Him we owe it to."

"I am rejoiced to think that. How often when God designs a special kindness to us He puts the kindness into the heart of a fellow-man—perhaps the last fellow-man we should have thought of; but in blessing him we thank God who inspired him. Now, my dear friends, I know that you all three suspect me of being the agent whom God chose for His benefits. You fancy that it was from me came the loan which enabled you to leave Graveleigh and settle here. You are mistaken—you look incredulous."

"It could not be the Squire," exclaimed Jessie. "Miss Travers assured me that it was neither he nor herself. Oh, it must be you, sir. I beg pardon, but who else could it be?"

"Your husband shall guess. Suppose, Will, that you had behaved ill to some one who was nevertheless dear to you, and on thinking over it afterwards felt very sorry and much ashamed of yourself, and suppose that later you had the opportunity and the power to render a service to that person, do you think you would do it?"

"I should be a bad man if I did not."

"Bravo! And supposing that when the person you thus served came to know it was you who rendered the service, he did not feel thankful, he did not think it handsome of you, thus to repair any little harm he might have done you before, but became churlish, and sore, and cross-grained, and with a wretched false pride said that because he had offended you once he resented your taking the liberty of befriending him now, would not you think that person an ungrateful fellow,—ungrateful not only to you his fellow-man—that is of less moment—but ungrateful to the God who put it into your heart to be His human agent in the benefit received?"

"Well, sir, yes, certainly," said Will, with all the superior refinement of his intellect to that of Jessie, unaware of what Kenelm was driving at; while Jessie, pressing her hands tightly together, turning pale, and with a frightened hurried glance towards Will's face, answered, impulsively—

"Oh, Mr. Chillingly, I hope you are not thinking, not speaking of Mr. Bowles?"

"Whom else should I think, or speak of?"

Will rose nervously from his chair, all his features writhing.

"Sir, sir, this is a bitter blow—very bitter, very."

Jessie rushed to Will, flung her arms round him and sobbed.

Kenelm turned quietly to old Mrs. Somers, who had suspended the work on which since supper she had been employed, knitting socks for the baby—

"My dear Mrs. Somers, what is the good of being a grandmother and knitting socks for baby grandchildren, if you cannot assure those silly children of yours that they are too happy in each other to harbour any resentment against a man who would have parted them, and now repents?"

Somewhat to Kenelm's admiration, I dare not say surprise, old Mrs. Somers, thus appealed to, rose from her seat, and, with a dignity of thought or of feeling no one could have anticipated from the quiet peasant woman, approached the wedded pair, lifted Jessie's face with one hand, laid the other on Will's head, and said, "If you don't long to see Mr. Bowles again and say 'the Lord bless you, sir!' you don't deserve the Lord's blessing upon you." Therewith she went back to her seat, and resumed her knitting.

"Thank Heaven, we have paid back the best part of the loan," said Will, in very agitated tones, "and I think, with a little pinching, Jessie, and with selling off some of the stock, we might pay the rest; and then"—and then he turned to Kenelm—"and then, sir, we will" (here a gulp) "thank Mr. Bowles."

"This don't satisfy me at all, Will," answered Kenelm; "and since I helped to bring you two together, I claim the right to say I would never have done so could I have guessed you could have trusted your wife so little as to allow a remembrance of Mr. Bowles to be a thought of pain. You did not feel humiliated when you imagined that it was to me you owed some moneys which you have been honestly paying off. Well, then, I will lend you whatever trifle remains to discharge your whole debts to Mr. Bowles, so that you may sooner be able to say to him, 'Thank you.' But between you and me, Will, I think you will be a finer fellow and a manlier fellow if you decline to borrow that trifle of me; if you feel you would rather say 'Thank you' to Mr. Bowles, without the silly notion that when you have paid him his money you owe him nothing for his kindness."

Will looked away, irresolutely. Kenelm went on: "I have received a letter from Mr. Bowles to-day: He has come into a fortune, and thinks of going abroad for a time; but before he goes, he says he should like to shake hands with Will, and be assured by Jessie that all his old rudeness is forgiven. He had no notion that I should blab about the loan; he wished that to remain always a secret. But between friends there need be no secrets. What say you, Will? As head of this household, shall Mr. Bowles be welcomed here as a friend or not?"

"Kindly welcome," said old Mrs. Somers, looking up from the socks.

"Sir," said Will, with sudden energy, "look here; you have never been in love, I dare say. If you had, you would not be so hard on me. Mr. Bowles was in love with my wife there. Mr. Bowles is a very fine man, and I am a cripple."

"Oh, Will! Will!" cried Jessie.

"But I trust my wife with my whole heart and soul; and, now that the first pang is over, Mr. Bowles shall be, as mother says, kindly welcome—heartily welcome."

"Shake hands. Now you speak like a man, Will. I hope to bring Bowles here to supper before many days are over."

And that night Kenelm wrote to Mr. Bowles:

"My Dear Tom,—Come and spend a few days with me at Cromwell Lodge, Moleswich. Mr. and Mrs. Somers wish much to see and to thank you. I could not remain for ever degraded in order to gratify your whim. They would have it that I bought their shop, &c., and I was forced in self-defence to say who it was. More on this and on travels when you come.

"Your true friend,
"K. C."

CHAPTER XVI.

MRS. CAMERON was seated alone in her pretty drawing-room, with a book lying open, but unheeded, on her lap. She was looking away from its pages, seemingly into the garden without, but rather into empty space.

To a very acute and practised observer, there was in her countenance an expression which baffled the common eye.

To the common eye it was simply vacant; the expression of a quiet, humdrum woman, who might have been thinking of some quiet humdrum household detail—found that too much for her, and was now not thinking at all.

But to the true observer, there were in that face indications of a troubled past, still haunted with ghosts never to be laid at rest—indications, too, of a character in herself that had undergone some revolutionary change; it had not always been the character of a woman quiet and humdrum. The delicate outlines of the lip and nostril evinced sensibility, and the deep and downward curve of it bespoke habitual sadness. The softness of the look into space did not tell of a vacant mind, but rather of a mind subdued and overburthened by the weight of a secret sorrow. There was also about her whole presence, in the very quiet which made her prevalent external characteristic, the evidence of manners formed in a highbred society—the society in which quiet is connected with dignity and grace. The poor understood this better than her rich acquaintances at Moleswich, when they said, "Mrs. Cameron was every inch a lady." To judge by her features she must once have been pretty, not a showy prettiness, but decidedly pretty. Now, as the features were small, all prettiness had faded away in cold gray colourings, and a sort of tamed and slumbering timidity of aspect. She was not only not demonstrative, but must have imposed on herself as a duty the suppression of demonstration. Who could look at the formation of those lips, and not see that they belonged to the nervous, quick, demonstrative temperament? And yet, observing her again more closely, that suppression of the constitutional tendency to candid betrayal of emotion, would the more enlist your curiosity or interest; because, if physiognomy and phrenology have any truth in them, there was little strength in her character. In the womanly yieldingness of the short curved upper lip, the pleading timidity of the *regard*, the disproportionate but elegant slenderness of the head between the ear and the neck, there were the tokens of one who cannot resist the will, perhaps the whim, of another whom she either loves or trusts.

The book open on her lap is a serious book on the doctrine of grace, written by a popular clergyman of what is termed "the Low Church." She seldom read any but serious books, except where such care as she gave to Lily's education compelled her to read 'Outlines of History and Geography,' or the elementary French books used in seminaries for young ladies. Yet if any one had decoyed Mrs. Cameron into familiar conversation, he would have discovered that she must early have received the education given to young ladies of station. She could speak and write French and Italian as a native. She had read, and still remembered, such classic authors in either language as are conceded to the use of pupils by the well-regulated taste of orthodox governesses. She had a knowledge of botany, such as botany was taught twenty years ago. I am not sure that, if her memory had been fairly aroused, she might not have come out strong in divinity and political economy, as expounded by the popular manuals of Mrs. Marcet. In short, you could see in her a thoroughbred English lady, who had been taught in a generation before Lily's, and immeasurably superior in culture to the ordinary run of English young ladies taught now-a-days. So, in what after all are very minor accomplishments—now made major accomplishments—such as music, it was impossible that a connoisseur should hear her play on the piano without remarking, "That woman has had the best masters of her time." She could only play pieces that belonged to her generation. She had learned nothing since. In short, the whole intellectual culture had come to a dead stop long years ago, perhaps before Lily was born.

Now, while she is gazing into space Mrs. Braefield is announced. Mrs. Cameron does not start from reverie. She never starts. But she makes a weary movement of annoyance, resettles herself, and lays the serious book on the sofa table. Elsie enters, young, radiant, dressed in all the perfection of the fashion, that is, as ungracefully as in the eyes of an artist any gentlewoman can be; but rich merchants who are proud of their wives so insist, and their wives, in that respect, submissively obey them.

The ladies interchange customary salutations, enter into the customary preliminaries of talk, and, after a pause, Elsie begins in earnest.

"But shan't I see Lily? Where is she?"

"I fear she has gone into the town. A poor little boy, who did our errands, has met with an accident—fallen from a cherry-tree."

"Which he was robbing?"

"Probably."

"And Lily has gone to lecture him?"

"I don't know as to that; but he is much hurt, and Lily has gone to see what is the matter with him."

Mrs. Braefield, in her frank outspoken way—

"I don't take much to girls of Lily's age in general, though I am passionately fond of children. You know how I do take to Lily; perhaps because she is so like a child. But she must be an anxious charge to you."

Mrs. Cameron replied by an anxious "No. She is still a child, a very good one; why should I be anxious?"

Mrs. Braefield, impulsively—

"Why, your child must now be eighteen."

Mrs. Cameron—

"Eighteen—is it possible! How time flies! though in a life so monotonous as mine, time does not seem to fly, it slips on like the lapse of water. Let me think—eighteen? No, she is but seventeen—seventeen last May?"

Mrs. Braefield—"Seventeen! A very anxious age for a girl; an age in which dolls cease and lovers begin."

Mrs. Cameron, not so languidly, but still quietly—

"Lily never cared much for dolls—never much for lifeless pets; and as to lovers, she does not dream of them."

Mrs. Braefield, briskly—

"There is no age after six in which girls do not dream of lovers. And here another question arises. When a girl so lovely as Lily is eighteen next birthday, may not a lover dream of her?"

Mrs. Cameron, with that wintry cold tranquillity of manner, which implies that in putting such questions an interrogator is taking a liberty—

"As no lover has appeared, I cannot trouble myself about his dreams."

Said Elsie, inly to herself, "This is the stupidest woman I ever met!" and aloud to Mrs. Cameron—

"Do you not think that your neighbour, Mr. Chillingly, is a very fine young man?"

"I suppose he would be generally considered so. He is very tall."

"A handsome face?"

"Handsome, is it? I dare say."

"What does Lily say?"

"About what?"

"About Mr. Chillingly. Does she not think him handsome?"

"I never asked her."

"My dear Mrs. Cameron, would it not be a very pretty match for Lily? The Chillinglys are among the oldest families in 'Burke's Landed Gentry,' and I believe his father, Sir Peter, has a considerable property."

For the first time in this conversation Mrs. Cameron betrayed emotion. A sudden flush overspread her countenance, and then left it paler than before. After a pause she recovered her accustomed composure, and replied, rudely,

"It would be no friend to Lily who could put such notions into her head; and there is no reason to suppose that they have entered into Mr. Chillingly's."

"Would you be sorry if they did? Surely you would like your niece to marry well, and there are few chances of her doing so at Moleswich."

"Pardon me, Mrs. Braefield, but the question of Lily's marriage I have never discussed, even with her guardian. Nor, considering the childlike nature of her tastes and habits, rather than the years she has numbered, can I think the time has yet come for discussing it at all."

Elsie, thus rebuked, changed the subject to some newspaper topic which interested the public mind at the moment, and very soon rose to depart. Mrs. Cameron detained the hand that her visitor held out, and said in low tones, which, though embarrassed, were evidently earnest, "My dear Mrs. Braefield, let me trust to your good sense and the affection with which you have honoured my niece, not to incur the risk of unsettling her mind by a hint of the ambitious projects for her future on which you have spoken to me. It is extremely improbable that a young man of Mr. Chillingly's expectations would entertain any serious thoughts of marrying out of his own sphere of life, and——"

"Stop, Mrs. Cameron, I must interrupt you. Lily's personal attractions and grace of manner would adorn any station; and have I not rightly understood you to say that though her guardian, Mr. Melville, is, as we all know, a man who has risen above the rank of his parents, your niece, Miss Mordaunt, is like yourself, by birth a gentlewoman."

"Yes, by birth a gentlewoman," said Mrs. Cameron, raising her head with a sudden pride. But she added, with as sudden a change to a sort of freezing humility, "What does that matter? A girl without fortune, without connection, brought up in this little cottage, the ward of a professional artist, who was the son of a city clerk, to whom she owes even the home she has found, is not in the same sphere of life as Mr. Chillingly, and his parents could not approve of such an alliance for him. It would be most cruel to her, if you were to change the innocent pleasure she may take in the conversation of a clever and well-informed stranger, into the troubled interest which, since you remind me of her age, a girl even so childlike and beautiful as Lily, might conceive in one represented to her as the possible partner of her life. Don't commit that cruelty; don't—don't, I implore you!"

"Trust me," cried the warm-hearted Elsie, with tears rushing to her eyes. "What you say so sensibly, so nobly, never struck me before. I do not know much of the world—knew nothing of it till I married—and being very fond of Lily, and having a strong regard for Mr. Chillingly, I fancied I could not serve both better than—than—but I see now; he is very young, very peculiar; his parents might object, not to Lily herself, but to the circumstances you name. And you would not wish her to enter any family where she was not as cordially welcomed as she deserves to be. I am glad to have had this talk with you. Happily, I have done no mischief as yet. I will do none. I had come to propose an excursion to the remains of the Roman Villa, some miles off, and to invite you and Mr. Chillingly. I will no longer try to bring him and Lily together."

"Thank you. But you still misconstrue me. I do not think that Lily cares half so much for Mr. Chillingly as she does for a new butterfly. I do not fear their coming together, as you call it, in the light in which she now regards him, and in which, from all I observe, he regards her. My only fear is that a hint might lead her to regard him in another way, and that way impossible."

Elsie left the house extremely bewildered, and with a profound contempt for Mrs. Cameron's knowledge of what may happen to two young persons "brought together."

CHAPTER XVII.

NOW, on that very day, and about the same hour in which the conversation just recorded between Elsie and Mrs. Cameron took place, Kenelm, in his solitary noonday wanderings, entered the burial-ground in which Lily had, some short time before, surprised him. And there he found her, standing beside the flower border which she had placed round the grave of the child whom she had tended and nursed in vain.

The day was clouded and sunless; one of those days that so often instil a sentiment of melancholy into the heart of an English summer.

"You come here too often, Miss Mordaunt," said Kenelm, very softly, as he approached.

Lily turned her face to him, without any start of surprise, with no brightening change in its pensive expression—an expression rare to the mobile play of her features.

"Not too often. I promised to come as often as I could; and, as I told you before, I have never broken a promise yet."

Kenelm made no answer. Presently the girl turned from the spot, and Kenelm followed her silently till she halted before the old tombstone with its effaced inscription.

"See," she said, with a faint smile, "I have put fresh flowers there. Since the day we met in this churchyard, I have thought much of that tomb, so neglected, so forgotten, and——" she paused a moment, and went on abruptly,—"do you not often find, that you are much too—what is the word? ah! too egotistical, considering, and pondering, and dreaming greatly too much about yourself?"

"Yes, you are right there; though, till you so accused me, my conscience did not detect it."

"And don't you find that you escape from being so haunted by the thought of yourself, when you think of the dead? they can never have any share in your existence *here*. When you say, 'I shall do this or that to-day;' when you dream, 'I may be this or that to-morrow,' you are thinking and dreaming, all by yourself, for yourself. But you are out of yourself, beyond yourself, when you think and dream of the dead, who can have nothing to do with your to-day or your to-morrow."

As we all know, Kenelm Chillingly made it one of the rules of his life never to be taken by surprise. But when the speech I have written down came from the lips of that tamer of butterflies, he was so startled that all it occurred to him to say, after a long pause, was—

"The dead are the past; and with the past rests all in the present or the future that can take us out of our natural selves. The past decides our present. By the past we divine our future. History, poetry, science, the welfare of states, the advancement of individuals, are all connected with tombstones of which inscriptions are effaced. You are right to honour the mouldered tombstones with fresh flowers. It *is* only in the companionship of the dead that one ceases to be an egotist."

If the imperfectly educated Lily had been above the quick comprehension of the academical Kenelm in her speech, so Kenelm was now above the comprehension of Lily. She too paused before she replied—

"If I knew you better, I think I could understand you better. I wish you knew Lion. I should like to hear you talk with him."

While thus conversing, they had left the burial-ground, and were in the pathway trodden by the common wayfarer.

Lily resumed.

"Yes, I should so like to hear you talk with Lion."

"You mean your guardian, Mr. Melville."

"Yes, you know that."

"And why should you like to hear me talk to him?"

"Because there are some things in which I doubt if he was altogether right, and I would ask you to express my doubts to him; you would, would not you?"

"But why can you not express them yourself to your guardian; are you afraid of him?"

"Afraid, no indeed! But—ah, how many people there are coming this way! There is some tiresome public meeting in the town to-day. Let us take the ferry, the other side of the stream is much pleasanter, we shall have it more to ourselves."

Turning aside to the right while she thus spoke, Lily descended a gradual slope to the margin of the stream, on which they found an old man dozily reclined in his ferry-boat.

As, seated side by side, they were slowly borne over the still waters under a sunless sky, Kenelm would have renewed the subject which his companion had begun, but she shook her head, with a significant glance at the ferryman. Evidently what she had to say was too confidential to admit of a listener, not that the old ferryman seemed likely to take the trouble of listening to any talk that was not addressed to him. Lily soon did address her talk to him—
"So, Brown, the cow has quite recovered."

"Yes, Miss, thanks to you, and God bless you. To think of your beating the old witch like that!"

"'Tis not I who beat the witch, Brown; 'tis the fairy. Fairies, you know, are much more powerful than witches."

"So I find, Miss."

Lily here turned to Kenelm—"Mr. Brown has a very nice milch-cow that was suddenly taken very ill, and both he and his wife were convinced that the cow was bewitched."

"Of course it were, that stands to reason. Did not Mother Wright tell my old woman that she would repent of selling milk, and abuse her dreadful; and was not the cow taken with shivers that very night?"

"Gently, Brown. Mother Wright did not say that your wife would repent of selling milk, but of putting water into it."

"And how did she know that, if she was not a witch? We have the best of customers among the gentlefolks, and never an one that complained."

"And," answered Lily to Kenelm, unheeding this last observation, which was made in a sullen manner, "Brown had a horrid notion of enticing Mother Wright into his ferry-boat, and throwing her into the water, in order to break the spell upon the cow. But I consulted the fairies, and gave him a fairy charm to tie round the cow's neck. And the cow is quite well now, you see. So, Brown, there was no necessity to throw Mother Wright into the water, because she said you put some of it into the milk. But," she added, as the boat now touched the opposite bank, "shall I tell you, Brown, what the fairies said to me this morning?"

"Do, Miss."

"It was this: If Brown's cow yields milk without any water in it, and if water gets into it when the milk is sold, we, the fairies, will pinch Mr. Brown black and blue; and when Brown has his next fit of rheumatics he must not look to the fairies to charm it away."

Herewith Lily dropped a silver groat into Brown's hand, and sprang lightly ashore, followed by Kenelm.

"You have quite converted him, not only as to the existence, but as to the beneficial power of fairies," said Kenelm.

"Ah," answered Lily very gravely, "ah, but would it not be nice if there were fairies still? good fairies, and one could get at them? tell them all that troubles and puzzles us, and win from them charms against the witchcraft we practise on ourselves?"

"I doubt if it would be good for us to rely on such supernatural counsellors. Our own souls are so boundless, that the more we explore them the more we shall find worlds spreading upon worlds into infinities; and among the worlds is Fairyland." He added, inly to himself, "Am I not in Fairyland now?"

"Hush!" whispered Lily. "Don't speak more yet awhile, I am thinking over what you have just said, and trying to understand it."

Thus walking silently they gained the little summer-house which tradition dedicated to the memory of Izaak Walton.

Lily entered it and seated herself; Kenelm took his place beside her. It was a small octagon building which, judging by its architecture, might have been built in the troubled reign of Charles I.; the walls plastered within were thickly covered with names, and dates, and inscriptions, in praise of angling, in tribute to Izaak, or with quotations from his books. On the opposite side they could see the lawn of Grasmere, with its great willows dipping into the water. The stillness of the place, with its associations of the angler's still life, were in harmony with the quiet day, its breezeless air, and cloud-vested sky.

"You were to tell me your doubts in connection with your guardian, doubts if he were right in something which you left unexplained, which you could not yourself explain to him."

Lily started as from thoughts alien to the subject thus re-introduced. "Yes, I cannot mention my doubts to him because they relate to me, and he is so good. I owe him so much that I could not bear to vex him by a word that might seem like reproach or complaint. You remember"—here she drew nearer to him; and, with that ingenuous confiding look and movement which had, not unfrequently, enraptured him at the moment, and saddened him on reflection—too ingenuous, too confiding, for the sentiment with which he yearned to inspire her—she turned towards him her frank untimorous eyes, and laid her hand on his arm: "you remember that I said in the burial-ground how much I felt that one is constantly thinking too much of one's self. That must be wrong. In talking to you only about myself I know I am wrong, but I cannot help it; I must do so. Do not think ill of me for it. You see I have not been brought up like other girls. Was my guardian right in that? Perhaps if he had insisted upon not letting me have my own wilful way, if he had made me read the books which Mr. and Mrs. Emlyn wanted to force on me, instead of the poems and fairy tales which he gave me, I should have had so much more to think of that I should have thought less of myself. You said that the dead were the past; one forgets one's self when one thinks of the dead. If I had read more of the past, had more subjects of interest in the dead whose history it tells, surely I should be less shut up, as it were, in my own small, selfish heart? It is only very lately I have thought of this, only very lately that I have felt sorrow and shame in the thought that I am so ignorant of what other girls know, even little Clemmy. And I dare not say this to Lion when I see him next, lest he should blame himself, when he only meant to be kind, and used to say, 'I don't want Fairy to be learned, it is enough for me to think she is happy.' And oh, I was so happy, till—till of late!"

"Because till of late you only knew yourself as a child. But, now that you feel the desire of knowledge, childhood is vanishing. Do not vex yourself. With the mind which nature has bestowed on you, such learning as may fit you to converse with those dreaded 'grown-up folks' will come to you very easily and quickly. You will acquire more in a month now than you would have acquired in a year when you were a child, and taskwork was loathed, not courted. Your aunt is evidently well instructed, and if I might venture to talk to her about the choice of books——"

"No, don't do that. Lion would not like it."

"Your guardian would not like you to have the education common to other young ladies?"

"Lion forbade my aunt to teach me much that I rather wished to learn. She wanted to do so, but she has given it up at his wish.

She only now teases me with those horrid French verbs, and that I know is a mere make-belief. Of course on Sunday it is different; then I must not read anything but the Bible and sermons. I don't care so much for the sermons as I ought, but I could read the Bible all day, every week-day as well as Sunday; and it is from the Bible that I learn that I ought to think less about myself."

Kenelm involuntarily pressed the little hand that lay so innocently on his arm.

"Do you know the difference between one kind of poetry and another?" asked Lily abruptly.

"I am not sure. I ought to know when one kind is good and another kind is bad. But in that respect I find many people, especially professed critics, who prefer the poetry which I call bad to the poetry I think good."

"The difference between one kind of poetry and another, supposing them both to be good," said Lily positively, and with an air of triumph, "is this—I know, for Lion explained it to me. In one kind of poetry the writer throws himself entirely out of his existence, he puts himself into other existences quite strange to his own. He may be a very good man, and he writes his best poetry about very wicked men; he would not hurt a fly, but he delights in describing murderers. But in the other kind of poetry the writer does not put himself into other existences, he expresses his own joys and sorrows, his own individual heart and mind. If he could not hurt a fly, he certainly could not make himself at home in the cruel heart of a murderer. There, Mr. Chillingly, that is the difference between one kind of poetry and another."

"Very true," said Kenelm, amused by the girl's critical definitions. "The difference between dramatic poetry and lyrical. But may I ask what that definition has to do with the subject into which you so suddenly introduced it?"

"Much—for when Lion was explaining this to my aunt, he said, 'A perfect woman is a poem; but she can never be a poem of the one kind, never can make herself at home in the hearts with which she has no connection, never feel any sympathy with crime and evil; she must be a poem of the other kind, weaving out poetry from her own thoughts and fancies.' And, turning to me, he said, smiling, 'That is the poem I wish Lily to be. Too many dry books would only spoil the poem.' And you now see why I am so ignorant, and so unlike other girls, and why Mr. and Mrs. Emlyn look down upon me."

"You wrong at least Mr. Emlyn, for it was he who first said to me, 'Lily Mordaunt is a poem.'"

"Did he? I shall love him for that. How pleased Lion will be!"

"Mr. Melville seems to have an extraordinary influence over your mind," said Kenelm, with a jealous pang.

"Of course. I have neither father nor mother, Lion has been both to me. Aunty has often said, 'You cannot be too grateful to your guardian; without him I should have no home to shelter you, no bread to give you.' *He* never said that—he would be very angry with aunty if he knew she had said it. When he does not call me Fairy he calls me Princess. I would not displease him for the world."

"He is very much older than you, old enough to be your father, I hear."

"I dare say. But if he were twice as old I could not love him better."

Kenelm smiled — the jealousy was gone. Certainly not thus could any girl, even Lily, speak of one with whom, however she might love him, she was likely to fall in love.

Lily now rose up, rather slowly and wearily. "It is time to go home; aunty will be wondering what keeps me away—come."

They took their way towards the bridge opposite to Cromwell Lodge.

It was not for some minutes that either broke silence. Lily was the first to do so, and with one of those abrupt changes of topic which were common to the restless play of her secret thoughts.

"You have father and mother still living, Mr. Chillingly?"

"Thank Heaven, yes."

"Which do you love the best?"

"That is scarcely a fair question. I love my mother very much; but my father and I understand each other better than——"

"I see—it is so difficult to be understood. No one understands me."

"I think I do."

Lily shook her head, with an energetic movement of dissent.

"At least as well as a man can understand a young lady."

"What sort of young lady is Miss Cecilia Travers?"

"Cecilia Travers! When and how did you ever hear that such a person existed?"

"That big London man whom they call Sir Thomas mentioned her name the day we dined at Braefieldville."

"I remember—as having been at the Court ball."

"He said she was very handsome."

"So she is."

"Is she a poem, too?"

"No; that never struck me."

"Mr. Emlyn, I suppose, would call her perfectly brought up—well educated. He would not raise his eyebrows at her as he does at me, poor me, Cinderella!"

"Ah, Miss Mordaunt, you need not envy her. Again let me say that you could very soon educate yourself to the level of any young ladies who adorn the Court balls."

"Ay; but then I should not be a poem," said Lily, with a shy arch side-glance at his face.

They were now on the bridge, and before Kenelm could answer, Lily resumed quickly, "You need not come any farther, it is out of your way."

"I cannot be so disdainfully dismissed, Miss Mordaunt; I insist on seeing you to, at least your garden gate."

Lily made no objection, and again spoke—

"What sort of country do you live in when at home—is it like this?"

"Not so pretty; the features are larger, more hill and dale and woodland; yet there is one feature in our grounds which reminds me a little of this landscape: a light stream, somewhat wider, indeed, than your brooklet; but here and there the banks are so like those by Cromwell Lodge that I sometimes start and fancy myself at home. I have a strange love for rivulets, and all running waters, and in my foot wanderings I find myself magnetically attracted towards them."

Lily listened with interest, and after a short pause said with a half-suppressed sigh, "Your home is much finer than any place here, even than Braefieldville, is it not? Mrs. Braefield says your father is very rich."

"I doubt if he is richer than Mr. Braefield, and though his house may be larger than Braefieldville, it is not so smartly furnished, and has no such luxurious hothouses and conservatories. My father's tastes are like mine, very simple. Give him his library, and he would scarcely miss his fortune if he lost it. He has in this one immense advantage over me."

"You would miss fortune?" said Lily, quickly.

"Not that; but my father is never tired of books. And shall I own it? there are days when books tire me almost as much as they do you."

They were now at the garden gate. Lily, with one hand on the latch held out the other to Kenelm, and her smile lit up the dull sky like a burst of sunshine, as she looked in his face and vanished.

BOOK VII.

CHAPTER I.

KENELM did not return home till dusk, and just as he was sitting down to his solitary meal there was a ring at the bell, and Mrs. Jones ushered in Mr. Thomas Bowles.

Though that gentleman had never written to announce the day of his arrival, he was not the less welcome.

"Only," said Kenelm, "if you preserve the appetite I have lost, I fear you will find meagre fare to-day. Sit down, man."

"Thank you, kindly, but I dined two hours ago in London, and I really can eat nothing more."

Kenelm was too well-bred to press unwelcome hospitalities. In a very few minutes his frugal repast was ended, the cloth removed, the two men were left alone.

"Your room is here, of course, Tom; that was engaged from the day I asked you, but you ought to have given me a line to say when to expect you, so that I could have put our hostess on her mettle as to dinner or supper. You smoke still, of course : light your pipe."

"Thank you, Mr. Chillingly, I seldom smoke now; but if you will excuse a cigar," and Tom produced a very smart cigar-case.

"Do as you would at home. I shall send word to Will Somers that you and I sup there to-morrow. You forgive me for letting out your secret. All straightforward now and henceforth. You come to their hearth as a friend, who will grow dearer to them both every year. Ah, Tom, this love for woman seems to me a very wonderful thing. It may sink a man into such deeps of evil, and lift a man into such heights of good."

"I don't know as to the good," said Tom, mournfully, and laying aside his cigar.

"Go on smoking; I should like to keep you company; can you spare me one of your cigars?"

Tom offered his case. Kenelm extracted a cigar, lighted it, drew a few whiffs, and when he saw that Tom had resumed his own cigar, recommenced conversation.

"You don't know as to the good; but tell me honestly, do you think if you had not loved Jessie Wiles, you would be as good a man as you are now?"

"If I am better than I was, it is not because of my love for the girl."

"What then?"

"The loss of her."

Kenelm started, turned very pale, threw aside the cigar, rose and walked the room to and fro with very quick but very irregular strides.

Tom continued quietly. "Suppose I had won Jessie and married her, I don't think any idea of improving myself would have entered my head. My uncle would have been very much offended at my marrying a day-labourer's daughter, and would not have invited me to Luscombe. I should have remained at Graveleigh, with no ambition of being more than a common farrier, an ignorant, noisy, quarrelsome man; and if I could not have made Jessie as fond of me as I wished, I should not have broken myself of drinking, and I shudder to think what a brute I might have been, when I see in the newspapers an account of some drunken wife-beater. How do we know but what that wife-beater loved his wife dearly before marriage, and she did not care for him? His home was unhappy, and so he took to drink and to wife-beating."

"I was right, then," said Kenelm, halting his strides, "when I told you it would be a miserable fate to be married to a girl whom you loved to distraction, and whose heart you could never warm to you, whose life you could never render happy."

"So right!"

"Let us drop that part of the subject at present," said Kenelm, reseating himself, "and talk about your wish to travel. Though contented that you did not marry Jessie, though you can now, without anguish, greet her as the wife of another, still there are some lingering thoughts of her that make you restless; and you feel that you could more easily wrench yourself from these thoughts in a marked change of scene and adventure, that you might bury them altogether in the soil of a strange land. Is it so?"

"Ay, something of that, sir."

Then Kenelm roused himself to talk of foreign lands, and to map out a plan of travel that might occupy some months. He was pleased to find that Tom had already learned enough of French to make himself understood at least upon commonplace matters, and still more pleased to discover that he had been not only reading the proper guide-books or manuals descriptive of the principal places in

Europe worth visiting, but that he had acquired an interest in the places; interest in the fame attached to them by their history in the past, or by the treasures of art they contained.

So they talked far into the night, and when Tom retired to his room, Kenelm let himself out of the house noiselessly, and walked with slow steps towards the old summer-house in which he had sat with Lily. The wind had risen, scattering the clouds that had veiled the preceding day, so that the stars were seen in far chasms of the sky beyond—seen for a while in one place, and when the swift clouds rolled over them there, shining out elsewhere. Amid the varying sounds of the trees, through which swept the night gusts, Kenelm fancied he could distinguish the sigh of the willow on the opposite lawn of Grasmere.

CHAPTER II.

KENELM despatched a note to Will Somers early the next morning, inviting himself and Mr. Bowles to supper that evening. His tact was sufficient to make him aware that in such social meal there would be far less restraint for each and all concerned than in a more formal visit from Tom during the day-time; and when Jessie, too, was engaged with customers to the shop.

But he led Tom through the town and showed him the shop itself, with its pretty goods at the plate-glass windows, and its general air of prosperous trade; then he carried him off into the lanes and fields of the country, drawing out the mind of his companion, and impressed with great admiration of its marked improvement in culture, and in the trains of thought which culture opens out and enriches.

But throughout all their multiform range of subject Kenelm could perceive that Tom was still preoccupied and abstracted; the idea of the coming interview with Jessie weighed upon him.

When they left Cromwell Lodge at nightfall, to repair to the supper at Will's, Kenelm noticed that Bowles had availed himself of the contents of his carpet bag, to make some refined alterations in his dress. The alterations became him.

When they entered the parlour, Will rose from his chair with the evidence of deep emotion on his face, advanced to Tom, took his hand and grasped and dropped it without a word. Jessie saluted both guests alike, with drooping eyelids and an elaborate curtsey.

The old mother alone was perfectly self-possessed and up to the occasion.

"I am heartily glad to see you, Mr. Bowles," said she, "and so all three of us are, and ought to be; and if baby was older, there would be four."

"And where on earth have you hidden baby?" cried Kenelm. "Surely he might have been kept up for me to-night, when I was expected; the last time I supped here I took you by surprise, and therefore had no right to complain of baby's want of respect to her parents' friends."

Jessie raised the window-curtain, and pointed to the cradle behind it. Kenelm linked his arm in Tom's, led him to the cradle, and leaving him alone to gaze on the sleeping inmate, seated himself at the table, between old Mrs. Somers and Will. Will's eyes were turned away towards the curtain, Jessie holding its folds aside, and the formidable Tom, who had been the terror of his neighbourhood, bending smiling over the cradle; till at last he laid his large hand on the pillow, gently, timidly, careful not to awake the helpless sleeper, and his lips moved, doubtless with a blessing; then he too came to the table, seating himself, and Jessie carried the cradle upstairs.

Will fixed his keen intelligent eyes on his bygone rival; and noticing the changed expression of the once aggressive countenance, the changed costume in which, without tinge of rustic foppery, there was the token of a certain gravity of station scarcely compatible with a return to old loves and old habits in the village world, the last shadow of jealousy vanished from the clear surface of Will's affectionate nature.

"Mr. Bowles," he exclaimed, impulsively, "you have a kind heart, and a good heart, and a generous heart. And your coming here to-night on this friendly visit is an honour which—which"—
"Which," interrupted Kenelm, compassionating Will's enbarrassment, "is on the side of us single men. In this free country a married man who has a male baby may be father to the Lord Chancellor or the Archbishop of Canterbury. But—well, my friends, such a meeting as we have to-night does not come often; and after supper let us celebrate it with a bowl of punch. If we have headaches the next morning none of us will grumble."

Old Mrs. Somers laughed out jovially. "Bless you, sir, I did not think of the punch; I will go and see about it," and, baby's socks still in her hands, she hastened from the room.

What with the supper, what with the punch, and what with Kenelm's art of cheery talk on general subjects, all reserve, all awkwardness, all shyness between the convivialists, rapidly disappeared. Jessie mingled in the talk; perhaps (excepting only Kenelm) she talked more than the others, artlessly, gaily, no vestige of the old coquetry; but, now and then, with a touch of genteel finery, indicative of her rise in life, and of the contact of the fancy shopkeeper with noble customers. It was a pleasant evening—Kenelm had resolved that it should be so. Not a hint of the obligations to Mr. Bowles escaped until Will, following his visitor to the door, whispered to Tom, "You don't want thanks, and I can't express them. But when we say our prayers at night, we have always asked God to bless him who brought us together, and has since made us so prosperous—I mean Mr. Chillingly. To-night there will be another besides him, for whom we shall pray, and for whom baby, when he is older, will pray too."

Therewith Will's voice thickened; and he prudently receded, with no unreasonable fear lest the punch might make him too demonstrative of emotion if he said more.

Tom was very silent on the return to Cromwell Lodge; it did not seem the silence of depressed spirits, but rather of quiet meditation, from which Kenelm did not attempt to rouse him.

It was not till they reached the garden pales of Grasmere that Tom, stopping short, and turning his face to Kenelm, said—

"I am very grateful to you for this evening—very."

"It has revived no painful thoughts, then?"

"No; I feel so much calmer in mind than I ever believed I could have been, after seeing her again."

"Is it possible!" said Kenelm, to himself. "How should I feel if I ever saw in Lily the wife of another man: the mother of his child?" At that question he shuddered, and an involuntary groan escaped from his lips. Just then having, willingly in those precincts, arrested his steps, when Tom paused to address him, something softly touched the arm which he had rested on the garden pale. He looked and saw that it was Blanche. The creature, impelled by its instincts towards night-wanderings, had, somehow or other, escaped from its own bed within the house, and hearing a voice that had grown somewhat familiar to its ear, crept from among the shrubs behind upon the edge of the pale. There it stood, with arched back, purring low as in pleased salutation.

Kenelm bent down and covered with kisses the blue ribbon which Lily's hand had bound round the favourite's neck. Blanche submitted to the caress for a moment, and then catching a slight rustle among the shrubs, made by some awaking bird, sprang into the thick of the quivering leaves and vanished.

Kenelm moved on with a quick impatient stride, and no further words were exchanged between him and his companion till they reached their lodging and parted for the night.

CHAPTER III.

THE next day, towards noon, Kenelm and his visitor, walking together along the brook-side, stopped before Izaak Walton's summer-house, and, at Kenelm's suggestion, entered therein to rest, and more at their ease to continue the conversation they had begun.

"You have just told me," said Kenelm, "that you feel as if a load were taken off your heart, now that you have again met Jessie Somers, and that you find her so changed that she is no longer the woman you loved. As to the change, whatever it be, I own, it seems to me for the better, in person, in manners, in character; of course I should not say this, if I were not convinced of your perfect sincerity when you assured me that you are cured of the old wound. But I feel so deeply interested in the question how a fervent love, once entertained and enthroned in the heart of a man so earnestly affectionate and so warm-blooded as yourself, can be, all of a sudden, at a single interview, expelled or transferred into the calm sentiment of friendship, that I pray you to explain?"

"That is what puzzles me, sir," answered Tom, passing his hand over his forehead. "And I don't know if I can explain it."

"Think over it, and try."

Tom mused for some moments and then began. "You see, sir, that I was a very different man myself when I fell in love with Jessie Wiles, and said, 'Come what may, that girl shall be my wife. Nobody else shall have her.'"

"Agreed; go on."

"But while I was becoming a different man, when I thought of her—and I was always thinking of her—I still pictured her to myself as the same Jessie Wiles; and though, when I did see her again at Graveleigh, after she had married—the day—"

"You saved her from the insolence of the squire."

"—She was but very recently married. I did not realize her as married. I did not see her husband, and the difference within myself was only then beginning. Well, so all the time I was reading and thinking, and striving to improve my old self at Luscombe, still Jessie Wiles haunted me as the only girl I had ever loved, ever could love; I could not believe it possible that I could ever marry any one else. And lately I have been much pressed to marry some one else; all my family wish it; but the face of Jessie rose up before me, and I said to myself, 'I should be a base man if I married one woman, while I could not get another woman out of my head.' I must see Jessie once more, must learn whether her face is now really the face that haunts me when I sit alone; and I have seen her, and it is not that face; it may be handsomer, but it is not a girl's face, it is the face of a wife and a mother. And, last evening, while she was talking with an open-heartedness which I had never found in her before, I became strangely conscious of the difference in myself that had been silently at work within the last two years or so. Then, sir, when I was but an ill-conditioned, uneducated, petty village farrier, there was no inequality between me and a peasant girl; or, rather, in all things except fortune, the peasant girl was much above me. But last evening I asked myself, on watching her and listening to her talk, "If Jessie were now free, should I press her to be my wife?" and I answered myself 'No.'"

Kenelm listened with rapt attention, and exclaimed briefly, but passionately, "Why?"

"It seems as if I were giving myself airs to say why. But, sir, lately I have been thrown among persons, women as well as men, of a higher class than I was born in; and in a wife I should want a companion up to their mark, and who would keep me up to mine; and ah, sir, I don't feel as if I could find that companion in Mrs. Somers."

"I understand you now, Tom. But you are spoiling a silly romance of mine. I had fancied the little girl with the flower face would grow up to supply the loss of Jessie; and, I am so ignorant of the human heart, I did think it would take all the years required for the little girl to open into a woman, before the loss of the old love could be supplied. I see now that the poor little child with the flower face has no chance."

"Chance? Why, Mr. Chillingly," cried Tom, evidently much nettled, "Susy is a dear little thing, but she is scarcely more than a mere charity girl. Sir, when I last saw you in London you touched on that matter as if I were still the village farrier's son, who might marry a village labourer's daughter. But," added Tom, softening down his irritated tone of voice, "even if Susy were a lady born, I think a man would make a very great mistake, if he thought he could bring up a little girl to regard him as a father; and then, when she grew up, expect her to accept him as a lover."

"Ah, you think that!" exclaimed Kenelm eagerly, and turning eyes that sparkled with joy towards the lawn of Grasmere. "You think that; it is very sensibly said—well—and you have been pressed to marry, and have hung back till you had seen again Mrs. Somers. Now you will be better disposed to such a step; tell me about it?"

"I said, last evening, that one of the principal capitalists at Luscombe, the leading corn-merchant, had offered to take me into partnership. And, sir, he has an only daughter, she is a very amiable girl, has had a first-rate education, and has such pleasant manners and way of talk, quite a lady. If I married her I should soon be the first man at Luscombe, and Luscombe, as you are no doubt aware, returns two members to Parliament; who knows, but that some day the farrier's son might be——" Tom stopped abruptly—abashed at the aspiring thought which, while speaking, had deepened his hardy colour and flashed from his honest eyes.

"Ah!" said Kenelm, almost mournfully, "is it so; must each man in his life play many parts? Ambition succeeds to love, the reasoning brain to the passionate heart. True, you are changed; my Tom Bowles is gone."

"Not gone in his undying gratitude to you, sir," said Tom, with great emotion. "Your Tom Bowles would give up all his dreams of wealth or of rising in life, and go through fire and water to serve the friend who first bid him be a new Tom Bowles! Don't despise me as your own work: you said to me that terrible day, when madness was on my brow and crime within my heart, 'I will be to you the truest friend man ever found in man.' So you have been. You commanded me to read, you commanded me to think, you taught me that body should be the servant of mind."

"Hush, hush, times are altered; it is you who can teach me now. Teach me, teach me; how does ambition replace love? How does the desire to rise in life become the all-mastering passion, and, should it prosper, the all-atoning consolation of our life? We can never be as happy, though we rose to the throne of the Cæsars, as we dream that we could have been, had Heaven but permitted us to dwell in the obscurest village, side by side with the woman we love."

Tom was exceedingly startled by such a burst of irrepressible passion from the man who had told him, that though friends were found only once in a life, sweethearts were as plentiful as blackberries.

Again he swept his hand over his forehead, and replied hesitatingly. "I can't pretend to say what may be the case with others. But to judge by my own case, it seems to be this: a young man who, out of his own business, has nothing to interest or excite him, finds content, interest, and excitement when he falls in love; and then, whether for good or ill, he thinks there is nothing like love in the world, he don't care a fig for ambition then. Over and over again did my poor uncle ask me to come to him at Luscombe, and represent all the worldly advantage it would be to me; but I could not leave the village in which Jessie lived, and, besides, I felt myself unfit to be anything higher than I was. But when I had been some time at Luscombe, and gradually got accustomed to another sort of people, and another sort of talk, then I began to feel interest in the same objects that interested those about me; and when, partly by mixing with better educated men, and partly by the pains I took to educate myself, I felt that I might now more easily rise above my uncle's rank of life than two years ago I could have risen above a farrier's forge, then the ambition to rise did stir in me, and grew stronger every day. Sir, I don't think you can wake up a man's intellect but what you wake with it emulation. And, after all, emulation is ambition."

"Then, I suppose, I have no emulation in me, for certainly I have no ambition."

"That I can't believe, sir; other thoughts may cover it over and keep it down for a time. But sooner or later, it will force its way to the top, as it has done with me. To get on in life, to be respected by those who know you, more and more as you grow older, I call that a manly desire. I am sure it comes as naturally to an Englishman as—as——"

"As the wish to knock down some other Englishman who stands in his way, does. I perceive now that you were always a very ambitious man, Tom; the ambition has only taken another direction. Cæsar might have been

'But the first wrestler on the green.'

"And now, I suppose, you abandon the idea of travel; you will return to Luscombe, cured of all regret for the loss of Jessie; you will marry the young lady you mention, and rise, through progressive steps of alderman and mayor, into the rank of Member for Luscombe."

"All that may come in good time," answered Tom, not resenting the tone of irony in which he was addressed, "but I still intend to travel; a year so spent must render me all the more fit for any station I aim at. I shall go back to Luscombe to arrange my affairs, come to terms with Mr. Leland the corn-merchant against my return, and——"

"The young lady is to wait till then."

"Emily."

"Oh, that is the name? Emily! a much more elegant name than Jessie."

"Emily," continued Tom, with an unruffled placidity, which, considering the aggravating bitterness for which Kenelm had exchanged his wonted dulcitudes of indifferentism, was absolutely saintlike, "Emily knows that if she were my wife I should be proud of her, and will esteem me the more if she feels how resolved I am that she shall never be ashamed of me."

"Pardon me, Tom," said Kenelm, softened and laying his hand on his friend's shoulder with brotherlike tenderness. "Nature has made you a thorough gentleman; and you could not think and speak more nobly if you had come into the world as the head of all the Howards."

CHAPTER IV.

TOM went away the next morning. He declined to see Jessie again, saying curtly, "I don't wish the impression made on me the other evening to incur a chance of being weakened."

Kenelm was in no mood to regret his friend's departure. Despite all the improvement in Tom's manners and culture, which raised him so much nearer to equality with the polite and instructed heir of the Chillinglys, Kenelm would have felt more in sympathy, and *rapport*, with the old disconsolate fellow-wanderer who had reclined with him on the grass, listening to the Minstrel's talk or verse, than he did with the practical, rising citizen of Luscombe. To the young lover of Lily Mordaunt there was a discord, a jar, in the knowledge that the human heart admits of such well-reasoned, well-justified transfers of allegiance; a Jessie to-day, or an Emily to-morrow— "*La reine est morte; vive la reine.*"

An hour or two after Tom had gone, Kenelm found himself almost mechanically led towards Braefieldville. He had instinctively divined Elsie's secret wish with regard to himself and Lily, however skilfully she thought she had concealed it.

At Braefieldville he should hear talk of Lily, and in the scenes where Lily had been first beheld.

He found Mrs. Braefield alone in the drawing-room, seated by a table covered with flowers, which she was assorting and intermixing for the vases to which they were destined.

It struck him that her manner was more reserved than usual and somewhat embarrassed; and when, after a few preliminary matters of small talk, he rushed boldly *in medias res*, and asked if she had seen Mrs. Cameron lately, she replied briefly, "Yes, I called there the other day," and immediately changed the conversation to the troubled state of the Continent.

Kenelm was resolved not to be so put off, and presently returned to the charge.

"The other day you proposed an excursion to the site of the Roman villa, and said you would ask Mrs. Cameron to be of the party. Perhaps you have forgotten it?"

"No; but Mrs. Cameron declines. We can ask the Emlyns instead. He will be an excellent *cicerone*."

"Excellent! Why did Mrs. Cameron decline?"

Elsie hesitated, and then lifted her clear brown eyes to his face, with a sudden determination to bring matters to a crisis.

"I cannot say why Mrs. Cameron declined, but in declining she acted very wisely and very honourably. Listen to me, Mr. Chillingly. You know how highly I esteem, and how cordially I like you, and judging by what I felt for some weeks, perhaps longer, after we parted at Tor Hadham——" Here again she hesitated, and with a half laugh and a slight blush, again went resolutely on. "If I were Lily's aunt or elder sister, I should do as Mrs. Cameron does; decline to let Lily see much more of a young gentleman too much above her in wealth and station for——"

"Stop," cried Kenelm, haughtily, "I cannot allow that any man's wealth or station would warrant his presumption in thinking himself above Miss Mordaunt."

"Above her in natural grace and refinement, certainly not. But in the world there are other considerations which, perhaps, Sir Peter and Lady Chillingly might take into account."

"You did not think of that before you last saw Mrs. Cameron."

"Honestly speaking, I did not. Assured that Miss Mordaunt was a gentlewoman by birth, I did not sufficiently reflect upon other disparities."

"You know, then, that she is by birth a gentlewoman?"

"I only know it as all here do, by the assurance of Mrs. Cameron, whom no one could suppose not to be a lady. But there are different degrees of lady and of gentleman, which are little heeded in the ordinary intercourse of society, but become very perceptible in questions of matrimonial alliance; and Mrs. Cameron herself says very plainly that she does not consider her niece to belong to that station in life from which Sir Peter and Lady Chillingly would naturally wish their son should select his bride. Then (holding out her hand) pardon me if I have wounded or offended you. I speak as a true friend to you and to Lily both. Earnestly I advise you, if Miss Mordaunt be the cause of your lingering here, earnestly I advise you to leave while yet in time for her peace of mind and your own."

"Her peace of mind," said Kenelm, in low faltering tones, scarcely hearing the rest of Mrs. Braefield's speech. "Her peace of mind. Do you sincerely think that she cares for me—could care for me—if I stayed?"

"I wish I could answer you decidedly. I am not in the secrets of her heart. I can but conjecture that it might be dangerous for the peace of any young girl to see too much of a man like yourself, to divine that he loved her, and not to be aware that he could not, with the approval of his family, ask her to become his wife."

Kenelm bent his face down, and covered it with his right hand. He did not speak for some moments. Then he rose, the fresh cheek very pale, and said—

"You are right. Miss Mordaunt's peace of mind must be the first consideration. Excuse me if I quit you thus abruptly. You have given me much to think of, and I can only think of it adequately when alone."

CHAPTER V.

FROM KENELM CHILLINGLY TO SIR PETER CHILLINGLY.

"MY FATHER, MY DEAR FATHER,—This is no reply to your letters. I know not if itself can be called a letter. I cannot yet decide whether it be meant to reach your hands. Tired with talking to myself, I sit down to talk to you. Often have I reproached myself for not seizing every fitting occasion to let you distinctly know how warmly I love, how deeply I reverence you; you, O friend, O father. But we Chillinglys are not a demonstrative race. I don't remember that you, by words, ever expressed to me the truth that you love your son infinitely more than he deserves. Yet, do I not know that you would send all your beloved old books to the hammer, rather than I should pine in vain for some untried, if sinless, delight on which I had set my heart? And do you not know, equally well, that I would part with all my heritage, and turn day-labourer, rather than you should miss the beloved old books?

"That mutual knowledge is taken for granted in all that my heart yearns to pour forth to your own. But, if I divine aright, a day is coming when, as between you and me, there must be a sacrifice on the part of one to the other. If so, I implore that the sacrifice may come from you. How is this? How am I so ungenerous, so egotistical, so selfish, so ungratefully unmindful of all I already owe to you, and may never repay? I can only answer, 'It is fate, it is nature, it is love'—

* * * * *

"Here I must break off. It is midnight, the moon halts opposite to the window at which I sit, and on the stream that runs below there is a long narrow track on which every wave trembles in her light; on either side of the moonlit track all the other waves, running equally to their grave in the invisible deep, seem motionless and dark. I can write no more."

* * * *

Dated two days later.

"They say she is beneath us in wealth and station. Are we, my father—we, two well-born gentlemen—coveters of gold or lackeys of the great? When I was at College, if there were any there more heartily despised than another, it was the parasite and the tuft-hunter; the man who chose his friends according as their money or their rank might be of use to him. If so mean where the choice is so little important to the happiness and career of a man who has something of manhood in him, how much more mean to be the parasite and tuft-hunter in deciding what woman to love, what woman to select as the sweetener and ennobler of one's everyday life! Could she be to my life that sweetener, that ennobler? I firmly believe it. Already life itself has gained a charm that I never even guessed in it before; already I begin, though as yet but faintly and vaguely, to recognize that interest in the objects and aspirations of my fellow-men which is strongest in those whom posterity ranks among its ennoblers. In this quiet village it is true that I might find examples enough to prove that man is not meant to meditate upon life, but to take active part in it, and in that action to find his uses. But I doubt if I should have profited by such examples; if I should not have looked on this small stage of the world as I have looked on the large one, with the indifferent eyes of a spectator on a trite familiar play carried on by ordinary actors, had not my whole being suddenly leapt out of philosophy into passion, and, at once made warmly human, sympathized with humanity wherever it burned and glowed. Ah, is there to be any doubt of what station, as mortal bride, is due to her—her, my princess, my

Fairy? If so, how contented you shall be, my father, with the worldly career of your son! how perseveringly he will strive (and when did perseverance fail?) to supply all his deficiencies of intellect, genius, knowledge, by the energy concentrated on a single object which—more than intellect, genius, knowledge, unless they attain to equal energy equally concentrated—commands what the world calls honours.

"Yes, with her, with her as the bearer of my name, with her to whom I, whatever I might do of good or of great, could say, 'It is thy work,' I promise that you shall bless the day when you took to your arms a daughter.

*   *   *   *   *

"'Thou art in contact with the beloved in all that thou feelest elevated above thee.' So is it written by one of those weird Germans who search in our bosoms for the seeds of buried truths, and conjure them into flowers before we ourselves were even aware of the seeds.

"Every thought that associates itself with my beloved seems to me born with wings.

*   *   *   *   *

I have just seen her, just parted from her. Since I had been told—kindly, wisely told—that I had no right to hazard her peace of mind unless I were privileged to woo and to win her, I promised myself that I would shun her presence until I had bared my heart to you, as I am doing now, and received that privilege from yourself; for even had I never made the promise that binds my honour, your consent and blessing must hallow my choice. I do not feel as if I could dare to ask one so innocent and fair to wed an ungrateful, disobedient son. But this evening I met her, unexpectedly, at the vicar's, an excellent man, from whom I have learned much; whose precepts, whose example, whose delight in his home, and his life at once active and serene, are in harmony with my own dreams when I dream of her.

"I will tell you the name of the beloved—hold, it is as yet a profound secret between you and me. But oh for the day when I may hear you call her by that name, and print on her forehead the only kiss by man of which I should not be jealous.

"It is Sunday, and after the evening service it is my friend's custom to gather his children round him, and, without any formal sermon or discourse, engage their interest in subjects harmonious to associations with the sanctity of the day; often not directly bearing upon religion; more often, indeed, playfully starting from some little incident or some slight story-book which had amused the children in the course of the past week, and then gradually winding into reference to some sweet moral precept or illustration from some divine example. It is a maxim with him that, while much that children must learn they can only learn well through conscious labour, and as positive task-work, yet Religion should be connected in their minds, not with labour and task-work, but should become insensibly infused into their habits of thought, blending itself with memories and images of peace and love; with the indulgent tenderness of the earliest teachers, the sinless mirthfulness of the earliest home; with consolation in after sorrows, support through after trials, and never parting company with its twin sister, Hope.

"I entered the vicar's room this evening just as the group had collected round him. By the side of his wife sat a lady in whom I feel a keen interest. Her face wears that kind of calm which speaks of the lassitude bequeathed by sorrow. She is the aunt of my beloved one. Lily had nestled herself on a low ottoman, at the good pastor's feet, with one of his little girls, round whose shoulder she had wound her arm. She is much more fond of the companionship of children than that of girls of her own age. The vicar's wife, a very clever woman, once, in my hearing, took her to task for this preference, asking her why she persisted in grouping herself with mere infants who could teach her nothing? Ah! could you have seen the innocent, angel-like expression of her face when she answered simply, 'I suppose because with them I feel safer, I mean nearer to God.'

"Mr. Emlyn—that is the name of the vicar—deduced his homily this evening from a pretty fairy tale which Lily had been telling to his children the day before, and which he drew her on to repeat.

"Take, in brief, the substance of the story:—

"Once on a time, a king and queen made themselves very unhappy because they had no heir to their throne; and they prayed for one; and lo, on some bright summer morning, the Queen, waking from sleep, saw a cradle beside her bed, and in the cradle a beautiful sleeping babe. Great day throughout the kingdom! But as the infant grew up, it became very wayward and fretful; it lost its beauty, it would not learn its lessons, it was as naughty as a child could be. The parents were very sorrowful; the heir, so longed for, promised to be a great plague to themselves and their subjects. At last one day, to add to their trouble, two little bumps appeared on the Prince's shoulders. All the doctors were consulted as to the cause and the cure of this deformity. Of course they tried the effect of back-bands and steel machines, which gave the poor little Prince great pain, and made him more unamiable than ever.

The bumps, nevertheless, grew larger, and as they increased, so the Prince sickened and pined away. At last a skilful surgeon proposed, as the only chance of saving the Prince's life, that the bumps should be cut out, and the next morning was fixed for that operation. But at night the Queen saw, or dreamed she saw, a beautiful shape standing by her bedside. And it said to her reproachfully, 'Ungrateful woman! How wouldst thou repay me for the precious boon that my favour bestowed on thee? In me behold the Queen of the Fairies. For the heir to thy kingdom, I consigned to thy charge an infant from Fairyland, to become a blessing to thee and to thy people; and thou wouldst inflict upon it a death of torture by the surgeon's knife.' And the Queen answered: 'Precious indeed thou mayest call the boon! A miserable, sickly, feverish changeling.'

"'Art thou so dull,' said the beautiful visitant, 'as not to comprehend that the earliest instincts of the fairy child would be those of discontent, at the exile from its native home? and in that discontent it would have pined itself to death, or grown up, soured and malignant, a fairy still in its power but a fairy of wrath and evil, had not the strength of its inborn nature sufficed to develop the growth of its wings. That which thy blindness condemns as the deformity of the human-born, is to the fairy-born the crowning perfection of its beauty. Woe to thee, if thou suffer not the wings of the fairy child to grow.'

"And the next morning the Queen sent away the surgeon when he came with his horrible knife, and removed the back-board and the steel machines from the Prince's shoulders, though all the doctors predicted that the child would die. And from that moment the royal heir began to recover bloom and health. And when at last, out of those deforming bumps, budded delicately forth the plumage of snow-white wings, the wayward peevishness of the Prince gave place to sweet temper. Instead of scratching his teachers, he became the quickest and most docile of pupils, grew up to be the joy of his parents and the pride of their people; and the people said, 'In him we shall have hereafter such a king as we have never yet known.'

"Here ended Lily's tale. I cannot convey to you a notion of the pretty playful manner in which it was told. Then she said, with a grave shake of the head, 'But you do not seem to know what happened afterwards. Do you suppose that the Prince never made use of his wings? Listen to me. It was discovered by the courtiers who attended on His Royal Highness that on certain nights, every week, he disappeared. In fact, on these nights, obedient to the instinct of the wings, he flew from palace halls into Fairyland; coming back thence all the more lovingly disposed towards the human home from which he had escaped for awhile.'

"'Oh, my children,' interposed the preacher earnestly, 'the wings would be given to us in vain if we did not obey the instinct which allures us to soar; vain, no less, would be the soaring, were it not towards the home whence we came, bearing back from its native airs a stronger health, and a serener joy; more reconciled to the duties of earth by every new flight into heaven.'

"As he thus completed the moral of Lily's fairy tale, the girl rose from her low seat, took his hand, kissed it reverently, and walked away towards the window. I could see that she was affected even to tears, which she sought to conceal. Later in the evening, when we were dispersed on the lawn, for a few minutes before the party broke up, Lily came to my side timidly and said, in a low whisper:

"'Are you angry with me? what have I done to displease you?'

"'Angry with you; displeased? How can you think of me so unjustly?'

"'It is so many days since you have called, since I have seen you,' she said so artlessly, looking up at me with eyes in which tears still seemed to tremble.

"Before I could trust myself to reply, her aunt approached, and noticing me with a cold and distant 'Good-night,' led away her niece.

"I had calculated on walking back to their home with them, as I generally have done when we met at another house. But the aunt had probably conjectured I might be at the vicarage that evening, and in order to frustrate my intention, had engaged a carriage for their return. No doubt she has been warned against permitting further intimacy with her niece.

"My father, I must come to you at once, discharge my promise, and receive from your own lips your consent to my choice; for you will consent, will you not? But I wish you to be prepared beforehand, and I shall therefore put up these disjointed fragments of my commune with my own heart and with yours, and post them tomorrow. Expect me to follow them, after leaving you a day free to consider them alone—alone, my dear father; they are meant for no eye but yours.

"K. C."

CHAPTER VI.

THE next day Kenelm walked into the town, posted his voluminous letter to Sir Peter, and then looked in at the shop of Will Somers, meaning to make some purchases of basket-work or trifling fancy goods in Jessie's pretty store of such articles, that might please the taste of his mother.

On entering the shop his heart beat quicker. He saw two young forms bending over the counter, examining the contents of a glass case. One of these customers was Clemmy; in the other there was no mistaking the slight graceful shape of Lily Mordaunt. Clemmy was exclaiming, "Oh it is so pretty, Mrs. Somers; but," turning her eyes from the counter to a silk purse in her hand, she added, sorrowfully, "I can't buy it. I have not got enough, not by a great deal."

"And what is it, Miss Clemmy?" asked Kenelm.

The two girls turned round at his voice, and Clemmy's face brightened.

"Look here," she said, "is it not too lovely?"

The object thus admired and coveted was a little gold locket, enriched by a cross composed of small pearls.

"I assure you, miss," said Jessie, who had acquired all the coaxing arts of her trade, "it is really a great bargain. Miss Mary Burrows, who was here just before you came, bought one not nearly so pretty, and gave ten shillings more for it."

Miss Mary Burrows was the same age as Miss Clementina Emlyn, and there was a rivalry as to smartness between those youthful beauties. "Miss Burrows!" sighed Clemmy very scornfully.

But Kenelm's attention was distracted from Clemmy's locket to a little ring which Lily had been persuaded by Mrs. Somers to try on, and which she now drew off and returned with a shake of the head. Mrs. Somers, who saw that she had small chance of selling the locket to Clemmy, was now addressing herself to the elder girl more likely to have sufficient pocket-money, and whom, at all events, it was quite safe to trust.

"The ring fits you so nicely, Miss Mordaunt, and every young lady of your age wears at least one ring; allow me to put it up?" She added in a lower voice, "Though we only sell the articles in this case on commission, it is all the same to us whether we are paid now or at Christmas."

"'Tis no use tempting me, Mrs. Somers," said Lily, laughing, and then with a grave air, "I promised Lion, I mean my guardian, never to run into debt, and I never will."

Lily turned resolutely from the perilous counter, taking up a paper that contained a new ribbon she had bought for Blanche, and Clemmy reluctantly followed her out of the shop.

Kenelm lingered behind and selected very hastily a few trifles, to be sent to him that evening with some specimens of basket-work left to Will's tasteful discretion; then purchased the locket on which Clemmy had set her heart; but all the while his thoughts were fixed on the ring which Lily had tried on. It was no sin against etiquette to give the locket to a child like Clemmy, but would it not be a cruel impertinence to offer a gift to Lily?

Jessie spoke:

"Miss Mordaunt took a great fancy to this ring, Mr. Chillingly. I am sure her aunt would like her to have it. I have a great mind to put it by on the chance of Mrs. Cameron's calling here. It would be a pity if it were bought by some one else."

"I think," said Kenelm, "that I will take the liberty of showing it to Mrs. Cameron. No doubt she will buy it for her niece. Add the price of it to my bill." He seized the ring and carried it off; a very poor little simple ring, with a single stone, shaped as a heart, not half the price of the locket.

Kenelm rejoined the young ladies just where the path split into two, the one leading direct to Grasmere, the other through the churchyard to the Vicarage. He presented the locket to Clemmy with brief kindly words which easily removed any scruple she might have had in accepting it; and, delighted with her acquisition, she bounded off to the Vicarage, impatient to show the prize to her mamma and sisters, and more especially to Miss Mary Burrows, who was coming to lunch with them.

Kenelm walked on slowly by Lily's side.

"You have a good heart, Mr. Chillingly," said she, somewhat abruptly. "How it must please you to give such pleasure! Dear little Clemmy!"

This artless praise, and the perfect absence of envy or thought of self evinced by her joy that her friend's wish was gratified, though her own was not, enchanted Kenelm.

"If it pleases to give pleasure," said he, "it is your turn to be pleased now; you can confer such pleasure upon me."

"How?" she asked, falteringly, and with quick change of colour.

"By conceding to me the same right your little friend has allowed."

And he drew forth the ring.

Lily reared her head with a first impulse of haughtiness. But when her eyes met his the head drooped down again, and a slight shiver ran through her frame.

"Miss Mordaunt," resumed Kenelm, mastering his passionate longing to fall at her feet and say, "But, oh! in this ring it is my love that I offer—it is my troth that I pledge!" "Miss Mordaunt, spare me the misery of thinking that I have offended you; least of all would I do so on this day, for it may be some little while before I see you again. I am going home for a few days upon a matter which may affect the happiness of my life, and on which I should be a bad son and an unworthy gentleman if I did not consult him who, in all that concerns my affections, has trained me to turn to him, the father; in all that concerns my honour to him, the gentleman."

A speech more unlike that which any delineator of manners and morals in the present day would put into the mouth of a lover, no critic in 'The Londoner' could ridicule. But, somehow or other, this poor little tamer of butterflies and teller of fairy tales comprehended on the instant all that this most eccentric of human beings thus frigidly left untold. Into her innermost heart it sank more deeply than would the most ardent declaration put into the lips of the boobies or the scamps in whom delineators of manners in the present day too often debase the magnificent chivalry embodied in the name of 'Lover.'

Where these two had, while speaking, halted on the path along the brook-side, there was a bench, on which it so happened that they had seated themselves weeks before. A few moments later on that bench they were seated again.

And the trumpery little ring with its turquoise heart was on Lily's finger, and there they continued to sit for nearly half an hour; not talking much, but wondrously happy; not a single vow of troth interchanged. No, not even a word that could be construed into "I love." And yet when they rose from the bench, and went silently along the brook-side, each knew that the other was beloved.

When they reached the gate that admitted into the garden of Grasmere, Kenelm made a slight start. Mrs. Cameron was leaning over the gate. Whatever alarm at the appearance Kenelm might have felt was certainly not shared by Lily; she advanced lightly before him, kissed her aunt on the cheek, and passed on across the lawn with a bound in her step and the carol of a song upon her lips.

Kenelm remained by the gate, face to face with Mrs. Cameron. She opened the gate, put her arm in his, and led him back along the brook-side.

"I am sure, Mr. Chillingly," she said, "that you will not impute to my words any meaning more grave than that which I wish them to convey, when I remind you that there is no place too obscure to escape from the ill-nature of gossip, and you must own that my niece incurs the chance of its notice if she be seen walking alone in these by-paths with a man of your age and position, and whose sojourn in the neighbourhood, without any ostensible object or motive, has already begun to excite conjecture. I do not for a moment assume that you regard my niece in any other light than that of an artless child, whose originality of tastes or fancy may serve to amuse you; and still less do I suppose that she is in danger of misrepresenting any attentions on your part. But for her sake I am bound to consider what others may say. Excuse me then if I add that I think that you are also bound in honour and in good feeling to do the same. Mr. Chillingly, it would give me a great sense of relief if it suited your plans to move from the neighbourhood."

"My dear Mrs. Cameron," answered Kenelm, who had listened to this speech with imperturbable calm of visage; "I thank you much for your candour, and I am glad to have this opportunity of informing you that I am about to move from this neighbourhood, with the hope of returning to it in a very few days and rectifying your mistake as to the point of view in which I regard your niece. In a word," here the expression of his countenance and the tone of his voice underwent a sudden change, "it is the dearest wish of my heart to be empowered by my parents to assure you of the warmth with which they will welcome your niece as their daughter, should she deign to listen to my suit and intrust me with the charge of her happiness."

Mrs. Cameron stopped short, gazing into his face with a look of inexpressible dismay.

"No! Mr. Chillingly," she exclaimed, "this must not be—cannot be. Put out of your mind an idea so wild. A young man's senseless romance. Your parents cannot consent to your union with my niece; I tell you beforehand they cannot."

"But why?" said Kenelm, with a slight smile, and not much impressed by the vehemence of Mrs. Cameron's adjuration.

"Why?" she repeated passionately; and then recovering something of her habitual weariness of quiet. "The why is easily explained. Mr. Kenelm Chillingly is the heir of a very ancient house and, I am told, of considerable estates. Lily Mordaunt is a nobody, an orphan, without fortune, without connection, the ward of a humbly born artist, to whom she owes the roof that shelters her; she is without the ordinary education of a gentlewoman; she has seen nothing of the world in which you move. Your parents have not the right to allow a son so young as yourself to throw himself out of his proper sphere by a rash and imprudent alliance. And, never would I consent, never would Walter Melville consent, to her entering into any family reluctant to receive her. There—that is enough. Dismiss the notion so lightly entertained. And farewell."

"Madam," answered Kenelm very earnestly, "believe me, that had I not entertained the hope approaching to conviction that the reasons you urge against my presumption will not have the weight with my parents which you ascribe to them, I should not have spoken to you thus frankly. Young though I be, still I might fairly claim the right to choose for myself in marriage. But I gave to my father a very binding promise that I would not formally propose to any one till I had acquainted him with my desire to do so, and obtained his approval of my choice; and he is the last man in the world who would withhold that approval where my heart is set on it as it is now. I want no fortune with a wife, and should I ever care to advance my position in the world, no connection could help me like the approving smile of the woman I love. There is but one qualification which my parents would deem they had the right to exact from my choice of one who is to bear our name. I mean that she should have the appearance, the manners, the principles —and my mother at least might add—the birth of a gentlewoman. Well, as to appearance and manners, I have seen much of fine society from my boyhood, and found no one among the highest born who can excel the exquisite refinement of every look, and the inborn delicacy of every thought, in her of whom, if mine, I shall be as proud as I shall be fond. As to defects in the frippery and tinsel of a boarding-school education, they are very soon remedied. Remains only the last consideration—birth. Mrs. Braefield informs me that you have assured her that, though circumstances into which as yet I have no right to inquire, have made her the ward of a man of humble origin, Miss Mordaunt is of gentle birth. Do you deny that?"

"No," said Mrs. Cameron, hesitating, but with a flash of pride in her eyes as she went on. "No. I cannot deny that my niece is descended from those who, in point of birth, were not unequal to your own ancestors. But what of that?" she added, with a bitter despondency of tone. "Equality of birth ceases when one falls into poverty, obscurity, neglect, nothingness!"

"Really this is a morbid habit on your part. But since we have thus spoken so confidentially, will you not empower me to answer the question which will probably be put to me, and the answer to which will, I doubt not, remove every obstacle in the way of my happiness. Whatever the reasons which might very sufficiently induce you to preserve, whilst living so quietly in this place, a discreet silence as to the parentage of Miss Mordaunt and your own— and I am well aware that those whom altered circumstances of fortune have compelled to altered modes of life, may disdain to parade to strangers the pretensions to a higher station than that to which they reconcile their habits—whatever, I say, such reasons for silence to strangers, should they preclude you from confiding to me, an aspirant to your niece's hand, a secret which, after all, cannot be concealed from her future husband?"

"From her future husband? of course not," answered Mrs. Cameron. "But I decline to be questioned by one whom I may never see again, and of whom I know so little. I decline, indeed, to assist in removing any obstacle to an union with my niece, which I hold to be in every way unsuited to either party. I have no cause even to believe that my niece would accept you if you were free to propose to her. You have not, I presume, spoken to her as an aspirant to her hand. You have not addressed to her any declaration of your attachment, or sought to extract from her inexperience any words that warrant you in thinking that her heart will break if she never sees you again."

"I do not merit such cruel and taunting questions," said Kenelm, indignantly. "But I will say no more now. When we again meet let me hope you will treat me less unkindly. Adieu!"

"Stay, sir. A word or two more. You persist in asking your father and Lady Chillingly to consent to your proposal to Miss Mordaunt?"

"Certainly I do."

"And you will promise me, on your word as a gentleman, to state fairly all the causes which might fairly operate against their consent; the poverty, the humble rearing, the imperfect education of my niece; so that they might not hereafter say you had entrapped their consent, and avenge themselves for your deceit by contempt for her?"

"Ah, madam, madam, you really try my patience too far. But take my promise, if you can hold that of value from one whom you can suspect of deliberate deceit."

"I beg your pardon, Mr. Chillingly. Bear with my rudeness. I have been so taken by surprise, I scarcely know what I am saying. But let us understand each other completely before we part. If your parents withhold their consent you will communicate it to me;

me only, not to Lily. I repeat I know nothing of the state of her affections. But it might embitter any girl's life to be led on to love one whom she could not marry."

"It shall be as you say. But if they do consent?"

"Then you will speak to me before you seek an interview with Lily, for then comes another question: Will her guardian consent? —and—and——"

"And what?"

"No matter. I rely on your honour in this request, as in all else. Good-day."

She turned back with hurried footsteps, muttering to herself, "But they will not consent. Heaven grant that they will not consent, or if they do, what—what is to be said or done? Oh, that Walter Melville were here, or that I knew where to write to him!"

On his way back to Cromwell Lodge, Kenelm was overtaken by the vicar.

"I was coming to you, my dear Mr. Chillingly, first to thank you for the very pretty present with which you have gladdened the heart of my little Clemmy, and next to ask you to come with me quietly to-day to meet Mr. ——, the celebrated antiquarian, who came to Moleswich this morning at my request, to examine that old Gothic tomb in our churchyard. Only think,—though he cannot read the inscription any better than we can, he knows all about its history. It seems that a young knight renowned for feats of valour in the reign of Henry IV. married a daughter of one of those great Earls of Montfichet who were then the most powerful family in these parts. He was slain in defending the church from an assault by some disorderly rioters of the Lollard faction; he fell on the very spot where the tomb is now placed. That accounts for its situation in the churchyard, not within the fabric. Mr. —— discovered this fact in an old memoir of the ancient and once famous family to which the young knight Albert belonged, and which came, alas! to so shameful an end, the Fletwodes, Barons of Fletwode and Malpas. What a triumph over pretty Lily Mordaunt, who always chose to imagine that the tomb must be that of some heroine of her own romantic invention! Do come to dinner; Mr. —— is a most agreeable man, and full of interesting anecdote."

"I am so sorry I cannot. I am obliged to return home at once for a few days. That old family of Fletwode! I think I see before me while we speak, the gray tower in which they once held sway; and the last of the race following Mammon along the Progress of the Age—a convicted felon! What a terrible satire on the pride of birth!"

Kenelm left Cromwell Lodge that evening, but he still kept on his apartments there, saying he might be back unexpectedly any day in the course of the next week.

He remained two days in London, wishing all that he had communicated to Sir Peter in writing to sink into his father's heart before a personal appeal to it.

The more he revolved the ungracious manner in which Mrs. Cameron had received his confidence, the less importance he attached to it. An exaggerated sense of disparities of fortune in a person who appeared to him to have the pride so common to those who have known better days, coupled with a nervous apprehension lest his family should ascribe to her any attempt to ensnare a very young man of considerable worldly pretensions into a marriage with a penniless niece, seemed to account for much that had at first perplexed and angered him. And if, as he conjectured, Mrs. Cameron had once held a much higher position in the world than she did now —a conjecture warranted by a certain peculiar conventional undeniable elegance which characterized her habitual manner—and was now, as she implied, actually a dependant on the bounty of a painter who had only just acquired some professional distinction, she might well shrink from the mortification of becoming an object of compassion to her richer neighbours; nor, when he came to think of it, had he any more right than those neighbours to any confidence as to her own or Lily's parentage, so long as he was not formally entitled to claim admission into her privity.

London seemed to him intolerably dull and wearisome. He called nowhere except at Lady Glenalvon's: he was glad to hear from the servants that she was still at Exmundham. He relied much on the influence of the queen of the Fashion with his mother, whom he knew would be more difficult to persuade than Sir Peter, nor did he doubt that he should win to his side that sympathizing and warm-hearted queen.

CHAPTER VII.

IT is somewhere about three weeks since the party invited by Sir Peter and Lady Chillingly assembled at Exmundham, and they are still there, though people invited to a country house have seldom compassion enough for the dulness of its owner to stay more than three days. Mr. Chillingly Mivers, indeed, had not exceeded that orthodox limit. Quietly observant, during his stay, of young Gordon's manner towards Cecilia, and hers towards him, he had satisfied himself that there was no cause to alarm Sir Peter, or induce the worthy baronet to regret the invitation he had given to that clever kinsman. For all the visitors remaining, Exmundham had a charm.

To Lady Glenalvon, because in the hostess she met her most familiar friend when both were young girls, and because it pleased her to note the interest which Cecilia Travers took in the place so associated with memories of the man to whom it was Lady Glenalvon's hope to see her united. To Gordon Chillingly, because no opportunity could be so favourable for his own well-concealed designs on the hand and heart of the heiress. To the heiress herself the charm needs no explanation.

To Leopold Travers the attractions of Exmundham were unquestionably less fascinating. Still even he was well pleased to prolong his stay. His active mind found amusement in wandering over an estate the acreage of which would have warranted a much larger rental, and lecturing Sir Peter on the old-fashioned system of husbandry which that good-natured easy proprietor permitted his tenants to adopt, as well as on the number of superfluous hands that were employed on the pleasure-grounds and in the general management of the estate, such as carpenters, sawyers, woodmen, bricklayers, and smiths.

When the squire said, "You could do just as well with a third of those costly dependants," Sir Peter, unconsciously plagiarizing the answer of the old French grand seigneur, replied, "Very likely. But the question is, could the rest do just as well without me?"

Exmundham, indeed, was a very expensive place to keep up. The house, built by some ambitious Chillingly three centuries ago, would have been large for an owner of thrice the revenues; and though the flower-garden was smaller than that at Braefieldville, there were paths and drives through miles of young plantations and old woodlands that furnished lazy occupation to an army of labourers. No wonder that, despite his nominal ten thousand a-year, Sir Peter was far from being a rich man. Exmundham devoured at least half the rental. The active mind of Leopold Travers also found ample occupation in the stores of his host's extensive library. Travers, never much of a reader, was by no means a despiser of learning, and he soon took to historical and archæological researches with the ardour of a man who must always throw energy into any pursuit that occasion presents as an escape from indolence. Indolent, Leopold Travers never could be. But, more than either of these resources of occupation, the companionship of Chillingly Gordon excited his interest and quickened the current of his thoughts. Always fond of renewing his own youth in the society of the young, and of the sympathizing temperament which belongs to cordial natures, he had, as we have seen, entered very heartily into the ambition of George Belvoir, and reconciled himself very pliably to the humours of Kenelm Chillingly. But the first of these two was a little too commonplace, the second a little too eccentric, to enlist the complete good-fellowship which, being alike very clever and very practical, Leopold Travers established with that very clever and very practical representative of the rising generation, Chillingly Gordon. Between them there was this meeting ground, political and worldly, a great contempt for innocuous old-fashioned notions; added to which, in the mind of Leopold Travers, was a contempt—which would have been complete, but that the contempt admitted dread—of harmful new-fashioned notions which, interpreted by his thoughts, threatened ruin to his country and downfall to the follies of existent society, and which, interpreted by his language, tamed itself into the man of the world's phrase, "Going too far for me." Notions which, by the much more cultivated intellect and the immeasurably more soaring ambition of Chillingly Gordon, might be viewed and criticized thus : " Could I accept these doctrines? I don't see my way to being Prime Minister of a country in which religion and capital are still powers to be consulted. And, putting aside religion and capital, I don't see how, if these doctrines passed into law, with a good coat on my back I should not be a sufferer. Either I, as having a good coat, should have it torn off my back as a capitalist, or, if I remonstrated in the name of moral honesty, be put to death as a religionist."

Therefore when Leopold Travers said "Of course we must go on," Chillingly Gordon smiled and answered, "Certainly, go on." And when Leopold Travers added, "But we may go too far," Chillingly Gordon shook his head, and replied, "How true that is! Certainly, too far."

Apart from the congeniality of political sentiment, there were other points of friendly contact between the older and younger man. Each was an exceedingly pleasant man of the world ; and, though Leopold Travers could not have plumbed certain deeps in Chillingly Gordon's nature—and in every man's nature there are deeps which his ablest observer cannot fathom—yet he was not wrong when he said to himself, "Gordon is a gentleman."

Utterly would my readers misconceive that very clever young man, if they held him to be a hypocrite like Blifil or Joseph Surface. Chillingly Gordon, in every private sense of the word, was a gentleman. If he had staked his whole fortune on a rubber at whist, and an undetected glance at his adversary's hand would have made the difference between loss and gain, he would have turned away his head and said, "Hold up your cards." Neither, as I have had occasion to explain before, was he actuated by any motive in common with the vulgar fortune-hunter in his secret resolve to win the hand of the heiress. He recognized no inequality of worldly gifts between them. He said to himself, "Whatever she may give me in money, I shall amply repay in worldly position if I succeed, and succeed I certainly shall. If I were as rich as Lord Westminster, and still cared about being Prime Minister, I should select her as the most fitting woman I have seen for a Prime Minister's wife."

It must be acknowledged that this sort of self-commune, if not that of a very ardent lover, is very much that of a sensible man setting high value on himself, bent on achieving the prizes of a public career, and desirous of securing in his wife a woman who would adorn the station to which he confidently aspired. In fact, no one so able as Chillingly Gordon would ever have conceived the ambition of being Minister of England if, in all that, in private life, constitutes the English gentleman, he could be fairly subject to reproach.

He was but in public life what many a gentleman honest in private life has been before him, an ambitious, resolute egotist, by no means without personal affections, but holding them all subordinate to the objects of personal ambition, and with no more of other principle than that of expediency in reference to his own career, than would cover a silver penny. But expediency in itself he deemed the statesman's only rational principle. And to the consideration of expediency he brought a very unprejudiced intellect, quite fitted to decide whether the public opinion of a free and enlightened people was for turning St. Paul's Cathedral into an Agapemone or not.

During the summer weeks he had thus vouchsafed to the turfs and groves of Exmundham, Leopold Travers was not the only person whose good opinion Chillingly Gordon had ingratiated. He had won the warmest approbation from Mrs. Campion. His conversation reminded her of that which she had enjoyed in the house of her departed spouse. In talking with Cecilia she was fond of contrasting him to Kenelm, not to the favour of the latter, whose humours she utterly failed to understand, and whom she pertinaciously described as "so affected." "A most superior young man Mr. Gordon, so well informed, so sensible, above all, so natural." Such was her judgment upon the unavowed candidate to Cecilia's hand; and Mrs. Campion required no avowal to divine the candidature. Even Lady Glenalvon had begun to take friendly interest in the fortunes of this promising young man. Most women can sympathize with youthful ambition. He impressed her with a deep conviction of his abilities, and still more with respect for their concentration upon practical objects of power and renown. She too, like Mrs. Campion, began to draw comparisons unfavourable to Kenelm between the two cousins; the one who seemed so slothfully determined to hide his candle under a bushel, the other so honestly disposed to set his light before men. She felt also annoyed and angry that Kenelm was thus absenting himself from the paternal home at the very time of her first visit to it, and when he had so felicitous an opportunity of seeing more of the girl in whom he knew that Lady Glenalvon deemed he might win, if he would properly woo, the wife that would best suit him. So that when one day Mrs. Campion, walking through the gardens alone with Lady Glenalvon, while from the gardens into the park went Chillingly Gordon, arm-in-arm with Leopold Travers, abruptly asked, "Don't you think that Mr. Gordon is smitten with Cecilia, though he, with his moderate fortune, does not dare to say so? And don't you think that any girl, if she were as rich as Cecilia will be, would be more proud of such a husband as Chillingly Gordon than of some silly Earl?"

Lady Glenalvon answered curtly, but somewhat sorrowfully—
"Yes."

After a pause, she added, "There *is* a man with whom I did once think she would have been happier than with any other. One man who ought to be dearer to me than Mr. Gordon, for he saved the life of my son, and who, though perhaps less clever than Mr. Gordon, still has a great deal of talent within him, which might come forth and make him—what shall I say?—a useful and distinguished member of society, if married to a girl so sure of raising any man she marries as Cecilia Travers. But if I am to renounce that hope, and look through the range of young men brought under my notice, I don't know one, putting aside consideration of rank and fortune, I should prefer for a clever daughter who went heart and soul with the ambition of a clever man. But, Mrs. Campion, I have not yet quite renounced my hope; and, unless I do, I yet think there is one man to whom I would rather give Cecilia, if she were my daughter."

Therewith Lady Glenalvon so decidedly broke off the subject of conversation, that Mrs. Campion could not have renewed it without such a breach of the female etiquette of good breeding as Mrs. Campion was the last person to adventure.

Lady Chillingly could not help being pleased with Gordon. He was light in hand, served to amuse her guests, and made up a rubber of whist in case of need.

There were two persons, however, with whom Gordon made no ground, viz., Parson John and Sir Peter. When Travers praised him one day, for the solidity of his parts and the soundness of his judgment, the Parson replied snappishly, "Yes, solid and sound as one of those tables you buy at a broker's; the thickness of the varnish hides the defects in the joints; the whole framework is rickety." But when the Parson was indignantly urged to state the reason by which he arrived at so harsh a conclusion, he could only reply by an assertion which seemed to his questioner a declamatory burst of parsonic intolerance.

"Because," said Parson John, "he has no love for man, and no reverence for God. And no character is sound and solid which enlarges its surface at the expense of its supports."

On the other hand, the favour with which Sir Peter had at first regarded Gordon gradually vanished, in proportion as, acting on the hint Mivers had originally thrown out but did not deem it necessary to repeat, he watched the pains which the young man took to insinuate himself into the good graces of Mr. Travers and Mrs. Campion, and the artful and half-suppressed gallantry of his manner to the heiress.

Perhaps Gordon had not ventured thus "to feel his way" till after Mivers had departed; or perhaps Sir Peter's parental anxiety rendered him, in this instance, a shrewder observer than was the man of the world, whose natural acuteness was, in matters of affection, not unfrequently rendered languid by his acquired philosophy of indifferentism.

More and more every day, every hour, of her sojourn beneath his roof, did Cecilia become dearer to Sir Peter, and stronger and stronger became his wish to secure her for his daughter-in-law. He was inexpressibly flattered by her preference for his company; ever at hand to share his customary walks, his kindly visits to the cottages of peasants, or the homesteads of petty tenants; wherein both were sure to hear many a simple anecdote of Master Kenelm in his childhood, anecdotes of whim or good nature, of considerate pity or reckless courage.

Throughout all these varieties of thought or feeling in the social circle around her, Lady Chillingly preserved the unmoved calm of her dignified position. A very good woman certainly, and very ladylike. No one could detect a flaw in her character, or a fold awry in her flounce. She was only like the gods of Epicurus, too good to trouble her serene existence with the cares of us simple mortals. Not that she was without a placid satisfaction in the tribute which the world laid upon her altars; nor was she so supremely goddess-like as to soar above the household affections which humanity entails on the dwellers and denizens of earth. She liked her husband as much as most elderly wives like their elderly husbands. She bestowed upon Kenelm a liking somewhat more warm, and mingled with compassion. His eccentricities would have puzzled her, if she had allowed herself to be puzzled; it troubled her less to pity them. She did not share her husband's desire for his union with Cecilia. She thought that her son would have a higher place in the county if he married Lady Jane, the Duke of Clanville's daughter; and "that is what he ought to do," said Lady Chillingly to herself. She entertained none of the fear that had induced Sir Peter to extract from Kenelm the promise not to pledge his hand before he had received his father's consent. That the son of Lady Chillingly should make a *mésalliance*, however crotchety he might be in other respects, was a thought that it would have so disturbed her to admit, that she did not admit it.

Such was the condition of things at Exmundham, when the lengthy communication of Kenelm reached Sir Peter's hands.

BOOK VIII.

CHAPTER I.

NEVER in his whole life had the mind of Sir Peter been so agitated as it was during, and after, the perusal of Kenelm's flighty composition. He had received it at the breakfast-table, and, opening it eagerly, ran his eye hastily over the contents, till he very soon arrived at sentences which appalled him. Lady Chillingly, who was fortunately busied at the tea-urn, did not observe the dismay on his countenance. It was visible only to Cecilia and to Gordon. Neither guessed who that letter was from.

"Not bad news, I hope," said Cecilia, softly.

"Bad news," echoed Sir Peter. "No, my dear, no; a letter on business. It seems terribly long," and he thrust the packet into his pocket, muttering, "see to it by-and-bye."

"That slovenly farmer of yours, Mr. Nostock, has failed, I suppose," said Mr. Travers, looking up and observing a quiver on his host's lip. "I told you he would—a fine farm too. Let me choose you another tenant."

Sir Peter shook his head with a wan smile.

"Nostock will not fail. There have been six generations of Nostocks on the farm."

"So I should guess," said Travers, dryly.

"And—and," faltered Sir Peter, "if the last of the race fails, he must lean upon me, and—if one of the two break down—it shall not be——"

"Shall not be that cross-cropping blockhead, my dear Sir Peter. This is carrying benevolence too far."

Here the tact and *savoir vivre* of Chillingly Gordon came to the rescue of the host. Possessing himself of the 'Times' newspaper, he uttered an exclamation of surprise, genuine or simulated, and read aloud an extract from the leading article, announcing an impending change in the Cabinet.

As soon as he could quit the breakfast-table, Sir Peter hurried into his library and there gave himself up to the study of Kenelm's unwelcome communication. The task took him long, for he stopped at intervals, overcome by the struggle of his heart, now melted into sympathy with the passionate eloquence of a son hitherto so free from amorous romance, and now sorrowing for the ruin of his own cherished hopes. This uneducated country girl would never be such a helpmate to a man like Kenelm as would have been Cecilia Travers. At length, having finished the letter, he buried his head between his clasped hands, and tried hard to realize the situation that placed the father and son into such direct antagonism.

"But," he murmured, "after all it is the boy's happiness that must be consulted. If he will not be happy in my way, what right have I to say that he shall not be happy in his?"

Just then Cecilia came softly into the room. She had acquired the privilege of entering his library at will, sometimes to choose a book of his recommendation, sometimes to direct and seal his letters —Sir Peter was grateful to any one who saved him an extra trouble —and sometimes, especially at this hour, to decoy him forth into his wonted constitutional walk.

He lifted his face at the sound of her approaching tread and her winning voice, and the face was so sad that the tears rushed to her eyes on seeing it. She laid her hand on his shoulder, and said pleadingly, "Dear Sir Peter, what is it—what is it?"

"Ah—ah, my dear," said Sir Peter, gathering up the scattered sheets of Kenelm's effusion with hurried trembling hands. "Don't ask—don't talk of it; 'tis but one of the disappointments that all of us must undergo, when we invest our hopes in the uncertain will of others."

Then, observing that the tears were trickling down the girl's fair, pale cheeks, he took her hand in both his, kissed her forehead, and said, whisperingly, "Pretty one, how good you have been to me! Heaven bless you. What a wife you will be to some man!"

Thus saying, he shambled out of the room through the open casement. She followed him impulsively, wonderingly; but before she reached his side he turned round, waved his hand with a gently repelling gesture, and went his way alone through dense fir groves which had been planted in honour of Kenelm's birth.

CHAPTER II.

KENELM arrived at Exmundham just in time to dress for dinner. His arrival was not unexpected, for the morning after his father had received his communication, Sir Peter had said to Lady Chillingly "that he had heard from Kenelm to the effect that he might be down any day."

"Quite time he should come," said Lady Chillingly.

"Have you his letter about you?"

"No, my dear Caroline. Of course he sends you his kindest love, poor fellow."

"Why poor fellow? Has he been ill?"

"No; but there seems to be something on his mind. If so we must do what we can to relieve it. He is the best of sons, Caroline."

"I am sure I have nothing to say against him, except," added her Ladyship, reflectively, "that I do wish he were a little more like other young men."

"Hum—like Chillingly Gordon, for instance?"

"Well, yes; Mr. Gordon is a remarkably well-bred, sensible young man. How different from that disagreeable, bearish father of his, who went to law with you!"

"Very different indeed, but with just as much of the Chillingly blood in him. How the Chillinglys ever gave birth to a Kenelm is a question much more puzzling."

"Oh, my dear Sir Peter, don't be metaphysical. You know how I hate puzzles."

"And yet, Caroline, I have to thank you for a puzzle which I can never interpret by my brain. There are a great many puzzles in human nature which can only be interpreted by the heart."

"Very true," said Lady Chillingly. "I suppose Kenelm is to have his old room, just opposite to Mr. Gordon's."

"Ay—ay, just opposite. Opposite they will be all their lives. Only think, Caroline, I have made a discovery!"

"Dear me; I hope not. Your discoveries are generally very expensive, and bring us in contact with such very odd people."

"This discovery shall not cost us a penny, and I don't know any people so odd as not to comprehend it. Briefly it is this: To genius the first requisite is heart; it is no requisite at all to talent. My dear Caroline, Gordon has as much talent as any young man I know, but he wants the first requisite of genius. I am not by any

O

means sure that Kenelm has genius, but there is no doubt that he has the first requisite of genius—heart. Heart is a very perplexing, wayward, irrational thing; and that perhaps accounts for the general incapacity to comprehend genius, while any fool can comprehend talent. My dear Caroline, you know that it is very seldom, not more than once in three years, that I presume to have a will of my own against a will of yours; but should there come a question in which our son's heart is concerned, then (speaking between ourselves) my will must govern yours."

"Sir Peter is growing more odd every day," said Lady Chillingly to herself when left alone. "But he does not mean ill, and there are worse husbands in the world."

Therewith she rang for her maid, gave requisite orders for the preparing of Kenelm's room, which had not been slept in for many months, and then consulted that functionary as to the adaptation of some dress of hers, too costly to be laid aside, to the style of some dress which Lady Glenalvon had imported from Paris as *la dernière mode*.

On the very day on which Kenelm arrived at Exmundham, Chillingly Gordon had received this letter from Mr. Gerard Danvers:

"DEAR GORDON,—In the ministerial changes announced as rumour in the public papers, and which you may accept as certain, that sweet little cherub * * * is to be sent to sit up aloft and pray there for the life of poor Jack—viz., of the government he leaves below. In accepting the peerage, which I persuaded him to do, * * * creates a vacancy for the borough of ——, just the place for you, far better in every way than Saxborough. * * * promises to recommend you to his committee. Come to town at once.—Yours, &c.   G. DANVERS."

Gordon showed this letter to Mr. Travers, and, on receiving the hearty good wishes of that gentleman, said, with emotion partly genuine partly assumed, "You cannot guess all that the realization of your good wishes would be. Once in the House of Commons, and my motives for action are so strong that—do not think me very conceited if I count upon Parliamentary success."

"My dear Gordon, I am as certain of your success as I am of my own existence."

"Should I succeed—should the great prizes of public life be within my reach—should I lift myself into a position that would warrant my presumption, do you think I could come to you and say, 'There is an object of ambition dearer to me than power and office—the hope of attaining which was the strongest of all my motives of action? And in that hope shall I also have the good wishes of the father of Cecilia Travers?"

"My dear fellow, give me your hand; you speak manfully and candidly as a gentleman should speak. I answer in the same spirit. I don't pretend to say that I have not entertained views for Cecilia which included hereditary rank and established fortune in a suitor to her hand, though I never should have made them imperative conditions. I am neither potentate nor *parvenu* enough for that; and I can never forget" (here every muscle in the man's face twitched) "that I myself married for love, and was so happy. How happy Heaven only knows! Still, if you had thus spoken a few weeks ago, I should not have replied very favourably to your question. But now that I have seen so much of you, my answer is this: If you lose your election—if you don't come into Parliament at all, you have my good wishes all the same. If you win my daughter's heart, there is no man on whom I would more willingly bestow her hand. There she is, by herself too, in the garden. Go and talk to her."

Gordon hesitated. He knew too well that he had not won her heart, though he had no suspicion that it was given to another. And he was much too clever not to know also how much he hazards, who, in affairs of courtship, is premature.

"Ah!" he said, "I cannot express my gratitude for words so generous, encouragement so cheering. But I have never yet dared to utter to Miss Travers a word that would prepare her even to harbour a thought of me as a suitor. And I scarcely think I should have the courage to go through this election with the grief of her rejection on my heart."

"Well, go in and win the election first; meanwhile, at all events, take leave of Cecilia."

Gordon left his friend, and joined Miss Travers, resolved not indeed to risk a formal declaration, but to sound his way to his chances of acceptance.

The interview was very brief. He did sound his way skilfully, and felt it very unsafe for his footsteps. The advantage of having gained the approval of the father was too great to be lost altogether, by one of these decided answers on the part of the daughter which allow of no appeal, especially to a poor gentleman who woos an heiress.

He returned to Travers, and said simply, "I bear with me her good wishes as well as yours. That is all. I leave myself in your kind hands."

Then he hurried away to take leave of his host and hostess, say a few significant words to the ally he had already gained in Mrs. Campion, and within an hour was on his road to London, passing on his way the train that bore Kenelm to Exmundham. Gordon was in high spirits. At least he felt as certain of winning Cecilia as he did of winning his election.

"I have never yet failed in what I desired," said he to himself, "because I have ever taken pains not to fail."

The cause of Gordon's sudden departure created a great excitement in that quiet circle, shared by all except Cecilia and Sir Peter.

CHAPTER III.

KENELM did not see either father or mother till he appeared at dinner. Then he was seated next to Cecilia. There was but little conversation between the two; in fact, the prevalent subject of talk was general and engrossing, the interest in Chillingly Gordon's election; predictions of his success, of what he would do in Parliament. "Where," said Lady Glenalvon, "there is such a dearth of rising young men, that if he were only half as clever as he is he would be a gain."

"A gain to what?" asked Sir Peter, testily. "To his country? about which I don't believe he cares a brass button."

To this assertion Leopold Travers replied warmly, and was not less warmly backed by Mrs. Campion.

"For my part," said Lady Glenalvon, in conciliatory accents, "I think every able man in Parliament is a gain to the country; and he may not serve his country less effectively because he does not boast of his love for it. The politicians I dread most are those so rampant in France nowadays, the bawling patriots. When Sir Robert Walpole said, 'All those men have their price,' he pointed to the men who called themselves 'patriots.'"

"Bravo!" cried Travers.

"Sir Robert Walpole showed his love for his country by corrupting it. There are many ways besides bribing for corrupting a country," said Kenelm, mildly, and that was Kenelm's sole contribution to the general conversation.

It was not till the rest of the party had retired to rest that the conference, longed for by Kenelm, dreaded by Sir Peter, took place in the library. It lasted deep into the night; both parted with lightened hearts and a fonder affection for each other. Kenelm had drawn so charming a picture of the Fairy, and so thoroughly convinced Sir Peter that his own feelings towards her were those of no passing youthful fancy, but of that love which has its roots in the innermost heart, that though it was still with a sigh, a deep sigh, that he dismissed the thought of Cecilia, Sir Peter did dismiss it; and, taking comfort at last from the positive assurance that Lily was of gentle birth, and the fact that her name of Mordaunt was that of ancient and illustrious houses, said, with half a smile, "It might have been worse, my dear boy. I began to be afraid that, in spite of the teachings of Mivers and Welby, it was 'The Miller's Daughter,' after all. But we still have a difficult task to persuade your poor mother. In covering your first flight from our roof I unluckily put into her head the notion of Lady Jane, a duke's daughter, and the notion has never got out of it. That comes of fibbing."

"I count on Lady Glenalvon's influence on my mother in support of your own," said Kenelm. "If so accepted an oracle in the great world pronounce in my favour, and promise to present my wife at Court and bring her into fashion, I think that my mother will consent to allow us to reset the old family diamonds for her next re-appearance in London. And then, too, you can tell her that I will stand for the county. I will go into Parliament, and if I meet there our clever cousin, and find that he does not care a brass button for the country, take my word for it, I will lick him more easily than I licked Tom Bowles."

"Tom Bowles! Who is he?—ah! I remember some letter of yours in which you spoke of a Bowles, whose favourite study was mankind, a moral philosopher."

"Moral philosophers," answered Kenelm, "have so muddled their brains with the alcohol of new ideas that their moral legs have become shaky, and the humane would rather help them to bed than give them a licking. My Tom Bowles is a muscular Christian, who became no less muscular, but much more Christian, after he was licked."

And in this pleasant manner these two oddities settled their conference, and went up to bed with arms wrapped round each other's shoulder.

CHAPTER IV.

KENELM found it a much harder matter to win Lady Glenalvon to his side than he had anticipated, With the strong interest she had taken in Kenelm's future, she could not but revolt from the idea of his union with an obscure portionless girl whom he had only known a few weeks, and of whose very parentage he seemed to know nothing, save an assurance that she was his equal in birth. And, with the desire, which she had cherished almost as fondly as Sir Peter, that Kenelm might win a bride in every way so worthy of his choice as Cecilia Travers, she felt not less indignant than regretful at the overthrow of her plans.

At first, indeed, she was so provoked that she would not listen to his pleadings. She broke away from him with a rudeness she had never exhibited to any one before, refused to grant him another interview in order to re-discuss the matter, and said that so far from using her influence in favour of his romantic folly, she would remonstrate well with Lady Chillingly and Sir Peter against yielding their assent to his "thus throwing himself away."

It was not till the third day after his arrival that, touched by the grave but haughty mournfulness of his countenance, she yielded to the arguments of Sir Peter in the course of a private conversation with that worthy baronet. Still it was reluctantly (she did not fulfil her threat of remonstrance with Lady Chillingly) that she conceded the point, that a son who, succeeding to the absolute fee simple of an estate, had volunteered the resettlement of it on terms singularly generous to both his parents, was entitled to some sacrifice of their inclinations on a question in which he deemed his happiness vitally concerned ; and that he was of age to choose for himself, independently of their consent, but for a previous promise extracted from him by his father, a promise which, rigidly construed, was not extended to Lady Chillingly, but confined to Sir Peter as the head of the family and master of the household. The father's consent was already given, and, if in his reverence for both parents Kenelm could not dispense with his mother's approval, surely it was the part of a true friend to remove every scruple from his conscience, and smooth away every obstacle to a love not to be condemned because it was disinterested.

After this conversation, Lady Glenalvon sought Kenelm, found him gloomily musing on the banks of the trout-stream, took his arm, led him into the sombre glades of the fir grove, and listened patiently to all he had to say. Even then her woman's heart was not won to his reasonings, until he said pathetically, "You thanked me once for saving your son's life; you said then that you could never repay me; you can repay me tenfold. Could your son who is now, we trust, in heaven, look down and judge between us, do you think he would approve you if you refuse?"

Then Lady Glenalvon wept, and took his hand, kissed his forehead as a mother might kiss it, and said, "You triumph; I will go to Lady Chillingly at once. Marry her whom you so love, on one condition; marry her from my house."

Lady Glenalvon was not one of those women who serve a friend by halves. She knew well how to propitiate and reason down the apathetic temperament of Lady Chillingly; she did not cease till that lady herself came into Kenelm's room, and said very quietly,

"So you are going to propose to Miss Mordaunt, the Warwickshire Mordaunts I suppose. Lady Glenalvon says she is a very lovely girl, and will stay with her before the wedding. And, as the young lady is an orphan, Lady Glenalvon's uncle the Duke, who is connected with the eldest branch of the Mordaunts, will give her away. It will be a very brilliant affair. I am sure I wish you happy, it is time you should have sown your wild oats."

Two days after the consent thus formally given, Kenelm quitted Exmundham. Sir Peter would have accompanied him to pay his respects to the intended, but the agitation he had gone through brought on a sharp twinge of the gout, which consigned his feet to flannels.

After Kenelm had gone, Lady Glenalvon went into Cecilia's room. Cecilia was seated very desolately by the open window; she had detected that something of an anxious and painful nature had been weighing upon the minds of father and son, and had connected it with the letter which had so disturbed the even mind of Sir Peter; but she did not divine what the something was, and if mortified by a certain reserve, more distant than heretofore, which had characterized Kenelm's manner towards herself, the mortification was less sensibly felt than a tender sympathy for the sadness she had observed on his face, and yearned to soothe. His reserve had, however, made her own manner more reserved than of old, for which she was now rather chiding herself than reproaching him.

Lady Glenalvon put her arms round Cecilia's neck and kissed her, whispering, "That man has so disappointed me, he is so unworthy of the happiness I had once hoped for him!"

"Whom do you speak of?" murmured Cecilia, turning very pale.

"Kenelm Chillingly. It seems that he has conceived a fancy for some penniless girl whom he has met in his wanderings, has come here to get the consent of his parents to propose to her, has obtained their consent, and is gone to propose."

Cecilia remained silent for a moment with her eyes closed, then she said, "He is worthy of all happiness, and he would never make an unworthy choice. Heaven bless him—and—and——" She would have added, "his bride," but her lips refused to utter the word bride.

"Cousin Gordon is worth ten of him," cried Lady Glenalvon, indignantly.

She had served Kenelm, but she had not forgiven him.

CHAPTER V.

KENELM slept in London that night, and, the next day being singularly fine for an English summer, he resolved to go to Moleswich on foot. He had no need this time to encumber himself with a knapsack; he had left sufficient change of dress in his lodgings at Cromwell Lodge.

It was towards the evening when he found himself in one of the prettiest rural villages by which

"Wanders the hoary Thames along
His silver-winding way."

It was not in the direct road from London to Moleswich, but it was a pleasanter way for a pedestrian. And when, quitting the long street of the sultry village, he came to the shelving margin of the river, he was glad to rest awhile, enjoy the cool of the rippling waters, and listen to their placid murmurs amid the rushes in the bordering shallows. He had ample time before him. His rambles while at Cromwell Lodge had made him familiar with the district for miles round Moleswich, and he knew that a footpath through the fields at the right would lead him, in less than an hour, to the side of the tributary brook on which Cromwell Lodge was placed, opposite the wooden bridge which conducted to Grasmere and Moleswich.

To one who loves the romance of history, English history, the whole course of the Thames is full of charm. Ah! could I go back to the days in which younger generations than that of Kenelm Chillingly were unborn, when every wave of the Rhine spoke of history and romance to me, what fairies should meet on thy banks, O thou our own Father Thames! Perhaps some day a German pilgrim may repay tenfold to thee the tribute rendered by the English kinsman to the Father Rhine.

Listening to the whispers of the reeds, Kenelm Chillingly felt the haunting influence of the legendary stream. Many a poetic incident or tradition in antique chronicle, many a votive rhyme in song, dear to forefathers whose very names have become a poetry to us, thronged dimly and confusedly back to his memory, which had little cared to retain such graceful trinkets in the treasure-house of love. But everything that, from childhood upward, connects itself with romance—revives with yet fresher bloom in the memories of him who loves.

And to this man, through the first perilous season of youth, so abnormally safe from youth's most wonted peril,—to this would-be pupil of realism, this learned adept in the schools of a Welby or a Mivers,—to this man, Love came at last as with the fatal powers of the fabled Cytherèa; and with that love all the realisms of life became ideals, all the stern lines of our commonplace destinies undulating into curves of beauty, all the trite sounds of our everyday life attuned into delicacies of song. How full of sanguine yet dreamy bliss was his heart,—and seemed his future,—in the gentle breeze and the softened glow of that summer eve! He should see Lily the next morn, and his lips were now free to say all that they had as yet suppressed.

Suddenly he was aroused from the half-awake, half-asleep happiness that belongs to the moments in which we transport ourselves into Elysium, by the carol of a voice more loudly joyous than that of his own heart—

"Singing—singing,
Lustily singing,
Down the road, with his dogs before,
Came the Ritter of Nierestein."

Kenelm turned his head so quickly that he frightened Max, who had for the last minute been standing behind him inquisitively with one paw raised, and sniffing, in some doubt whether he recognized an old acquaintance; but at Kenelm's quick movement the animal broke into a nervous bark, and ran back to his master.

The Minstrel, little heeding the figure reclined on the bank, would have passed on with his light tread and his cheery carol, but Kenelm rose to his feet, and holding out his hand, said, "I hope you don't share Max's alarm at meeting me again?"

"Ah, my young philosopher, is it indeed you?"

"If I am to be designated a philosopher it is certainly not I. And, honestly speaking, I am not the same. I, who spent that pleasant day with you among the fields round Luscombe two years ago——"

"Or who advised me at Tor Hadham to string my lyre to the praise of a beefsteak. I, too, am not quite the same, I, whose dog presented you with the begging-tray."

"Yet you still go through the world singing."

"Even that vagrant singing time is pretty well over. But I disturbed you from your repose. I would rather share it; you are probably not going my way, and as I am in no hurry, I should not like to lose the opportunity chance has so happily given me of renewing acquaintance with one who has often been present to my thoughts since we last met." Thus saying, the Minstrel stretched himself at ease on the bank, and Kenelm followed his example.

There certainly was a change in the owner of the dog with the begging-tray, a change in costume, in countenance, in that indescribable self-evidence which we call "manner." The costume was not that Bohemian attire in which Kenelm had first encountered the Wandering Minstrel, nor the studied, more graceful garb, which so well became his shapely form, during his visit to Luscombe. It was now neatly simple, the cool and quiet summer dress any English gentleman might adopt in a long rural walk. And as he uncovered his head to court the cooling breeze, there was a graver dignity in the man's handsome Rubens-like face, a line of more concentrated thought in the spacious forehead, a thread or two of gray shimmering here and there through the thick auburn curls of hair and beard. And in his manner, though still very frank, there was just perceptible a sort of self-assertion, not offensive, but manly; such as does not misbecome one of maturer years, and of some established position, addressing another man much younger than himself, who in all probability has achieved no position at all beyond that which the accident of birth might assign to him.

"Yes," said the Minstrel, with a half-suppressed sigh, "the last year of my vagrant holidays has come to its close. I recollect that the first day we met by the road-side fountain, I advised you to do like me, seek amusement and adventure as a foot traveller. Now, seeing you, evidently a gentleman by education and birth, still a foot traveller, I feel as if I ought to say, 'You have had enough of such experience; vagabond life has its perils as well as charms; cease it and settle down.'"

"I think of doing so," replied Kenelm, laconically.

"In a profession?—army—law—medicine?"

"No."

"Ah, in marriage then. Right; give me your hand on that. So a petticoat indeed has at last found its charm for you in the actual world, as well as on the canvas of a picture?"

"I conclude," said Kenelm,—evading any direct notice of that playful taunt,—"I conclude from your remark that it is in marriage you are about to settle down."

"Ay, could I have done so before I should have been saved from many errors, and been many years nearer to the goal which dazzled my sight through the haze of my boyish dreams."

"What is that goal—the grave?"

"The grave! That which allows of no grave—Fame."

"I see—despite of what you just now said—you still mean to go through the world seeking a poet's fame."

"Alas! I resign that fancy," said the Minstrel, with another half-sigh. "It was not indeed wholly, but in great part the hope of the poet's fame that made me a truant in the way to that which destiny, and such few gifts as nature conceded to me, marked out for my proper and only goal. But what a strange, delusive Will-o'-the-Wisp the love of verse-making is! How rarely a man of good sense deceives himself as to other things for which he is fitted, in which he can succeed; but let him once drink into his being the charm of verse-making, how the glamour of the charm bewitches his understanding! how long it is before he can believe that the world will not take his word for it, when he cries out to sun, moon, and stars, 'I, too, am a poet.' And with what agonies, as if at the wrench of soul from life, he resigns himself at last to the conviction, that whether he or the world be right, it comes to the same thing. Who can plead his cause before a court that will not give him a hearing?"

It was with an emotion so passionately strong, and so intensely painful, that the owner of the dog with the begging-tray thus spoke, that Kenelm felt, through sympathy, as if he himself were torn asunder by the wrench of life from soul. But then, Kenelm was a mortal so eccentric, that, if a single acute suffering endured by a fellow-mortal could be brought before the evidence of his senses, I doubt whether he would not have suffered as much as that fellow-mortal. So that, though if there were a thing in the world which Kenelm Chillingly would care not to do, it was verse-making, his mind involuntarily hastened to the arguments by which he could best mitigate the pang of the verse-maker.

Quoth he—"According to my very scanty reading, you share the love of verse-making with men the most illustrious in careers which have achieved the goal of fame. It must, then, be a very noble love—Augustus, Pollio, Varius, Mæcenas—the greatest statesmen of their day; they were verse-makers. Cardinal Richelieu was a verse-maker; Walter Raleigh and Philip Sidney; Fox, Burke, Sheridan, Warren Hastings, Canning—even the grave William Pitt; all were verse-makers. Verse-making did not retard—no doubt the qualities essential to verse-making accelerated—their race to the goal of fame. What great painters have been verse-makers! Michael Angelo, Leonardo da Vinci, Salvator Rosa"—and Heaven knows how many other great names Kenelm Chillingly might have proceeded to add to his list, if the Minstrel had not here interposed.

"What! all those mighty painters were verse-makers?"

"Verse-makers so good, especially Michael Angelo—the greatest painter of all—that they would have had the fame of poets, if, unfortunately for that goal of fame, their glory in the sister art of painting did not outshine it. But when you give to your gift of song the modest title of verse-making, permit me to observe that your gift is perfectly distinct from that of the verse-maker. Your gift, whatever it may be, could not exist without some sympathy with the non-verse-making human heart. No doubt, in your foot-travels, you have acquired not only observant intimacy with external nature in the shifting hues at each hour of a distant mountain, in the lengthening shadows which yon sunset casts on the waters at our feet, in the habits of the thrush dropped fearlessly close beside me, in that turf moistened by its neighbourhood to those dripping rushes, all of which I could describe no less accurately than you—as a Peter Bell might describe them no less accurately than a William Wordsworth. But in such songs of yours as you have permitted me to hear, you seem to have escaped out of that elementary accidence of the poet's art, and to touch, no matter how slightly, on the only lasting interest which the universal heart of man can have in the song of the poet—viz., in the sound which the poet's individual sympathy draws forth from the latent chords in that universal heart. As for what you call 'the world,' what is it more than the fashion of the present day? How far the judgment of that is worth a poet's brain I can't pretend to say. But of one thing I am sure, that while I could as easily square the circle as compose a simple couplet addressed to the heart of a simple audience with sufficient felicity to decoy their praises into Max's begging-tray, I could spin out by the yard the sort of verse-making which characterizes the fashion of the present day."

Much flattered, and not a little amused, the Wandering Minstrel turned his bright countenance, no longer dimmed by a cloud, towards that of his lazily-reclined consoler, and answered gaily—

"You say that you could spin out by the yard verses in the fashion of the present day. I wish you would give me a specimen of your skill in that handiwork."

"Very well; on one condition, that you will repay my trouble by a specimen of your own verses, not in the fashion of the present day,—something which I can construe. I defy you to construe mine."

"Agreed."

"Well, then, let us take it for granted that this is the Augustan age of English poetry, and that the English language is dead, like the Latin. Suppose I am writing for a prize-medal, in English, as I wrote at college for a prize-medal, in Latin; of course, I shall be successful in proportion as I introduce the verbal elegances peculiar to our Augustan age, and also catch the prevailing poetic characteristic of that classical epoch.

"Now I think that every observant critic will admit that the striking distinctions of the poetry most in the fashion of the present day, viz., of the Augustan age, are—first, a selection of such verbal elegances as would have been most repulsive to the barbaric taste of the preceding century; and, secondly, a very lofty disdain of all prosaic condescensions to common-sense, and an elaborate cultivation of that element of the sublime which Mr. Burke defines under the head of obscurity.

"These premises conceded, I will only ask you to choose the metre. Blank verse is very much in fashion just now."

"Pooh!—blank verse indeed—I am not going so to free your experiment from the difficulties of rhyme."

"It is all one to me," said Kenelm, yawning; "Rhyme be it: heroic, or lyrical?"

"Heroics are old-fashioned; but the Chaucer couplet, as brought to perfection by our modern poets, I think the best adapted to dainty leaves and uncrackable nuts. I accept the modern Chaucerian."

"The subject?"

"Oh, never trouble yourself about that. By whatever title your Augustan verse-maker labels his poem, his genius, like Pindar's, disdains to be cramped by the subject. Listen, and don't suffer Max to howl, if he can help it. Here goes."

And in an affected, but emphatic, sing-song, Kenelm began:—

> 'In Attica the gentle Pythias dwelt.
> Youthful he was, and passing rich: he felt
> As if nor youth nor riches could suffice
> For bliss. Dark-eyed Sophronia was a nice

> Girl: and one summer day, when Neptune drove
> His sea-car slowly and the olive grove
> That skirts Ilissus, to thy shell, Harmonia,
> Rippled, he said 'I love thee' to Sophronia.
> Crocus and iris, when they heard him, wagg'd
> Their pretty heads in glee: the honey-bagg'd
> Bees became altars: and the forest dove
> Her plumage smooth'd. Such is the charm of love.
> Of this sweet story do ye long for more?
> Wait till I publish it in volumes four;
> Which certain critics, my good friends, will cry
> Up beyond Chaucer. Take their word for't. I
> Say 'Trust them: but not read,—or you'll not buy.'"

"You have certainly kept your word," said the Minstrel, laughing. "And if this be the Augustan age, and the English were a dead language, you deserve to win the prize medal."

"You flatter me," said Kenelm, modestly. "But if I, who never before strung two rhymes together, can improvise so readily in the style of the present day, why should not a practical rhymester like yourself dash off at a sitting a volume or so in the same style; disguising completely the verbal elegances borrowed, adding to the delicacies of the rhyme by the frequent introduction of a line that will not scan, and towering yet more into the sublime by becoming yet more unintelligible. Do that, and I promise you the most glowing panegyric in 'The Londoner,' for I will write it myself."

"'The Londoner!'" exclaimed the Minstrel, with an angry flush on his cheek and brow. "My bitter, relentless enemy."

"I fear, then, you have as little studied the critical press of the Augustan age as you have imbued your Muse with the classical spirit of its verse. For the art of writing a man must cultivate himself. The art of being reviewed consists in cultivating the acquaintance of reviewers. In the Augustan age criticism is cliquism. Belong to a clique, and you are Horace or Tibullus. Belong to no clique, and, of course, you are Bavius or Mævius. 'The Londoner' is the enemy of no man—it holds all men in equal contempt. But as, in order to amuse, it must abuse, it compensates the praise it is compelled to bestow upon the members of its clique by heaping additional scorn upon all who are cliqueless. Hit him hard, he has no friends."

"Ah," said the Minstrel, "I believe that there is much truth in what you say. I never had a friend among the cliques. And Heaven knows with what pertinacity those from whom I, in utter ignorance of the rules which govern the so-called organs of opinion, had hoped, in my time of struggle, for a little sympathy,—a kindly encouragement,—have combined to crush me down. They succeeded long. But at last I venture to hope that I am beating them. Happily, Nature endowed me with a sanguine, joyous, elastic temperament. He who never despairs seldom completely fails."

This speech rather perplexed Kenelm, for had not the Minstrel declared that his singing days were over, that he had decided on the renunciation of verse-making? What other path to fame, from which the critics had not been able to exclude his steps, was he, then, now pursuing? he whom Kenelm had assumed to belong to some commercial money-making firm. No doubt some less difficult prose-track; probably a novel. Everybody writes novels nowadays, and as the public will read novels without being told to do so, and will not read poetry unless they are told that they ought, possibly novels are not quite so much at the mercy of cliques, as are the poems of our Augustan age.

However, Kenelm did not think of seeking for further confidence on that score. His mind at that moment, not unnaturally, wandered from books and critics to love and wedlock.

"Our talk," said he, "has digressed into fretful courses—permit me to return to the starting-point. You are going to settle down into the peace of home. A peaceful home is like a good conscience. The rains without do not pierce its roof, the winds without do not shake its walls. If not an impertinent question, is it long since you have known your intended bride?"

"Yes, very long."

"And always loved her?"

"Always, from her infancy. Out of all womankind, she was designed to be my life's playmate, and my soul's purifier. I know not what might have become of me, if the thought of her had not walked beside me as my guardian angel. For, like many vagrants from the beaten high-roads of the world, there is in my nature something of that lawlessness which belongs to high animal spirits, to the zest of adventure, and the warm blood which runs into song, chiefly because song is the voice of a joy. And, no doubt, when I look back on the past years I must own that I have too often been led astray from the objects set before my reason, and cherished at my heart, by erring impulse or wanton fancy."

"Petticoat interest, I presume," interposed Kenelm dryly.

"I wish I could honestly answer 'No,'" said the Minstrel, colouring high. "But from the worst, from all that would have permanently blasted the career to which I entrust my fortunes, all that would have rendered me unworthy of the pure love that now, I trust, awaits and crowns my dreams of happiness, I have been saved by the haunting smile in a sinless infantine face. Only once was I in great peril—that hour of peril I recall with a shudder. It was at Luscombe."

"At Luscombe!"

"In the temptation of a terrible crime I thought I heard a voice say—'Mischief! Remember the little child.' In that supervention which is so readily accepted as a divine warning, when the imagination is morbidly excited, and when the conscience, though lulled asleep for a moment, is still asleep so lightly that the sigh of a breeze, the fall of a leaf, can awake it with a start of terror, I took the voice for that of my guardian angel. Thinking over it later, and coupling the voice with the moral of those weird lines you repeated to me so appositely the next day, I conclude that I am not mistaken when I say it was from your lips that the voice which preserved me came."

"I confess the impertinence—you pardon it!"

The Minstrel seized Kenelm's hand and pressed it earnestly.

"Pardon it! Oh, could you but guess what cause I have to be grateful, everlastingly grateful! That sudden cry, the remorse and horror of my own self that it struck into me—deepened by those rugged lines which the next day made me shrink in dismay from 'the face of my darling sin!' Then came the turning-point of my life. From that day, the lawless vagabond within me was killed. I mean not, indeed, the love of nature and of song which at first allured the vagabond, but the hatred of steadfast habits and of serious work—*that* was killed. I no longer trifled with my calling, I took to it as a serious duty. And when I saw her, whom fate has reserved and reared for my bride, her face was no longer in my eyes that of the playful child; the soul of the woman was dawning into it. It is but two years since that day, to me so eventful. Yet my fortunes are now secured. And if fame be not established, I am at last in a position which warrants my saying to her I love, 'The time has come when, without fear for thy future, I can ask thee to be mine.'"

The man spoke with so fervent a passion that Kenelm silently left him to recover his wonted self-possession,—not unwilling to be silent—not unwilling, in the softness of the hour, passing from roseate sunset into starry twilight, to murmur to himself, "And the time, too, has come for me!"

After a few moments the Minstrel resumed lightly and cheerily—

"Sir, your turn—pray have you long known—judging by our former conversation you cannot have long loved—the lady whom you have wooed and won?"

As Kenelm had neither as yet wooed nor won the lady in question, and did not deem it necessary to enter into any details on the subject of love particular to himself, he replied by a general observation—

"It seems to me that the coming of love is like the coming of spring—the date is not to be reckoned by the calendar. It may be slow and gradual; it may be quick and sudden. But in the morning, when we wake and recognize a change in the world without, verdure on the trees, blossoms on the sward, warmth in the sunshine, music in the air, then we say Spring has come!"

"I like your illustration. And if it be an idle question to ask a lover how long he has known the beloved one, so it is almost as idle to ask if she be not beautiful. He cannot but see in her face the beauty she has given to the world without."

"True; and that thought is poetic enough to make me remind you that I favoured you with the maiden specimen of my verse-making on condition that you repaid me by a specimen of your own practical skill in the art. And I claim the right to suggest the theme. Let it be——"

"Of a beef-steak?"

"Tush, you have worn out that tasteless joke at my expense. The theme must be of love, and if you could improvise a stanza or two expressive of the idea you just uttered I shall listen with yet more pleased attention."

"Alas! I am no improvisatore. Yet I will avenge myself on your former neglect of my craft by chanting to you a trifle somewhat in unison with the thought you ask me to versify, but which you would not stay to hear at Tor Hadham (though you did drop a shilling into Max's tray)—it was one of the songs I sang that evening, and it was not ill-received by my humble audience.

THE BEAUTY OF THE MISTRESS IS IN THE LOVER'S EYE.

"Is she not pretty, my Mabel May?
  Nobody ever yet called her so.
Are not her lineaments faultless, say?
  If I must answer you plainly—No.

"Joy to believe that the maid I love
  None but myself as she is can see;
Joy that she steals from her Heaven above,
  And is only revealed on this earth to me!"

As soon as he had finished this very artless ditty, the Minstrel rose and said—

"Now I must bid you good-bye. My way lies through those meadows, and yours, no doubt, along the high-road."

"Not so. Permit me to accompany you. I have a lodging not

far from hence, to which the path through the fields is the shortest way."

The Minstrel turned a somewhat surprised and somewhat inquisitive look towards Kenelm. But feeling, perhaps, that having withheld from his fellow-traveller all confidence as to his own name and attributes, he had no right to ask any confidence from that gentleman not voluntarily made to him, he courteously said "that he wished the way were longer, since it would be so pleasantly halved," and strode forth at a brisk pace.

The twilight was now closing into the brightness of a starry summer night, and the solitude of the fields was unbroken. Both these men, walking side by side, felt supremely happy. But happiness is like wine; its effect differing with the differing temperaments on which it acts. In this case garrulous and somewhat vaunting with the one man, warm-coloured, sensuous, impressionable to the influences of external nature, as an Æolian harp to the rise or fall of a passing wind; and, with the other man, taciturn and somewhat modestly expressed, saturnine, meditative, not indeed dull to the influences of external nature, but deeming them of no value, save where they passed out of the domain of the sensuous into that of the intellectual, and the soul of man dictated to the soul-less nature its own questions and its own replies.

The Minstrel took the talk on himself, and the talk charmed his listener. It became so really eloquent in the tones of its utterance, in the frank play of its delivery, that I could no more adequately describe it than a reporter, however faithful to every word a true orator may say, can describe that which, apart from all words, belongs to the presence of the orator himself.

Not, then, venturing to report the language of this singular itinerant, I content myself with saying that the substance of it was of the nature on which it is said most men can be eloquent: it was personal to himself. He spoke of aspirations towards the achievement of a name, dating back to the dawn of memory; of early obstacles in lowly birth, stinted fortunes; of a sudden opening to his ambition while yet in boyhood, through the generous favour of a rich man, who said, "The child has genius, I will give it the discipline of culture, one day it shall repay to the world what it owes to me;" of studies passionately begun, earnestly pursued, and mournfully suspended in early youth. He did not say how or wherefore: he rushed on to dwell upon the struggles for a livelihood for himself and those dependent on him; how in such struggles he was compelled to divert toil and energy from the systematic pursuit of the object he had once set before him; the necessities for money were too urgent to be postponed to the visions of fame. "But even," he exclaimed passionately, "even in such hasty and crude manifestations of what is within me, as circumstances limited my powers, I know that I ought to have found from those who profess to be authoritative judges the encouragement of praise. How much better, then, I should have done if I had found it! How a little praise warms out of a man the good that is in him, and the sneer of a contempt which he feels to be unjust chills the ardour to excel! However, I forced my way, so far as was then most essential to me, the sufficing breadmaker for those I loved; and in my holidays of song and ramble I found a delight that atoned for all the rest. But still the desire of fame, once conceived in childhood, once nourished through youth, never dies but in our grave. Foot and hoof may tread it down, bud, leaf, stalk; its root is too deep below the surface for them to reach, and year after year stalk and leaf and bud re-emerge. Love may depart from our mortal life; we console ourselves—the beloved will be re-united to us in the life to come. But if he who sets his heart on fame loses it in this life, what can console him?"

"Did you not say a little while ago that fame allowed of no grave?"

"True; but if we do not achieve it before we ourselves are in the grave, what comfort can it give to us? Love ascends to heaven, to which we hope ourselves to ascend; but fame remains on the earth, which we shall never again revisit. And it is because fame is earth-born that the desire for it is the most lasting, the regret for the want of it the most bitter, to the child of earth. But I shall achieve it now; it is already in my grasp."

By this time the travellers had arrived at the brook, facing the wooden bridge beside Cromwell Lodge.

Here the Minstrel halted; and Kenelm, with a certain tremble in his voice, said, "Is it not time that we should make ourselves known to each other by name? I have no longer any cause to conceal mine, indeed I never had any cause stronger than whim —Kenelm Chillingly, the only son of Sir Peter, of Exmundham, ——shire."

"I wish your father joy of so clever a son," said the Minstrel with his wonted urbanity. "You already know enough of me to be aware that I am of much humbler birth and station than you; but if you chance to have visited the exhibition of the Royal Academy this year—ah! I understand that start—you might have recognized a picture of which you have seen the rudimentary sketch, 'The girl with the flower-ball,' one of three pictures very severely handled by 'The Londoner,' but, in spite of that potent enemy, ensuring fortune and promising fame to the Wandering Minstrel, whose name, if the sight of the pictures had induced you to inquire into that, you would have found to be Walter Melville. Next January I hope, thanks to that picture, to add, 'Associate of the Royal Academy.' The public will not let them keep me out of it, in spite of 'The Londoner.' You are probably an expected guest at one of the more imposing villas from which we see the distant lights. I am going to a very humble cottage, in which henceforth I hope to find my established home. I am there now only for a few days, but pray let me welcome you there before I leave. The cottage is called Grasmere."

CHAPTER VI.

THE Minstrel gave a cordial parting shake of the hand to the fellow-traveller whom he had advised to settle down, not noticing how very cold had become the hand in his own genial grasp. Lightly he passed over the wooden bridge, preceded by Max, and merrily, when he had gained the other side of the bridge, came upon Kenelm's ear, through the hush of the luminous night, the verse of the uncompleted love song—

" Singing—singing,
Lustily singing,
Down the road with his dogs before,
Came the Ritter of Nierestein."

Love song, uncompleted—why uncompleted? It was not given to Kenelm to divine the why. It was a love song versifying one of the prettiest fairy tales in the world, which was a great favourite with Lily, and which Lion had promised Lily to versify, but only to complete it in her presence, and to her perfect satisfaction.

CHAPTER VII.

IF I could not venture to place upon paper the exact words of an eloquent coveter of fame, the earth-born, still less can I dare to place upon paper all that passed through the voiceless heart of a coveter of love, the heaven-born. From the hour in which Kenelm Chillingly had parted from

Walter Melville, until somewhere between sunrise and noon the next day, the summer joyousness of that external nature which does now and then, though, for the most part, deceitfully, address to the soul of man questions and answers all her soul-less own, laughed away the gloom of his misgivings.

No doubt this Walter Melville was the beloved guardian of Lily; no doubt it was Lily whom he designated as reserved and reared to become his bride. But on that question Lily herself had the sovereign voice. It remained yet to be seen whether Kenelm had deceived himself in the belief that had made the world so beautiful to him since the hour of their last parting. At all events it was due to her, due even to his rival, to assert his own claim to her choice. And the more he recalled all that Lily had ever said to him of her guardian, so openly, so frankly, proclaiming affection, admiration, gratitude, the more convincingly his reasonings allayed his fears, whispering, "So might a child speak of a parent; not so does the maiden speak of the man she loves; she can scarcely trust herself to praise."

In fine, it was not in despondent mood, nor with dejected looks, that, a little before noon, Kenelm crossed the bridge and re-entered the enchanted land of Grasmere. In answer to his inquiries, the servant who opened the door said that neither Mr. Melville nor Miss Mordaunt were at home; they had but just gone out together for a walk. He was about to turn back, when Mrs. Cameron came into the hall, and, rather by gesture than words, invited him to enter. Kenelm followed her into the drawing-room, taking his seat beside her. He was about to speak, when she interrupted him in a tone of voice so unlike its usual languor, so keen, so sharp, that it sounded like a cry of distress.

"I was just about to come to you. Happily, however, you find me alone, and what may pass between us will be soon over. But first tell me—you have seen your parents; you have asked their consent to wed a girl such as I described; tell me, oh tell me that that consent is refused!"

"On the contrary, I am here with their full permission to ask the hand of your niece."

Mrs. Cameron sank back in her chair, rocking herself to and fro in the posture of a person in great pain.

"I feared that. Walter said he had met you last evening; that you, like himself, entertained the thought of marriage. You, of course, when you learnt his name, must have known with whom his thought was connected. Happily, he could not divine what was the choice to which your youthful fancy had been so blindly led."

"My dear Mrs. Cameron," said Kenelm, very mildly, but very firmly, "you were aware of the purpose for which I left Moleswich a few days ago, and it seems to me that you might have forestalled my intention, the intention which brings me thus early to your house. I come to say to Miss Mordaunt's guardian, 'I ask the hand of your ward. If you also woo her, I have a very noble rival. With both of us no consideration for our own happiness can be comparable to the duty of consulting hers. Let her choose between the two.'"

"Impossible!" exclaimed Mrs. Cameron; "impossible! You know not what you say; know not, guess not, how sacred are the claims of Walter Melville to all that the orphan whom he has protected from her very birth can give him in return. She has no right to a preference for another; her heart is too grateful to admit of one. If the choice were given to her between him and you, it is he whom she would choose. Solemnly I assure you of this. Do not, then, subject her to the pain of such a choice. Suppose, if you will, that you had attracted her fancy, and that now you proclaimed your love and urged your suit, she would not, must not, the less reject your hand, but you might cloud her happiness in accepting Melville's. Be generous. Conquer your own fancy; it can be but a passing one. Speak not to her, nor to Mr. Melville, of a wish which can never be realized. Go hence, silently, and at once."

The words and the manner of the pale imploring woman struck a vague awe into the heart of her listener. But he did not the less resolutely answer, "I cannot obey you. It seems to me that my honour commands me to prove to your niece that, if I mistook the nature of her feelings towards me, I did not, by word or look, lead her to believe mine towards herself were less in earnest than they are; and it seems scarcely less honourable towards my worthy rival to endanger his own future happiness, should he discover later that his bride would have been happier with another. Why be so mysteriously apprehensive? If, as you say, with such apparent conviction, there is no doubt of your niece's preference for another, at a word from her own lips I depart, and you will see me no more. But that word must be said by her; and if you will not permit me to ask for it in your own house, I will take my chance of finding her now, on her walk with Mr. Melville; and, could he deny me the right to speak to her alone, that which I would say can be said in his presence. Ah! madam, have you no mercy for the heart that you so needlessly torture? If I must bear the worst, let me learn it, and at once."

"Learn it, then, from my lips," said Mrs. Cameron, speaking

with voice unnaturally calm, and features rigidly set into stern composure. "And I place the secret you wrung from me under the seal of that honour, which you so vauntingly make your excuse for imperilling the peace of the home I ought never to have suffered you to enter. An honest couple, of humble station and narrow means, had an only son, who evinced in early childhood talents so remarkable that they attracted the notice of the father's employer, a rich man of very benevolent heart and very cultivated taste. He sent the child, at his expense, to a first-rate commercial school, meaning to provide for him later in his own firm. The rich man was the head partner of an eminent bank; but very infirm health, and tastes much estranged from business, had induced him to retire from all active share in the firm, the management of which was confined to a son whom he idolized. But the talents of the *protégé* he had sent to school, there took so passionate a direction towards art, and estranged from trade; and his designs in drawing, when shown to connoisseurs, were deemed so promising of future excellence; that the patron changed his original intention, entered him as a pupil in the studio of a distinguished French painter, and afterwards bade him perfect his taste by the study of Italian and Flemish masterpieces."

"He was still abroad, when—" here Mrs. Cameron stopped, with visible effort, suppressed a sob, and went on, whisperingly, through teeth clenched together—"when a thunderbolt fell on the house of the patron, shattering his fortunes, blasting his name. The son, unknown to the father, had been decoyed into speculations, which proved unfortunate; the loss might have been easily retrieved in the first instance, unhappily he took the wrong course to retrieve it, and launched into new hazards. I must be brief. One day the world was startled by the news that a firm, famed for its supposed wealth and solidity, was bankrupt. Dishonesty was alleged, was proved, not against the father,—he went forth from the trial, censured indeed for neglect, not condemned for fraud, but a penniless pauper. The—son—the son—the idolized son—was removed from the prisoner's dock, a convicted felon, sentenced to penal servitude. Escaped that sentence by—by—you guess—you guess. How could he escape except through death?—death by his own guilty deed."

Almost as much overpowered by emotion as Mrs. Cameron herself, Kenelm covered his bended face with one hand, stretching out the other blindly to clasp her own, but she would not take it.

A dreary foreboding. Again before his eyes rose the old gray tower—again in his ears thrilled the tragic tale of the Fletwodes.

What was yet left untold held the young man in spell-bound silence. Mrs. Cameron resumed—

"I said the father was a penniless pauper; he died lingeringly bed-ridden. But one faithful friend did not desert that bed; the youth to whose genius his wealth had ministered. He had come from abroad with some modest savings from the sale of copies or sketches made in Florence. These savings kept a roof over the heads of the old man and the two helpless, broken-hearted women —paupers like himself,—his own daughter and his son's widow. When the savings were gone, the young man stooped from his destined calling, found employment somehow, no matter how alien to his tastes, and these three whom his toil supported never wanted a home or food. Well, a few weeks after her husband's terrible death, his young widow (they had not been a year married) gave birth to a child—a girl. She did not survive the exhaustion of her confinement many days. The shock of her death snapped the feeble thread of the poor father's life. Both were borne to the grave on the same day. Before they died, both made the same prayer to their sole two mourners, the felon's sister, the old man's young benefactor. The prayer was this, that the new-born infant should be reared, however humbly, in ignorance of her birth, of a father's guilt and shame. She was not to pass a suppliant for charity to rich and high-born kinsfolk, who had vouchsafed no word even of pity to the felon's guiltless father and as guiltless wife. That promise has been kept till now. I am that daughter. The name I bear, and the name which I gave to my niece, are not ours, save as we may indirectly claim them through alliances centuries ago. I have never married. I was to have been a bride, bringing to the representative of no ignoble house what was to have been a princely dower; the wedding day was fixed, when the bolt fell. I have never again seen my betrothed. He went abroad and died there. I think he loved me, he knew I loved him. Who can blame him for deserting me? Who could marry the felon's sister? Who would marry the felon's child? Who, but one? The man who knows her secret, and will guard it; the man who, caring little for other education, has helped to instil into her spotless childhood so steadfast a love of truth, so exquisite a pride of honour, that did she know such ignominy rested on her birth, she would pine herself away."

"Is there only one man on earth," cried Kenelm, suddenly, rearing his face—till then concealed and downcast—and with a loftiness of pride on its aspect, new to its wonted mildness,—"is there only one man who would deem the virgin, at whose feet he desires to kneel and say, 'Deign to be the queen of my life,' not far too noble in herself to be debased by the sins of others before she was even born; is there only one man who does not think that the love of truth and the pride of honour are most royal attributes of woman or of man, no matter whether the fathers of the woman or the man were pirates as lawless as the fathers of Norman kings, or liars as unscrupulous, where their own interests were concerned, as have been the crowned representatives of lines as deservedly famous as Cæsars and Bourbons, Tudors and Stuarts? Nobility, like genius, is inborn. One man alone guard *her* secret!—guard a secret that if made known could trouble a heart that recoils from shame! Ah, madam, we Chillinglys are a very obscure undistinguished race, but for more than a thousand years we have been English gentlemen. Guard her secret rather than risk the chance of discovery that could give her a pang? I would pass my whole life by her side in Kamtchatka, and even there I would not snatch a glimpse of the secret itself with mine own eyes, it should be so closely muffled and wrapped round by the folds of reverence and worship."

This burst of passion seemed to Mrs. Cameron the senseless declamation of an inexperienced, hot-headed young man, and putting it aside, much as a great lawyer dismisses as balderdash the florid rhetoric of some junior counsel, rhetoric in which the great lawyer had once indulged, or as a woman for whom romance is over dismisses as idle verbiage some romantic sentiment that befools her young daughter, Mrs. Cameron simply replied, "All this is hollow talk, Mr. Chillingly; let us come to the point. After all I have said, do you mean to persist in your suit to my niece?"

"I persist."

"What!" she cried, this time indignantly, and with generous indignation; "what, even were it possible that you could win your parents' consent to marry the child of a man condemned to penal servitude, or, consistently with the duties a son owes to parents, conceal that fact from them, could you, born to a station on which every gossip will ask, 'Who and what is the name of the future Lady Chillingly?' believe that the who and the what will never be discovered! Have you, a mere stranger, unknown to us a few weeks ago, a right to say to Walter Melville, 'Resign to me that which is your sole reward for the sublime sacrifices, for the loyal devotion, for the watchful tenderness of patient years!'"

"Surely, madam," cried Kenelm, more startled, more shaken in soul by this appeal, than by the previous revelations—"surely, when we last parted, when I confided to you my love for your niece, when you consented to my proposal to return home, and obtain my father's approval of my suit,—surely then was the time to say, 'No; a suitor with claims paramount and irresistible has come before you.'"

"I did not then know, Heaven is my witness, I did not then even suspect, that Walter Melville ever dreamed of seeking a wife in the child who had grown up under his eyes. You must own, indeed, how much I discouraged your suit; I could not discourage it more without revealing the secret of her birth, only to be revealed as an extreme necessity. But my persuasion was, that your father would not consent to your alliance with one so far beneath the expectations he was entitled to form, and the refusal of that consent would terminate all further acquaintance between you and Lily, leaving her secret undisclosed. It was not till you had left, only indeed two days ago, that I received from Walter Melville a letter, which told me what I had never before conjectured. Here is the letter, read it, and then say if you have the heart to force yourself into rivalry, with—with——" She broke off, choked by her exertion, thrust the letter into his hands, and with keen, eager, hungry stare watched his countenance while he read.

"—— STREET, BLOOMSBURY.

"MY DEAR FRIEND,—Joy and triumph! My picture is completed; the picture on which, for so many months, I have worked night and day in this den of a studio, without a glimpse of the green fields, concealing my address from every one, even from you, lest I might be tempted to suspend my labours. The picture is completed—it is sold; guess the price? Fifteen hundred guineas, and to a dealer—a dealer! Think of that! It is to be carried about the country, exhibited by itself. You remember those three little landscapes of mine which two years ago I would gladly have sold for ten pounds, only neither Lily nor you would let me. My good friend and earliest patron, the German merchant at Luscombe, who called on me yesterday, offered to cover them with guineas thrice piled over the canvas. Imagine how happy I felt when I forced him to accept them as a present. What a leap in a man's life it is when he can afford to say, 'I give!' Now then, at last, at last I am in a position which justifies the utterance of the hope which has for eighteen years been my solace, my support; been the sunbeam that ever shone through the gloom, when my fate was at the darkest; been the melody that buoyed me aloft as in the song of the skylark, when in the voices of men I heard but the laugh of scorn. Do you remember the night on which Lily's mother besought us to bring up her child in ignorance of her parentage, not even communicate to unkind and disdainful relatives that such a child was born? do you remember how plaintively, and yet how proudly, she so nobly born, so luxuriously nurtured, clasping my hand when I ventured to remonstrate, and say that her own family could not condemn her child because of the father's guilt,—she, the proudest woman I ever knew, she whose smile I can at rare moments detect in Lily, raised her head from her pillow, and gasped forth—

"'I am dying—the last words of the dying are commands. I command you to see that my child's lot is not that of a felon's daughter transported to the hearth of nobles. To be happy, her lot must be humble—no roof too humble to shelter, no husband too humble to wed, the felon's daughter.'

"From that hour I formed the resolve that I would keep hand and heart free, that when the grandchild of my princely benefactor grew up into womanhood I might say to her, 'I am humbly born, but thy mother would have given thee to me.' The new-born, consigned to our charge, has now ripened into woman, and I have now so assured my fortune that it is no longer poverty and struggle that I should ask her to share. I am conscious that, were her fate not so exceptional, this hope of mine would be a vain presumption—conscious that I am but the creature of her grandsire's bounty, and that from it springs all I ever can be—conscious of the disparity in years—conscious of many a past error and present fault. But, as fate so ordains, such considerations are trivial; I am her rightful choice. What other choice, compatible with these necessities which weigh, dear and honoured friend, immeasurably more on your sense of honour than they do upon mine, and yet mine is not dull? Granting, then, that you, her nearest and most responsible relative, do not contemn me for presumption, all else seems to me clear. Lily's childlike affection for me is too deep and too fond not to warm into a wife's love. Happily, too, she has not been reared in the stereotyped boarding-school shallownesses of knowledge and vulgarities of gentility; but educated, like myself, by the free influences of nature, longing for no halls and palaces save those that we build as we list, in fairyland; educated to comprehend and to share the fancies, which are more than book-lore to the worshipper of art and song. In a day or two, perhaps the day after you receive this, I shall be able to escape from London, and most likely shall come on foot as usual. How I long to see once more the woodbine on the hedgerows, the green blades of the corn-fields, the sunny lapse of the river, and dearer still the tiny falls of our own little noisy rill! Meanwhile I entreat you, dearest, gentlest, most honoured of such few friends as my life has hitherto won to itself, to consider well the direct purport of this letter. If you, born in a grade so much higher than mine, feel that it is unwarrantable insolence in me to aspire to the hand of my patron's grandchild, say so plainly; and I remain not less grateful for your friendship, than I was to your goodness when dining for the first time at your father's palace. Shy and sensitive and young, I felt that his grand guests wondered why I was invited to the same board as themselves. You, then courted, admired, you had sympathetic compassion on the raw, sullen boy; left those, who then seemed to me like the gods and goddesses of a heathen Pantheon, to come and sit beside your father's *protégé*, and cheeringly whisper to him such words as make a low-born ambitious lad go home light-hearted, saying to himself, 'Some day or other.' And what it is to an ambitious lad, fancying himself lifted by the gods and goddesses of a Pantheon, to go home light-hearted muttering to himself 'Some day or other,' I doubt if even you can divine.

"But should you be as kind to the presumptuous man as you were to the bashful boy, and say, 'Realized be the dream, fulfilled be the object of your life! take from me as her next of kin, the last descendant of your benefactor,' then I venture to address to you this request. You are in the place of mother to your sister's child, act for her as a keeper now, to prepare her mind and heart for the coming change in the relations between her and me. When I last saw her, six months ago, she was still so playfully infantine that it half seems to me I should be sinning against the reverence due to a child, if I said too abruptly, 'You are woman, and I love you not as child but as woman.' And yet, time is not allowed to me for long, cautious, and gradual slide from the relationship of friend into that of lover. I now understand what the great master of my art once said to me, 'A career is a destiny.' By one of those merchant princes who now at Manchester, as they did once at Genoa or Venice, reign alike over those two civilizers of the world which to dull eyes seem antagonistic, Art and Commerce, an offer is made to me for a picture on a subject which strikes his fancy; an offer so magnificently liberal that his commerce must command my art; and the nature of the subject compels me to seek the banks of the Rhine as soon as may be. I must have all the hues of the foliage in the meridian glories of summer. I can but stay at Grasmere a very few days; but before I leave I must know this, am I going to work for Lily or am I not? On the answer to that question depends all. If not to work for her, there would be no glory in the summer, no triumph in art to me: I refuse the offer. If she says,

'Yes; it is for me you work,' then she becomes my destiny. She assures my career. Here I speak as an artist: nobody who is not an artist can guess how sovereign over even his moral being, at a certain critical epoch in his career of artist or his life of man, is the success or the failure of a single work. But I go on to speak as man. My love for Lily is such for the last six months, that though if she rejected me I should still serve art, still yearn for fame, it would be as an old man might do either. The youth of my life would be gone.

"As man I say, all my thoughts, all my dreams of happiness, distinct from Art and fame, are summed up in the one question—'Is Lily to be my wife or not?'

"Yours affectionately,
"W. M."

Kenelm returned the letter without a word.

Enraged by his silence, Mrs. Cameron exclaimed, "Now, sir, what say you? You have scarcely known Lily five weeks. What is the feverish fancy of five weeks' growth to the life-long devotion of a man like this! Do you now dare to say, 'I persist'?"

Kenelm waved his hand very quietly, as if to dismiss all conception of taunt and insult, and said with his soft melancholy eyes fixed upon the working features of Lily's aunt, "This man is more worthy of her than I. He prays you, in his letter, to prepare your niece for that change of relationship which he dreads too abruptly to break to her himself. Have you done so?"

"I have; the night I got the letter."

"And—you hesitate; speak truthfully, I implore. And—she——"

"She," answered Mrs. Cameron, feeling herself involuntarily compelled to obey the voice of that prayer—"she seemed stunned at first, muttering, 'This is a dream—it cannot be true—cannot! I Lion's wife—I—I! I, his destiny! In me his happiness!' And then she laughed her pretty child's laugh, and put her arms round my neck, and said, 'You are jesting, aunty. He could not write thus!' So I put that part of his letter under her eyes; and when she had convinced herself, her face became very grave, more like a woman's face than I ever saw it; and after a pause she cried out passionately, 'Can you think me—can I think myself—so bad, so ungrateful, as to doubt what I should answer, if Lion asked me whether I would willingly say or do anything that made him unhappy? If there be such a doubt in my heart, I would tear it out by the roots, heart and all!' Oh! Mr. Chillingly. There would be no happiness for her with another, knowing that she had blighted the life of him to whom she owes so much, though she never will learn how much more she owes." Kenelm not replying to this remark, Mrs. Cameron resumed—"I will be perfectly frank with you, Mr. Chillingly. I was not quite satisfied with Lily's manner and looks the next morning, that is, yesterday. I did fear there might be some struggle in her mind in which there entered a thought of yourself. And when Walter, on his arrival here in the evening, spoke of you as one he had met before in his rural excursions, but whose name he only learned on parting at the bridge by Cromwell Lodge, I saw that Lily turned pale, and shortly afterwards went to her own room for the night. Fearing that any interview with you, though it would not alter her resolve, might lessen her happiness on the only choice she can and ought to adopt, I resolved to visit you this morning, and make that appeal to your reason and your heart which I have done now—not, I am sure, in vain. Hush! I hear his voice!"

Melville entered the room, Lily leaning on his arm. The artist's comely face was radiant with an ineffable joyousness. Leaving Lily, he reached Kenelm's side as with a single bound, shook him heartily by the hand, and saying—"I find that you have already been a welcomed visitor in this house. Long may you be so, so say I, so (I answer for her) says my fair betrothed, to whom I need not present you."

Lily advanced, and held out her hand very timidly. Kenelm touched rather than clasped it. His own strong hand trembled like a leaf. He ventured but one glance at her face. All the bloom had died out of it, but the expression seemed to him wondrously, cruelly tranquil.

"Your betrothed—your future bride!" he said to the artist, with a mastery over his emotion rendered less difficult by the single glance at that tranquil face. "I wish you joy. All happiness to you, Miss Mordaunt. You have made a noble choice."

He looked round for his hat; it lay at his feet, but he did not see it; his eyes wandering away with uncertain vision, like those of a sleep-walker.

Mrs. Cameron picked up the hat and gave it to him.

"Thank you," he said meekly; then with a smile half sweet, half bitter, "I have so much to thank you for, Mrs. Cameron."

"But you are not going already—just as I enter too. Hold! Mrs. Cameron tells me you are lodging with my old friend Jones. Come and stop a couple of days with us, we can find you a room; the room over your butterfly cage, eh, Fairy?"

"Thank you, too. Thank you all. No; I must be in London by the first train."

Speaking thus, he had found his way to the door, bowed with the quiet grace that characterized all his movements, and was gone.

"Pardon his abruptness, Lily; he too loves; he too is impatient to find a betrothed," said the artist gaily: "but now he knows my dearest secret, I think I have a right to know his; and I will try."

He had scarcely uttered the words before he too had quitted the room and overtaken Kenelm just at the threshold.

"If you are going back to Cromwell Lodge—to pack up, I suppose —let me walk with you as far as the bridge."

Kenelm inclined his head assentingly and tacitly as they passed through the garden-gate, winding backward through the lane which skirted the garden-pales; when, at the very spot in which the day after their first and only quarrel Lily's face had been seen brightening through the evergreen, that day on which the old woman, quitting her, said, "God bless you!" and on which the vicar, walking with Kenelm, spoke of her fairy charms; well, just in that spot Lily's face appeared again, not this time *brightening* through the evergreens, unless the palest gleam of the palest moon can be said to brighten. Kenelm saw, started, halted. His companion, then in the rush of a gladsome talk, of which Kenelm had not heard a word, neither saw nor halted; he walked on mechanically, gladsome, and talking.

Lily stretched forth her hand through the evergreens. Kenelm took it reverentially. This time it was not his hand that trembled.

"Good-bye," she said in a whisper, "good-bye for ever in this world. You understand—you do understand me. Say that you do."

"I understand. Noble child—noble choice. God bless you. God comfort me!" murmured Kenelm. Their eyes met. Oh, the sadness; and, alas! oh the love in the eyes of both.

Kenelm passed on.

All said in an instant. How many Alls are said in an instant! Melville was in the midst of some glowing sentence, begun when Kenelm dropped from his side, and the end of the sentence was this:

"Words cannot say how fair seems life: how easy seems conquest of fame, dating from this day—this day"—and in his turn he halted, looked round on the sunlit landscape, and breathed deep, as if to drink into his soul all of the earth's joy and beauty which his gaze could compass, and the arch of the horizon bound.

"They who knew her even the best," resumed the artist, striding on, "even her aunt, never could guess how serious and earnest, under all her infantine prettiness of fancy, is that girl's real nature. We were walking along the brook-side, when I began to tell how solitary the world would be to me if I could not win her to my side; while I spoke she had turned aside from the path we had taken, and it was not till we were under the shadow of the church in which we shall be married that she uttered the words that gives to every cloud in my fate the silver lining; implying thus how solemnly connected in her mind was the thought of love with the sanctity of religion."

Kenelm shuddered—the church—the burial-ground—the old Gothic tomb—the flowers round the infant's grave!

"But I am talking a great deal too much about myself," resumed the artist. "Lovers are the most consummate of all egotists, and the most garrulous of all gossips. You have wished me joy on my destined nuptials, when shall I wish you joy on yours? Since we have begun to confide in each other, you are in my debt as to a confidence."

They had now gained the bridge. Kenelm turned round abruptly, "Good day; let us part here. I have nothing to confide to you that might not seem to your ears a mockery when I wish you joy. So saying, so obeying in spite of himself the anguish of his heart, Kenelm wrung his companion's hand with the force of an uncontrollable agony, and speeded over the bridge before Melville recovered his surprise.

The artist would have small claim to the essential attribute of genius—viz., the intuitive sympathy of passion with passion—if that secret of Kenelm's which he had so lightly said "he had acquired the right to learn," was not revealed to him as by an electric flash. "Poor fellow!" he said to himself, pityingly; "how natural that he should fall in love with Fairy! but happily he is so young, and such a philosopher, that it is but one of those trials through which, at least ten times a-year, I have gone with wounds that leave not a scar."

Thus soliloquizing, the warm-blooded worshipper of Nature returned homeward, too blest in the triumph of his own love to feel more than a kindly compassion for the wounded heart, consigned with no doubt of the healing result to the fickleness of youth and the consolations of philosophy. Not for a moment did the happier rival suspect that Kenelm's love was returned; that an atom in the heart of the girl who had promised to be his bride could take its light or shadow from any love but his own. Yet, more from delicacy of respect to the rival so suddenly self-betrayed than from any more prudential motive, he did not speak even to Mrs. Cameron of Kenelm's secret and sorrow; and certainly neither she nor Lily was disposed to ask any question that concerned the departed visitor.

In fact the name of Kenelm Chillingly was scarcely, if at all, mentioned in that household during the few days which elapsed before Walter Melville quitted Grasmere for the banks of the Rhine, not to return till the autumn, when his marriage with Lily was to take place. During those days Lily was calm and seemingly cheerful —her manner towards her betrothed, if more subdued, not less affectionate than of old. Mrs. Cameron congratulated herself on having so successfully got rid of Kenelm Chillingly.

CHAPTER VIII.

SO, then, but for that officious warning, uttered under the balcony at Luscombe, Kenelm Chillingly might never have had a rival in Walter Melville. But ill would any reader construe the character of Kenelm, did he think that such a thought increased the bitterness of his sorrow. No sorrow in the thought that a noble nature had been saved from the temptation to a great sin.

The good man does good merely by living. And the good he does may often mar the plans he formed for his own happiness. But he cannot regret that Heaven has permitted him to do good.

What Kenelm did feel is perhaps best explained in the letter to Sir Peter, which is here subjoined.

"MY DEAREST FATHER,—Never till my dying day shall I forget that tender desire for my happiness with which, overcoming all worldly considerations, no matter at what disappointment to your own cherished plans or ambition for the heir to your name and race, you sent me away from your roof, these words ringing in my ear like the sound of joy-bells, "Choose as you will, with my blessing on your choice. I open my heart to admit another child—your wife shall be my daughter." It is such an unspeakable comfort to me to recall those words now. Of all human affections gratitude is surely the holiest; and it blends itself with the sweetness of religion when it is gratitude to a father. And, therefore, do not grieve too much for me, when I tell you that the hopes which enchanted me when we parted are not to be fulfilled. Her hand is pledged to another— another with claims upon her preference to which mine cannot be compared; and he is himself, putting aside the accidents of birth and fortune, immeasurably my superior. In that thought—I mean the thought that the man she selects deserves her more than I do, and

P

that in his happiness she will blend her own—I shall find comfort, so soon as I can fairly reason down the first all-engrossing selfishness that follows the sense of unexpected and irremediable loss. Meanwhile you will think it not unnatural that I resort to such aids for change of heart as are afforded by change of scene. I start for the Continent to-night, and shall not rest till I reach Venice, which I have not yet seen. I feel irresistibly attracted towards still canals and gliding gondolas. I will write to you and to my dear mother the day I arrive. And I trust to write cheerfully, with full accounts of all I see and encounter. Do not, dearest father, in your letters to me revert or allude to that grief, which even the tenderest word from your own tender self might but chafe into pain more sensitive. After all, a disappointed love is a very common lot. And we meet every day men—ay, and women too—who have known it, and are thoroughly cured.

"The manliest of our modern lyrical poets has said very nobly and, no doubt, very justly,

"'To bear is to conquer our fate.'

"Ever your loving son,
"K. C."

CHAPTER IX.

NEARLY a year and a half has elapsed since the date of my last chapter. Two Englishmen were—the one seated, the other reclined at length—on one of the mounds that furrow the ascent of Posilippo. Before them spread the noiseless sea, basking in the sunshine, without visible ripple; to the left there was a distant glimpse through gaps of brushwood of the public gardens and white water of the Chiaja. They were friends who had chanced to meet abroad—unexpectedly—joined company, and travelled together for many months, chiefly in the East. They had been but a few days in Naples. The elder of the two had important affairs in England which ought to have summoned him back long since. But he did not let his friend know this; his affairs seemed to him less important than the duties he owed to one for whom he entertained that deep and noble love which is something stronger than brotherly, for with brotherly affection it combines gratitude and reverence. He knew, too, that his friend was oppressed by a haunting sorrow, of which the cause was divined by one, not revealed by the other.

To leave him, so beloved, alone with that sorrow in strange lands, was a thought not to be cherished by a friend so tender; for in the friendship of this man there was that sort of tenderness which completes a nature, thoroughly manlike, by giving it a touch of the woman's.

It was a day which in our northern climates is that of winter; in the southern clime of Naples it was mild as an English summer day, lingering on the brink of autumn. The sun sloping towards the west, and already gathering around it roseate and purple fleeces. Elsewhere the deep blue sky was without a cloudlet.

Both had been for some minutes silent; at length the man reclined on the grass—it was the younger man—said suddenly, and with no previous hint of the subject introduced, "Lay your hand on your heart, Tom, and answer me truly. Are your thoughts as clear from regrets as the heavens above us are from a cloud? Man takes regret from tears that have ceased to flow, as the heaven takes cloud from the rains that have ceased to fall."

"Regrets? Ah, I understand, for the loss of the girl I once loved to distraction! No; surely I made that clear to you many, many, many months ago, when I was your guest at Moleswich."

"Ay, but I have never, since then, spoken to you on that subject. I did not dare. It seems to me so natural that a man, in the earlier struggle between love and reason, should say, 'reason shall conquer, and has conquered;' and yet—and yet—as time glides on, feel that the conquerors who cannot put down rebellion have a very uneasy reign. Answer me not as at Moleswich, during the first struggle, but now, in the after-day, when reaction from struggle comes."

"Upon my honour," answered the friend, "I have had no reaction at all. I was cured entirely, when I had once seen Jessie again, another man's wife, mother to his child, happy in her marriage; and, whether she was changed or not—very different from the sort of wife I should like to marry, now that I am no longer a village farrier."

"And, I remember, you spoke of some other girl whom it would suit you to marry. You have been long abroad from her. Do you ever think of her—think of her still as your future wife? Can you love her? Can you, who have once loved so faithfully, love again?"

"I am sure of that. I love Emily better than I did when I left England. We correspond. She writes such nice letters." Tom hesitated, blushed, and continued timidly, "I should like to show you one of her letters."

"Do."

Tom drew forth the last of such letters from his breast pocket.

Kenelm raised himself from the grass, took the letter, and read slowly, carefully, while Tom watched in vain for some approving smile to brighten up the dark beauty of that melancholy face.

Certainly it was the letter a man in love might show with pride to a friend; the letter of a lady, well educated, well brought up, evincing affection modestly, intelligence modestly too; the sort of letter in which a mother who loved her daughter, and approved the daughter's choice, could not have suggested a correction.

As Kenelm gave back the letter, his eyes met his friend's. Those were eager eyes—eyes hungering for praise. Kenelm's heart smote him for that worst of sins in friendship—want of sympathy; and that uneasy heart forced to his lips congratulations, not perhaps quite sincere, but which amply satisfied the lover. In uttering them, Kenelm rose to his feet, threw his arm round his friend's shoulder, and said, "Are you not tired of this place, Tom? I am. Let us go back to England to-morrow." Tom's honest face brightened vividly. "How selfish and egotistical I have been!" continued Kenelm; "I ought to have thought more of you, your career, your marriage—pardon me——"

"Pardon you—pardon! Don't I owe to you all—owe to you Emily herself. If you had never come to Graveleigh, never said, 'Be my friend,' what should I have been now? what—what?"

The next day the two friends quitted Naples *en route* for England, not exchanging many words by the way. The old loquacious crotchety humour of Kenelm had deserted him. A duller companion than he was you could not have conceived. He might have been the hero of a young lady's novel.

It was only when they parted in London, that Kenelm evinced more secret purpose, more external emotion than one of his heraldic Daces shifting from the bed to the surface of a waveless pond.

"If I have rightly understood you, Tom, all this change in you, all this cure of torturing regret, was wrought—wrought lastingly—wrought so as to leave you heart-free for the world's actions and a home's peace, on that eve when you saw her whose face till then had haunted you, another man's happy wife, and in so seeing her, either her face was changed, or your heart became so."

"Quite true. I might express it otherwise, but the fact remains the same."

"God bless you, Tom; bless you in your career without, in your home within," said Kenelm, wringing his friend's hand at the door of the carriage that was to whirl to love, and wealth, and station, the whilom bully of a village, along the iron groove of that contrivance, which, though now the tritest of prosaic realities, seemed once too poetical for a poet's wildest visions.

CHAPTER X.

A WINTER'S evening at Moleswich. Very different from a winter sunset at Naples. It is intensely cold. There has been a slight fall of snow, accompanied with severe, bright, clear frost, a thin sprinkling of white on the pavements. Kenelm Chillingly entered the town on foot, no longer a knapsack on his back. Passing through the main street, he paused a moment at the door of Will Somers. The shop was closed. No, he would not stay there to ask in a roundabout way for news. He would go in straightforwardly and manfully to Grasmere. He would take the inmates there by surprise. The sooner he could bring Tom's experience home to himself, the better. He had schooled his heart to rely on that experience, and it brought him back the old elasticity of his stride. In his lofty carriage and buoyant face were again visible the old haughtiness of the indifferentism that keeps itself aloof from the turbulent emotions and conventional frivolities of those whom its philosophy pities and scorns.

"Ha! ha!" laughed he who like Swift never laughed aloud, and often laughed inaudibly. "Ha! ha! I shall exorcise the ghost of my grief. I shall never be haunted again. If that stormy creature whom love might have maddened into crime, if *he* were cured of love at once by a single visit to the home of her whose face was changed to him—for the smiles and the tears of it had become the property of another man—how much more should I be left without a scar! I, the heir of the Chillinglys! I, the kinsman of a Mivers! I, the pupil of a Welby! I—I, Kenelm Chillingly, to be thus—thus——" Here, in the midst of his boastful soliloquy, the well-remembered brook rushed suddenly upon eye and ear, gleaming and moaning under the wintry moon. Kenelm Chillingly stopped, covered his face with his hands, and burst into a passion of tears.

Recovering himself slowly, he went along the path, every step of which was haunted by the form of Lily.

He reached the garden gate of Grasmere, lifted the latch, and entered. As he did so, a man, touching his hat, rushed beside, and advanced before him—the village postman. Kenelm drew back, allowing the man to pass to the door, and as he thus drew back, he caught a side view of lighted windows looking on the lawn—the windows of the pleasant drawing-room in which he had first heard Lily speak of her guardian.

The postman left his letters, and regained the garden gate, while Kenelm still stood wistfully gazing on those lighted windows. He had, meanwhile, advanced along the whitened sward to the light, saying to himself, "Let me just see her and her happiness, and then I will knock boldly at the door, and say, 'Good evening, Mrs. Melville.'"

So Kenelm stole across the lawn, and stationing himself at the angle of the wall, looked into the window.

Melville, in dressing-robe and slippers, was seated alone by the fireside. His dog was lazily stretched on the hearth-rug. One by one the features of the room, as the scene of his vanished happiness, grew out from its stillness; the delicately-tinted walls, the dwarf bookcase, with its feminine ornaments on the upper shelf; the piano standing in the same place. Lily's own small low chair; *that* was not in its old place, but thrust into a remote angle, as if it had passed into disuse. Melville was reading a letter, no doubt one of those which the postman had left. Surely the contents were pleasant, for his fair face, always frankly expressive of emotion, brightened wonderfully as he read on. Then he rose with a quick, brisk movement and pulled the bell hastily.

A neat maid-servant entered—a strange face to Kenelm. Melville gave her some brief message. "He has had joyous news," thought Kenelm. "He has sent for his wife that she may share his joy." Presently the door opened, and entered not Lily, but Mrs. Cameron.

She looked changed. Her natural quietude of mien and movement the same, indeed, but with more languor in it. Her hair had become gray. Melville was standing by the table as she approached him. He put the letter into her hands with a gay, proud smile, and looked over her shoulder while she read it, pointing with his finger as to some lines that should more emphatically claim her attention.

When she had finished her face reflected his smile. They exchanged a hearty shake of the hand, as if in congratulation. "Ah," thought Kenelm, "the letter is from Lily. She is abroad. Perhaps the birth of a first-born."

Just then Blanche, who had not been visible before, emerged from under the table, and as Melville reseated himself by the fireside, sprang into his lap, rubbing herself against his breast. The expression of his face changed; he uttered some low exclamation. Mrs. Cameron took the creature from his lap, stroking it quietly, carried it across the room, and put it outside the door. Then she

seated herself beside the artist, placing her hand in his, and they
conversed in low tones, till Melville's face again grew bright, and
again he took up the letter.

A few minutes later the maid-servant entered with the tea-things,
and after arranging them on the table approached the window.
Kenelm retreated into the shade, the servant closed the shutters
and drew the curtains—that scene of quiet home comfort vanished
from the eyes of the looker-on.

Kenelm felt strangely perplexed. What had become of Lily?
was she indeed absent from her home? Had he conjectured rightly,
that the letter which had evidently so gladdened Melville was from
her, or was it possible—here a thought of joy seized his heart and
held him breathless—was it possible, that, after all, she had not
married her guardian; had found a home elsewhere—was free?
He moved on farther down the lawn, towards the water, that he
might better bring before his sight that part of the irregular building in which Lily formerly had her sleeping-chamber, and her
"own—own room." All was dark there; the shutters inexorably
closed. The place with which the childlike girl had associated her
most childlike fancies, taming and tending the honey drinkers destined to pass into fairies, that fragile tenement was not closed against
the winds and snows; its doors were drearily open; gaps in the
delicate wire-work; of its dainty draperies a few tattered shreds
hanging here and there; and on the depopulated floor the moonbeams resting cold and ghostly. No spray from the tiny fountain;
its basin chipped and mouldering; the scanty waters therein frozen.
Of all the pretty wild ones that Lily fancied she could tame, not
one. Ah! yes, there was one, probably not of the old familiar
number; a stranger that might have crept in for shelter from the
first blasts of winter, and now clung to an angle in the farther wall,
its wings folded—asleep, not dead. But Kenelm saw it not; he
noticed only the general desolation of the spot.

"Natural enough," thought he. "She has outgrown all such
pretty silliness. A wife cannot remain a child. Still, if she had
belonged to me——" The thought choked even his inward, un-
spoken utterance. He turned away, paused a moment under the
leafless boughs of the great willow still dipping into the brook, and
then with impatient steps strode back towards the garden gate.

"No—no—no. I cannot now enter that house and ask for Mrs.
Melville. Trial enough for one night to stand on the old ground.
I will return to the town. I will call at Jessie's, and there I can
learn if she indeed be happy."

So he went on by the path along the brook-side, the night

momently colder and colder, and momently clearer and clearer, while the moon noiselessly glided into loftier heights. Wrapt in his abstracted thoughts, when he came to the spot in which the path split in twain he did not take that which led more directly to the town. His steps, naturally enough following the train of his thoughts, led him along the path with which the object of his thoughts was associated. He found himself on the burial ground, and in front of the old ruined tomb with its effaced inscription.

"Ah! child—child!" he murmured almost inaudibly, "what depths of woman tenderness lay concealed in thee! In what loving sympathy with the past—sympathy only vouchsafed to the tenderest women and the highest poets—didst thou lay thy flowers on the tomb, to which thou didst give a poet's history interpreted by a woman's heart, little dreaming that beneath the stone slept a hero of thine own fallen race."

He passed beneath the shadow of the yews, whose leaves no winter wind can strew, and paused at the ruined tomb—no flower now on its stone, only a sprinkling of snow at the foot of it—sprinklings of snow at the foot of each humbler grave mound. Motionless in the frosty air rested the pointed church spire, and through the frosty air, higher and higher up the arch of heaven, soared the unpausing moon. Around, and below, and above her, the stars which no science can number; yet not less difficult to number are the thoughts, desires, aspirations, which, in a space of time briefer than a winter's night, can pass through the infinite deeps of a human soul.

From his stand by the Gothic tomb, Kenelm looked along the churchyard for the infant's grave, which Lily's pious care had bordered with votive flowers. Yes, in that direction there was still a gleam of colour; could it be of flowers in that biting winter time —the moon is so deceptive, it silvers into the hue of the jessamines the green of the everlastings.

He passed towards the white grave mound. His sight had duped him; no pale flower, no green "everlasting" on its neglected border —only brown mould, withered stalks, streaks of snow.

"And yet," he said sadly, "she told me she had never broken a promise; and she had given a promise to the dying child. Ah! she is too happy now to think of the dead."

So murmuring, he was about to turn towards the town, when close by that child's grave he saw another. Round that other there were pale "everlastings," dwarfed blossoms of the laurestinus; at the four angles the drooping bud of a Christmas rose; at the head of the grave was a white stone, its sharp edges cutting into the starlit air; and on the head, in fresh letters, were inscribed these words:—

To the Memory of
L. M.
Aged 17,
Died October 29, A.D. 18—,
This stone, above the grave to which her mortal remains are consigned, beside that of an infant not more sinless, is consecrated by those who most mourn and miss her,
ISABEL CAMERON,
WALTER MELVILLE.
"Suffer the little children to come unto me."

CHAPTER XI.

THE next morning Mr. Emlyn, passing from his garden to the town of Moleswich, descried a human form stretched on the burial-ground, stirring restlessly but very slightly, as if with an involuntary shiver, and uttering broken sounds, very faintly heard, like the moans that a man in pain strives to suppress and cannot.

The rector hastened to the spot. The man was lying, his face downward, on a grave-mound, not dead, not asleep.

"Poor fellow! overtaken by drink, I fear," thought the gentle pastor; and as it was the habit of his mind to compassionate error even more than grief, he accosted the supposed sinner in very soothing tones—trying to raise him from the ground—and with very kindly words.

Then the man lifted his face from its pillow on the grave-mound, looked round him dreamily into the gray, blank air of the cheerless morn, and rose to his feet quietly and slowly.

The vicar was startled; he recognized the face of him he had last seen in the magnificent affluence of health and strength. But the character of the face was changed—so changed! its old serenity of expression, at once grave and sweet, succeeded by a wild trouble in the heavy eyelids and trembling lips.

"Mr. Chillingly—you! Is it possible?"

"Varus, Varus," exclaimed Kenelm, passionately, "what hast thou done with my legions?"

At that quotation of the well-known greeting of Augustus to his unfortunate general, the scholar recoiled. Had his young friend's mind deserted him—dazed, perhaps, by over-study?

He was soon reassured; Kenelm's face settled back into calm, though a dreary calm, like that of a wintry day.

"I beg pardon, Mr. Emlyn; I had not quite shaken off the hold of a strange dream. I dreamed that I was worse off than Augustus; he did not lose the world when the legions he had trusted to another vanished into the grave."

Here Kenelm linked his arm in that of the rector—on which he leaned rather heavily—and drew him on from the burial-ground into the open space where the two paths met.

"But how long have you returned to Moleswich?" asked Emlyn; "and how come you to choose so damp a bed for your morning slumbers?"

"The wintry cold crept into my veins when I stood in the burial-ground, and I was very weary; I had no sleep at night. Do not let me take you out of your way; I am going on to Grasmere. So I see, by the record on a grave-stone, that it is more than a year ago since Mr. Melville lost his wife."

"Wife? He never married."

"What!" cried Kenelm. "Whose, then, is that grave-stone—'L. M.'?"

"Alas! it is our poor Lily's."

"And she died unmarried?"

As Kenelm said this he looked up, and the sun broke out from the gloomy haze of the morning. "I may claim thee, then," he thought within himself—"claim thee as mine when we meet again."

"Unmarried—yes," resumed the vicar. "She was indeed betrothed to her guardian; they were to have been married in the autumn, on his return from the Rhine. He went there to paint on the spot itself his great picture, which is now so famous—'Roland, the Hermit Knight, looking towards the convent lattice for a sight of the Holy Nun.' Melville had scarcely gone before the symptoms of the disease which proved fatal to poor Lily betrayed themselves; they baffled all medical skill—rapid decline. She was always very delicate, but no one detected in her the seeds of consumption. Melville only returned a day or two before her death. Dear child-like Lily! how we all mourned for her!—not least the poor, who believed in her fairy charms."

"And least of all, it appears, the man she was to have married."

"He?—Melville? How can you wrong him so? His grief was intense—overpowering—for the time."

"For the time! what time?" muttered Kenelm, in tones too low for the pastor's ear.

They moved on silently. Mr. Emlyn resumed:

"You noticed the text on Lily's grave-stone—'Suffer the little children to come unto me?' She dictated it herself the day before she died. I was with her then, so I was at the last."

"Were you—were you—at the last—the last? Good-day, Mr. Emlyn; we are just in sight of the garden gate. And—excuse me—I wish to see Mr. Melville alone."

"Well, then, good-day; but if you are making any stay in the neighbourhood, will you not be our guest? We have a room at your service."

"I thank you gratefully; but I return to London in an hour or so. Hold, a moment. You were with her at the last? She was resigned to die?"

"Resigned! that is scarcely the word. The smile left upon her lips was not that of human resignation; it was the smile of a divine joy."

CHAPTER XII.

"YES, sir, Mr. Melville is at home, in his studio."

Kenelm followed the maid across the hall into a room not built at the date of Kenelm's former visits to the house: the artist, making Grasmere his chief residence after Lily's death, had added it at the back of the neglected place wherein Lily had encaged "the souls of infants unbaptized."

A lofty room, with a casement partially darkened, to the bleak north; various sketches on the walls; gaunt specimens of antique furniture, and of gorgeous Italian silks, scattered about in confused disorder; one large picture on its easel, curtained; another as large, and half finished, before which stood the painter. He turned quickly, as Kenelm entered the room unannounced, let fall brush and palette, came up to him eagerly, grasped his hand, drooped his head on Kenelm's shoulder, and said, in a voice struggling with evident and strong emotion:

"Since we parted, such grief! such a loss!"

"I know it; I have seen her grave. Let us not speak of it. Why so needlessly revive your sorrow? So—so—your sanguine hopes are fulfilled—the world has at last done you justice? Emlyn tells me that you have painted a very famous picture."

Kenelm had seated himself as he thus spoke. The painter still stood with dejected attitude on the middle of the floor, and brushed his hand over his moistened eyes once or twice before he answered,

"Yes, wait a moment, don't talk of fame yet. Bear with me; the sudden sight of you unnerved me."

The artist here seated himself also on an old worm-eaten Gothic chest, rumpling and chafing the golden or tinselled threads of the embroidered silk, so rare and so time-worn, flung over the Gothic chest, so rare also, and so worm-eaten.

Kenelm looked through half-closed lids at the artist, and his lips, before slightly curved with a secret scorn, became gravely compressed. In Melville's struggle to conceal emotion the strong man recognized a strong man—recognized, and yet only wondered; wondered how such a man, to whom Lily had pledged her hand, could so soon after the loss of Lily go on painting pictures, and care for any praise bestowed on a yard of canvas.

In a very few minutes Melville recommenced conversation—no more reference to Lily than if she had never existed. "Yes, my last picture has been indeed a success—a reward complete, if tardy, for all the bitterness of former struggles made in vain, for the galling sense of injustice, the anguish of which only an artist knows, when unworthy rivals are ranked before him.

'Foes quick to blame, and friends afraid to praise.'

True that I have still much to encounter; the clique still seek to disparage me, but between me and the cliques there stands at last the giant form of the public, and at last critics of graver weight than the cliques have deigned to accord to me a higher rank than even the public yet acknowledge. Ah! Mr. Chillingly, you do not profess to be a judge of paintings, but, excuse me, just look at this letter. I received it only last night from the greatest connoisseur of my art, certainly in England, perhaps in Europe." Here Melville drew, from the side pocket of his picturesque *moyen âge* surtout, a letter signed by a name authoritative to all who—being painters themselves—acknowledge authority in one who could no more paint a picture himself than Addison, the ablest critic of the greatest poem modern Europe has produced, could have written ten lines of the Paradise Lost—and thrust the letter into Kenelm's hand. Kenelm read it listlessly, with an increased contempt for an artist who could so find in gratified vanity consolation for the life gone from earth. But, listlessly as he read the letter, the sincere and fervent enthusiasm of the laudatory contents impressed him, and the pre-eminent authority of the signature could not be denied.

The letter was written on the occasion of Melville's recent election to the dignity of R.A., successor to a very great artist whose death had created a vacancy in the Academy. He returned the letter to

Melville, saying, "This is the letter I saw you reading last night as I looked in at your window. Indeed, for a man who cares for the opinion of other men, this letter is very flattering; and for the painter who cares for money, it must be very pleasant to know by how many guineas every inch of his canvas may be covered." Unable longer to control his passions of rage, of scorn, of agonizing grief, Kenelm then burst forth,—"Man, Man, whom I once accepted as a teacher on human life, a teacher to warm, to brighten, to exalt mine own indifferent, dreamy, slow-pulsed self! has not the one woman whom thou didst select out of this over-crowded world to be bone of thy bone, flesh of thy flesh, vanished evermore from the earth—little more than a year since her voice was silenced, her heart ceased to beat? But how slight is such loss to thy life, compared to the worth of a compliment that flatters thy vanity!"

The artist rose to his feet with an indignant impulse. But the angry flush faded from his cheek as he looked on the countenance of his rebuker. He walked up to him, and attempted to take his hand, but Kenelm snatched it scornfully from his grasp.

"Poor friend," said Melville, sadly and soothingly, "I did not think you loved her thus deeply. Pardon me." He drew a chair close to Kenelm's, and after a brief pause went on thus, in very earnest tones—"I am not so heartless, not so forgetful of my loss as you suppose. But reflect, you have but just learned of her death, you are under the first shock of grief. More than a year has been given to me for gradual submission to the decree of Heaven. Now listen to me, and try to listen calmly. I am many years older than you, I ought to know better the conditions on which man holds the tenure of life. Life is composite, many-sided, nature does not permit it to be lastingly monopolized by a single passion, or while yet in the prime of its strength, to be lastingly blighted by a single sorrow. Survey the great mass of our common race, engaged in the various callings, some the humblest, some the loftiest, by which the business of the world is carried on,—can you justly despise as heartless the poor trader, or the great statesman, when, it may be but a few days after the loss of some one nearest and dearest to his heart, the trader reopens his shop, the statesman reappears in his office? But in me, the votary of art, in me you behold but the weakness of gratified vanity—if I feel joy in the hope that my art may triumph, and my country may add my name to the list of those who contribute to her renown—where and whenever lived an artist not sustained by that hope, in privation, in sickness, in the sorrows he must share with his kind? Nor is this hope that of a feminine vanity, a sicklier craving for applause; it identifies itself with glorious services to our land, to our race, to the children of all after time. Our art cannot triumph, our name cannot live, unless we achieve a something that tends to beautify or ennoble the world in which we accept the common heritage of toil and of sorrow, in order, therefrom, to work out for successive multitudes a recreation and a joy."

While the artist thus spoke Kenelm lifted towards his face eyes charged with suppressed tears. And the face, kindling as the artist vindicated himself from the young man's bitter charge, became touchingly sweet in its grave expression at the close of the not ignoble defence.

"Enough," said Kenelm, rising. "There is a ring of truth in what you say. I can conceive the artist's, the poet's escape from this world, when all therein is death and winter, into the world he creates and colours at his will with the hues of summer. So, too, I can conceive how the man whose life is sternly fitted into the grooves of a trader's calling, or a statesman's duties, is borne on by the force of custom, afar from such brief halting-spot as a grave. But I am no poet, no artist, no trader, no statesman; I have no calling, my life is fixed into no grooves. Adieu."

"Hold a moment. Not now, but somewhat later, ask yourself whether any life can be permitted to wander in space, a monad detached from the lives of others. Into some groove or other, sooner or later, it must be settled, and be borne on obedient to the laws of nature and the responsibility to God."

CHAPTER XIII.

KENELM went back alone, and with downcast looks, through the desolate flowerless garden, when at the other side of the gate a light touch was laid on his arm. He looked up, and recognized Mrs. Cameron.

"I saw you," she said, "from my window coming to the house, and I have been waiting for you here. I wished to speak to you alone. Allow me to walk beside you."

Kenelm inclined his head assentingly, but made no answer.

They were nearly midway between the cottage and the burial-ground when Mrs. Cameron resumed, her tones quick and agitated, contrasting her habitual languid quietude—

"I have a great weight on my mind; it ought not to be remorse. I acted as I thought in my conscience for the best. But oh, Mr.

Chillingly, if I erred—if I judged wrongly—do say at least you forgive me." She seized his hand, pressing it convulsively. Kenelm muttered inaudibly—a sort of dreary stupor had succeeded to the intense excitement of grief. Mrs. Cameron went on—

"You could not have married Lily—you know you could not. The secret of her birth could not, in honour, have been concealed from your parents. They could not have consented to your marriage; and even if you had persisted, without that consent and in spite of that secret, to press for it—even had she been yours——"

"Might she not be living now?" cried Kenelm, fiercely.

"No—no; the secret must have come out. The cruel world would have discovered it; it would have reached her ears. The shame of it would have killed her. How bitter then would have been her short interval of life! As it is, she passed away—resigned and happy. But I own that I did not, could not, understand her, could not believe her feeling for you to be so deep. I did think, that when she knew her own heart, she would find that love for her guardian was its strongest affection. She assented, apparently without a pang, to become his wife; and she seemed always so fond of him, and what girl would not be? But I was mistaken—deceived. From the day you saw her last, she began to fade away; but then Walter left a few days after, and I thought that it was his absence she mourned. She never owned to me that it was yours—never till too late—too late—just when my sad letter had summoned him back, only three days before she died. Had I known earlier while yet there was hope of recovery, I must have written to you, even though the obstacles to your union with her remained the same. Oh, again I implore you, say that if I erred you forgive me. She did, kissing me so tenderly. She did forgive me. Will not you? It would have been her wish."

"Her wish? Do you think I could disobey it? I know not if I have anything to forgive. If I have, now could I not forgive one who loved her? God comfort us both."

He bent down and kissed Mrs. Cameron's forehead. The poor woman threw her arm gratefully, lovingly round him, and burst into tears.

When she had recovered her emotion, she said—

"And now, it is with so much lighter a heart that I can fulfil her commission to you. But, before I place this in your hands, can you make me one promise? Never tell Melville how she loved you. She was so careful he should never guess that. And if he knew it was the thought of union with him which had killed her, he would never smile again."

"You would not ask such a promise if you could guess how sacred from all the world I hold the secret that you confide to me. By that secret the grave is changed into an altar. Our bridals now are only awhile deferred."

Mrs. Cameron placed a letter in Kenelm's hand, and murmuring in accents broken by a sob, "She gave it to me the day before her last," left him, and with quick vacillating steps hurried back towards the cottage. She now understood *him*, at last, too well not to feel that on opening that letter he must be alone with the dead.

It is strange that we need have so little practical household knowledge of each other to be in love. Never till then had Kenelm's eyes rested upon Lily's handwriting. And he now gazed at the formal address on the envelope with a sort of awe. Unknown handwriting coming to him from an unknown world—delicate, tremulous handwriting—handwriting not of one grown up, yet not of a child who had long to live.

He turned the envelope over and over—not impatiently, as does the lover whose heart beats at the sound of the approaching footstep, but lingeringly, timidly. He would not break the seal.

He was now so near the burial-ground. Where should the first letter ever received from her—the sole letter he ever could receive—be so reverentially, lovingly read, as at her grave?

He walked on to the burial-ground, sat down by the grave, broke the envelope; a poor little ring, with a poor little single turquoise, rolled out and rested at his feet. The letter contained only these words:

"The ring comes back to you. I could not live to marry another. I never knew how I loved you—till, till I began to pray that you might not love me too much. Darling! darling! good-bye, darling!
"LILY.

"Don't let Lion ever see this, or ever know what it says to you. He is so good, and deserves to be so happy. Do you remember the day of the ring? Darling! darling!"

CHAPTER XIV.

SOMEWHAT more than another year has rolled away. It is early spring in London. The trees in the parks and squares are budding into leaf and blossom. Leopold Travers has had a brief but serious conversation with his daughter, and is now gone forth on horseback. Handsome and graceful still, Leopold Travers when in London is pleased to find himself scarcely less the fashion with the young than he was when himself in youth. He is now riding along the banks of the Serpentine, no one better mounted, better dressed, better looking, or talking with greater fluency on the topics which interest his companions.

Cecilia is in the smaller drawing-room, which is exclusively appropriated to her use—alone with Lady Glenalvon.

LADY GLENALVON. "I own, my dear, dear Cecilia, that I arrange myself at last on the side of your father. How earnestly at one time I had hoped that Kenelm Chillingly might woo and win the bride that seemed to me most fitted to adorn and to cheer his life, I need not say. But when at Exmundham he asked me to befriend his choice of another, to reconcile his mother to that choice—evidently not a suitable one—I gave him up. And though that affair is at an end, he seems little likely ever to settle down to practical duties and domestic habits, an idle wanderer over the face of the earth, only heard of in remote places and with strange companions. Perhaps he may never return to England."

CECILIA.—"He is in England now, and in London."

LADY GLENALVON.—"You amaze me! Who told you so?"

CECILIA.—"His father, who is with him. Sir Peter called yesterday, and spoke to me so kindly." Cecilia here turned aside her face to conceal the tears that had started to her eyes.

LADY GLENALVON.—"Did Mr. Travers see Sir Peter?"

CECILIA.—"Yes; and I think it was something that passed between them which made my father speak to me—for the first time—almost sternly."

LADY GLENALVON.—"In urging Gordon Chillingly's suit."

CECILIA.—"Commanding me to reconsider my rejection of it. He has contrived to fascinate my father."

LADY GLENALVON.—"So he has me. Of course you might choose among other candidates for your hand one of much higher worldly rank, of much larger fortune, yet as you have already rejected them, Gordon's merits become still more entitled to a fair hearing. He has already leapt into a position that mere rank and mere wealth cannot attain. Men of all parties speak highly of his parliamentary abilities. He is already marked in public opinion as a coming man—a future minister of the highest grade. He has youth and good looks, his moral character is without a blemish, yet his manners are so free from affected austerity, so frank, so genial. Any woman might be pleased with his companionship; and you, with your intellect, your culture,—you, so born for high station,—

you of all women might be proud to partake the anxieties of his career, and the rewards of his ambition."

CECILIA (clasping her hands tightly together).—"I cannot, I cannot. He may be all you say—I know nothing against Mr. Chillingly Gordon—but my whole nature is antagonistic to his, and even were it not so——"

She stopped abruptly, a deep blush warming up her fair face, and retreating to leave it coldly pale.

LADY GLENALVON (tenderly kissing her).—"You have not, then, even yet conquered the first maiden fancy; the ungrateful one is still remembered?"

Cecilia bowed her head on her friend's breast, and murmured imploringly, "Don't speak against him, he has been so unhappy. How much he must have loved!"

"But it is not you whom he loved."

"Something here, something at my heart, tells me that he will love me yet; and if not, I am contented to be his friend."

CHAPTER XV.

WHILE the conversation just related took place between Cecilia and Lady Glenalvon, Gordon Chillingly was seated alone with Mivers in the comfortable apartment of the cynical old bachelor. Gordon had breakfasted with his kinsman, but that meal was long over; the two men having found much to talk about on matters very interesting to the younger, nor without interest to the elder one.

It is true that Chillingly Gordon had, within the very short space of time that had elapsed since his entrance into the House of Commons, achieved one of those reputations which mark out a man for early admission into the progressive career of office—not a very showy reputation, but a very solid one. He had none of the gifts of the genuine orator, no enthusiasm, no imagination, no imprudent bursts of fiery words from a passionate heart. But he had all the gifts of an exceedingly telling speaker—a clear metallic voice; well-bred, appropriate action, not less dignified for being somewhat too quiet; readiness for extempore replies; industry and method for prepared expositions of principle or fact. But his principal merit with the chiefs of the assembly was in the strong good sense and worldly tact which made him a safe speaker For this merit he was largely indebted to his frequent conferences with Chillingly Mivers. That gentleman, owing whether to his social qualities or to the influence of the 'Londoner' on public opinion, enjoyed an intimate acquaintance with the chiefs of all parties, and was up to his ears in the wisdom of the world. "Nothing," he would say, "hurts a young Parliamentary speaker like violence in opinion, one way or the other. Shun it. Always allow that much may be said on both sides. When the chiefs of your own side suddenly adopt a violence, you can go with them or against them, according as best suits your own book."

"So," said Mivers, reclined on his sofa, and approaching the end of his second Trabuco (he never allowed himself more than two), "so I think we have pretty well settled the tone you must take in your speech to-night. It is a great occasion."

"True. It is the *first* time in which the debate has been arranged so that I may speak at ten o'clock or later. That in itself is a great leap; and it is a Cabinet minister whom I am to anwer—luckily, he is a very dull fellow. Do you think I might hazard a joke—at least a witticism?"

"At his expense? Decidedly not. Though his office compels him to introduce this measure, he was by no means in its favour when it was discussed in the Cabinet; and though, as you say, he is dull, it is precisely that sort of dulness which is essential to the formation of every respectable Cabinet. Joke at *him*, indeed! Learn that gentle dulness never loves a joke—at its own expense. Vain man! seize the occasion which your blame of his measure affords you to secure his praise of yourself; compliment him. Enough of politics. It never does to think too much over what one has already decided to say. Brooding over it, one may become too much in earnest, and commit an indiscretion. So Kenelm has come back?"

"Yes. I heard that news last night, at White's, from Travers. Sir Peter had called on Travers."

"Travers still favours your suit to the heiress?"

"More, I think, than ever. Success in Parliament has great effect on a man who has success in fashion and respects the opinion of clubs. But last night he was unusually cordial. Between you and me, I think he is a little afraid that Kenelm may yet be my rival. I gathered that from a hint he let fall of the unwelcome nature of Sir Peter's talk to him."

"Why has Travers conceived a dislike to poor Kenelm? He seemed partial enough to him once."

"Ay, but not as a son-in-law, even before I had a chance of

becoming so. And when, after Kenelm appeared at Exmundham while Travers was staying there, Travers learned, I suppose from Lady Chillingly, that Kenelm had fallen in love with and wanted to marry some other girl, who it seems rejected him, and still more when he heard that Kenelm had been subsequently travelling on the Continent in company with a low-lived fellow, the drunken, riotous son of a farrier, you may well conceive how so polished and sensible a man as Leopold Travers would dislike the idea of giving his daughter to one so little likely to make an agreeable son-in-law. Bah! I have no fear of Kenelm. By the way, did Sir Peter say if Kenelm had quite recovered his health? He was at death's door some eighteen months ago, when Sir Peter and Lady Chillingly were summoned to town by the doctors."

"My dear Gordon, I fear there is no chance of your succession to Exmundham. Sir Peter says that his wandering Hercules is as stalwart as ever, and more equable in temperament, more taciturn and grave—in short, less odd. But when you say you have no fear of Kenelm's rivalry, do you mean only as to Cecilia Travers?"

"Neither as to that nor as to anything in life; and as to the succession to Exmundham, it is his to leave as he pleases, and I have cause to think that he would never leave it to me. More likely to Parson John or the parson's son—or why not to yourself? I often think that for the prizes immediately set before my ambition I am better off without land: land is a great obfuscator."

"Humph, there is some truth in that. Yet the fear of land and obfuscation does not seem to operate against your suit to Cecilia Travers?"

"Her father is likely enough to live till I may be contented to 'rest and be thankful' in the upper house; and I should not like to be a landless peer."

"You are right there; but I should tell you that, now Kenelm has come back, Sir Peter has set his heart on his son's being your rival."

"For Cecilia?"

"Perhaps; but certainly for Parliamentary reputation. The senior member for the county means to retire, and Sir Peter has been urged to allow his son to be brought forward—from what I hear, with the certainty of success."

"What! in spite of that wonderful speech of his on coming of age?"

"Pooh! that is now understood to have been but a bad joke on the new ideas, and their organs, including the 'Londoner.' But if Kenelm does come into the House, it will not be on your side of the question; and unless I greatly overrate his abilities—which very likely I do—he will not be a rival to despise. Except, indeed, that he may have one fault which in the present day would be enough to unfit him for public life."

"And what is that fault?"

"Treason to the blood of the Chillinglys. This is the age, in England, when one cannot be too much of a Chillingly. I fear that if Kenelm does become bewildered by a political abstraction— call it, no matter what, say, 'love of his country,' or some such old-fashioned crotchet—I fear—I greatly fear—that he may be—in earnest."

CHAPTER THE LAST.

IT was a field night in the House of Commons—an adjourned debate, opened by George Belvoir, who had been, the last two years, very slowly creeping on in the favour, or rather the indulgence of the House, and more than justifying Kenelm's prediction of his career. Heir to a noble name and vast estates, extremely hard-working, very well-informed, it was impossible that he should not creep on. That night he spoke sensibly enough, assisting his memory by frequent references to his notes; listened to courteously, and greeted with a faint "Hear, hear!" of relief when he had done.

Then the House gradually thinned till nine o'clock, at which hour it became very rapidly crowded. A cabinet minister had solemnly risen, deposited on the table before him a formidable array of printed papers, including a corpulent blue-book. Leaning his arm on the red box, he commenced with this awe-compelling sentence:

"Sir,—I join issue with the right honourable gentleman opposite. He says this is not raised as a party question. I deny it. Her Majesty's Government are put upon their trial."

Here there were cheers, so loudly, and so rarely greeting a speech from that cabinet minister, that he was put out, and had much to "hum" and to "ha," before he could recover the thread of his speech. Then he went on, with unbroken but lethargic fluency; read long extracts from the public papers, inflicted a whole page from the blue book, wound up with a peroration of respectable platitudes, glanced at the clock, saw that he had completed the hour which a cabinet minister who does not profess to be oratorical is expected to speak, but not to exceed ; and sat down.

Up rose a crowd of eager faces, from which the Speaker, as previously arranged with the party whips, selected one—a young face, hardy, intelligent, emotionless.

I need not say that it was the face of Chillingly Gordon.

His position that night was one that required dexterous management and delicate tact. He habitually supported the Government; his speeches had been hitherto in their favour. On this occasion he differed from the Government. The difference was known to the chiefs of the Opposition, and hence the arrangement of the whips, that he should speak for the first time after ten o'clock, and for the first time in reply to a cabinet minister. It is a position in which a young party man makes or mars his future. Chillingly Gordon spoke from the third row behind the Government; he had been duly cautioned by Mivers not to affect a conceited independence, or an adhesion to "violence" in ultra-liberal opinions, by seating himself below the gangway. Speaking thus, amid the rank and file of the Ministerial supporters, any opinion at variance with the mouthpieces of the Treasury Bench would be sure to produce a more effective sensation than if delivered from the ranks of the mutinous Bashi Bazouks divided by the gangway from better disciplined forces. His first brief sentences enthralled the House, conciliated the Ministerial side, kept the Opposition side in suspense. The whole speech was, indeed, felicitously adroit, and especially in this, that while in opposition to the Government as a whole, it expressed the opinions of a powerful section of the cabinet, which, though at present a minority, yet being the most enamoured of a New Idea, the progress of the age would probably render a safe investment for the confidence which honest Gordon reposed in its chance of beating its colleagues.

It was not, however, till Gordon had concluded, that the cheers of his audience—impulsive and hearty as are the cheers of that assembly, when the evidence of intellect is unmistakable—made manifest to the gallery and the reporters the full effect of the speech he had delivered. The chief of the Opposition whispered to his next neighbour, "I wish we could get that man." The cabinet minister whom Gordon had answered—more pleased with a personal compliment to himself than displeased with an attack on the measure his office compelled him to advocate—whispered to his chief, "That is a man we must not lose."

Two gentlemen in the Speaker's gallery, who had sat there from the opening of the debate, now quitted their places. Coming into the lobby, they found themselves commingled with a crowd of members who had also quitted their seats, after Gordon's speech, in order to discuss its merits, as they gathered round the refreshment table for oranges or soda-water. Among them was George Belvoir, who, on sight of the younger of the two gentlemen issuing from the Speaker's gallery, accosted him with friendly greeting :

"Ha! Chillingly, how are you? Did not know you were in town. Been here all the evening? Yes; very good debate. How did you like Gordon's speech?"

"I liked yours much better."

"Mine!" cried George, very much flattered and very much surprised. "Oh! mine was a mere humdrum affair, a plain statement of the reasons for the vote I should give. And Gordon's was anything but that. You did not like his opinions?"

"I don't know what his opinions are. But I did not like his ideas."

"I don't quite understand you. What ideas?"

"The new ones; by which it is shown how rapidly a great state can be made small."

Here Mr. Belvoir was taken aside by a brother member, on an important matter to be brought before the committee on salmon fisheries, on which they both served; and Kenelm, with his companion, Sir Peter, threaded his way through the crowded lobby, and disappeared. Emerging into the broad space, with its lofty clock tower, Sir Peter halted, and pointing towards the old Abbey, half in shadow half in light, under the tranquil moonbeams, said :

"It tells much for the duration of a people, when it accords with the instinct of immortality in a man; when an honoured tomb is deemed recompense for the toils and dangers of a noble life. How much of the history of England, Nelson summed up in the simple words—' Victory or Westminster Abbey.'"

"Admirably expressed, my dear father," said Kenelm, briefly.

"I agree with your remark, which I overheard, on Gordon's speech," resumed Sir Peter. "It was wonderfully clever; yet I should have been sorry to hear you speak it. It is not by such sentiments that Nelsons become great. If such sentiments should ever be national, the cry will not be 'Victory or Westminster Abbey!' but 'Defeat and the Three per Cents!'"

Pleased with his own unwonted animation, and with the sympathizing half-smile on his son's taciturn lips, Sir Peter then proceeded more immediately to the subjects which pressed upon his heart. Gordon's success in Parliament, Gordon's suit to Cecilia Travers, favoured, as Sir Peter had learned, by her father, rejected as yet by herself, were somehow inseparably mixed up in Sir Peter's mind and his words, as he sought to kindle his son's emulation. He dwelt on the obligations which a country imposed on its citizens, especially on the young and vigorous generation to which the destinies of those to follow were intrusted; and with these stern obligations he combined all the cheering and tender associations which an English public man connects with an English home: the wife with a smile to soothe the cares, and a mind to share the aspirations, of a life that must go through labour to achieve renown; thus, in all he said, binding together, as if they could not be disparted, Ambition and Cecilia.

His son did not interrupt him by a word: Sir Peter in his eagerness not noticing that Kenelm had drawn him aside from the direct thoroughfare, and had now made halt in the middle of Westminster Bridge, bending over the massive parapet and gazing abstractedly upon the waves of the starlit river. On the right the stately length of the people's legislative palace, so new in its date, so elaborately in each detail ancient in its form, stretching on towards the lowly and jagged roofs of penury and crime. Well might these be so near to the halls of a people's legislative palace;—near to the heart of every legislator for a people must be the mighty problem how to increase a people's splendour and its virtue, and how to diminish its penury and its crime.

"How strange it is," said Kenelm, still bending over the parapet, "that throughout all my desultory wanderings I have ever been attracted towards the sight and the sound of running waters, even those of the humblest rill! Of what thoughts, of what dreams, of what memories, colouring the history of my past, the waves of the humblest rill could speak, were the waves themselves not such supreme philosophers—roused indeed on their surface, vexed by a check to their own course, but so indifferent to all that makes gloom or death to the mortals who think and dream and feel beside their banks."

"Bless me," said Peter to himself, "the boy has got back to his old vein of humours and melancholies. He has not heard a word I have been saying. Travers is right. He will never do anything in life. Why did I christen him Kenelm? he might as well have been christened Peter." Still, loth to own that his eloquence had been expended in vain, and that the wish of his heart was doomed to expire disappointed, Sir Peter said aloud, "You have not listened to what I said; Kenelm, you grieve me."

"Grieve you! you! do not say that, father, dear father. Listen to you! Every word you have said has sunk into the deepest deep of my heart. Pardon my foolish, purposeless snatch of talk to myself—it is but my way, only my way, dear father!"

"Boy, boy," cried Sir Peter, with tears in his voice, "if you could get out of those odd ways of yours I should be so thankful. But if you cannot, nothing you can do shall grieve me. Only, let me say this; running waters have had a great charm for you. With a humble rill you associate thoughts, dreams, memories in your past. But now you halt by the stream of the mighty river—before you the senate of an empire wider than Alexander's; behind you the market of a commerce to which that of Tyre was a pitiful trade. Look farther down, those squalid hovels, how much there to redeem or to remedy; and out of sight, but not very distant, the nation's Walhalla: 'Victory or Westminster Abbey!' The humble rill has witnessed your past. Has the mighty river no effect on your future? The rill keeps no record of your past, shall the river keep no record of your future? Ah, boy, boy, I see you are dreaming still—no use talking. Let us go home."

"I was not dreaming, I was telling myself that the time had come to replace the old Kenelm with the new ideas, by a New Kenelm with the Ideas of Old. Ah! perhaps we must—at whatever cost to ourselves,—we must go through the romance of life before we clearly detect what is grand in its realities. I can no longer lament that I stand estranged from the objects and pursuits of my race. I have learned how much I have with them in common. I have known love; I have known sorrow."

Kenelm paused a moment, only a moment, then lifted the head which, during that pause, had drooped, and stood erect at the full height of his stature, startling his father by the change that had passed over his face; lip—eye—his whole aspect eloquent with a resolute enthusiasm, too grave to be the flash of a passing moment.

"Ay, ay," he said, "Victory or Westminster Abbey! The world is a battle-field in which the worst wounded are the deserters, stricken as they seek to fly, and hushing the groans that would betray the secret of their inglorious hiding-place. The pain of wounds received in the thick of the fight is scarcely felt in the joy of service to some honoured cause, and is amply atoned by the reverence for noble scars. My choice is made. Not that of deserter, that of soldier in the ranks."

"It will not be long before you rise from the ranks, my boy, if you hold fast to the Idea of Old, symbolized in the English battle-cry—'Victory or Westminster Abbey.'"

So saying, Sir Peter took his son's arm, leaning on it proudly; and so, into the crowded thoroughfares, from the halting-place on the modern bridge that spans the legendary river, passes the Man of the Young Generation to fates beyond the verge of the horizon to which the eyes of *my* generation must limit their wistful gaze.

THE END.

Richard Clay and Sons, London and Bungay.

www.ingramcontent.com/pod-product-compliance
Lightning Source LLC
Chambersburg PA
CBHW020525300426
44111CB00008B/549